British Economic Policy

British Economic Policy

A Modern Introduction

edited by

PAUL HARE

and

LESLIE SIMPSON

HARVESTER
WHEATSHEAF

New York   London   Toronto   Sydney   Tokyo   Singapore

First published 1993 by
Harvester Wheatsheaf
Campus 400, Maylands Avenue
Hemel Hempstead
Hertfordshire, HP2 7EZ
A division of
Simon & Schuster International Group

Designed by Claire Brodmann

Typeset in 9½/12pt Century Schoolbook
by Photoprint, Torquay, Devon

Printed and bound in Great Britain
by Hartnolls, Bodmin, Cornwall.

British Library Cataloguing in Publication Data

A catalogue record for this book is available
from the British Library

ISBN 0–7450–1328–7 (hbk)
ISBN 0–7450–1329–5 (pbk)

1 2 3 4 5   97 96 95 94 93

Contents

About the authors vii
List of figures and tables ix
Preface xiii

1 Economic policy: the major themes
   PAUL HARE 1

Part I Macroeconomic policy

2 Fiscal policy and the Public Sector Deficit
   STUART SAYER 23

3 Monetary policy and inflation
   GEOFFREY WYATT 44

4 Financial markets and public policy
   IAN HIRST 61

5 Unemployment
   PRABIR BHATTACHARYA 87

6 The UK external sector
   HUGH FLEMING 102

7 The European Community's impact on UK
   economic policy
   ANDREW SCOTT 117

Part II Microeconomic issues

8 Industrial economic policy
   PETER CLARKE 141

9 The role of services in the economy
   PATRICK O'FARRELL 165

v

10 Privatisation
    PAUL HARE   189

11 Trade unions and industrial relations
    IAN PATERSON AND LESLIE SIMPSON   204

12 Controlling environmental pollution
    LESLIE SIMPSON   221

13 Public expenditure and taxation
    PHILIP WELHAM   236

14 The distribution of income and wealth
    PHILIP WELHAM   256

15 Local government finance
    DOUGLAS MAIR   272

    Index   289

About the authors

Note: all authors are in the Heriot-Watt Business School unless otherwise indicated.

The editors

PROFESSOR PAUL HARE, former head of the Economics Department (1985–90), now mainly occupied with research on Eastern Europe and part-time at the London School of Economics. He has also worked on public finance issues, and on UK economic policy, especially to do with privatisation.

LESLIE SIMPSON, lecturer in economics, with interests in environmental economics, macroeconomics and some aspects of public sector economics.

The authors

PRABIR BHATTACHARYA, lecturer in economics. He has done substantial research in development economics, mainly to do with unemployment and migration problems.

PETER CLARKE, lecturer in economics, with research interests in the aerospace industry, transport economics and health economics.

HUGH FLEMING, lecturer in economics. His major interests are exchange rate policy and the international financial markets.

IAN HIRST, Professor of Finance in the Department of Accountancy and Finance. He has previously researched on the financial markets, as well as on investment evaluation techniques.

PROFESSOR DOUGLAS MAIR, Economics Department, working on Kaleckian models applied to local taxation issues; he is also interested in the history of economic thought.

PROFESSOR PATRICK O'FARRELL, Economics Department. He carries out research on comparative productivity levels of firms in different areas and, more recently, on business services and their impact on industrial performance.

IAN PATERSON, lecturer in economics, specialising in industrial relations, trade union studies and labour market issues.

STUART SAYER, lecturer in economics at Edinburgh University. Author of books and articles on macroeconomic issues.

ANDREW SCOTT, lecturer in economics, with extensive research on the European Community including several contracts for the Commission; editor of *Journal of Common Market Studies*.

PHILIP WELHAM, senior lecturer in economics and Deputy Head of Department (1990–3), working on inter-temporal aspects of income and wealth distribution, and with a general interest in public finance.

GEOFFREY WYATT, present head of the Economics Department (1990–93) and a senior lecturer, with books and articles on technological change, and a study of financial options and futures markets. More recently, he has been investigating techniques of graphical representation of macroeconomic models.

List of figures and tables

Figures

2.1 Public Sector Deficit as a percentage of GDP   24

2.2 Tax revenues and general government expenditure as a
percentage of GDP   25

2.3a Public sector consumption and transfer payments   26

2.3b Public sector investment and debt interest   27

2.4 Public sector asset sales   28

2.5 Government debt as a percentage of GDP   30

3.1 Historical trend of consumer price inflation in the
United Kingdom   45

3.2 Short- and long-term interest rates   53

4.1 Average inflation and standard deviation of inflation   71

4.2 Risk and real return in the UK market for three classes
of financial asset   72

4.3 Rates of stock market capitalisation of GDP   73

4.4 The network of major shareholdings relating to the
French mineral water company, Source Perrier, in 1992   74

4.5 International comparisons of company gearing   75

4.6 Share prices and takeovers   76

4.7 Foreign direct investment per capita, 1983–7   77

5.1 UK unemployment   90

5.2 Equilibrium with flexible money wages   92

6.1 Exchange rate determination   110

6.2 Dollar/pound exchange rate   112

6.3 Deutschmark/pound exchange rate   113

6.4   Exchange rate determination in the ERM   114
10.1 Pricing and investment in nationalised industries   191
11.1 Perfect competition model   206
11.2 Monopsonist model   208
12.1 Optimal pollution control   222
12.2 Pollution tax   226
13.1 Demand for public and private goods   238
13.2 Effect of a tax on a good   247
14.1 A Lorenz curve   257
14.2 Incidence of a tax on income   261

Tables

1.1   GDP and its components in the United Kingdom and
      other OECD countries   12
1.2   Consumption price deflator in the United Kingdom and
      other OECD countries   14
3.1   Personal sector wealth composition   51
3.2   Medium-term financial strategy   54
4.1   Share ownership in the United Kingdom   73
5.1   OECD standardised unemployment rates   91
6.1   Sectoral financial positions   105
6.2   Personal sector   106
6.3   Dollar/pound and Deutschmark/pound exchange rates   110
8.1   Share of world merchandise trade for the United
      Kingdom   143
8.2   UK visible trade and import penetration   144
8.3   Government expenditure on regional preferential
      assistance to industry   158
9.1   Employees in employment in Great Britain, 1981 and
      1991   168
9.2   The regional distribution of other business service
      employment in the United Kingdom, 1981–9   177
9.3   The eligibility for regional policy assistance of producer
      services: 1984 scheme   183
10.1 UK privatisation – progress in the 1980s   195
10.2 New regulatory bodies established in the United
      Kingdom   196
11.1 Trade union membership and density in the United
      Kingdom, 1968–89   205

11.2 Stoppages of work due to industrial disputes in the
United Kingdom, 1965–89 214
12.1 Ceilings and reduction targets for emission of SO_2 from
existing plant 231
13.1 General government expenditure, 1978/9 to 1990/1 240
13.2 General government expenditure on services 243
13.3 Government revenue from taxation 250
14.1 Distribution of family income before tax 259
14.2 Effects of taxes and benefits on the distribution of
household income in the United Kingdom 263
14.3 Gini coefficients for the distribution of income at each
stage of the tax benefit system 264
14.4 The distribution of wealth 266
15.1 Gross local tax bills 282
15.2 Local tax bills, net of rebates and rebate entitlements 282
15.3 Valuation bands and tax ratios 284

Preface

In teaching economics it is not easy, especially at the introductory level, to find good books on economic policy which cover the most relevant topics in an interesting and illuminating way, using some theory, presenting some data and stimulating further interest in the subject. There is a tendency to regard economic policy as 'too difficult' for an introductory treatment, and most textbooks reflect this by providing excellent coverage of basic economic theory but relatively little applied or policy-related material. However, we disagree with this view of policy. Rather, we believe that a course in economics which includes a strand of economic policy is likely to be greatly appreciated both by students and their teachers. Not only that, but we consider that many policy issues can usefully be studied with the aid of quite simple economic theory, and that the interplay between theory and policy can be beneficial to both.

This book is intended to demonstrate these points. Its level is introductory, so that it should be suitable for the more advanced school students (taking 'A' levels or Scottish Highers and CSYS) as well as for first-year university and college students. While it uses theory, it does not purport to be a theory text. Accordingly, it should normally be used alongside one of the many good textbooks on introductory economic theory.

The book was originally conceived as the second edition of *Introduction to British Economic Policy*, edited by Paul Hare and Maurice Kirby in 1984. However, by the time a second edition was being seriously considered, both original editors had left Stirling University, where the first edition was written, and Maurice Kirby was too busy with other commitments to take part in this project. As a result, it was decided to base the new book at Heriot-Watt University, and to take on a new editor, Leslie Simpson.

Since the world of UK economic policy has changed so much since the early 1980s, it was not possible to produce the present book merely by updating the old one. Instead, everything has been written from scratch, reflecting the most up-to-date information now available about the UK economy, as well as the changed policy agenda and priorities. This book deals with several topics not covered at all in the first edition, including the impact of the European Community on UK economic policy, the distribution of income and wealth, and the economics of services. Chapters on the labour market and de-industrialisation from the first edition are no longer included here (though we do discuss industrial relations and industrial policy), not because the topics are no longer important or interesting, but simply because something had to go to make way for the new material and a different approach was considered more appropriate.

For Heriot-Watt University's Economics Department, writing this book has been an enormously successful, co-operative venture. As can be seen from the information provided about the authors, all but two come from the Economics Department. It is also the case that almost everyone in the Economics Department has contributed to the book. Early meetings about the book revealed widespread enthusiasm for the project, and a surprising willingness to agree to fairly tight deadlines in the preparation of draft chapters and the implementation of revisions requested by the editors. Even more surprising, to the editors at least, was the outcome. For all authors not only made promises but they actually delivered the goods, more or less on time. In our experience, this is extremely unusual for edited books.

Doing this obviously required considerable co-operation from the authors, as indicated, but also substantial support from the secretarial staff who typed some of the chapters and prepared many of the figures and diagrams. We owe particular thanks, in this regard, to the Economics Department's two secretaries, Mrs Jean Roberts and Mrs Pat Chrystal for their valiant efforts.

As editors, we took full advantage of modern word-processing technology by ensuring that all chapters were submitted to us both on paper and on disk. This enabled us to carry out a lot of minor (and some major) editing without referring back to the individual authors, and to print out revised versions of each chapter. We hope that all authors will be content with the changes we have made to their chapters, and that they can still recognise their own work despite our revisions. In any case, we certainly owe many thanks to our enthusiastic and dedicated authors, both for their own chapters, and for the helpful comments and suggestions they provided about other chapters.

Finally, especially in the last weeks of preparing this book, the heavy demands of editorial work inevitably placed great strain on the editors' families. We would like to thank our respective wives and children for their support and tolerance during this especially busy period, and hope they agree with us that the results are worthwhile.

PAUL HARE *and* LESLIE SIMPSON
Edinburgh, July 1992

Chapter 1

Economic policy: the major themes

PAUL HARE

1.1 Introduction

The conduct and nature of economic policy in Britain are very different in the early 1990s from what they were in the 1970s and even from the early 1980s. Several factors have contributed to what amounts to an enormous shift in the policy environment in which Britain now operates, and with which it must come to terms. Many of these factors are related to political and institutional developments in Britain and the world, including Britain's evolving relationship with the European Community (EC), but some of the changes are also associated with developments in economic thinking, with the ways in which we conceptualise the working of policy instruments both in the short run, and in terms of an ultimate influence on longer-term performance (such as through growth rates).

1.2 Political and institutional factors

Some of these factors are essentially domestic (though even these have often reflected, or paralleled, developments elsewhere). For instance, the government's more restricted conception of the role of macroeconomic policy in actively guiding the economy in the last decade or so contrasts quite strikingly with more interventionist approaches pursued formerly (by both of the main political parties). Within this, conceptions of fiscal policy have assigned greater importance than before to stability and balance in the government's spending and revenue plans, as against the active use of fiscal levers to promote short-term stabilisation. At the same time, monetary policy was largely used to promote price rather than output stability during the 1980s (prices here including both the domestic price level and the exchange rate), with money supply targets and interest rate targets being emphasised more or less strongly at different times.

1

Another domestic factor is the greatly increased emphasis on using markets and the private sector to deliver goods and services as against the more traditional reliance on public provision for many items. This has influenced wide areas of policy in the last decade. Associated with this theme is the whole question of the privatisation of housing, public services and public enterprises, as well as the liberalisation of the financial markets, and the several stages of legislation on trade unions. Despite this marked change in the philosophy of government, however, the 1980s actually witnessed a *rise* in the share of general government spending in gross domestic product (GDP), as we detail later.

The United Kingdom's economic policy environment has also been increasingly influenced by external factors. In the past, some of these might well have been regarded as constraints on domestic policy-making, and to some extent this is correct, of course. However, several of the aspects of policy which are either determined externally or subject to external influence are in policy domains where the most appropriate level of determination nowadays is wider than the nation state. Trade policy, exchange rate policy (including the United Kingdom's membership of the European Monetary System (EMS), and the implications of that), the liberalisation associated with the '1992' programme, and the recent development of EC, G7 or G24[1] policies towards Eastern Europe are just a few of the domains in this category. Hence it is more relevant, now, to think of the United Kingdom's policy environment in a very wide sense, with different types of policy being determined, quite properly, at different levels. Recognition of this situation has not proved easy for the United Kingdom.

One consequence, though, is that it is no longer possible to discuss most important issues in United Kingdom policy without making some reference at least to the European Community, and in some cases to wider areas. This is why, in the chapters that follow, many of them have an 'EC dimension' reflecting the influence of European institutions on what would previously have been considered domestic policy. Moreover, this influence is evident not only in the familiar areas of macroeconomic policy, referred to above, but increasingly in microeconomic policy too, including such matters as regional policy, environmental policy, science and technology policy, and many others.

Through its efforts to promote mobility across the Community – of goods, services and people – the European Community is also contributing towards a process of harmonisation which is having increasingly noticeable effects in the individual member states. Whereas in the past, the European Community sought to ensure harmonisation by convergence to common standards, a process fraught with political and technical difficulties (and, sometimes, absurdities), it now seeks to make progress through the mutual recognition of standards adopted in different countries, combined, where relevant, with definitions of accepted minimum standards. This approach is proving more acceptable to member states, but in many cases it still requires considerable adaptation of their respective domestic policies.

Aside from the increasing impact of the European Community, other international agreements and organisations also influence domestic policy in the United Kingdom, such as the General Agreement on Tariffs and Trade (GATT) in relation to trade policy (though at present there is great uncertainty about the outcome of the present Uruguay Round of trade negotiations[2]) and various international conventions on environmental issues. In the international oil market, the Organisation of Petroleum Exporting Countries (OPEC) remains influential, though its role and policies may well be influenced by the longer-term effects of the 1991 Gulf War to expel Iraq from Kuwait. The world oil market will also be influenced by the serious economic situation in the former Soviet Union. Since the United Kingdom is a major oil producer itself, the oil price is important for it both in terms of public revenues (a higher price yields higher profits to the producers, and hence more tax revenue) and in terms of costs of production throughout the economy (a lower price obviously helps user industries and sectors).

1.3 Conceptual developments and policy aims

Economic policy used to be thought of in very simple terms, with a list of reasonably widely agreed policy objectives to be achieved by the application of a limited range of macroeconomic policy instruments – monetary and fiscal policy, exchange rate policy. At the level of formal policy analysis relatively little attention was paid to microeconomic issues and economists (as well as policy-makers) believed that some variant of the standard Keynesian model provided an adequate basis for discussion. None of this holds today; indeed, much of it was either rejected or found to be seriously deficient by the early 1980s.

Typical policy objectives included the achievement of full employment, low (and preferably stable) rates of inflation, a satisfactory balance of payments and satisfactory growth, though in practice most attention was focused on the so-called internal and external balances. Internal balance essentially means full employment, but the term is also sometimes used to encompass objectives to do with inflation, as well as with the balance between government income and expenditure. External balance just refers to the balance of payments, including, of course, both the current and capital accounts.

Influenced by Keynesian ideas, for much of the postwar period it was taken for granted that, in response to short-term fluctuations in output and employment, the government should and could use a judiciously chosen combination of fiscal and monetary policy, supplemented by exchange rate policy, to reduce their amplitude and duration. It is no longer so clear that this is a viable approach (if it ever was) or, in any case, whether it is desirable. For one thing, this approach was predicated on a conviction that certain empirically established relationships, such as the Phillips curve, could be relied on to be tolerably stable under a wide range of alternative economic policies. For another, it involved accepting the notion of a private sector which, while it responded to what the government actually did, was assumed to be rather unsophisticated in that it did not attempt to forecast government actions. This passive conception of the private sector is not accepted nowadays.

Instead, the private sector is regarded as forming a model of the economy which includes views about the government's own behaviour (and, as is well known from the work of Lucas and others on rational expectations models, this can imply the complete ineffectiveness of government policy under certain conditions). Given this, it becomes important for the government's policies, and its statements about its likely future actions, to have credibility and consistency. Among other things, this tends to favour relatively stable, slowly changing policy; it also favours policies which involve some pre-commitment by the government, so that private sector agents can see that the government would incur significant political and/or economic costs by making unexpected changes.

In addition to its role in the macro-economy, Keynesian thinking predisposed governments of both major parties towards intervention in other areas of economic life, though to a rather greater extent under Labour governments. This is clear in the nationalised industries (which Conservative governments did not extend, but also did not seek to privatise before 1979, with the sole exception of steel), where large monopolies enjoyed statutory protection extending well beyond areas where arguments about economies of scale could have justified them. In some sectors, such as housing and civil engineering (as well as defence, of course), the government was a dominant or major customer and was thereby able to influence the conditions of operation in these sectors. It did so partly by determining the technical conditions of what it purchased, sometimes without regard to what private sector customers might have wanted (e.g. the serious and costly 'mistakes' in public sector housing), and sometimes through fluctuations in the level and composition of public spending. The latter could easily create conditions of boom or bust in the sectors most closely related to government demands, and at times the resulting instability made planning and long-term investment appear very risky.

The government, at both national and local levels, also acted as a regulator in regard to many aspects of private sector activity, including safety, consumer protection, planning and building controls and environmental controls. Intervention of this sort is essential in a modern economy, since private sector agents, left to themselves, cannot be expected to take proper account of the potentially harmful externalities arising from their decisions, and the need for it did not disappear as Keynesian thinking lost its dominance in the United Kingdom. Nevertheless, there have been widespread criticisms about the bureaucratic, and sometimes overpoliticised way in which such controls are implemented in the United Kingdom, especially now that they are increasingly influenced by European Community policies emanating from Brussels.

Increasing awareness of these and other shortcomings of the standard Keynesian package influenced conceptions of the most appropriate policy aims, and approach to economic policy, for the government to pursue. At the macro-level, rather than seeking to achieve the short-term stabilisation of output by using the traditional, Keynesian instruments of economic policy, the government increasingly took the view that its role was to provide a stable policy environment within which the private sector could (and presumably would) flourish. The key element of this stability was considered to be the rate of inflation which, accordingly, became the principal policy target from the end of the 1970s onwards. This does not, of course, imply that policy was wholly successful in this regard, as we shall see in the next section. Nor does it imply that the government was no longer concerned about the traditional, Keynesian objectives for the economy – full employment, growth and balance of payments equilibrium.

The instruments used to control inflation changed over the decade, influenced by the prevailing exchange rate regime. For most of the 1980s, the exchange rate was, in theory, floating (albeit, a managed float), and the domestic money stock (defined in many different ways) was the principal intermediate policy target, with interest rates being used as the main instrument to achieve it (along with the general stance of the public sector, naturally). Later, the exchange rate of the pound sterling (£) was informally linked to the Deutschmark (DM), and eventually the United Kingdom joined the Exchange Rate Mechanism (ERM) of the European Monetary System (though not within the narrow bands; see below for fuller discussion). Thus interest rates were then used to keep the pound within its agreed limits in the EMS. To the extent that the financial markets had confidence in these exchange rates, the DM/£ exchange rate effectively provided a nominal anchor to the United Kingdom price level, to which United Kingdom producers (and consumers) must adapt themselves. However, speculative pressure in the international currency markets forced the government to leave the ERM in mid-September. At the time of writing, no clear alternative policy had emerged.

Aside from seeking to control inflation, it is important to consider the most suitable wages/incomes policy for the United Kingdom. The government has tended to assert that there is no wages policy, and that 'markets must decide'. But this is clearly absurd. For the government is, directly and indirectly, the largest employer in the country, and hence its own approach to wage settlements unavoidably influences the behaviour of the private sector. Conversely, major private sector wage settlements are bound to influence or constrain what the government must pay. Given existing policies towards inflation (and the present nominal anchor just referred to), the real question is how much unemployment must be tolerated in order to make the desired inflation rate 'stick'. Unfortunately, this is an area where the government has been relatively ineffective in developing new policy in the last decade, with the result that the level of unemployment may have to remain higher than would be necessary with more satisfactory wage-setting arrangements.

Although the 1960s and 1970s did witness an active micro-policy, for instance in areas like regional policy and industrial policy, this was not really in keeping with the typically neoclassical approach to microeconomic issues that could be found in most economics textbooks of the time. Interestingly, while the neoclassical approach gained greater acceptance among policy-makers in the 1980s, in association with the ascendance of monetarist ideas in macroeconomics, it was accompanied by a new emphasis on what came to be called supply-side economics. This is not easy to define precisely, but the basic idea is simple enough.

Supply-side economics recognises that, even in an essentially competitive economy, certain markets may not work perfectly. This can be due to high taxation (distortions), formal or informal restrictions on competition, or externalities of various sorts, including those due to imperfect information. Politically, supply-side economics was strongly associated with Mrs Thatcher and her advisers in the United Kingdom, and with President Reagan in the United States, but many of its tenets were adopted by other industrialised countries of all political persuasions during the 1980s.

An important aspect of supply-side economics was a strong push to lower tax rates, both on corporations and on personal incomes, in order to stimulate more effective and efficient use of economic resources. Such a trend was evident in many western countries during the 1980s, including the United Kingdom, though ironically, the United Kingdom's reductions in income taxation were almost wholly offset by rises in value added tax (VAT). Given that, it is questionable whether the supposed incentive effects of lower income taxes can have been very significant.

In addition, training and education policy have both received attention as means of improving the general level of skills, and improving labour market mobility and flexibility. In practice, though, much of the new training provided by government agencies was of a rather low level, and educational reforms, including those in higher education, were limited by increasingly stringent budgetary constraints. Trade union legislation was introduced to limit restrictive practices and make the effective use of strikes more difficult. In the capital market, one of the first steps taken by the Conservative government in 1979 was to abolish all remaining United Kingdom controls over capital movements. Other countries also gradually relaxed their controls during the 1980s, and the decade witnessed an enormous expansion in the international flow of capital, both for portfolio investment and for investment in new plant and equipment. Within the United Kingdom itself, particular attention was paid to the needs of small firms (which were 'fashionable' for a time, and considered to be 'neglected' by the capital market), as well as to de-regulation in the financial markets. Finally, public support for research and development (R&D), while much criticised in the United Kingdom for its over-emphasis on military R&D, was focused on information technology and other so-called generic technologies where externality arguments could be deployed to justify it. The United Kingdom lost its technological advantage in some areas, such as electronics and nuclear power, while gaining in such areas as chemicals, drugs and food. As in many other policy domains, R&D was a field that came to be increasingly dominated by EC-level policies from the mid-1980s onwards.

Particularly in the United Kingdom, the housing market has been seen as restricting mobility, partly through problems of local authority tenants finding new accommodation in an area to which they might wish to move, partly because of highly differentiated house prices across the United Kingdom in the privately owned sector. Both sectors of the market have been distorted by subsidies of various kinds, which governments have been slow to recognise or remove. So this is an aspect of supply-side policy where there has been little real change recently, aside from a vigorous pursuit of privatisation: much of the local-authority-owned housing stock was privatised during the 1980s, mainly by sale to existing residents on favourable terms.

Another important issue affecting labour supply, wages and unemployment is social security (including housing benefit) and social welfare policy. This has changed over the 1980s, with typical social security payments falling in relation to average money wages, and several elements of policy being more sharply focused on those deemed to be in greatest need. The result of this, and the tax cuts already referred to, has been to increase the inequality of incomes in the United Kingdom during the 1980s.

Partly as a supply-side policy, partly as a means of promoting greater efficiency (and sometimes competition), we must refer to the government's privatisation programme. After a slow start this gathered pace and resulted in the transfer to private hands of about 10 per cent of the nation's capital stock during the 1980s, leaving very little productive capital outside the private sector. The programme is expected to continue at least for the first few years of the 1990s, and is gradually being extended to new areas.

With the Conservative government re-elected in spring 1992 and the domestic economy still in deep recession, and with increasing strains associated with its continuing membership of the Exchange Rate Mechanism of the European Monetary System, the world financial markets became increasingly turbulent in August and early September 1992. Despite frequent restatements of its determination to remain in the ERM at the existing exchange rate for sterling, weeks of pressure eventually forced the government to leave the ERM, as noted above. The result has been to leave the country with a policy vacuum, though the government continues to express its determination to reduce inflation even further, the pound has fallen by over 10 per cent against major European currencies, and interest rates have started to decline. Given this unexpected outcome of recent government policy, can it be said that the economic policies of the 1980s have left behind a favourable legacy for the remainder of this century?

Towards the end of 1992, the main economic indicators were mixed, though mainly rather gloomy: the good news was that inflation was continuing to come down, and that many firms in the United Kingdom were far more competitive than they had been a decade earlier; but against this, output was still static or declining, the trade balance remained weak, government finances had moved into substantial deficit (forcing the government to restrict public spending despite the recession), unemployment was still rising towards the 3 million level, and until the country's sudden exit from the Exchange Rate Mechanism, interest rates were unable to fall because of the high level of German interest rates and the markets' lack of confidence in the exchange rate.

There are two possible interpretations of such a configuration of indicators. According to the first, policy – including withdrawal from the EMS – is substantially correct, but the United Kingdom (along with other industrialised countries) is in a recession not caused by government policy, and outside government control. On this view, it is simply (!) necessary to wait for a revival of private sector confidence, whereupon increases in private consumption and investment (and, it is to be hoped, exports) will drive recovery and growth for the next few years. On this view, the government's job, as stated earlier, is to maintain a monetary environment compatible with continuing low inflation. In particular, as the prime minister, John Major, recently asserted, there is no need to 'kick-start' the economy.

The second interpretation is somewhat different, however. This is that the recession was caused, and/or the recovery is being delayed, by policy errors. Thus one can easily cite the over-rapid reduction in income taxation which stimulated excessive consumer spending in the late 1980s and helped to foster a new round of inflationary pressure in the United Kingdom, accompanied by massive increases in property prices. The recession left many people with abnormally high debts which they are still striving to reduce, while property prices continue to fall. In addition, the

United Kingdom's late entry into the ERM, at a point when United Kingdom inflation was much faster than Germany's, and at a DM/£ rate that was widely considered too high even at the time of entry into the mechanism, created serious difficulties. For although the ERM provided the United Kingdom economy with a nominal anchor to restrain inflation (in the absence of effective domestic policies to achieve this outcome), its effectiveness depended on credibility. In the ERM, therefore, the government was locked into a position where, for reasons of inflation control then and in the future, it did not believe that it should change sterling's exchange rate in the ERM; but not doing so would have entailed very high unemployment in order to bring the United Kingdom price level into line with competitor countries'. Yet for exporters a realignment of currencies in the ERM appeared desirable, to stimulate export demand and make imports relatively more expensive. Such a realignment would have the additional benefit of enabling United Kingdom interest rates to be cut much further than was possible before October 1992, so helping to stimulate domestic demand. Moreover, given the depth of recession, it is very likely that a modest depreciation of sterling would not even give a significant impulse to inflation. In the event, rather than a managed realignment of currencies, market forces compelled the government to leave the ERM. The realignment just discussed then took place outside the ERM framework. Moreover, it appears that the government does not intend to return to the ERM very quickly.

Before the United Kingdom so ignominiously exited from the ERM, we (that is, the editors) were inclined to favour a realignment of currencies within the ERM which, if it had occurred as part of a general adjustment and not merely as something to help this country, need not even have markedly dented the UK government's policy credibility. However, as we now know, such a managed adjustment is not at all what happened in September 1992, and in late 1992 the government faced a new and largely unexpected situation. How it reacts will still depend, though, on its underlying philosophy of the powers and duties of the government in relation to the economy. If it returns to earlier, Keynesian conceptions, it could allow the public sector deficit to rise for counter-cyclical reasons to help to boost aggregate demand, reduce interest rates fairly fast (if necessary allowing the currency to depreciate somewhat faster than it would otherwise have done), and thereby *actively* stimulate the economy. Alternatively, it could adhere to its monetarist principles (even if we no longer hear much about monetary targets and the like), restrict public spending despite the rising deficit, focus on controlling inflation, and otherwise rely on the creation of a stable economic environment to raise confidence and hence private sector spending; in this way, a relatively *passive* approach would be adopted towards stimulating the economy. Given the diverse political pressures both within the Conservative party itself, and within the country in general, it will be very interesting to observe how this difficult policy dilemma is resolved in the next year or two.

1.4 Economic performance in the 1980s

The 1980s started badly with a very deep recession, and ended badly with another recession, from which recovery was barely perceptible at the time of writing (October 1992). In between, the United Kingdom enjoyed a period of rapid growth of output and, for many of those in full-time employment, rapidly improving incomes and real living standards. Tighter monetary control was supposed to 'squeeze inflation out of the system', changes in taxation were expected to improve incentives, and those firms which survived the tough conditions of the early 1980s should have been 'leaner and fitter'. No doubt many of them were, and still are, though the cost in terms of bankruptcies and unemployment was very high. The question is whether, in the 1990s, the policies of the last decade will turn out to have brought about a fundamental change in the United Kingdom's economic behaviour, and, therefore, whether their costs will be considered justified in the light of superior United Kingdom performance in the coming years.

At present, this does not appear likely, since the immediate prospect is of very slow growth at best, with the United Kingdom's high marginal propensity to import ensuring that much of the additional demand benefits foreign rather than United Kingdom producers (hence continuing the recent run of poor foreign trade results), with high interest rates and the aftermath of the recent property boom holding back investment, and with the government itself striving to hold down the public sector deficit. Moreover, the government is so concerned to win 'the battle against inflation' that it is prepared to maintain a very tight monetary policy even in the depths of a recession. These and other issues are referred to in later chapters (but see also Michie, 1992; Smith, 1992), so here I confine myself to a brief review of the main macroeconomic indicators for the 1980s, including some comparisons with other industrialised countries. Many indicators not covered here are discussed fully in the chapters that follow (e.g. unemployment, balance of payments, money supply, etc.).

For the period from 1978 to 1991, Table 1.1 shows gross domestic product and its main expenditure components for the United Kingdom and five other developed countries: the chosen comparator countries are the United States, Japan, France, Germany and Italy. For the same period, and the same six countries, Table 1.2 shows how the consumer price index (consumption price deflator in the table) has moved in each country.

From the data shown in the tables, the evidence for a British economic miracle in the 1980s is quite mixed. Indeed, over the whole period shown, the United Kingdom experienced slower overall economic growth (i.e. growth of GDP) than any other country in the tables, and consumer prices rose faster on average than anywhere except Italy. Taking a somewhat shorter period, from 1981 to 1990, however, during which time the United Kingdom economy enjoyed unbroken growth, GDP growth was faster than any country in the table except Japan, averaging 2.9 per cent per annum.

Like all the other OECD countries exhibited, except the United States, growth of public consumption (government expenditure on goods and services) was slower than that of GDP as a whole. This reflects a tendency throughout the developed world to restrict government spending in recent years, in line with monetarist philosophy which, as we saw above, favoured reducing the role of the government in the economy. On the other hand, the United Kingdom and Italy were the only countries in the tables in which private consumption grew noticeably faster than GDP as a whole. In the case of the United Kingdom, this reflects a tendency for booms to be led by private consumption spending. Thus living standards rise for a time, but investment and exports are too weak to sustain the expansion without encountering capacity constraints (in the case of investment) and inflationary pressures, as well as a worsening trade balance. All of this was apparent in the United Kingdom in the second half of the 1980s.

Table 1.1 shows that the United Kingdom's export performance has been the weakest of the countries shown over the 1980s. Thus even when world trade grows rapidly, as it did for much of the 1980s, the United Kingdom enjoys export growth while losing market share to more dynamic competitors, both within the OECD (as in the table) and outside (e.g. Hong Kong, China, etc.). For United Kingdom industry, this trend is very worrying, since it implies that in an increasing range of branches and product groups, United Kingdom firms are unable to compete effectively in world markets.

One reason for this is undoubtedly the low rates of investment which characterise the United Kingdom. It is interesting that, with the exception of the United States whose underlying economic situation is even more difficult than that of the United Kingdom, investment by OECD countries grew much faster than GDP as a whole during the 1980s. In the United Kingdom, investment enjoyed a short-lived boom in the late 1980s, but has fallen back substantially since 1989. Meanwhile, our principal competitors continue to invest at a higher rate, partly because their investment has grown faster than GDP in the last decade, partly because even at the start of this process they were already investing a higher proportion of their GDP. On both counts, the United Kingdom is being left behind.

Turning, finally, to inflation, we have already noted the United Kingdom's poor inflation record in the last decade (see Table 1.2). However, this record is better than that achieved in the United Kingdom during the 1970s. Already, inflation in 1992 is expected to be little more than 4 per

Table 1.1 GDP and its components in the United Kingdom and other OECD countries

Country	United Kingdom						United States						Japan					
Item Year	GDP	C	G	I	X	M	GDP	C	G	I	X	M	GDP	C	G	I	X	M
1978	90.9	86.2	92.7	91.0	83.8	77.3	86.5	83.5	83.2	86.7	87.4	66.0	75.9	79.7	80.7	84.4	53.7	86.0
1979	93.0	89.9	94.5	93.5	87.0	84.8	88.7	85.4	84.7	90.7	94.9	66.9	80.1	84.9	84.2	89.6	57.9	98.5
1980	91.2	90.0	96.0	88.5	86.8	81.7	88.2	85.4	86.6	83.3	103.7	63.8	82.9	85.8	87.0	89.6	67.8	93.5
1981	90.2	90.1	96.3	80.0	86.2	79.4	89.8	86.4	87.7	83.8	105.5	66.9	85.7	87.2	91.1	91.7	77.4	97.6
1982	91.4	91.0	97.1	84.4	86.9	83.3	87.9	87.4	89.0	77.1	95.9	66.9	88.7	91.0	93.0	91.6	80.4	96.9
1983	94.9	95.1	99.0	88.6	88.6	88.7	91.3	91.4	91.4	82.2	92.5	75.2	91.1	94.1	95.7	90.7	81.9	91.3
1984	96.4	96.6	100.0	96.2	94.4	97.5	96.9	95.8	94.3	95.3	98.9	94.1	95.1	96.7	98.3	95.0	94.0	101.0
1985	100.0	100.0	100.0	100.0	100.0	100.0	100.0	100.0	100.0	100.0	100.0	100.0	100.0	100.0	100.0	100.0	100.0	100.0
1986	104.0	106.2	101.8	102.4	104.7	106.9	102.9	103.6	105.2	100.4	106.6	106.6	102.6	103.4	104.5	104.8	94.6	100.6
1987	108.8	111.8	103.0	112.3	110.7	115.2	106.1	106.5	108.4	99.9	117.7	111.5	107.1	107.8	104.9	114.8	99.0	111.3
1988	113.4	120.1	103.6	127.0	110.7	129.4	110.3	110.3	109.0	104.1	136.3	115.6	113.8	113.4	107.2	128.5	109.6	135.0
1989	116.0	124.3	104.6	135.6	115.4	139.0	113.0	112.5	110.7	104.5	151.7	119.9	119.3	118.3	109.3	140.4	126.0	164.8
1990	117.1	125.4	107.8	132.4	121.1	140.4	114.1	113.8	114.2	102.8	163.5	122.5	125.5	123.3	111.4	153.6	139.5	184.6
1991	114.7	123.2	110.4	118.8	122.0	136.3	113.3	113.7	115.2	95.0	173.9	122.9	131.0	126.5	115.2	159.0	146.5	179.5

Country	France						Germany						Italy					
Item Year	GDP	C	G	I	X	M	GDP	C	G	I	X	M	GDP	C	G	I	X	M
1978	88.4	86.9	83.9	100.7	78.6	84.4	89.7	93.8	89.1	97.3	69.6	79.9	83.6	81.0	82.4	90.3	83.1	79.6
1979	91.3	89.6	86.4	103.8	84.5	93.0	93.4	96.7	92.1	104.1	73.0	87.7	88.6	86.9	84.9	95.5	90.2	88.9
1980	92.7	90.6	88.6	106.6	86.8	95.3	94.3	97.8	94.5	106.6	76.9	91.4	93.3	92.1	87.2	104.5	82.8	88.1
1981	93.8	92.5	91.3	104.6	90.0	93.3	94.5	97.3	96.2	101.6	83.3	90.2	93.8	93.5	89.1	101.2	89.4	87.4
1982	96.2	95.7	94.7	103.1	88.5	95.7	93.3	95.7	95.3	95.9	86.0	90.0	94.0	94.6	91.5	96.5	87.2	86.9
1983	96.9	96.6	96.7	99.4	91.7	93.2	95.1	97.0	95.6	99.1	85.2	90.1	94.9	95.2	94.6	95.9	89.3	85.7
1984	98.2	97.5	97.8	96.9	98.1	95.6	98.0	98.5	97.9	99.4	92.9	95.0	97.5	97.1	96.7	99.4	96.9	96.2
1985	100.0	100.0	100.0	100.0	100.0	100.0	100.0	100.0	100.0	100.0	100.0	100.0	100.0	100.0	100.0	100.0	100.0	100.0
1986	102.5	103.9	101.7	104.5	98.6	107.1	102.2	103.4	102.5	103.4	99.9	103.3	102.9	103.7	102.6	102.2	102.5	102.9
1987	104.8	106.9	104.6	106.5	101.6	115.4	103.6	106.8	104.1	105.4	130.5	107.3	106.1	108.0	106.1	107.3	107.0	112.0
1988	109.5	110.4	108.2	120.1	109.8	125.3	107.2	109.4	106.4	110.1	106.1	113.3	110.5	112.5	109.1	114.8	113.1	119.9
1989	114.0	114.0	108.5	128.5	121.0	135.6	111.3	111.7	104.6	117.8	118.6	123.2	113.7	116.5	110.0	119.7	123.0	129.0
1990	116.6	117.3	110.5	132.2	127.7	144.4	116.6	116.8	106.8	128.8	132.2	138.2	116.2	119.8	111.4	123.6	132.6	139.1
1991	118.1	119.1	114.0	131.5	132.8	148.5	120.3	119.7	107.6	137.4	148.2	155.4	117.9	123.2	113.4	124.8	131.6	143.1

Notes: [1] All data are presented in index form in constant prices of 1985, with 1985 values = 100.

[2] Notation is standard, so C = private consumption, G = public consumption, I = investment, X = exports, M = imports.

Source: Quarterly National Accounts, 1992(1), Paris: OECD.

Table 1.2 Consumption price deflator in the United Kingdom and other
OECD countries. (All figures are expressed as percentages of the 1985
consumer price level for each country.)

Country Year	United Kingdom	United States	Japan	France	Germany	Italy
1978	54.0	63.8	78.4	50.6	74.7	37.4
1979	61.3	69.5	81.2	56.0	77.9	42.8
1980	71.3	76.7	87.3	63.5	82.4	51.6
1981	79.3	83.6	91.2	71.8	87.7	60.9
1982	86.2	88.4	93.6	80.1	92.3	71.3
1983	90.4	92.6	95.5	87.8	95.4	81.9
1984	94.8	96.3	97.8	94.6	98.0	91.7
1985	100.0	100.0	100.0	100.0	100.0	100.0
1986	104.4	103.1	100.4	102.7	99.5	106.3
1987	108.9	107.4	100.6	105.9	100.1	111.9
1988	114.3	112.0	100.5	108.7	101.5	118.3
1989	121.0	117.3	102.3	112.5	104.6	125.8
1990	127.7	123.2	105.0	115.8	107.3	133.5
1991	137.2	128.2	107.7	119.4	111.1	142.7*

Note: * 1991, third quarter.
Source: As Table 1.1.

cent, with further falls likely thereafter. However, as we discuss later, the
costs of this achievement may turn out to have been very high.

1.5 Brief introductions to individual chapters

In order to guide the reader through what follows, this section provides
some brief introductory remarks on each chapter. Like the book as a whole,
the comments are grouped into two sub-sections, on macroeconomic and
microeconomic policy respectively.

1.5.1 Macroeconomic policy

Part I opens with Stuart Sayer's chapter on fiscal policy and the Public
Sector Deficit. This argues that in order to understand the stance of fiscal
policy it is necessary to consider what has been happening to the Public
Sector Deficit. Whether a particular deficit is sustainable depends on how it
is financed – by asset sales, bond issues or by monetary emission – and on
its relation to GDP both now and in the future. The latter, of course,
depends both on cyclical factors and on longer-run growth trends. After
discussing a variety of possible cases, including the effects of political
pressures and expectations, the chapter ends with a useful checklist of
factors to look for in assessing the likely impact of fiscal policy in general,

and the chancellor's budget statements and public expenditure statements in particular.

For much of the period since 1979, controlling inflation has been the government's top priority, but large reductions in inflation were only achieved at very high cost in terms of output and employment, as Geoffrey Wyatt emphasises in Chapter 3. While the government attempted to use monetary targeting to control inflation in the early 1980s, it was doing so at a time when financial markets were undergoing both rapid innovation as well as de-regulation. This made it very hard to operate monetary policy effectively, and to interpret monetary indicators. By the end of the decade, the United Kingdom had abandoned its own independent approach to monetary policy, opting instead for membership of the ERM of the European Monetary System. This gave the German Bundesbank the greatest influence over monetary conditions, and meant that the United Kingdom had to use interest rates and other policy instruments to maintain the exchange rate. Though this was not sustained for more than two years, it remains to be seen whether a future re-entry to the ERM, at a more viable exchange rate, will prove to be more successful than the former approach to monetary policy.

As Ian Hirst emphasises in Chapter 4, the United Kingdom financial markets changed rapidly during the 1980s. He concentrates on the corporate sector, reviewing the banks, the equity market and the bond markets, as well as important issues to do with takeovers, mergers and corporate governance. There is now less distinction between different types of financial institution than there used to be (which is a mixed blessing, since it gives up some of the benefits of specialisation), greater competition and tougher regulation to protect investors. Whether the reformed system of financial markets functions more effectively as a supplier of risk capital to the corporate sector is not yet clear, since the reforms have not been in place for long, and a recession does not provide the best occasion to assess market performance.

Partly as a result of the monetary policy pursued in the 1980s, the United Kingdom experienced its highest unemployment rates since the 1930s. This gave rise to much debate about the nature of the resulting unemployment, and in particular about how high unemployment needed to rise in order to restrain and bring down inflation. The policy issues involved here are both important and complex. They are examined in Chapter 5, by Prabir Bhattacharya. He argues that reducing unemployment entails the use of supply-side policies to reduce wage pressure, while aggregate demand is also increased. The inflationary effects of the latter are minimised if new job opportunities can be made available to the long term-unemployed.

In Chapter 6, Hugh Fleming analyses both the balance of payments and the exchange rate. In contrast to the 1960s and 1970s, even though the balance of trade was often in substantial deficit in the 1980s, it did not provoke government intervention: it was certainly not one of the key policy targets, since it was considered to be largely the outcome of a myriad of separate private sector decisions. The chapter outlines the accounting framework which makes clear the connection between the overseas balance and private and public sector financial balances. On the exchange rate, it focuses on the $/£ and DM/£ rates, which at various times did become targets of government policy. Study of the record of the 1980s shows that for quite long periods the government can indeed control the exchange rate rather effectively. It then becomes crucial to assess what a suitable target would be. In particular, it appears that the United Kingdom entered the ERM at a DM/£ exchange rate which left much of United Kingdom industry relatively uncompetitive.

The final chapter in Part I, Andrew Scott's Chapter 7 on the European Community, could have been placed in either part, since it deals with both macroeconomic and microeconomic issues. Its inclusion in the book reflects the enormous importance of EC policy for the United Kingdom nowadays, not only in connection with the EMS, which was already referred to above, but also in connection with agriculture (the Common Agricultural Policy, or CAP), regional policy, technology policy and the whole package of policies to do with the Single European Market (sometimes called the 1992 Initiative, but actually due to be fully in effect from January 1993). The last of these entails removing many of the remaining EC barriers to the movement of goods, capital and people within the European Community.

1.5.2   Microeconomic policy

In Part II, we begin with chapters on two unfashionable but important topics. The first, Peter Clarke's Chapter 8 on industrial policy, covers a diverse field of policy in which any government intervention extending beyond the minimal requirement to set the parameters within which the private sector would operate was generally considered undesirable during the 1980s. The second, Patrick O'Farrell's Chapter 9 on the role of services, charts a crucial area of the economy (now providing over two-thirds of total employment in the United Kingdom) which has been surprisingly neglected by government policy.

After reviewing alternative approaches to industrial policy, notably the neoclassical and 'Austrian' approaches, Chapter 8 sets out the framework of industrial policy in the United Kingdom. In doing so, it reviews the areas of competition policy, regional policy, public support for research and development, and policy on international trade. Starting from the premise that the function of industrial policy should be to promote international competitiveness, the chapter finds that United Kingdom policy has probably had very little net impact in the last decade, even though the existence of the relevant legislation and institutions might help to discourage certain forms of anti-competitive behaviour. Some aspects of industrial policy, such as merger and takeover issues, and some aspects of R&D policy, now fall within the ambit of EC policy. While this can enable a wider, EC, view to be taken of industrial concentration, for instance, it can also give rise to conflicts of interest between the European Community and member states.

Since services have received so little attention from policy-makers, and are so rarely covered in economics textbooks, it is appropriate for Chapter 9 to provide some definitions. Some of the key features of services are highlighted, including the increasing interchangeability between goods and services, and the nature of the interaction between supplier and customer: some types of specialised manufacturing become increasingly like services, while some services (e.g. fast-food outlets) become more like a production line. Although hard to measure, there is evidence that United Kingdom service sector productivity has risen far faster than that of manufacturing in recent decades, while the sector generated over 2 million new jobs in the 1980s. Only a small part of United Kingdom regional policy spending has supported services, and at EC level the main emphasis has been on de-regulation and the promotion of competition.

Aside from policy towards private industry and the services sector, the 1980s witnessed a massive programme of privatisation of state-owned firms and industries in the United Kingdom. This transformation is described in Paul Hare's Chapter 10. Even as late as the 1970s, the nationalised sector in the United Kingdom was expanding as new firms were brought into public ownership. At the same time, the government sought to establish a general framework of control over the sector, with policies concerning pricing, investment criteria, and financial limits. Increasingly, both public perceptions and comparative analysis agreed that the nationalised sector was not performing well and, as monetarist thinking came to the fore in macroeconomics, so privatisation became an increasingly central plank in the government's microeconomic policy. In the course of implementing the programme, many United Kingdom citizens became shareholders for the first time. Especially in the public utilities, which remained as virtual monopolies after privatisation, the government established new regulatory bodies to control their pricing and other aspects of their economic behaviour. Towards the end of the 1980s, the government was starting to extend the idea of privatisation to new areas: schooling, the universities, the health service, local authority services and so on. In the early 1990s, it was apparent that the re-elected Conservative government would continue in the same direction.

In contrast to services, the trade unions did attract substantial amounts of attention from the government in the 1980s, as documented in Chapter 11, by Leslie Simpson and Ian Paterson. They outline the basic labour market theory which makes it possible to assess the impact of trade unions, and review the empirical evidence for the United Kingdom which suggests that the impact has been quite small in practice (despite government assertions to the contrary). In stages during the 1980s, industrial relations legislation was passed to limit trade union powers and immunities, requiring pre-strike ballots, and ending the protection previously given to union closed shops. Although union membership has declined, as has the extent of national pay bargaining in the United Kingdom, the government seems set to introduce a further round of legislation very soon.

Increasingly important at both United Kingdom and EC levels of policy is the control over environmental pollution. As Leslie Simpson emphasises in Chapter 12, the 'common sense' view that all such pollution is a bad thing is simply mistaken. Instead, it is essential to consider both the costs and benefits of pollution, which together enable us to determine the 'optimal' level of pollution. Because of the high costs of eliminating some forms of pollution, this optimal level is unlikely to be zero. Nevertheless, since pollution is not normally traded (no price is attached to it), markets left to themselves are most likely to generate more than the optimal level of it (firms treat it as costless, even though it generates social costs). This is why governments seek to regulate pollution. They can do so either through the price mechanism (using taxes and subsidies), or by direct controls and standards. Although the former is usually preferable in theory, the latter is most often employed in practice. The chapter reviews air and water pollution control policy in the United Kingdom, as well as recent legislation to establish an integrated pollution control system. EC environmental policies, as well as measures resulting from the recent Earth Summit, are likely to have a substantial impact on the United Kingdom's pollution controls in the 1990s.

The remaining three chapters in Part II deal with issues related to government expenditure and taxation, government being broadly inter-preted to include the local authorities. Thus Chapter 13, by Philip Welham, deals with public expenditure and taxation, Chapter 14, also by Philip Welham reviews the distribution of income and wealth, with particular reference to the impact of tax and expenditure policies upon these distributions. Finally, Chapter 15, by Douglas Mair, analyses local government finance, including that biggest political misjudgement of modern times, namely the so-called poll tax (officially, the Community Charge). Between them, these chapters cover two of the three traditional areas of public finance, to do with efficient resource allocation and questions of equity. The remaining area, stabilisation policy, is covered in Chapter 2 (see outline, above).

Chapter 13 studies the appropriate size of the public sector, the components of government expenditure and the way the tax base and tax rates affect firms' and households' decisions. It concludes that there has almost certainly been too little public spending on education, health and housing, and that despite substantial reductions in income taxation, the overall burden of taxation increased during the 1980s. In the 1990s, policy options will be constrained by concern over the government's total borrowing: thus even if income tax rates continue to fall, it will be at the cost of widening the tax base (by removing some existing tax concessions) or by cutting public expenditure.

As Chapter 14 shows, the United Kingdom experienced a reduction in income inequality in the period from 1945 to 1979, but in the 1980s inequality increased again, with further increases likely in the 1990s. Taken as a whole, the tax system has little effect on income distribution, but transfer payments redistribute annual income towards the poor. Nevertheless, the extent of poverty in the United Kingdom increased during the 1980s. The distribution of wealth in the United Kingdom was also becoming more equal in the postwar period, but this trend came to an end around 1976. Since then, it is most likely that the distribution has remained roughly stable.

The concluding Chapter 15 combines a review of general issues to do with local government spending and taxation, with an account of the astonishing story of the poll tax. The tax was introduced as a replacement for domestic rates, rates being a tax on property (or, in effect, on housing services) not greatly different in practice from the value added tax levied on many other items of personal expenditure. Although economically sound, the rates became politically unacceptable when the government realised that an impending property revaluation would result in massive increases in rates for some households. It therefore introduced an economically unsound tax, the Community Charge. This tax was also designed to ensure that all adult members of the community (including those on social security) should contribute to local services, though this feature could easily have been incorporated in the rates system. Nevertheless, as soon as the Community Charge became law, it was clear that its obvious injustices (the requirement that even the poorest should pay something, and its generous treatment of the rich) would make it highly unpopular. So strong was the popular resistance to the tax that its collection costs became embarrassingly high, many people failed to register for the tax, and eventually the government was obliged to return to a modified form of the rates, the Council Tax, which comes into effect in 1993. All governments make mistakes, and all too frequently they do so with the help of bad economics: the poll tax fiasco is the most spectacular recent instance of this phenomenon.

Questions for discussion

1. How did the United Kingdom government's approach to economic policy change in the 1980s?
2. Discuss the United Kingdom's economic performance in the 1980s in comparison with other industrialised countries.
3. 'Low income taxes strengthen work incentives, which in turn yield faster growth.' How far does the United Kingdom's experience support this view?
4. Is investment in the United Kingdom too low?
5. Discuss the main ways in which the world economic environment changed in the last decade. Were these changes favourable or unfavourable for the United Kingdom?

Notes

1. G7 refers to the group of seven most developed countries: the United States, Canada, Japan, Germany, France, Italy and the United Kingdom. G24 refers to the twenty-four most developed countries (which therefore includes G7), belonging to the Organisation for Economic Co-operation and Development (OECD), based in Paris. Both groups meet regularly to discuss a wide range of world economic and political issues.
2. At the time of writing, the completion of the Uruguay round of GATT negotiations is already a year overdue and there is still no sign of a completion date. These negotiations have been very prolonged and are very complex. They are the first major round of world trade negotiations to include services in the discussions and there are serious disagreements between the United States and the European Community over agricultural subsidies.

References and suggestions for further reading

Michie, J. (ed.) (1992), *The Economic Legacy 1979–1992*, London: Academic Press.
Smith, D. (1992), *From Boom to Bust: Trial and error in British economic policy*, London: Penguin.

Macroeconomic policy

Chapter 2

Fiscal policy and the Public Sector Deficit

STUART SAYER

2.1 Introduction

Fiscal policy directly concerns taxation, government expenditure on goods and services, and transfer payments such as welfare benefits paid to the unemployed or poor. As such, it has many facets that cannot be adequately dealt with in a short chapter. The focus of this chapter is on broad macroeconomic aspects of fiscal policy and its financial implications – somewhat similar in spirit to the opening sections of an annual budget speech. The discussion centres on the Public Sector Deficit (PSD), largely because this is the most useful measure of the overall stance of fiscal policy in the United Kingdom. Section 2.2 explains the PSD and provides a summary review of its behaviour in recent years. To assess this behaviour it is helpful to distinguish between long-run and short-run aspects, and these are considered in sections 2.3 and 2.4 respectively. Section 2.5 addresses some specific issues to do with political pressures and expectations, that provide an interesting perspective on recent fiscal history. Finally, section 2.6 concludes with a summary checklist that can be used to review the macroeconomic aspects of the annual budget.

2.2 The Public Sector Deficit

In simple terms, a deficit in the public sector arises from the difference between public sector outgoings and income over an accounting period. There are a number of different measures of the deficit based on different ways of measuring outgoings and income.

The most commonly used measure in the United Kingdom is the Public Sector Borrowing Requirement (PSBR). The PSBR directly measures the extent to which the public sector borrows from other sectors of the domestic economy or overseas. Many discussions, particularly in the media and political circles, treat the PSBR as the primary indicator of the state of the government's finances. This was formalised in the original version of the Medium Term Financial Strategy (MTFS) introduced in 1980, which set out explicit targets for reducing PSBR/GDP, and more recently the Maastricht treaty of the European Community set a guideline for PSBR/GDP (see section 2.5).

From 1987 to 1991 the PSBR was negative, so that instead of borrowing the public sector was repaying previous borrowing. This negative PSBR was sometimes referred to as a (positive) Public Sector Debt Repayment.

One problem with the PSBR as a measure of the underlying state of the public sector's finances concerns its treatment of the sale of public sector assets, such as the sale of publicly owned corporations (e.g. British Telecom) or the sale of council houses. The proceeds raised from public sector asset sales directly reduce the need for the public sector to borrow and hence reduce the PSBR, at least in the accounting period in which the sale takes place. When assessing the state of the public sector's finances, however, public sector asset sales are best thought of as a means of

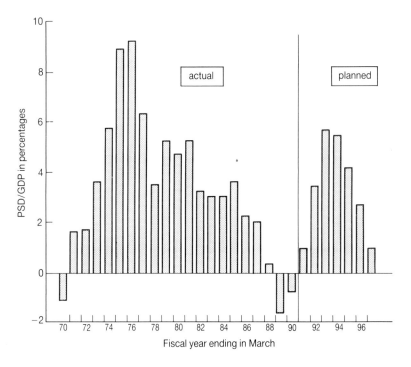

Figure 2.1 Public Sector Deficit as a percentage of GDP. (*Sources: Financial Statement and Budget Report,* and *Annual Abstract of Statistics*)

financing the deficit in the public sector rather than as a means of *reducing* it (see the discussion in section 2.3). To take account of this the proceeds from public sector asset sales ('privatisation proceeds') need to be added to the PSBR. This gives the measure of public sector finances known as the Public Sector Deficit.

Figure 2.1 shows the actual behaviour of the PSD between 1970 and 1990 and the plans announced in the 1992 Budget. It is presented as a percentage of GDP (PSD/GDP), since this provides a more meaningful scale than the basic numbers. Reading too much into these raw figures can be dangerous. The remaining sections of this chapter aim to elucidate this behaviour and, as should become apparent, first impressions may be misleading. Two features of Figure 2.1 are worth highlighting. First, PSD/GDP has varied markedly, ranging from a high of 9.3 per cent in the fiscal year 1975–6, to a surplus (i.e. a negative PSD/GDP) of 1.6 per cent in 1988–9. Second, when the plans for PSD/GDP up to the mid 1990s are taken into account, there does not appear to have been a particularly dramatic change in the state of public sector finances under the Conservative administrations that have been in power since 1979.

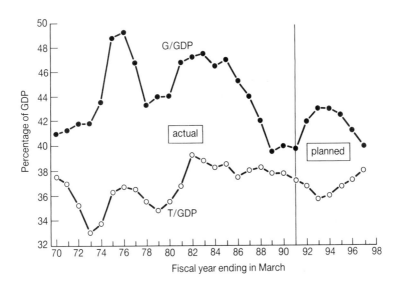

Notes: G/GDP is General Government Expenditure as a percentage of GDP.
T/GDP is tax revenue (including social security contributions but excluding North Sea taxes) as a percentage of GDP.

Figure 2.2 Tax revenues and general government expenditure as a percentage of GDP. (*Source: Financial Statement and Budget Report (1992–3)*)

A more detailed picture of what underlies the behaviour of PSD/GDP can be obtained by considering the behaviour of the public sector outgoings and income that give rise to the PSD. The main source of public sector income is tax revenues. The behaviour of tax revenues as a percentage of GDP (T/GDP) is depicted in Figure 2.2. An important point to note is that, despite the much publicised cuts in rates of personal income taxation and the political rhetoric of the period, the tax share of GDP was consistently higher throughout the 1980s than it was in the previous decade. This partly stems from 'fiscal drag' since tax thresholds, at which one starts to pay basic or higher rates of tax, have not risen in line with GDP, as well as from changes in the structure of taxation, for example, notably increases in the rate of VAT. In addition to tax revenue, public sector income also includes revenue from assets owned by the public sector. Although this makes a relatively small contribution to public sector income, it is of some importance when considering public sector asset sales as a source of finance for the deficit. The sale of public sector assets straightforwardly reduces the flow of revenue that the public sector would have received from these assets in future periods.

Turning to public sector outgoings, the main outgoings are classified as General Government Expenditure, which comprises expenditure by central and local government on consumption, capital investment, transfer payments, and interest payments on public sector debt. Figure 2.2 depicts

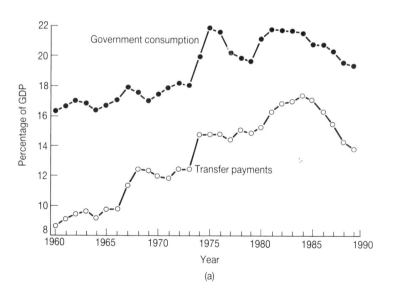

Figure 2.3a Public sector consumption and transfer payments (percentage of GDP). *(Source: Economic Trends)*

the behaviour of this measure of government expenditure as a percentage of GDP (G/GDP). Comparing Figures 2.1 and 2.2 there is a clear relationship between the behaviour of PSD/GDP and G/GDP. Both peak in 1974–6, fall in the latter part of the 1970s under the Labour government, rise in the early 1980s under the Conservatives, followed by a substantial fall in the latter part of the 1980s.

Breaking down General Government Expenditure into the four components listed above provides further insight (see Figures 2.3a, 2.3b). One important feature of Figure 2.3b that is worth highlighting is the very low level of general government investment expenditure throughout the 1980s. This is a potential cause for concern to which we return later.

Returning to the more aggregated picture provided by Figure 2.2, actual and planned G/GDP is now substantially lower than it was throughout much of the 1970s and early 1980s. The consideration of whether this change has been wholly or partly desirable raises complex and important issues to do with the scale and scope of government that we do not address directly in this chapter (though see Chapters 1, 10 and 14).[1] Our concern is primarily with the broader picture provided by the overall PSD, though the component parts that go to make up the PSD do, at times, have an important bearing on our discussion.

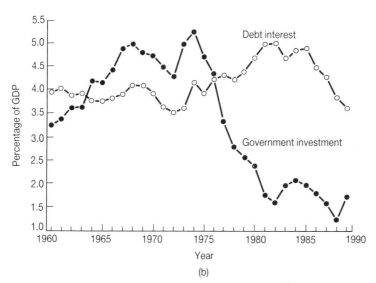

Note: Government investment is measured by General Government Expenditure on gross domestic fixed capital formation.

Figure 2.3b Public sector investment and debt interest (percentage of GDP). (*Source: Economic Trends*)

2.3   Deficits, money and debt in the long run

When assessing the PSD/GDP ratio from a long-run perspective the key issues concern the consequences of financing the PSD. Three main ways of financing the PSD can be distinguished, which we consider in turn.

1. *Public sector asset sales:*   Public sector asset sales, related to privatisation, have provided a significant source of finance during the 1980s (see Figure 2.4). As noted in section 2.2 these proceeds represent the difference between our measure of the PSD and the PSBR, so that subtracting public sector asset sales from the PSD gives the PSBR. Since public sector asset sales reduce the PSBR, at least in the accounting period in which the sale takes place, they have the attraction of improving the appearance of the government's finances as well as making it easier to meet targets for PSBR/GDP.

This appearance is, at least for the most part, cosmetic and misleading. In the first place, public sector asset sales can normally only provide a temporary rather than sustainable source of finance. Once the asset sales' programme is completed, this source of finance dries up.[2] At that time the PSD will either have to be reduced or financed by some other means. Secondly, the current reduction of the PSBR resulting from an asset sale is offset by the increase in the PSD and PSBR in all future time periods that results from the loss to the public sector of the income stream from the

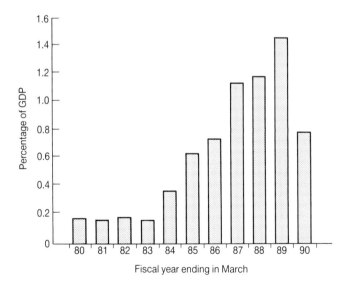

Figure 2.4   Public sector asset sales (percentage of GDP). (*Sources: Annual Abstract of Statistics* and *Financial Statement and Budget Report*)

asset. Thirdly, public sector asset sales absorb private sector savings in much the same way as the sale of interest-bearing government debt. Somewhat simplistically, since the adjustments to savings behaviour are more complex than this, individuals or institutions who might otherwise have purchased interest-bearing government debt to finance a given amount of the PSD may use the identical funds to purchase public sector assets and finance the PSD by an equivalent amount. Moreover, the loss in the public sector's revenue stream resulting from the asset sale is, in essence, similar to the interest stream payable on government debt.

2. *Increasing the monetary base or high powered money (money finance):* In simple terms this can be thought of as printing new money to finance the PSD, though the monetary base also includes bankers' balances at the Bank of England in addition to notes and coin. This method of financing the PSD utilises the seignorage gain that accrues to the issuer of money. Seignorage reflects the difference between the direct costs of creating new money, which, particularly for notes and bankers' balances, are relatively trivial, and the value of the goods and services for which the new money can be exchanged. At first sight this might seem an attractive and painless way of financing the PSD. However there are potentially serious drawbacks that stem from the inflationary consequences of excessive money creation.

3. *The sale of interest-bearing government debt:* The key feature of financing the current PSD by the sale of interest-bearing government debt is that this will result in a time stream of interest payments raising the PSD in all future time periods. The consequences of this for PSD/GDP depend on whether or not the rate of interest on government debt exceeds the rate of growth of GDP (as has been the case in recent years).

Government debt at some date is the sum of all loans made to central and local government which have not been repaid at that date. Financing the interest payments on outstanding government debt by the sale of new debt is potentially explosive, the government debt as a proportion of GDP (GD/GDP) would get larger and larger, and ultimately this is not sustainable.

However, far from exploding, the actual GD/GDP ratio in the United Kingdom has declined significantly over the last two decades (see Figure 2.5). Whether this decline has been altogether desirable is a complex and contentious issue. Reducing the GD/GDP ratio has transitional effects which we discuss in section 2.4. In general they can be thought of as requiring taxes to be higher or government expenditure lower than they would otherwise be. Given the GD/GDP ratio we have inherited from the past, the current cost of reducing it may outweigh any (suitably discounted) future benefits. This argument applies with particular force to the current situation in the United Kingdom, since the United Kingdom's GD/GDP ratio is now low by both historical and international standards.

Comparing Figures 2.1 and 2.5 suggests a puzzle. Even though the PSD/GDP ratio has been substantially positive for most of the period, the GD/GDP ratio has fallen from 63 per cent in 1975 to 35 per cent in 1990. The solution to the puzzle hinges on the fact that the capital value of most government debt is fixed in money terms. In consequence, the value of outstanding debt does not rise automatically in line with either real GDP growth or inflation, so that the GD/GDP ratio automatically falls as nominal GDP grows unless new debt is issued.

A simple calculation, set out in Buiter (1985), gives a rough guide to the numbers involved. Suppose the GD/GDP ratio is to remain stable at 50 per cent, and the annual real growth rate of GDP is 2.5 per cent. With zero inflation, new debt issues of 1.25 per cent of GDP would be required (i.e. the 50 per cent GD/GDP ratio times the real growth rate of 2.5 per cent). Whereas, if the stable inflation target were 5 per cent, there would need to be additional new government debt issues of 2.5 per cent of GDP to offset the effects of inflation (i.e. the 50 per cent GD/GDP ratio times the 5 per cent inflation rate). Overall, new debt issues amounting to 3.75 per cent of GDP would be needed to maintain the stable GD/GDP ratio in the 5 per cent inflation case.

This analysis sheds an interesting light on the medium-term plans of the current government. These plans envisage maintaining a zero PSBR/GDP on average over the medium term. The consequences of this strategy for GD/GDP depend on inflation. Even assuming a zero inflation rate, this

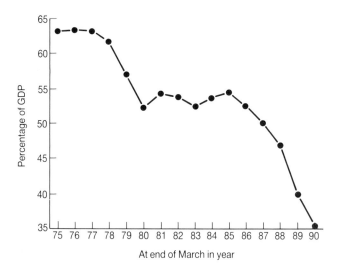

Figure 2.5 Government debt as a percentage of GDP. (*Source: Annual Abstract of Statistics*)

strategy may involve further reductions in the GD/GDP ratio. A more realistic assumption about inflation is that it will be low but positive (e.g. between 2 per cent and 5 per cent), broadly in line with the inflation rate of our partners within the European Monetary System (see section 2.5). This implies even more strongly that the medium-term strategy set out by the government involves further reductions in the GD/GDP ratio. Given that the GD/GDP ratio is already low, the merits of this strategy are questionable.

2.4   Short-term variations in PSD/GDP

Relative to some benchmark level of a stable GD/GDP ratio, a reduction in GD/GDP, requires the current PSD/GDP to be lower than it would otherwise be. In future periods the reduced GD/GDP ratio will mean that interest payments on outstanding debt are lower, so that a given PSD/GDP target allows for either lower revenues or some other component of public sector outgoings to be greater. For simplicity we will concentrate on tax revenues, so that a reduction in GD/GDP involves an increase in current tax revenues and a reduction in future tax revenues, relative to the benchmark. Conversely, an increase in GD/GDP involves a cut in current tax revenues and an increase in future tax revenues. In effect, changes in the GD/GDP ratio redistribute the tax burden over time.

How should the government make use of this ability to redistribute the tax burden over time? We focus on two broad cases that serve to illustrate the basic principles and shed light on recent fiscal policy in the United Kingdom (e.g. the planned increase in PSD/GDP in the early 1990s depicted in Figure 2.1).

1. *Exceptional public sector investment:*   The focus on exceptional invest-ment is important. 'Normal' public sector investment should take place at a more or less even rate over time. Exceptional situations may, however, arise from time to time. Two pertinent examples are unforeseen disasters, such as an environmental catastrophe or war, and the cumulative effect of past underinvestment by the public sector which may have stemmed from the political pressures for short–sightedness that are considered in section 2.5. Assuming the exception is genuine, then some increase in the GD/GDP ratio to finance the investment at least partially would normally be justified. One simple justification is that the timing of the tax burden should be related to the timing of the benefits that accrue in the future from the investment. Further, by smoothing the tax burden over time, rather than wholly financing the exceptional expenditure by a rise in current taxation, debt financing can help the private sector to even out

consumption over time (this is spelled out in more detail in the second case below).

Consideration of this case can provide interesting insights into the arguments surrounding cutting rates of income tax. One beguiling argument runs as follows. Cutting income tax rates improves incentives. So although the impact effect of a cut in income tax rates will be to reduce revenue, at a given level of economic activity, over time the improvement of incentives will raise the level of activity to offset this effect, or even generate higher tax revenues from lower tax rates. If this argument were true, cutting income tax rates has obvious attractions. It effectively raises the size of the national cake in the long run, giving scope for both higher public and private sector expenditure. Though in the short run, until incentive effects have raised the tax base sufficiently, tax revenues will fall, and this temporary fall in tax revenues will need to be financed. One approach is to allow PSD/GDP to rise and use government debt finance, and this can be justified along the lines discussed above by thinking of the tax cut as an exceptional investment.

Although this argument, in various guises, has received widespread currency in recent years, it suffers from a fundamental weakness. This is that there is no evidence to support the belief that cutting income tax rates has the substantial effects on incentives envisaged by the above argument. Cuts in the basic rate of income tax appear to have no significant effects on the incentive to work and unambiguously reduce tax revenues. The effect of cuts in higher rates of income tax is less clear, partly because the available information on higher-rate tax payers is limited. Again the balance of the evidence suggests that there is little or no effect on work incentives, though the revenue effects are more complex since, for example, cuts in higher rates of taxes may alter the way in which taxpayers choose to be compensated. (See Brown, 1988; Dilnot and Kell, 1988.)

Some exponents of tax cuts argue that this evidence is limited because it neglects longer-term changes to the work and risk-taking culture, which they regard as important. The weight of the evidence seems clear that, at least at the rates that have prevailed in the United Kingdom, cutting the basic rate of income tax produces a permanent reduction in tax revenue below what it would otherwise have been. If the tax rate cut is to be sustained, there must be a permanent change to some other component of the public sector finances: for example, an increase in some other form of taxation (e.g. taxes on expenditure such as VAT) or a permanent reduction in government outgoings below what they otherwise would have been. Tax rate cuts do not provide a magic solution that will allow us to have our cake and eat it, though the attractions of this magic solution can be important in the context of the political issues introduced in section 2.5.

2. *Stabilisation over an economic cycle:* The second case concerns an economic cycle in which GDP fluctuates about its trend path. Standard economic analysis suggests that consumers plan to even out their consumption over the cycle. In a recession, where GDP is below its trend, they would choose to increase the proportion of current income devoted to consumption and finance this by borrowing or dissaving against the expectation of higher future income. Conversely, in a boom where GDP is above trend, they would reduce the proportion of income consumed and increase savings. The ability of the private sector to smooth their consumption in this way is limited by the operation of financial and credit markets. The spread (i.e. difference) between borrowing and lending rates available to private sector agents – particularly individuals and small- to medium-sized corporations – is often large. This can make it unattractive to borrow when times are bad and lend when times are good. In some cases individuals may be unable to obtain any credit at all (e.g. the unemployed in a recession) or be required to pay exorbitant rates of interest. Recent theoretical work on the operation of financial and credit markets suggests that there are good reasons, to do with information and risk, for these limitations on private sector borrowing and lending. For our purpose they have the important implication that it is generally easier for the government to reallocate income or spending power over time, by varying PSD/GDP, than it is for at least most private sector agents.

This argument suggests that PSD/GDP should be higher than normal in a cyclical recession. In effect the public sector increases its borrowing in a recession, and the tax payments made by the private sector are lower than they would need to be to maintain the normal PSD/GDP ratio. Since tax payments take a smaller share of current income, private sector agents can afford to devote a larger share of current income to consumption, limiting their need to borrow to finance consumption smoothing. Conversely, in a boom PSD/GDP should be lower than normal or even negative, with the tax payments made by the private sector being higher than they would need to be to maintain the normal PSD/GDP ratio.

At least loosely this is reflected in the behaviour of PSD/GDP in the late 1980s and early 1990s (see Figure 2.1). PSD/GDP was low or negative in the boom phase of the late 1980s, followed by a substantial increase in PSD/GDP in the recession of the early 1990s. Although this might appear to validate the fiscal policy of the period, this simple observation needs to be treated with caution.

In addition to the pure consumption smoothing argument, just outlined, resources may also be utilised inefficiently over the economic cycle, for instance as a result of various frictions inhibiting the operation of market forces. If resources are used inefficiently then a judicious use of fiscal policy may be able to improve efficiency. A relatively simple example is an economy where frictions result in underutilised or unemployed resources in a recession. One possible response might be to use current fiscal policy to improve the efficiency of resource use. For example, taxation might be increased on those in work, whose income might be little affected by the recession, in order to finance an increase in public sector expenditure that uses unemployed resources for some socially useful purpose. In general, though, it is more efficient to spread this tax burden over time by increasing PSD/GDP, since this enables both tax and consumption smoothing.

Ideally the timing of PSD/GDP changes should coincide with the timing of the income changes that they are designed to smooth. In practice, at least when the underlying disturbance that causes the income change is unpredicted, there is likely to be a lag before the PSD/GDP ratio can be adjusted. Further, it may take time for the change in fiscal policy to take effect, particularly in the presence of frictions. In the extreme, if this lag is sufficiently long relative to the length of the cycle the policy may itself be de-stabilising.

With regard to the appropriate size of PSD/GDP changes it is difficult to generalise. The ideal size depends on the nature of the cycle, the significance of impediments to borrowing and lending in the private sector, the timing and structure of the PSD/GDP change, as well as other components of the policy package, notably monetary, interest rate and exchange rate policy. The question of structure concerns the need for the underlying changes in government outgoings or taxation to be appropriately directed to those whose income or employment is affected by the cycle in order for variations in PSD/GDP actually to bring about income or employment smoothing. This question is often neglected in simple macroeconomic models which focus on aggregate income or employment. In practice the main effect of disturbances is commonly localised, either geographically or in particular industrial or employment sectors, or some sector or region may gain while others lose. Where the disturbance is localised, a general fiscal stimulus, such as a cut in income taxes, can exacerbate rather than dampen the fluctuations in income since the majority of the beneficiaries of the tax cut are unaffected by the disturbance. Some attempt at targeting, e.g. by subsidies or tax cuts directed at specific industries or regions, would normally be worthwhile, though information and administrative problems make it difficult for fiscal policy to be perfectly targeted.

A more specific, but important, complication concerns the distinction between temporary cyclical variations in income and employment, and permanent shocks that cause a permanent shift in the trend path of income and employment. The smoothing argument outlined above only applies straightforwardly to cyclical movements. By contrast, a permanent shock requires a permanent adjustment to consumption. The practical problem is that at the time they occur it may be difficult or impossible to distinguish between a temporary and a permanent shock. If a permanent shock is mistakenly thought to be temporary, a mistake that may be made by both public and private sectors, then both private sector borrowing and PSD/GDP may be set inappropriately high.

This scenario can provide some insight into recent fiscal history in the United Kingdom and elsewhere (see Roubini and Sachs, 1989). A widespread view is that the United Kingdom suffered from a permanent downward shock, or series of shocks, to potential output and employment in the late 1960s and early 1970s, reflected in a permanent increase in the non-accelerating inflation rate of unemployment or NAIRU (see Chapter 5 for further discussion). The initial response was to treat this permanent shock as if it were a temporary cyclical downturn in activity and increase PSD/GDP, most notably in the so-called Barber boom in 1973–4. In addition a substantial portion of the PSD was financed by money rather than debt. The consequences were high inflation and a depreciating exchange rate. Eventually, in the later 1970s and early 1980s, uncomfortable fiscal adjustments had to be made to take account of the permanent nature of the shock. The initially inappropriate response made these adjustments more uncomfortable than would have otherwise been the case.

It is misleading to think of the PSD/GDP ratio as directly under the control of the government. In practice both the PSD and GDP may differ quite markedly from the government's offical projections set out in the Budget. Further, the PSD will tend to be higher than expected when GDP is lower than expected, since lower GDP reduces tax revenues by reducing the tax base on which given rates of income and expenditure taxes are charged, and also increases expenditure on transfer payments (e.g. unemployment benefits, income supplement). In consequence, the effect of forecasting errors on the PSD/GDP ratio can be quite dramatic. For example, in recent years the average error in the forecast for the coming year's PSD has been around 1 per cent of GDP.

This automatic effect has some attractions when viewed as a response to an unforeseen cyclical disturbance. It is likely to be fairly well directed to the extent that those who suffer an unforeseen income loss pay lower taxes or receive transfer payments. The delays associated with legislative action to change tax rates or outgoings are avoided, but there is no guarantee that this automatic effect produces the right size of response to a particular disturbance. A rough guide to the size, based on recent Treasury estimates, is that a 1 per cent decline in GDP relative to trend, will 'automatically' increase PSD/GDP by 0.3 per cent in the first year and 0.7 per cent in the second year (see Davies, 1991).[3] Naturally, this automatic response does not distinguish between temporary and permanent movements in GDP, and for the latter it is likely to be inappropriate. Thus despite their prominence in recent budget speeches, 'automatic stabilisers' need to be treated with caution. The need for discretionary judgements about the appropriate stance of fiscal policy remains.

2.5   Government failure, political pressures and expectations

For a variety of reasons governments may tend to set the PSD/GDP ratio at an inappropriate level, or the underlying components of fiscal policy that give rise to the PSD may be poorly structured to deal with the current economic situation. This may result from more or less understandable errors of judgement. For example, misinterpreting a permanent shock as a transitory shock, as discussed in section 2.4; or anticipating a downturn in economic activity that does not materialise, e.g. following the October 1987 Stock Exchange crash. The consequences of inappropriate policy tend to be asymmetric. A prodigal policy – i.e. an excessive or poorly structured PSD/GDP – tends to generate a nominal boom, with higher inflation and a depreciating exchange rate, especially if a significant part of the PSD is money financed so that fiscal policy is reinforced by an 'accommodating' monetary policy. In contrast, an excessively tight fiscal policy tends to induce a real recession. Specific examples depend on one's underlying judgements about the appropriateness of policy. Many commentators regard the early 1980s as illustrating an excessively tight fiscal policy with an associated real recession, though see below for a subtly different view of this period. Similarly, many regard the 'Lawson boom' of 1987–8 as illustrating a prodigal policy with an associated resurgence of inflation.

The problems can be more serious if fiscal policy is subject to a systematic bias. To illustrate we concentrate on one fairly general and simple story that has been applied to recent fiscal history in the United Kingdom and elsewhere. The basis of the story is that decisions in practice are boundedly rational, i.e. they are based on limited information and a relatively short time horizon. In 'normal' times attention is focused on the immediate benefits of an increase in the GD/GDP ratio in terms of the current reduction in taxes or increase in government outgoings. Although at some future date the PSD/GDP ratio will have to be cut, for the long-run reasons discussed above, this does not cross information thresholds. In effect people act as if tomorrow never comes, or at least does not come in their own lifetime, so that the burden of cutting the PSD/GDP ratio will be borne by future generations and is not of immediate concern.

These perceptions give rise to political pressures, both from the electorate and interest groups, for a high and possibly rising PSD/GDP ratio, and policy–makers, who are also subject to bounded rationality, succumb to these pressures. Though for appearances' sake they may attempt to disguise this fiscal prodigality as a prudent response to the current economic situation (see Buchanan *et al.*, 1978, who also consider other aspects of the political system that may add to these pressures). As well as affecting the overall level of PSD/GDP, boundedly rational (and other) political pressures may also bias the fiscal components that give rise to the PSD. For example, policy may be focused on changes that give immediate and obvious benefits – e.g. cuts in income tax or increases in outgoings directed at powerful interest groups – at the expense of other areas – e.g. less visible taxes on expenditure, and public sector investment, especially where it yields indirect and long-term benefits. A further influential variant of this story argues that the pressures to increase the PSD/GDP ratio are particularly pronounced in the run-up to an election, giving rise to the notion of give-away election budgets and the political business cycle. Despite the popular attention given to political business cycles, however, the evidence in support of this notion, at least in a simple form, is at best weak (see Alesina, 1989).

Periodically, normal times are interrupted by crises when some key indicator, notably the rate of inflation, balance of payments and/or exchange rate, moves outside its accepted limits. The cause of the crisis may be the cumulative effects of an excessive PSD/GDP, but other factors may also be at work, e.g. major disturbances such as oil price shocks and excessive monetary growth. In some cases crises may even arise as a result of disturbances in financial markets that have little or no basis in fundamental economic activity (see Sayer, 1992). Once a crisis is perceived, fiscal policy is focused on responding to the crisis. Crisis rhetoric may emphasise a concern with long-run fiscal prudence, though the boundedly rational focus on the immediate crisis, allied to feelings of guilt about past profligacy and the need for harsh medicine, may give rise to a tougher fiscal stance than long-run fiscal prudence requires. Once the key indicators have fallen back below their information thresholds and feelings of guilt have receded, normal times return, until the next crisis unfolds.

This simple story has a certain intuitive appeal, though it is difficult to formulate and test in a rigorous fashion. One problem is that boundedly rational perceptions and pressures appear to change over time. In part this may reflect increasing recognition of and desire to avert the type of fiscal cycle that the story describes. But there are other apparent changes, for example in comparison to the 1970s, unemployment appears to have become more politically acceptable and inflation less (i.e. their respective crisis thresholds appear to have shifted), and the perceived benefits of income tax cuts, at the expense of other components of the PSD, appears to have increased. A further important issue concerns the increasing scale and sophistication of financial markets, which has made the reaction of financial markets to fiscal policy increasingly significant. Some argue that financial markets help to check fiscal prodigality. But others take a less benign view, arguing that the reactions of financial markets may be biased or unrelated to fundamental economic behaviour.

The consideration of expectations, whether in financial markets or elsewhere, adds a subtle twist to the above story. If fiscal policy is expected to be expansionary, which may be a reasonable expectation in the light of the above story, this expectation will itself tend to put upward pressure on inflation and interest rates and downward pressure on the exchange rate. Moreover, given such an expectation about policy, the best short-term response of the government may indeed be to pursue an expansionary fiscal policy. Failure to do so would cause a surprise or expectational error, which would be likely to depress output and employment. In effect the government may get caught in a trap where expectations of expansion become self–fulfilling. In order to get out of this trap, expectations of fiscal expansion need to be revised downwards. We briefly consider three approaches, which can also be interpreted more broadly in terms of the basic bounded rationality story.

First, despite the costs to output and employment, the government may pursue a tighter than expected fiscal policy in order to establish a reputation for fiscal prudence. This may be difficult if expectations of expansion are firmly entrenched, and there may remain a lurking suspicion that at some point the government will revert to its expansionary ways. A variant of this approach is to tighten dramatically fiscal policy to try to signal a clear break with the past. The immediate effects of such a regime shift on output and employment may be severe, but this may serve to reinforce the signal and allay suspicions, since a government that was not firmly committed to fiscal prudence might be thought to be unwilling to countenance these effects. This provides an interesting interpretation of the controversial 1981 Budget, where in the depths of a recession the budget changes were aimed at increasing tax revenues by about 1.6 per cent of GDP. This interpretation needs to be treated with a certain amount of care, since there are other aspects of the 1981 Budget that need to be considered to tell a complete story (see Allsopp, 1985; or Budd, 1991). It can also be of interest to consider the sequel to this budget. Having administered this sharp shock to expectations (or crisis response), did subsequent administrations maintain fiscal prudence or revert to expansion in a manner similar to that suggested by the bounded rationality story outlined above?

Second, the government may enter into a commitment that indirectly limits the scope for fiscal expansion. The Exchange Rate Mechanism of the European Monetary System can be thought of as such a commitment. The key feature of the ERM is that it limits the permitted normal movement of the exchange rate, for sterling against other member currencies, to within a fairly narrow band (see Chapter 6 for further details). In its present form the commitment is not fully binding. The ERM allows for the possibility of the target band being adusted in exceptional circumstances, and there is the option of withdrawing from the ERM (for example, the withdrawal of sterling in September 1992). This weakens the force of the commitment, since the government might choose to adjust its target exchange rate or even withdraw from the ERM rather than make the other adjustments needed to maintain the exchange rate. The proposed moves towards European Monetary Union (EMU) would effectively strengthen this commitment, as well as removing the scope for individual nations to decide unilaterally to increase monetary growth to provide more seignorage revenue to finance the deficit.

A full consideration of the ERM and EMU involves a number of important political and economic issues that would take us too far afield. We focus here on one relatively simple implication of the ERM for fiscal policy. This is that if fiscal policy puts downward pressure on the exchange rate, this will need to be offset by higher domestic interest rates (i.e. tighter monetary or interest rate policy) in order to maintain the exchange rate within its target band. In a sense the effects of an expansionary fiscal policy under the ERM become more concentrated on high domestic interest rates, and can no longer be dissipated in an exchange rate depreciation. The political and economic consequences of high interest rates may dampen the government's enthusiasm for fiscal expansion, though the effectiveness of this mechanism is questionable. In the eyes of a number of critics, fiscal policy in the late 1980s and early 1990s was expansionary, and the resulting exchange rate pressures meant that interest rates had to be maintained at undesirably high levels (see e.g. Vines, 1989).

Third, the government may enter into a commitment that directly limits the scope for fiscal expansion. A topical example is the guideline agreed as part of the EC Maastricht treaty of a PSBR/GDP ratio of 3 per cent. Again there are important wider aspects of this guideline that relate to the conduct of fiscal policy under full EMU, though we focus here on the narrower merits of such a guideline as a credible check on fiscal expansion. One basic point links back to the discussion of section 2.3: that is, since the target is expressed in terms of the PSBR rather than the PSD, this may encourage inappropriate public sector asset sales, to finance an expansionary fiscal policy within the 3 per cent guideline. However, even if the guideline had been stated in terms of PSD/GDP, problems would remain since the 3 per cent guideline may not always be appropriate. Explicitly if, in the light of the underlying economic situation, the appropriate PSBR/GDP were less than 3 per cent, this would leave some scope for fiscal expansion without breaching the guideline. On the other hand, situations may arise where the appropriate PSBR/GDP exceeds 3 per cent, so that if the guideline were strictly interpreted as an upper limit fiscal policy would be tighter than the underlying situation warrants. To avoid the latter problem exceptions may be allowed, and provision for this was made in the Maastricht treaty. Providing the exceptions are genuine, there is a clear sense to this provision. However, there is a corresponding danger that more dubious exceptions will be allowed, or be expected to be allowed, and this effectively weakens the credibility of the commitment.

2.6   Conclusions

A basic point that emerges from the foregoing discussion is that fiscal policy is complex. Simple prescriptions, such as maintaining a zero PSD on average over the medium term, or raising PSD/GDP in response to any downturn in economic activity, are too simple. Moreover, things are not always what they seem. 'Automatic stabilisers' may not always be stabilising, and a deficit may be consistent with a falling GD/GDP ratio. While it is important to recognise this complexity, and be sceptical of simplistic answers, it would be wrong to conclude that fiscal policy is an incomprehensible morass. At least as far as the macroeconomic aspects of fiscal policy are concerned, it is relatively easy to understand the main issues that should and do affect budget judgements. The following checklist provides a guide that is roughly based on the structure of this chapter.

Budget checklist
1. Assess the long-run target for PSD/GDP, taking into account the target for inflation, which is effectively determined within Europe in the context of the ERM.
2. Assess the components of PSD/GDP from a long-run perspective. What should be the long–run levels of different components of outgoings and revenue (as a proportion of GDP)? Is the tax share too high? Or is it too low to provide funding for adequate public sector expenditures and transfer payments? Is public sector investment too low?
3. Assess the underlying state of the economy at the time of the budget and over the future when budgetary actions will have their effects. Particular issues to consider include the following: the nature of disturbances and their consequences – e.g. are they temporary or permanent? Domestic or global? Supply or demand shocks? Concentrated on particular industries or regions, or general? Are resources unemployed or underutilised? Are there any genuine cases for exceptional public sector investment?
4. In the light of your assessment of points 1 to 3, what is the appropriate fiscal response? This should take into account your judgements about timing, size and structure. The relationship with other areas of policy, notably monetary policy and the exchange rate, should also be considered.
5. If the actual budget differs from your assessment, do not be surprised, but consider how these differences might be explained. Can they be explained by 'reasonable' differences in opinion about the above issues – e.g. different forecasts, different views about policy effects, etc.? In particular, when viewing a budget retrospectively, to what extent is

your judgement affected by hindsight, e.g. were forecasting errors understandable?
6. Consider the extent to which the actual budget judgement might have been affected by the issues raised in section 2.5. For example: political pressures for expansion, a crisis reaction, concern to establish a credible reputation for fiscal prudence, or more general concerns about the reaction of financial markets.

Assessing these issues, with regard to a particular budget or a longer period of fiscal history, is not easy, even with the benefit of hindsight. The study of economics certainly helps to clarify the issues and expose quack cures, but it does not, at least at present, provide all the answers. There remains considerable scope for differing judgements about the state of the economy and the appropriate stance of fiscal policy, as well as scope for further study to refine these judgements.

In broad terms my own judgements at the time of writing are the following:

1. The medium-term objective of a zero PSD, and the implied further reduction of GD/GDP (given European inflation rates) is inappropriate.
2. More contentiously, cuts in personal income tax rates have gone too far to provide adequate funding for an appropriately sized public sector. The belief in significant incentive effects from lowering income tax rates (given their current level) is mistaken. Given the visibility of personal income taxes, and the associated political pressures, it may be difficult to reverse this process. Other less visible forms of taxation may be more politically attractive.
3. Due to the low levels of public sector investment in recent years there is an incipient crisis in many areas of the public sector. There is a case for exceptional public sector investment expenditure, along the lines discussed in section 2.4. Care needs to be taken to smooth this over time to avoid a major demand disturbance.
4. More imaginative – less blunt and better directed – use of fiscal instruments could be used to stimulate economic activity in recessions. Again there has been an excessive emphasis on personal income taxation.
5. A tighter fiscal policy should have been adopted to dampen the Lawson boom (e.g. an increase in personal income taxation), reducing the emphasis placed on interest rates.
6 There are long-run structural problems in the United Kingdom (linked to the 'permanent' shock and rise in the NAIRU discussed in section 2.4), which might be addressed by more imaginative use of fiscal policy.
7. The scope for the use of fiscal policy is constrained by political pressures and the reaction of financial markets (as discussed in section 2.5), and this needs to be borne in mind when drawing up a feasible fiscal programme.

Questions for discussion

1. Why may the PSBR be a misleading indicator of the state of public sector finances when there is a major 'privatisation' sale of a public sector asset?
2. Critically assess the objective of maintaining a zero PSD over the medium term.
3. Use the checklist set out in section 2.6 to assess the following: (a) the latest budget; (b) the controversial budget of 1981; (c) the differing fiscal responses to recession reflected in the 1971, 1981 and 1991 Budgets (see Budd, 1991).
4. Critically assess the argument that the incentive effects of lower rates of income tax will enable us to afford improvements in public sector services.
5. Why might 'automatic stabilisers' be de-stabilising?
6. Is a cut in the basic rate of income tax an appropriate response to a (temporary) negative shock that has its primary impact on a particular industrial sector or region? Can you think of a better fiscal response?

Notes

1. It is interesting to consider these issues in an international perspective. Most industrialised countries have gone through a broadly similar period of retrenchment in the public sector as the United Kingdom (see Roubini and Sachs, 1989). In broad terms government outgoings and income as proportions of GDP in the United Kingdom are not out of line with those of other industrialised countries, nor were they in the 1970s. Space limits prevent a more detailed analysis, which is really needed for an adequate comparative study.
2. In principle some asset sales might be sustainable, e.g. ongoing public sector investment in housing which is subsequently sold to the private sector. However, the potential contribution of such sustainable asset sales is relatively small, particularly in comparison to the one-off asset sales that have taken place in the 1980s.
3. Estimates of the size of automatic effects are sometimes used to calculate the 'structural public sector deficit'. This purports to measure what the PSD would be if the economy were operating at some measure of potential output. In addition to the problems of estimating the size of automatic effects, mentioned in the text, estimates of the structural PSD also depend on what potential output is assumed to be. In consequence measures of the structural PSD are model dependent. They should be treated with considerable caution unless the underlying assumptions are clearly spelled out, and this is best done in the context of a macroeconomic model (see Buiter, 1985).

References and suggestions for further reading

Alesina, A. (1989), 'Politics and business cycles in industrial democracies', *Economic Policy*, April, pp. 56–98.

Allsopp, C. (1985), 'The assessment: Monetary and fiscal policy in the 1980s', *Oxford Review of Economic Policy*, March, pp. 1–20.

Allsopp, C., T. Jenkinson, and D. Morris (1991), 'The assessment: Macroeconomic policy in the 1980s', *Oxford Review of Economic Policy*, September, pp. 68–80.

Brown, C. (1988), 'Will the 1988 income tax cuts either increase work incentives or raise more revenue?', *Fiscal Studies*, May, pp. 93–107.

Buchanan, J., J. Burton, and R. Wagner (1978), *The Consequences of Mr Keynes*, (Hobart Paper 78), London: Institute of Economic Affairs.

Budd, A. (1991), 'The 1991 Budget in its historical context', *Fiscal Studies*, May, pp. 1–8.

Buiter, W. (1985), 'A guide to public sector debt and deficits', *Economic Policy*, November, pp. 13–79.

Davies, G. (1991), 'The 1991 Budget: Fiscal policy inside the ERM', *Fiscal Studies*, May, pp. 9–22.

Dilnot, A. and M. Kell (1988), 'Top-rate tax cuts and incentives: Some empirical evidence', *Fiscal Studies*, May, pp. 70–92.

Roubini, N. and J. Sachs (1989), 'Government spending and budget deficits in the industrial countries', *Economic Policy*, April, pp. 99–132.

Sayer, S. (1992), 'The city, power and economic policy in the UK', *International Review of Applied Economics*, May, pp. 125–51.

Vines, D. (1989), 'Is the "Thatcher experiment" still on course', *The Royal Bank of Scotland Review*, December, pp. 3–14.

Chapter 3

Monetary policy and inflation

GEOFFREY WYATT

3.1   Introduction and historical overview

Inflation is a persistent tendency for prices in general to rise, and this has occurred in the United Kingdom throughout the second half of the twentieth century. But there is no inevitability for the general level of prices to rise. Indeed in earlier periods the general level of prices was roughly constant, with price falls as frequent and as severe as price rises. A general fall in prices is a deflation, and when these occurred they were usually associated with declines in output and employment: slumps and depressions. But nowadays, while fluctuations in national output still take place (though generally with smaller amplitude than in earlier times), they are very rarely accompanied by actual falls in the general level of prices. So the term 'deflation' has come to mean a decline in real output and economic activity, the circumstances that used to be associated with the original meaning of the word, rather than an actual fall in the general price level.

As Figure 3.1 shows, inflation in the United Kingdom has been given sharp impulses at times of war, most notably the First World War and its immediate aftermath, but also with the onset of the Second World War, the Korean war in 1950 and after the six-day war in the Middle East in 1973 and the Islamic revolution in Iran in 1979. Each of these episodes led to strong rises in raw material prices, and notably large rises in oil prices in the two more recent cases of turbulence in the Middle East. But despite this common feature, it is unlikely that the mechanism by which these wars or revolutions affected consumer prices in the United Kingdom was the same in each case. The two world wars imposed an overriding need to finance the war effort in the United Kingdom, and the inflationary demand on domestic resources that this engendered was generated at home to some degree, possibly in the larger part. By contrast, the three blips in United

44

Kingdom inflation that have occurred since the Second World War originated externally, and their inflationary consequences were somehow imported into the United Kingdom.

The second feature of the history of inflation in the United Kingdom that Figure 3.1 points up is the upward step in inflation after the Second World War, to average levels that are systematically positive. It appears that the war ushered in a change in the way the economic system functions, giving it an inflationary bias. It is legitimate to ask whether this was induced by the new approach to economic management, with its macroeconomic focus. The pre-war era had assumed the macroeconomy to be self-regulating, and in terms of inflation it regulated itself around the zero mark. If government intervention by demand management has really regulated the economy, we might also ask whether the post-war inflation is an expression of public choice or an accidental side effect.

Whatever the reasons for the upward step in average inflation in the post-war era, it has surely affected the behaviour of all sorts of actors in the economy: individuals as consumers, workers, savers and investors, and businesses as well as government itself. This in turn has affected the way that economists think the economy functions. It is nowadays quite impossible to analyse the state of the macro-economy without taking expectations about inflation into account.

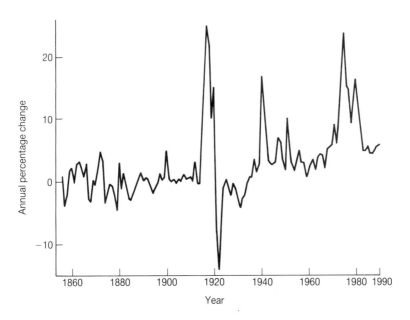

Figure 3.1 Historical trend of consumer price inflation in the United Kingdom

3.2 The measurement of inflation

Inflation is a rise in the general level of prices. To measure inflation we need to measure the general level of prices; that is, construct an appropriate price index. Generally, it is the prices faced by consumers that are considered to be relevant, so inflation is measured by the rate of change of the consumer price index (CPI). The CPI is the price deflator of consumers' expenditure in the National Accounts – nominal consumers' expenditure is converted to real consumers' expenditure by dividing by the CPI. This converts consumers' expenditure in current prices to consumers' expenditure in constant 1985 (or 1990 or 1995) prices, depending on the base year of the CPI.

In practice the CPI, or consumer expenditure deflator, is not the only available measure of the general price level. Another possibility would be the GDP deflator, which is the price index for national output, though this is less commonly quoted than the CPI. A further possibility, and one that is more frequently quoted than the CPI, is the retail price index (RPI). The RPI has the great advantage that it is compiled monthly rather than quarterly like the CPI, which accounts for its popularity. It is published in the *Employment Gazette*. However, the RPI is conceived as a measure of the 'cost of living', which is a concept somewhat removed from that of a price index for consumers' expenditure. Thus it ignores the expenditure patterns both of wealthy individuals and of certain pensioner households. Another important difference from the CPI is that the RPI makes an allowance for the interest cost of servicing a typical house mortgage. Though the RPI is different in concept from the CPI, and perhaps less suitable as a measure of inflation, the data that is collected for it is also used in the calculation of the CPI.

The construction of a general price index such as the RPI or the CPI involves two types of data: the first determining the composition of the 'basket' of goods and services that consumers actually consume, and the second being the prices of the individual items in the 'basket'. In the United Kingdom the first component is determined from the Family Expenditure Survey, which asks a stratified random sample of about 7000 households to record their outgoings over a particular fortnight. The second component involves getting the prices of some 130 000 goods and services every month. These two components are combined in a chained index which accurately reflects the changing composition of people's spending.

The rate of inflation at a given date is usually quoted as the percentage change of the relevant price index from its value a year earlier. This is of course a backward-looking measure, and does not necessarily reflect people's expectation about how it will develop in the future. But it is this latter notion which is relevant for most decisions, and is reflected in various contracts such as wage agreements, rentals and loans. Expectations are notoriously difficult to measure, but one possibility is to use the data in the rates of interest quoted on nominal and real bonds (known as 'index-linked' bonds in the United Kingdom) to extract the implicit expectation of future inflation.

3.3 Inflation control as an objective of policy

The principal macroeconomic target of policy since 1979, when Mrs Thatcher was first elected as prime minister, has been the rate of inflation. The other targets of macroeconomic policy, namely the levels and rates of growth of wealth, output, consumption and unemployment have all been subordinated to the control of inflation, largely because low and stable inflation has been thought of as a pre-condition for the achievement of these other goals. However, in terms of their contribution to people's well-being, those other goals are generally of more direct relevance than the rate of inflation. Inflation and unemployment are highly interconnected, as is discussed in Chapter 5, and reducing one is likely to increase the other in the short run (a year or two), though they are less closely coupled in the long run. But once inflation is in the system, it seems that a period of relatively high unemployment is an inevitable consequence of policies to eliminate it.

Because it is not at all obvious that inflation should rank so high among the objectives of economic policy, it is worth considering the matter further. To do so, we distinguish between anticipated and unanticipated inflation. If inflation is steady and predictable, we would expect people to allow for it in the decisions they make concerning their incomes. Thus it should be reflected in wage agreements, pension arrangement, tax thresholds, interest rates, company dividends and so on. In effect, all sources of income should be indexed to the rate of inflation. Why then should any particular rate of fully anticipated inflation be a cause for concern? There are some rather minor costs to note. One is the need to change price tags, and the faster the rate of anticipated inflation the more often such changes would be needed. Another cost of high inflation is the erosion in the value of nominal assets – assets whose value is expressed in money terms. Where inflation is fully anticipated, we should expect the price of all assets to be indexed to it; except, that is, money itself. So the higher the rate of anticipated inflation, the greater the incentive for people to reduce their holdings of money. This induces the so-called 'shoe leather cost' of anticipated inflation, as people are encouraged to make more frequent trips to the bank. The proportion of money in people's portfolios of assets tends thereby to diminish, and the general loss of liquidity inhibits people from making quick responses to buying opportunities. Thus the usefulness of money in making transactions and as a store of value is impaired. These costs are not trivial, but they pale in significance when set against the costs of unanticipated inflation.

When people are taken unawares by an increase in the general price level there are several consequences. To begin with, there is a strong redistribution of real income from savers to borrowers which comes about because the expected rate of inflation incorporated in the nominal interest rate is lower than the inflation that actually occurs. When inflation is less than people had anticipated, the transfer is from borrowers to savers. Since there is a systematic pattern of saving and borrowing over the life cycle, the redistributive consequences of unanticipated inflation (or its converse) tend to fall on particular age groups. Thus young adults, who are generally borrowers, possibly with recently acquired mortgages on their houses, tend to benefit from unanticipated inflation, and older people with accumulated savings tend to lose out.

Another effect of unexpected inflation is that it engenders confusion about relative price changes, and a consequent misallocation of resources due to decisions taken on misleading price signals. In order to avoid making costly mistakes, decision-makers may expend substantial effort on forecasting inflation, or by taking steps to mitigate possible errors. Higher rates of inflation are associated with greater variability, and hence greater unpredictability, of inflation. So the costs associated with unanticipated price changes tend to be more important in circumstances of high inflation. Even when it is clear that an erroneous assumption about inflation has been made, it may be difficult to correct quickly. Particularly important examples of this include wage contracts, which may be revised annually or biennially, and property rentals which may only be revised at even longer intervals of time – five years is not uncommon. Such 'sticky' prices tend to prolong misallocations of resources in times of high inflation.

It is clear from the foregoing that the consequences of inflation can badly damage the functioning of an economy. Since, as will be argued shortly, inflation can be controlled by government action, this would seem to be a proper objective of policy. But first we should consider a different angle on the subject, namely how it is that government may stimulate inflation by opting for a particular mode of financing its activities.

Governments can finance their spending in three ways: taxation, borrowing from the general public and 'printing money', which is shorthand for the process of borrowing from banks and thereby expanding the stock of money. Government revenue from taxes is normally by far the most important source of funding for its expenditure, and the other sources of finance are usually considered as devices to cover a deficit occasioned by a tax shortfall. While taxation and borrowing from the general public entail a direct transfer of resources from the private sector to the government (involuntary and voluntary respectively), the process of printing money appears to give the government control over real resources without a corresponding sacrifice by the private sector. This command over real resources derived from printing money is known as 'seigniorage'. However, unless the resources claimed by the government would otherwise be unused, as might be the case in a recession, this seigniorage adds to the general pressure of aggregate demand and eventually results in higher prices. To reflect this, the financing of government spending by printing money is sometimes called the 'inflation tax'. The tax is paid by people who had not anticipated the monetary expansion, and consequently suffer in the general transfer of real income from savers to borrowers that occurs with unanticipated inflation. Thus nominal interest rates are too low as they do not yet reflect the coming inflation due to the new pressure on resources, and the inflation tax falls on income from saving. The major beneficiaries are future taxpayers, for whom the burden of the National Debt is eroded by the unanticipated inflation.

3.4 Money and inflation

If the money price of all goods and services were doubled there would be no change in any relative price, but the general level of prices would clearly have doubled, and the purchasing power of a unit of currency would have halved. If this had happened over the course of a year the rate of inflation that year would have been 100 per cent. It is conceivable that this could have happened without any change in the amount of money in general circulation or the amount of goods and services purchased with that money, so that the given stock of money was being transferred from buyer to seller twice as fast. Conceivable, but not plausible. More likely, neither the velocity of circulation (the value of all transactions divided by the stock of money) nor the volume of sales were much different, but roughly twice as much money was in general circulation. This is the usual experience in inflations, so much so that Milton Friedman's dictum that 'inflation is always and everywhere a monetary phenomenon' is not seriously disputed as holding true over long periods of time, or in rapid inflations as in this example. In such circumstances inflation is always associated with an expansion in the stock of money held by the public. But over shorter periods of time more modest inflation can occur without much change in the stock of money, but with a fall in the volume of transactions or a rise in the velocity of circulation.

The 'quantity equation' is a famous tautology connecting the stock of money (M), the price level (P), the number of transactions (T) and the velocity of circulation (V) in the following equation: $MV = PT$. All of the variables in this identity may change over time, and the equation is only of serious empirical validity if the velocity of circulation of money is predictable. On the assumption that it is, a further step of reasoning is to assert that since the stock of money can be controlled by the government, this provides a mechanism through which it can influence the general level of prices and the rate of inflation. This is the beginning of the doctrine of 'monetarism' which assumed considerable importance for the first term of the Thatcher administration, from 1979 to 1983.

In the money market, if the supply of money is fixed, the demand for money is brought into equality with it by changes in the short-term interest rate. On the other hand, if the interest rate is fixed, which means that the central bank stands ready to meet whatever level of demand for cash that emerges, the supply of money becomes perfectly elastic at that rate of interest. If, as monetarists suppose, the demand for money is well determined as a stable and predictable function of a set of variables including the rate of interest and the level of income, and the interest elasticity of demand for money is low, then it should be possible to control the stock of money by central bank control of the interest rate. The monetarist view of the purpose of such control over the stock of money is not that it should be used to influence the level of demand in the economy in the short run, but that it should set a framework designed to lead to a steady and low rate of inflation in the longer term. Thus discretionary monetary policy should be eschewed in favour of a publicly declared rule of a constant, low rate of monetary growth, to which the central bank is committed.

The monetary authorities may control the money supply either directly, by open market operations which change the reserves of the commercial banks, or indirectly by changing the discount rate at which commercial banks can borrow from the central bank, which in turn influences short-term interest rates generally. But whichever method they adopt, they must be prepared for wide fluctuations in short-term interest rates as the demand for money fluctuates, because of the low interest elasticity of demand for money. Most empirical studies before the 1980s confirmed the assumed low elasticity. However, financial innovation and liberalisation has since then produced a spectrum of different forms of money, and differences in rates of return between them influence the form in which people hold their money if not the total amount of money-like liquid assets.

The transmission mechanism by which expansion in the money supply eventually translates into increased prices may take many paths, and it may vary from time to time and from country to country. The most direct route is the stimulation of expenditures through lower interest rates. This of course depends on the interest elasticity of such expenditure, and one would expect it to be confined to durable and investment goods. Prices generally are pushed upwards as aggregate demand presses on aggregate supply, which is determined by real variables such as the availability of factors of production and technological change.

Another channel of monetary influence is by a fall in the exchange rate which is brought about by the downward pressure on interest rates. Lower

Table 3.1 Personal sector wealth composition

	£ billion			% of net wealth		
	1980	1985	1990	1980	1985	1990
Net wealth	694	1167	2127	100.0	100.0	100.0
Non-financial assets	479	728	1403	69.0	62.4	65.9
Housing	401	635	1276	57.8	54.4	60.0
Net financial wealth	215	439	724	31.0	37.6	34.0
Notes and coin	8	10	13	1.2	0.9	0.6
Bank deposits	37	64	162	5.3	5.5	7.6
Building society deposits	50	104	159	7.2	8.9	7.5
Shareholdings	46	83	139	6.6	7.1	6.5
Pension and insurance funds	107	291	587	15.4	24.9	27.6
Mortgages (liability)	−53	−128	−288	−7.6	−11.0	−13.5
Bank lending (liability)	−15	−40	−87	−2.2	−3.4	−4.1

Sources: Central Statistical Office, *Economic Trends*, October 1991, and *Financial Statistics*, February 1992, HMSO.

domestic interest rates induce people to sell United Kingdom bonds and buy foreign bonds, reducing the demand for sterling in the process. The upshot is an increase in the price of imported goods. This channel comprises elements of both 'cost push' and 'demand pull' inflation, as the lower exchange rate also stimulates export demand.

A further channel of monetary influence, and one which monetarists tend to emphasise, is through adjustments in the composition of wealth. Although money is only a small fraction of people's tangible wealth, as can be seen from Table 3.1, the monetary expansion which pulls down short-term interest rates – interest rates on three-month Treasury Bills – tends to drag down other interest rates too, and as the implied interest rates on all sorts of assets, both financial and non-financial, drift down in sympathy, so the prices of those assets tend to rise. Thus people's nominal wealth rises, and thereby aggregate demand too. Another way of looking at this is in terms of the composition of wealth portfolios directly. When the central bank purchases gilt-edged stock from the public in an open market operation, the proportion of money in the aggregate portfolio of the private sector increases, and now exceeds the desired level. The people with excess cash will try to turn it into other assets, bidding up their price in the process. Thus there is an initial increase in the wealth of those who hold the substitute assets, some of which translates into spending.

Financial wealth accounts for roughly one-third of total tangible wealth of the personal sector in the United Kingdom, as is shown in Table 3.1, and most of the remaining two-thirds is in the form of house ownership or tenancy rights. Between 1980 and 1990, the proportion of notes and coin in total non-human wealth halved while the proportion of bank deposits increased by almost a half, and by 1990 stood roughly equal to building society deposits. Traditionally, bank deposits were considered as money, available for transactions, whereas building society deposits were mostly in savings accounts. In the first half of the 1980s, however, the building societies substantially increased their share of deposits as they entered into competition with the banks by offering very similar services. But the banks fought back by offering interest-bearing current accounts. Thus the earlier distinctions between banks and building societies were eroded, and the inclusion of bank deposits, but not building society deposits, in a wide definition of the money stock became questionable. On the other hand, assigning all deposits, of both banks and building societies, to a measure of the money stock is also inappropriate since an unknown proportion of both are really savings accounts.

The foregoing has pointed to an intimate connection between monetary expansions and short-term interest rates (Figure 3.2). Long-term interest rates, however, do not necessarily move in parallel with short-term rates. Two factors determine long-term rates, namely the real interest rate, i.e. the marginal product of capital, and expectations about inflation in future years. A switch in the monetary stance which involves a progressive slowing down of both the rate of monetary expansion and the rate of inflation over the medium term, should therefore imply a widening gap between short-term and long-term interest rates as the short-term rates rise in response to monetary tightness, and long-term rates fall in the expectation of the success of this policy in reducing the rate of inflation.

3.5 Monetary policy in the 1980s

The new Conservative government of 1979 had inherited a high and rising rate of inflation, and its main goal was to correct it. To do so, it adopted the previous Callaghan administration's practice of setting monetary targets, expressed as a range of growth rates for sterling M3 (£M3), which is currency in circulation plus bank deposits denominated in sterling. Such £M3 target ranges were intended to exert a gradual squeeze on the economy, forcing inflation down. However, direct control of the monetary base was eschewed in favour of manipulating short-term interest rates via the government's official discount rate, known as minimum lending rate (MLR). This decision stemmed from a judgement that direct control of the monetary base, which would have left interest rates to be determined entirely by market forces, would have implied very large fluctuations in interest rates, more than could be tolerated. Instead, the government set interest rates and allowed the money stock to respond indirectly, via the money demand function. In choosing greater stability for short-term

interest rates, it sacrificed stability in its ostensible target indicator, the
money stock.

In 1979 and 1980 the monetary squeeze, which required high interest
rates, combined with both a sharp rise in the price of oil and the emergent
self-sufficiency of the United Kingdom in oil to push the exchange value of
sterling sharply upwards. Although the rise in sterling was attenuated by
the abolition of exchange controls in October 1979, which encouraged a net
outflow of portfolio capital, it was nevertheless the main factor leading to
the severe recession of 1980 and 1981.

The formal expression of the Thatcher government's monetary policy
was the 'Medium-Term Financial Strategy' (MTFS) which was launched in
the 1980 Budget. This initiated a programme of rolling targets for
monetary growth and the public sector borrowing requirement (PSBR)
expressed as a proportion of GDP, over three- to five-year horizons from
each annual budget. The aim of the MTFS was clearly to create an
environment of relatively stable and predictable monetary conditions. But
it only partially succeeded in doing so. The success was with regard to the
PSBR, which by 1987 had turned into a surplus. However, the monetary
aggregates stubbornly refused to comply with the government's targets
throughout most of the period up to 1990, when monetary targeting was
effectively abandoned (see Table 3.2).

In order to succeed in monetary targeting through the indirect channel

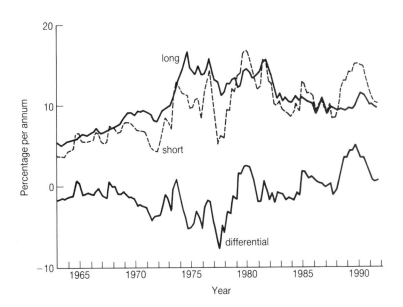

Figure 3.2 Short- and long-term interest rates

Table 3.2   Medium-term financial strategy (out-turn of key variables and their targets one year ahead)

| | Monetary growth, % change | | | | PSBR, % of GDP | |
| | £M3 | | M0 | | | |
	Target range	Out-turn	Target range	Out-turn	Target	Out-turn
1979/80	7 to 11	16.5			4.5	4.75
1980/1	7 to 11	19.5			3.75	5.5
1981/2	6 to 10	12.75			4.25	3.5
1982/3	8 to 12	10			3.5	3.25
1983/4	7 to 11	9.75			2.75	3.25
1984/5	6 to 10	9.5	4 to 8	5.2	2.25	3
1985/6	5 to 9	14.25	3 to 7	3.4	2	1.5
1986/7	11 to 15		2 to 6	4.6	1.75	1
1987/8			2 to 6	5.8	1	−0.75
1988/9			1 to 5	6.2	−0.75	−3
1989/90			1 to 5	6.2	−2.75	−1.5
1990/1			1 to 5	2.5	−1.25	0
1991/2			0 to 4	2	1.25	2.25
1992/3			0 to 4		4.5	

Sources: Financial Statement and Budget Reports, 1980 to 1992, London, HMSO.
Central Statistical Office, *Economic Trends, Annual Supplement*, 1992, London,
HMSO.

of interest rates, it is necessary to have reliable knowledge about the money demand function, or the determinants of the velocity of money circulation. This was the subject of considerable research at the Bank of England and in the Treasury during the 1970s and 1980s, but the forecasting accuracy of the estimated money demand functions tended to be rather poor. This was particularly true for the wider definitions of money such as £M3, and it was partly due to this that £M3 tended systematically to overshoot its MTFS targets. A further factor is that the government wished to target a measure of the personal sector's stock of liquid assets that would be used for expenditures as opposed to savings, but financial innovations made it difficult to maintain this distinction between different kinds of bank or building society accounts. As a consequence, after some experimentation with different definitions of money, both wide and narrow, the monetary focus for the MTFS switched in the mid-1980s from £M3 to the narrow definition of money stock as notes and coins in circulation plus commercial banks' deposits at the Bank of England, M0. However, M0 was treated less as a target than as an indicator of monetary conditions. And it was not the sole indicator – the exchange rate and short- and long-term interest rates were also used in that capacity. The underlying target became the growth of nominal GDP in 1987.

The Government's systematic inability to keep its chosen definition of money within the target range was probably due to a number of factors. Foremost among these were the rapid financial and technological innovations that took place in the 1980s, the removal of constraints on bank lending (the 'corset') and on international capital movements at the beginning of the period and the changing behaviour of the stock of money when it became a target indicator.

The 1980s was a decade of worldwide financial liberalisation and innovation, much of the demand for which was generated by the global monetary regime of fluctuating exchange rates and interest rates. Although institutions such as offshore banks, eurocurrency markets and derivative asset exchanges already existed at the beginning of the decade, they grew rapidly during the 1980s, and activities that had hitherto been the preserve of banks were for the first time engaged in by other financial institutions and also by the finance departments of large companies. This was enabled to a large extent by the developments in information technology and electronic communications. Commercial banks competed more vigorously for business than ever before, and were also forced to compete with other non-bank financial companies. A consequence of this competition was the blurring of the distinction between demand deposits and time deposits. Formerly only the latter paid interest, whereas by the 1990s nearly all bank deposit accounts earned interest. This has increased the interest sensitivity of demand for different types of liquid assets, including notes and coin as the opportunity cost of holding cash has risen. A further important factor reducing the demand for narrow money by the personal customers of banks (or increasing its velocity of circulation), was the proliferation of 24-hour cash dispensers. Simultaneously the demand for checking accounts was reduced by the rapid growth of credit cards, which enabled people to manage their liquid assets more effectively than before. All of these developments had an influence on the demand for monetary aggregates, and therefore, given the indirect method of control, on the stock of those self-same aggregates.

As an identity, any increase in the stock of narrow money is equal to the PSBR plus the overall balance of payments surplus minus sales of government debt to the non-bank public. So reducing the PSBR, which was the successful aspect of the MTFS of the 1980s, does not necessarily imply a reduced growth of the narrow money stock. It is largely a matter of how the deficit is financed. However, narrow money (M0) was reasonably well under control in the 1980s, so the failure to keep to the announced targets for wider money (£M3) can be attributed in large part to the government's failure to foresee the changes in the competitive behaviour of banks and of the general public who switched their financial assets into interest-bearing bank deposits.

By the end of the 1980s, after several years of quite fast growth which boosted tax revenue and reduced the level of unemployment and related benefit payments, the deficit (PSBR) was transformed into a surplus. With the onset of recession in 1990, however, these trends reversed and the PSBR emerged once more. This coincided with a two-year period during which monetary policy was assigned the task of maintaining the sterling exchange rate within the European Community's Exchange Rate Mechanism and monetary policy took a rear seat in the operation of the MTFS.

3.6   Exchange rate policy as an instrument to control inflation

The global system of exchange rates is a mixture of fixed and floating parities. From the middle 1970s to 1990 the exchange value of the pound sterling against other currencies was determined by the forces of supply and demand in the market for currencies. There was little intervention by the Bank of England in these markets in the form of buying or selling sterling, except to smooth out the very short-run fluctuations in the exchange rate. Sterling was floating against other currencies. The effect of this exchange rate regime was to de-couple domestic monetary conditions from the balance of payments since foreign exchange reserves at the Bank of England, which are part of the monetary base, are not affected by the balance of payments position. (With a fixed exchange rate these reserves would fluctuate, offsetting the overall balance of payments position.) This meant that the stock of money, and its rate of expansion, were determined by the government. Thus the government in effect chose the rate of inflation.

Between October 1990 and September 1992 the United Kingdom was a member of the Exchange Rate Mechanism of the European Community, and this constrained the extent to which sterling could fluctuate against the currencies of the other members of the ERM. The ERM is part of the European Community's European Monetary System, in which all members of the European Community participate. But membership of the ERM is not yet a mandatory component of the EMS. Indeed two members of the European Community – Greece and Portugal – have never participated in the ERM, and the terms of participation of those countries that are members are not uniform. The ERM was established in 1979 as a zone of monetary stability in Europe. Each participating country undertakes to maintain the exchange values of its currency against all other participants within a specified margin. For most participants the margin is ±2.25 per cent of the agreed bilateral parities, but for the United Kingdom and Spain, the margin was set at ±6 per cent. See Chapters 6 and 7 for more detail on the EMS.

Within the ERM, when the sterling exchange rate approached its lower limit against any other currency (so that the other currency approached its upper limit against sterling), both central banks concerned stood ready to buy sterling on the currency markets. For the United Kingdom this implied a loss of reserves of foreign currency, and therefore a contraction of the money supply because foreign currency reserves held by the Bank of England are a component of the monetary base. By contrast, the other European country experienced an expansion of its central bank's foreign currency reserves, and therefore of its money supply. Thus an automatic monetary contraction would be stimulated if the exchange rate depreciated to its floor, and an automatic monetary expansion would be set in train if it appreciated to its ceiling. If the original reason for the depreciation of the exchange rate to its floor was a general expectation of higher inflation here than abroad, then the induced monetary contraction here and the monetary expansion abroad would be appropriate offsetting responses. They should have the effect of narrowing the gap in inflationary expectations.

These effects at the floor or the ceiling of the permitted range of variation of the exchange rate within the ERM are similar to what happens when an exchange rate is fixed between two currencies. But within the limits the exchange rate is determined by the supply and demand for the currencies, which in turn depend on both the need to effect transactions and the rates of return obtainable from holding assets in that currency. A feature of today's current global financial system is that there are few limitations to the free flow of financial capital between countries. In these circumstances monetary assets are virtually fungible between currencies (i.e. they can be transformed into each other at very little cost). Consequently, the free market determination of the exchange rate ensures that it takes a value that equalises the expected rate of return in the two currencies, taking interest rates and expected future movements of the exchange rate into account. The monetary authorities could therefore stabilise the exchange rate within its ERM limits by setting the short-term interest rate at an appropriate level. Thus monetary policy became subservient to the exchange rate regime.

The ERM exchange rate regime is a hybrid, being neither purely floating nor rigidly fixed against some anchor. The monetary autonomy implied by the freedom of movement for the exchange rate within the allowed band is, at the most, of a short-run nature. Any divergent inflationary tendencies that it enables can only persist as long as the limits are not reached. It follows that in the medium to longer term, the ERM system is in effect a rather sophisticated variation on a fixed exchange rate regime. Within this system the inflation rates of the participants must converge. It was this inevitable process of convergence, and the pain that it implies for countries that have to disinflate rapidly, that justified the initial wider 6 per cent band for the more inflation-prone countries. But the process of convergence within the ERM made it natural to assume that these countries would also adopt the narrower 2.25 per cent band at some point. Indeed, Italy entered the ERM in 1979 on the wider 6 per cent band, but moved to the standard narrow band in 1990.

If a country cannot persist with the discipline required by the ERM, the system does allow for a possible realignment of its central exchange rates against those of the other member countries. However, resort to this device tends to undermine the credibility of the disinflationary policy, and may of itself encourage inflationary expectations to persist. This seems to be the view of policy-makers, who publicly eschew the realignment option. But in the longer term there may well be divergences in competitiveness which will require the use of this device. They can come about due to different rates of productivity growth or changes in the availability of factors of production or of the composition of demand. Such considerations suggest that the eventual goal of monetary union, namely a single EC currency, may be an inferior outcome for the member states of the European Community than the ERM system, which possesses many of the benefits of the post-war Bretton Woods system. But, like the Bretton Woods system, the ERM enables speculation against overvalued currencies.

The ERM can be characterised as a quasi-fixed currency regime for the participating countries. Its mode of operation implies that they will eventually have a common rate of inflation. This is likely to be determined by the monetary policy of the largest country, Germany, which in recent decades has also been the least inflationary country. However, the unification of Germany in October 1990, and the subsequent monetary unification in 1991, has been a source of inflationary pressure in Germany which is currently a cause for concern to its monetary authorities. It remains to be seen whether the much respected independence of the Bundesbank to preserve the value of the D-mark will be compromised.

In mid-September 1992 the currency markets were thrown into a state of turmoil as the divergent needs for higher interest rates in Germany and lower interest rates in a number of other European countries made adherence to the ERM currency bands unsustainable. First the Italian lira, then the pound sterling, came under pressure as huge volumes of speculative selling forced the central banks of both countries to buy their own currencies in exchange for foreign currency reserves. The German central bank was meanwhile obliged to sell Deutschmarks for lira and sterling, thus adding to its reserves. But all this intervention proved futile as it was overwhelmed by the transactions of speculators convinced of impending changes in the exchange rates, which duly transpired as Italy first devalued within the ERM, followed within days by the joint exit from the ERM of both the United Kingdom and Italy along with a devaluation of the Spanish peseta within the ERM. The pound sterling had been overvalued within the ERM as part of the government's strategy to bear down on inflation. However, the outcome of a lower exchange value should boost the level of demand and activity, and may not be excessively inflationary in an economy in the depths of recession. The United Kingdom government is committed to returning to the ERM, but this will not happen before the economies of Germany and the United Kingdom have 'converged', and it is by no means clear when that may be. In the meantime the situation has reverted to the *status quo ante*, with the United Kingdom monetary authorities monitoring narrow and broad money, and asset prices, including house prices and the exchange rate, as indicators of the tightness of monetary policy. However, their reluctance to set clear monetary targets in the immediate post-ERM setting leaves the stance of monetary policy somewhat unclear.

3.7 Conclusion

Although controlling inflation has been the government's top priority since 1979, it is not yet clear that it has been brought fully under control. The periods in which there were substantial reductions in inflation, that is the early 1980s and the early 1990s, corresponded to periods of record unemployment. Thus the control of inflation was bought at substantial cost in terms of output and employment, and yet it seems to have given only temporary relief – though the jury is still out on the experience of the 1990s. The big difference between the 1980s and the 1990s is the monetary environment. Throughout the 1980s monetary targeting of one form or another was in sway, initially with full conviction but with little success in adhering to the targets, and finally merely as a monitoring device. In retrospect it seems that the wholehearted espousal of monetarism was thwarted by the instabilities of an era of rapid financial innovation which made it virtually impossible for the authorities to read the runes. By contrast, independent monetary control had been abandoned by the 1990s in favour of a commitment to quasi-fixed exchange rates within a European context. For a period monetary conditions were set in Europe where the strongest influence was the German Bundesbank. However, the German central bank still had the objective to maintain the value of the German currency, without regard to the European partners. At the same time it was having to come to grips with the daunting task of maintaining stability in the newly unified Germany. The pressures induced by these imperatives forced the United Kingdom to leave the Exchange Rate Mechanism, though it remains an objective of policy to rejoin when conditions allow.

Questions for discussion

1. Why are asset prices inversely related to interest rates?
2. What are the strengths and weaknesses of the RPI as a basis for the measurement of inflation?

3. What are the 'costs of inflation'?
4. Describe three different mechanisms through which an expansion of the stock of money affects the general price level.
5. Why was it so difficult for the government to meet its monetary targets in the 1980s?
6. How are short- and long-term interest rates affected by an unforeseen monetary expansion?
7. How have changes in the exchange rate regime affected the conduct of monetary policy in recent years?

Suggestions for further reading

Central Statistical Office (annual), *Family Expenditure Survey*, London: HMSO.
Central Statistical Office (1987), *A Short Guide to the Retail Prices Index*, London: HMSO.
Department of Employment (monthly), *Employment Gazette*, London: HMSO.
Johnson, C. (1991), *The Economy under Mrs Thatcher, 1979–1990*, London: Penguin.
Maynard, G. (1988), *The Economy under Mrs Thatcher*, Oxford: Basil Blackwell.
Treasury and Civil Service Committee (1981), *Monetary Policy*, vol. II, *Minutes of Evidence*, (HC 163), London: HMSO.
Walters, A. (1990), *Sterling in Danger*, London: Fontana.

Chapter 4

Financial markets and public policy

IAN HIRST

4.1 Introduction

The most visible evidence of public policy towards the financial markets in the United Kingdom is the imposition of new legislation and new regulations. The 1980s were an active period in this regard. A short list of the most prominent changes in the United Kingdom since the return of a Conservative government in 1979 would run as follows:

- 1979 Exchange controls abolished.
- 1980 Supplementary Special Deposits scheme ended. This scheme, known as the 'corset', restricted the rate of growth of UK banks' deposits.
- 1982 Controls on consumer instalment credit ended.
- 1985 Company Securities (Insider Dealing) Act made insider trading a criminal offence.
- 1986 The 'Big Bang' reforms to the operation of The Stock Exchange take effect.
- 1986 The Financial Services Act setting up a new regulatory structure for parts of the financial services industry.

The main purpose of recent changes has been to make refinements and adjustments to a financial system whose basic features are long established. Many of the main features of the financial system in the United Kingdom have resulted from inflation, the tax system, the system of state benefits and the place of state ownership in the economy. The main aspects of public policy that have shaped the financial markets are not clearly labelled as such. Conversely, some of the changes in regulations which have received so much publicity have had comparatively little impact. The 1985 Act covering insider trading certainly created a new criminal offence. But insider trading was regarded as unethical before the Act, and leading financial institutions had their own house rules to prevent it. Since insider trading can be disguised in a number of ways, it is likely that a significant amount still goes on without detection. The new law was certainly welcome in principle, but it is not clear that it made any substantial change to the working of the financial markets in practice.

The 1986 Financial Services Act comes into the same category. This massive regulatory edifice was set up in response to financial scandals resulting from the operations of a few rogue companies. The great majority of reputable firms incurred the costs of a more formal and prescriptive environment without major changes in their activities.

The most significant regulatory change in the list, by a wide margin, was the abolition of exchange controls of 1979. This opened the United Kingdom financial markets to external competition in several areas. It made the Special Deposits Scheme ineffective and undermined the structure of The Stock Exchange. The new legislative and regulatory environment has been partly created by international agreements. The Banking Directives of the European Community will enable European banks to open branches throughout the community from 1993. An agreement reached under the auspices of the Bank for International Settlements in 1988 established the capital requirements for international banks for twelve major industrialised countries.

This chapter will not attempt to chronicle recent modifications to financial market regulations. Its main concern will be the effectiveness of United Kingdom financial markets. Because there are so many different markets, we must be selective. Priority will be given to company finance and to the supporting structure of the savings industry.

One of the curious features of financial markets is that the major industrial economies have very different financial systems. This contrasts with other industries where similar systems can be expected. In the automobile industry, for example, there is a strong similarity in the way cars are built in different parts of the world. One assembly line looks much like another. Financial markets and financial systems do not seem to follow the same logic. There are very substantial differences, which do not appear to be diminishing with time, between the corporate finance systems in the G5 countries (the United Kingdom, the United States, Japan, Germany, France). Sometimes the poor industrial performance of the UK and USA economies are attributed to their financial systems. So many variables contribute to industrial performance that it is difficult to isolate their different effects. It can also be argued that the sophistication and variety of the financial markets in the United Kingdom tend to counteract other factors which are the roots of Britain's industrial problems.

4.2 The economics of financial markets

The financial markets bring together savers and borrowers. Within the market sector of the economy, savers are economic agents who are willing to postpone the enjoyment (consumption) of their wealth in order to invest in financial assets. Borrowers are economic agents who wish to spend above the level that can be covered by their existing resources. The phrase 'economic agent' is carefully chosen. It covers both individuals and companies. Our discussion will centre on individuals as savers (in what follows, we commonly refer to such people, loosely, as investors) and companies as borrowers, although individuals can also be borrowers as in the consumer credit market.

4.2.1 The interest rate

The basic price in the financial markets is the interest rate. To individual investors, the interest rate is a reward for postponing consumption. To businesses, the interest rate is a cost incurred when using a production process which involves time. Body panels for modern cars are not produced by taking a sheet of steel and hammering it into a shape that fits. They are formed in giant presses using very carefully shaped dies. The job of designing and manufacturing the dies takes place many months before the resulting cars come to market. The production process is a 'roundabout' one. There are large set-up costs before production takes place. The production process is time intensive. The workers who manufacture the dies will need to be paid long before customers will pay for the cars. Capital, from individual investors (i.e. savers, see above) is needed to bridge this time gap. Where time-intensive (i.e. capital-using) methods of production are most efficient, capital has added value and the individuals who have supplied capital can expect to be rewarded with interest payments.

Offered a greater reward, a higher interest rate, individuals will normally be willing to save more and provide more capital. On the other hand, at a higher interest rate, businesses will look for ways to use less time in their production processes. A market–clearing interest rate will emerge at which the supply of savings from individuals will just match the borrowing requirements of businesses.

Markets have no respect for international boundaries. In the absence of barriers or discriminatory taxes the interest rate will be set at a rate that will clear the global capital market. Countries which have within their borders an excess of savers over borrowers will export capital. Other countries will be net importers.

4.2.2 Inflation

The explanation of interest rates given above is only valid in a world without inflation. With inflation, growth in money and growth in purchasing power will no longer be the same thing. Economic agents will have to decide whether to evaluate projects on the basis of the money amounts they will generate in the future or the amounts of purchasing power. It is not a hard decision. Money is not desired for its own sake. It is purchasing power that counts. The analysis must be modified in an inflationary environment to run in purchasing power units rather than amounts of money.

An interest rate can be regarded as an exchange rate. It is an exchange rate between an amount an individual investor can enjoy now (through present consumption) and the amount that investor could enjoy in the future if he or she is prepared to wait. The equilibrium rate which reconciles saving and borrowing behaviour is not the exchange rate between money now and money next year but an exchange rate between purchasing power now and purchasing power next year. The money-to-money rate is known as the nominal interest rate and is the kind of interest rate normally quoted in financial deals. The purchasing-power-to-purchasing-power rate is known as the real interest rate. Real interest rates are not normally quoted but the concept is familiar to most people. If the bank is giving you an 8 per cent (nominal) interest rate on your savings at a time when inflation is 13 per cent, you are getting poorer. Putting it another way, you are getting a negative real interest rate on your savings. It is real rates which tend to equality in different countries. Nominal rates will be different because of different levels of inflation.

4.2.3   Risk

The outcome of most business ventures is uncertain. A very simple business opportunity might involve a cash outflow of £100 now and an inflow of either £90 or £140 in one year's time, with each of these two possible outcomes being equally likely. The return, therefore, has a 50 per cent probability of being +40 per cent, and a 50 per cent probability of being −10 per cent. The expected return is simply the average of these two numbers, 15 per cent. The usual numerical measure of risk is the standard deviation, which is a measure of how far away from the expected return the actual return is likely to be. In the example, the return will either be 25 per cent above the expected return or 25 per cent below it. The standard deviation of return in this example is, not surprisingly, 25 per cent. Businesses cannot offer all investors a fixed rate of return on their investment. Someone must take the risk. One function of financial markets is to allocate risk efficiently.

A saver (i.e. an individual investor) will look at both the expected return of each project and its risk. Investors are risk averse. This means that, if two projects offer the same mean return, they will choose the one with the lower risk of return. They would prefer to get a guaranteed return of 15 per cent rather than an equal chance of a return of 40 per cent or -10 per cent. If the projects offer different mean returns, an investor may choose the one with the lower return if this disadvantage is counteracted by a lower risk.

To enable financial investors to control the level of risk in their investments (and for other reasons that will be discussed later) companies will split up the cash flow from their activities into different types of claim with different levels of risk. A good analogy comes from considering a dairy farmer. The milk comes out of the cows with a certain proportion of cream naturally included. Not all consumers want this particular mix. Some will want low-fat milk with the cream removed. Others want to buy pure cream to pour on their strawberries. The dairy industry will separate out the components of the raw milk to satisfy these different tastes.

It is the same with business projects. In the raw state they offer a mixture of return and risk, but these two elements can be separated out and savers can be offered both low-risk and high-risk opportunities. Consider our earlier example of the £100 cash outflow rewarded a year later by an inflow of either £90 or £140. This project might be financed by two different types of claim. One could be zero risk. Investors who put in £50 on this basis could be guaranteed that they would get £55 back. Their investment would offer a return of 10 per cent and a standard deviation of zero. The investors who put in the other £50 would take the risk. They would get back either £40 or £90 depending on which way the project turned out. They would get a mean return of 30 per cent and a standard deviation of return of 50 per cent. The risky investment will have to offer a higher return to attract investors.

A company is a legal entity which stands between individual investors and the business projects which they fund. Companies normally package the proceeds from projects into a very low-risk stream in the form of interest-bearing securities and/or bank loans, and a risky stream which goes to shareholders.

4.2.4 Diversification

One of the most visible characteristics of risk-averse behaviour by individual investors (savers) is that they will spread their holdings of shares over a wide range of different companies rather than plunging it all into one. By doing this the overall risk to which their investment is exposed will be reduced. Some shares will do well; some will do poorly but the overall return will not tend towards either extreme. The risk on a portfolio of shares can well be less than the risk on any single share taken in isolation.

There are limits to what diversification can achieve. The economic cycle in the United Kingdom will affect almost all business activities. Shares will tend to go up and down together in response. All United Kingdom shares have their price movements linked to the rise and fall of the stock market index. This component of risk cannot be diversified away other than by investing in non-UK-based businesses.

The remaining risk, the part that is specific to the individual company and quite independent of developments outside it, can be diversified away very effectively. If an investor spreads his or her money evenly over the shares of thirty different companies, this type of risk will have disappeared almost completely.

The implication of this is a surprising but important one in the theory of financial markets. For risk-averse investors, extra risk must be rewarded by extra return, but it is only the component of risk which is linked to the movement of the stock market as a whole which is rewarded. The remaining risk is diversified away by investors. It does not harm them and they do not require any extra return to persuade them to accept it.

4.2.5 Liquidity

Most business projects are long term. Once the initial investment has been made, the benefits will arise over a period of years and, sometimes, of decades. Investors often have a shorter time horizon. They often do not know, when they make an investment, how soon they will want to take their money out. They will be well aware that they might need to withdraw their money at almost any time, as a result of illness or unemployment, for example. In other words, they need their investments to be liquid.

There are two ways in which the financial markets can perform the conjuring trick of providing funds to borrowers on a long-term basis while simultaneously assuring savers that they can get their money back whenever they want. The first is the secondary market, such as that organised by The Stock Exchange. The second is financial intermediary organisations such as banks.

The Stock Exchange

A primary financial market is one in which investors provide funds to companies (and other bodies, such as governments) and receive financial assets such as shares or bonds in return. A secondary market is one in which investors trade these financial assets among themselves. Investor A wants to sell shares; investor B is willing to buy; their advisers or brokers will negotiate a price for the exchange; and the company and its business are unaffected.

The Stock Exchange is mainly a secondary market. Because shares in most companies are traded many times a day, price negotiation between buyers and sellers is much simplified. The starting point will be the price for the last deal and the new price will not move very far in either direction.

The natural tendency is for the trading of a particular company's shares to be concentrated in a single market and The London Stock Exchange has virtual monopoly in the trading of shares for most United Kingdom companies. This enables The Stock Exchange to control the primary market for company securities too. Investors will not buy securities in the primary market unless they are sure that there will be an adequate secondary market, i.e. that The Stock Exchange will list the security and supervise trading in it. The Stock Exchange is, therefore, in a position to set rules governing the issue of new securities which are supplementary to the legal requirements of the Prevention of Fraud Acts. It can change its rules to stop any emerging abuse much more quickly than the government can rewrite the law.

The secondary market in shares can only work well when companies are large and have a large number of shareholders who will generate a constant flow of orders to buy and sell. This will produce a continuous market with small price jumps between transactions. Anyone who wants to trade can be confident that there will be counterparties in the market. For small companies the system tends to break down; there can be buyers without sellers or sellers without buyers so that a shareholder can find that either he or she is 'locked in' to shares or can only dispose of them at an unattractive price.

Banks

A bank creates liquidity in a quite different way. The depositors are assured that they can get their money out on demand or at short notice; the borrowers, mainly companies, are assured that their loans only need to be repaid over a negotiated period which may be as long as five or seven years. The bank is performing an asset transformation by taking in short-term deposits and giving out long-term loans. The system relies on the bank's ability to attract new depositors to replace those who withdraw. Under normal circumstances this can be achieved by judicious use of marketing campaigns and new, more attractive types of account for depositors.

A bank will also need its own risk capital so that if some of its loans to businesses go bad the loss can be absorbed by the shareholders in the bank rather than the depositors. Under the Basle Concordat, there is now international agreement that banks must have risk capital equal to at least 8 per cent of their total assets.

In times of economic and financial crisis there remains the possibility that large losses on bad loans will undermine public confidence and a bank will not be able to keep its deposit base. Any banking system is, in this respect, inherently unstable. Implicitly or explicitly the government and the central bank will underpin the banking system by guaranteeing depositors against loss and by standing ready to buy high-quality assets from a bank that needs to raise cash urgently. Although the relationship between banks and governments is often not written down in black and white, it is very important in influencing bank behaviour and we shall later compare the system in the United Kingdom with that in other industrial countries.

Notice that where a business is financed by shares quoted on The Stock Exchange, these shares will be actively traded and any adverse information about the success of the business will show up clearly and directly in a fall in the value of the shares. Where the finance comes from a bank loan, the loan will not be traded and there will be no open-market price which would give an objective measure of what the loan is worth. For this reason the bank finance system cannot provide business with risk capital. The system would not generate the information needed to operate effectively. Banks are best suited to providing business with safe loans where the problem of constant re-evaluation in the light of new information does not arise.

The conclusion of this section discussing the creation of liquidity is that risk capital for a business (other than that provided by the founders and directors) has to be provided through The Stock Exchange. However, low-risk capital can be provided either through an open market, on which the companies' debt securities are traded, or through banks.

4.2.6   Information

It is a basic rule in financial markets that those who take the risk in a business venture will have the ultimate decision-making power. Investors will be reluctant to put up risk capital if they are powerless to correct management errors that put their wealth at risk. Consequently share-holders have votes for the selection of the company directors, and the bondholders or banks who have provided the rest of the capital do not. The United Kingdom has a 'winner-take–all' system for the selection of directors. Fifty-one per cent of the votes are enough to control all the seats on the board.

When shareholders accept risks they want to understand clearly what the risks are and they want to see how they can act to protect their investment if things go wrong. Generally investors will prefer to invest in a 'pure play', a company that concentrates on a particular industrial sector, rather than a conglomerate company which has its finger in lots of pies and is, therefore, much harder for outsiders to understand. Investors will be less enthusiastic about buying shares in companies where there is a controlling shareholder, perhaps the founder of the business and his or her family. They will be suspicious that the controlling shareholder may find ways of benefiting himself or herself at the expense of other shareholders.

They will also be aware that a controlling shareholder can block a take-over bid, so no relief from that quarter could be expected if the business performed poorly. Investors also dislike, for similar reasons, companies which own non-controlling shareholdings in other companies. Share-holders will generally prefer to have the shares (and votes) in their own hands rather than own them indirectly at one remove.

How are shareholders to know what is going on in the business? The Companies Acts require that shareholders be given a report and accounts every year. In the judgement of The Stock Exchange this is insufficient. Quoted companies must provide half-yearly accounts and inform share-holders of any significant acquisitions or disposals which may change the nature of the business. For large changes and for any transaction between the company and one of its directors they must seek their shareholders' approval in a vote.

These requirements will certainly improve shareholders' awareness of what is going on in their company. But it will remain true that the directors and managers are likely to have much more detailed and up-to-date information than anyone relying on published accounts. Furthermore, if the information available to shareholders is seriously deficient, the financial markets cannot perform their resource allocation role effectively.

The inequality (or 'asymmetry') of information between shareholders and directors/managers has a number of consequences. If the directors know better than any outsiders what the company's shares are really worth, they will be able to make profits by trading the shares in the secondary market. This is known as insider trading and its consequence is that the market will become unfair. The losses will fall in the first instance on the market-makers whose function is to quote on a continuous basis prices at which they are prepared to buy and sell. They will find, for example, that they have been 'stuffed' with shares by insiders just before bad news about the company becomes publicly available, and the share price falls. The market-makers take a loss. The only way that they can stay in business is by widening the difference between their buying price for shares and their selling price (the 'spread'). This means in effect that ordinary investors pay a larger commission or charge whenever they trade in the market. In this way the ordinary investors pay the insiders' winnings.

The wider price spread reduces the liquidity that The Stock Exchange exists to create. Investors will pay less for shares if the secondary market deteriorates and, in the end, the whole economy suffers because companies cannot raise new risk capital on such favourable terms.

As noted in the introduction, insider trading has always been unethical. Since 1985, as a result of the Insider Trading Act it has been illegal. But it is a difficult crime to prove and easy crime to conceal by, for example, dealing through an offshore nominee company. Insider trading may have

been reduced, but it would be naive to suggest that the new law has
eliminated it.

4.2.7 Moral hazard

The opportunities for unjust self-enrichment by company directors and
managers are not confined to trading on the stock market. There are also
opportunities for these individuals to do the following:

1. Pay themselves excessive salaries and pensions.
2. Provide themselves with excessive perks in the form of cars, yachts,
   corporate jets, luxurious corporate offices and other facilities.
3. Sell off corporate assets to companies that they own privately at low
   prices; to buy assets for the corporation from their own private interests
   at high prices.
4. To set an undemanding pace of work; to appoint staff on grounds other
   than fitness for the job; to keep colleagues in their jobs even when they
   have proved themselves incompetent.

In all these respects, shareholders are exposed to moral hazard, the risk of
being cheated. It is clearly sensible for the shareholders to take whatever
steps they can to prevent their wealth being damaged in these ways.

In economic theory this is known as the Principal–Agent problem. The
shareholders are the Principals; the directors and managers are the
Agents, appointed by the Principals to act in their interest, but who will
still be tempted to promote their own interests rather than those of the
Principal if they feel they can get away with it. The problem is
fundamental. It cannot be eradicated. The best that can be done is to
monitor management's activities (through the auditors) and to try and
devise incentive schemes for managers which will link their interests
closely with that of shareholders (e.g. through share option schemes).

There is a further problem. If management is identified as inefficient or
dishonest, who is going to incur the costs of energy and effort needed to put
together a new and better team to take their place? The natural tendency
of shareholders, as we saw earlier, is to reduce risk by spreading their
shareholdings across a wide range of companies. There are many companies where no individual shareholder has more than 1 or 2 per cent of the
shares. An investor is not in the business; he or she expects to take a
passive role and normally has no direct contact with other shareholders. So
although shareholders have, collectively, the power to use their votes to
replace poorly performing directors, in practice this power is unusable. The
shareholder body lacks co-ordination, leadership, and any method of
sharing the burden of the costs incurred. Although it is within the power,
and the collective interest, of the shareholders to act, the incentive for the
individual shareholder is to sit tight and hope someone else will take the lead.

The consequence of this is that boards of directors tend to become self-perpetuating oligarchies. When one member steps down, the remainder of the group will choose a replacement. And they will choose a congenial individual, one who will fit in with the mores of the group and who can be relied on not to make waves.

In the absence of any controlling or large shareholding, therefore, the only effective sanction against poor management will be the takeover bid. The unsuccessful company will become a victim. Another company, the aggressor, will offer to buy shares in the victim at a price above the previous market level. If it succeeds in acquiring more than 50 per cent of the shares, it can sweep away the existing board and put in its own team. If, under UK law, it acquires 90 per cent it can buy the remaining shares compulsorily and absorb the victim company fully into its own operations.

4.3 The UK financial markets: selected statistics

4.3.1 Interest rates and other returns

The first item to notice in Figure 4.1 is the high level of average inflation in the United Kingdom compared to other industrial countries. Not only is United Kingdom inflation high, but also the variability of inflation (measured by the standard deviation) has been higher. This variability has been largely unanticipated and has exacerbated the economic cycle in the United Kingdom.

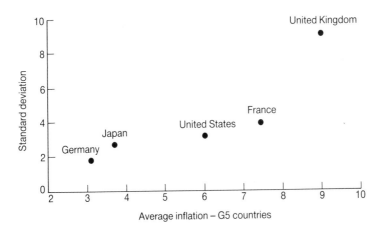

Figure 4.1 Average inflation and standard deviation of inflation, Q1 1976 to Q4 1991. (*Source: Datastream*)

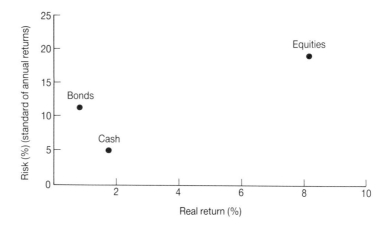

Figure 4.2 Risk and real return in the UK market for three classes of
financial asset, 1967–90. (*Source: Bank of England Quarterly Bulletin*, 1991)

Figure 4.2 shows the risk and return (both in real terms) for three classes
of asset in the United Kingdom. Equities have offered high return and high
risk as would be expected. Short-term assets (near-cash) have offered low
returns but still have a significant amount of risk because of the failure to
control United Kingdom inflation over the period. Bonds (medium- and
long-term fixed interest securities) have offered an intermediate level of
risk coupled with the lowest level of real return. This unattractive
combination, again caused by inflation, has made bonds unattractive to
both companies and investors. Companies cannot predict, in real terms,
what their liabilities will be and investors have no certainty about how
much they will receive.

4.3.2   The size of the UK Stock Exchange

The size of The Stock Exchange is perhaps the single most outstanding
feature of the United Kingdom system (see Figure 4.3). The comparison
with Japan is misleading. In the Japanese market cross-holdings between
quoted companies are common. About 40 per cent of the capitalisation of
the market is held in this way. A better comparison between the Japanese
market and the other markets in the figure is to multiply the Japanese
figure by 0.6. With this adjustment, the UK stock market is substantially
the largest in relative terms. In absolute terms it is as large as the German,
French, Italian and Spanish markets added together. The size of the UK
Stock Exchange made possible the privatisation in the 1980s of large state-
owned companies such as British Telecom and British Gas.

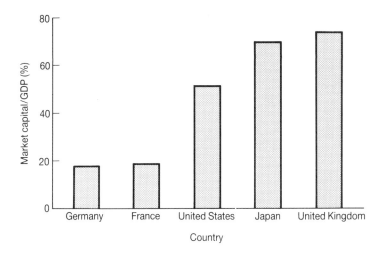

Figure 4.3 Rates of stock market capitalisation of GDP, 31 December 1991.
(*Source: Datastream*)

4.3.3 Share ownership in the United Kingdom

The growth of institutional investors, especially pension funds and insurance companies, has transformed The Stock Exchange in the last three decades. Private individuals now account for less than a quarter of the market value of quoted shares, as shown in Table 4.1. Pension funds and insurance companies accounted for 48.8 per cent in 1989 and it is believed that this figure has subsequently risen above 50 per cent. The policy of institutional investors is to avoid taking controlling stakes, nor do they ask for representation on boards of directors. They will keep their stakes in individual companies low. These small holdings can be quickly

Table 4.1 Share ownership in the United Kingdom (%)

	1963	1969	1975	1981	1989
Persons	54.0	47.4	37.5	28.2	21.3
Pension funds	6.4	9.0	16.8	26.7	30.4
Insurance companies	10.0	12.2	15.9	20.5	18.4
Unit and investment trusts	12.6	13.0	14.6	10.4	9.1
Other	17.0	18.4	15.2	14.2	20.8

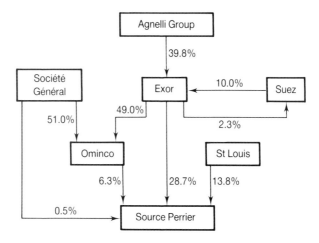

Note: The numbers show the percentage of the shares in one company which
      are held by another company in the network. For example, the Agnelli
      Group holds 39.8 per cent of the shares in Exor.

Figure 4.4 The network of major shareholdings relating to the French
mineral water company, Source Perrier, in 1992. (*Source: The Economist*)

and easily sold. Institutional investors will switch their holdings from one
company to another in accordance with their assessment of each company's
prospects. They have no long-term commitment to the company or its
management.

4.3.4   Ownership structures in continental Europe

Perrier, a French mineral water company, was the subject of a battle for
control in 1992. The ownership pattern is typical of many other companies
in continental Europe (see Figure 4.4). Many of the shares are held in large
blocks on a long-term basis. If there is more than one such block, control
will be exercised by an alliance between the interests involved. Banks often
hold blocks of shares. Cross holdings of shares can be used to strengthen
the grip of the controlling alliance. Any outsider who buys shares in The
Stock Exchange cannot expect that their voting rights will ever have any
significance. Notice the many differences between this structure and the
usual situation in the United Kingdom described earlier.

4.3.5   International comparisons of company gearing

Gearing is the proportion of a company's capital which is in the form of
debt. The implication of the large volume of share capital in the United

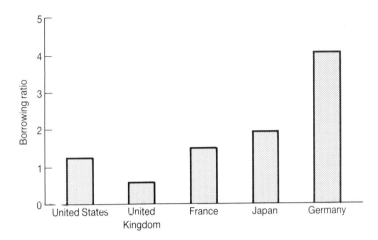

Figure 4.5 International comparisons of company gearing; average gearing 1987–91. (The borrowing ratio is the ratio of total loan capital to total equity capital employed. *Source: Datastream*)

Kingdom financial system is that the amount of debt will be correspondingly small. Figure 4.5 shows that this is the case. Companies in the United Kingdom have a conspicuously low level of gearing by international standards.

4.3.6 New issues and takeovers in the UK stock market

Figure 4.6 suggests that takeover activity, new issues of shares and the level of share prices tend to be linked. The state of the primary market for capital as measured by the capital issues of industrial and commercial companies follows the level of the stock market very closely. Both series show peaks in 1987 and 1991. The takeover series shows the same strong rise through the mid 1980s but sustained its growth through 1988 and 1989. It was not affected by the stock market crash of October 1987, largely because the government reacted to the crash by lowering interest rates and thus creating opportunities for profitable deal-making using borrowed money. The amount of takeover activity shown here greatly exceeds the level in any country in continental Europe.

The very large change in the level of new issues between, for example, 1979–80 and 1986–7 illustrates one of the main features of The Stock Exchange as a source of finance. It is unreliable. At times the institutional

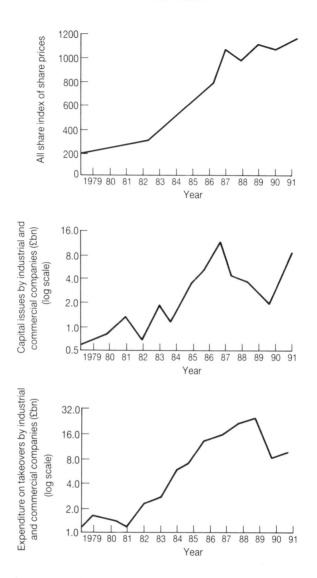

Figure 4.6 Share prices and takeovers. (*Source:* Bank of England)

investors are 'on feed' and willing to buy new issues. At other times they
are out of the market and even companies with a strong business case for
raising more risk capital are turned away. United Kingdom companies
tend to imitate camels as a result; fill up when you have the chance, it may
be a long way to the next oasis. The figures also show that takeover activity
in the United Kingdom is large and highly cyclical. If takeovers are

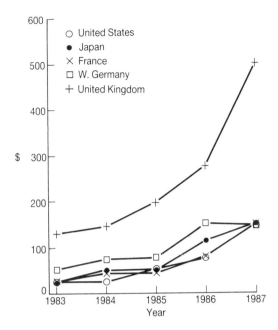

Figure 4.7 Foreign direct investment per capita, 1983–7 (1985 US dollars). (*Source:* D. Julius, *Datastream*)

motivated by the low efficiency of existing management, it is hard to see why the volume of takeovers should be so volatile.

4.3.7 Foreign direct investment

Backed by a plentiful supply of risk capital at home, UK companies have invested heavily overseas (see Figure 4.7). Some of the investment is physical (setting up new factories, etc.) but a large part comes from overseas acquisitions. United Kingdom companies have shown a much stronger tendency to develop into international players in their respective industries than their continental equivalents. In this area, the United Kingdom financial system may be helping British companies to establish a competitive advantage. A cynic, of course, might suggest that British companies are so keen to expand abroad because the economic prospects look so poor at home.

4.4 The logic of the UK markets

The statistics above have tended to show that the United Kingdom has a quite distinct system of corporate finance compared with other large industrial countries. The contrast between the United Kingdom and continental Europe is particularly marked. The purpose of this section is to explain how public policy decisions in the United Kingdom have produced the differences. We shall also want to discuss, briefly, how well public policy has served the public interest in the United Kingdom

4.4.1   UK banks

Let us start with banks. Why do they play such a small role in corporate finance when compared, for example, to their German counterparts? There are three main reasons. The first is the uncertainty produced by inflation. Inflation in the United Kingdom has been high, highly variable and highly unpredictable in comparison with Germany. Inflation is, as we have seen, a major component of interest rates. High inflation leads to high interest rates; unpredictable inflation leads to unpredictable interest rates. The general disturbance to financial market equilibrium resulting from this means that real interest rates will be volatile too.

All this is bad for banks. Depositors will not commit themselves to three- or five-year deposits at fixed interest rates if this exposes them to considerable risk from unforeseen inflation. If bank deposits are on a short-term basis with interest rates linked to short-term market rates, then loans to businesses must also be on a variable interest rate basis. A company which agrees a five year loan may start paying at 8 per cent; if economic conditions change it may find the cost goes up to 14 per cent. And this extra interest rate burden will come on top of a decline in orders as high interest rates tip the economy into recession.

For many purposes, companies would prefer to borrow money at fixed interest rates. If loans on this basis are not available they are likely to take their business away from the banks altogether and issue shares. And this leaves a smaller role for United Kingdom banks to play. One indication of the restricted role of United Kingdom banks is that they are inferior to building societies in the level of deposits they attract from investors.

A second reason for the weakness of UK banks comes from the interaction between inflation and the tax system. Because their assets are monetary (rather than real assets like factories, machinery and stocks) the effective (i.e. inflation-corrected) rate of tax can be considerably higher than the stated rate; so high, in fact, that no matter how hard the banks run, they find it difficult to avoid slipping backwards.

This point can be illustrated with a highly simplified example. Suppose the bank has the following four items on its balance sheet. Each item, other than shareholders' capital, has a real interest rate associated with it. The associated nominal interest rates depend on the assumed rate of inflation.

Balance sheet

Assets

Amount (£m)

75 Loans to companies,
    5 per cent real interest, 15.5 per cent nominal at 10 per cent
    inflation

25 Reserve assets,
    4 per cent real interest, 14.4 per cent nominal at 10 per cent
    inflation

——
100

Liabilities

90 Deposits,
    4 per cent real interest, 14.4 per cent nominal at 10 per cent
    inflation

10 Shareholders' capital
——
100

With *no inflation*, the interest being received and paid by the bank is simply the real rate. We assume a tax rate of 40 per cent on the bank's profits. The Profit and Loss statement is then:

Profit and loss account

	Amount (£m)
Interest received on loans to companies (75 × 0.05)	3.75
Interest received on Reserve Assets (25 × 0.04)	1.00
	4.75
Interest paid on deposits (90 × 0.04)	3.60
Taxable profit	1.15
Tax	0.46
After-tax profit	0.69

On shareholders capital of £10 million, the bank is earning an after-tax profit of almost 7 per cent. If the bank intends to grow at 4 per cent annually in real terms while maintaining the existing proportions on its balance sheet, then 0.40 of the after-tax profit needs to be kept in the business and the remainder can be paid out as a dividend to shareholders.

With 10 per cent inflation, the corresponding figures will be as follows:

	Amount (£m)
Interest received on loans to companies (75 × 0.155)	11.625
Interest received on reserve assets (25 × 0.144)	3.600
	15.225
Interest paid on deposits (90 × 0.144)	12.960

Taxable profit	2.265
Tax	0.906
After-tax profit	1.359

On first appearance, it looks as though inflation has made the bank more profitable. After-tax profit has apparently risen from £0.69 million to £1.359 million. But this is entirely misleading. With an inflation rate of 10 per cent, the shareholders' capital must go from £10 million to £11 million just in order to retain its real value. The only gain to shareholders is the remaining £0.359 million in end-of-year money which is only worth £0.326 million in beginning-of-the-year money. If the bank wants to increase its real capital base at 4 per cent per year it will be unable to pay any dividend to its shareholders. Either the bank will have to go to its shareholders from time to time to get injections of new capital (and the shareholders will hardly be enthusiastic) or the bank must accept that its growth must be stunted by the tax and inflation environment in which it operates.

One way of looking at the impact of inflation on banks is to say that, in this example, the effective tax rate has grown from 40 per cent with no inflation to 72 per cent with 10 per cent inflation. No business can flourish with effective tax rates at these very high levels.

Of course, there are many countries with significant inflation where the banking sector flourishes. There are two ways in which this may occur. One is the situation in which the government owns the major banks. This is the case in France, Italy and Spain. The banking sector can be used as an instrument of economic policy and can work behind the scenes to support particular industries in accordance with political priorities. In the United Kingdom the Bank of England did until 1971 operate direct credit controls designed to encourage banks to lend to particular sectors, for example to manufacturing industry rather than to property developers. The banking system tended to find ways round the controls and their effectiveness was limited.

Another approach is that banks should take equity stakes in companies. This gives them a 'real' asset which will tend to rise in value with inflation. German and Spanish banks, for example, have large shareholdings in industry. This certainly makes life easier for the banks, but it is not value-maximising for the bank's shareholders. We have already seen that they prefer to hold equity stakes directly rather than indirectly. So this escape route is not open to British banks. The German and Spanish banks are less sensitive to shareholders' interests and seem under no strong pressure to give up their equity holdings.

There are, therefore, good reasons for the poor health of UK banks. And the poor competitive position of the banks will be one factor leading to the size and success of The Stock Exchange in Britain. There are several others. In continental Europe, invasions, defeats and hyperinflation in the first half of the twentieth century have forced the rebuilding of the corporate structure from ground zero. British companies are typically older-established and have often come to The Stock Exchange as a result of inheritance taxes or the dispersion of shares to increasingly remote family descendants with no emotional or managerial links to the company. Family controlled large companies are still common in continental Europe.

4.4.2 The UK pension system

Pension arrangements in the United Kingdom also have a major influence on the financial markets. In contrast to policy in continental Europe, in the United Kingdom, the state only offers a small basic pension. Funded, mainly private, pension schemes make up the difference. Because most schemes offer pensions based on salary at retirement, they need to buy real (not monetary) assets to match this real liability. Shares fit this requirement well. Since contributions to pension schemes are tax-deductible for both employee and employer, and the returns earned by the fund are tax-free, pension funds are a very attractive way to save. Many individuals opt to make additional voluntary contributions (AVCs) to their occupational pension scheme rather than save directly on their own account.

Pension funds and other institutional investors have had a beneficial effect on the operations of the London Stock Exchange. Where individual investors tend to be passive, institutional investors are vocal and critical. They have been active in protecting shareholders' rights and in pressing for modernisation of Stock Exchange trading practices. The Take Over Panel (1968), the abolition of minimum commissions on sharedealing and the other 'Big Bang' reforms (1986), the prohibition of insider dealing (1985), the increase in the amount of information given in company accounts (a continuous process during the 1970s and 1980s) have all resulted from pressure from institutional investors. These reforms have put the London market some distance ahead of continental Europe. Evidence of this competitive advantage of the trading mechanisms of the London market can be seen in the growth of SEAQ (Stock Exchange Automatic Quotations) International, a system for trading the shares of non-UK companies in London. Some companies in continental Europe, particularly from Scandinavia, have been active in courting United Kingdom institutional investors.

4.4.3 Takeovers

Takeovers have been far more common in Britain than in continental Europe. Many takeovers are friendly but, equally, many are not. Because companies lack controlling shareholders, many United Kingdom companies are potential takeover targets. There is a 'market for corporate control' in which shareholders can oust existing managers if another management team offers a better deal. The defending management, and the challengers will put their arguments in circulars to shareholders and press advertisements. The whole process is very public and very expensive.

Unsuccessful managers are removed in other financial systems too. In Germany and Japan it would probably fall to the company's bankers, who would have a close long-term relationship with the company including representation on the board, to press for a management change. There would be much less publicity for this type of change. And the interests of the bankers, of course, will not be quite the same as the interests of the shareholders.

4.4.4 The case for UK financial market policies

Let us conclude by setting out briefly the arguments for and against the financial markets policies in the United Kingdom compared with those in Germany or other continental countries. The United Kingdom system has produced the largest market for risk capital in Europe. As a result, British companies have had a financial base on which to grow into world-class competitors, a development which was also encouraged by the abolition of all exchange controls in 1979. The level of Foreign Direct Investment from the United Kingdom illustrates this strength clearly.

Risk capital is available in Britain partly because shareholders are offered a fair deal. They can get rid of incompetent or self-serving management. The United Kingdom corporate world is a meritocracy. Promotion comes on the basis of talent and not because you were born into the right family or belong to the right political party.

The financial markets are generally clean and getting cleaner. The government has shown itself willing to pass reforming legislation and to act against abuses in the courts. The complex, expensive and well-publicised 'Guinness' and 'Blue Arrow' cases (both essentially concerned with events linked to take-overs) are evidence of this.

Shareholders are better at allocating their own funds than politicians or bankers are at doing it on their behalf. Shareholders have been brutally realistic in observing those sectors of the economy which were in long-term decline or in which Britain did not have a competitive advantage. They have steered the United Kingdom economy away from metal-bashing and textiles and towards service and leisure industries, branded consumer goods and health-care products (especially drugs). They have given the United Kingdom a strong position in the growth industries of the future.

The clearest evidence of the success of United Kingdom policy towards financial markets is the success of UK financial sector companies in selling their services overseas. London is the leading financial centre in Europe. It is a centre for international banking and share dealing and its expertise in privatisation and corporate restructuring are in demand throughout the world. A host of other high-value professional services – legal, accounting, property valuation, insurance, etc. – are flourishing on the basis of Britain's highly developed financial markets. The financial markets are the source of many well-paid jobs.

4.4.5   The case against UK financial market policies

So far as industrial and commercial development is concerned, the main task of the financial markets is to provide low-cost finance. This the United Kingdom system fails to do. Bank finance is the first choice for most companies. The transaction is simple and cheap. The borrower provides whatever information the lender needs. But bank finance is scarce in Britain and there is only a small market for corporate bonds. Companies are forced into the stock market to raise equity capital.

Equity from The Stock Exchange is expensive. It is expensive because it is risk capital and investors demand extra return for extra risk. In the United Kingdom the propensity of the economy to lurch from slump to boom and back again adds to risk and so adds to the expense. Equity is also expensive because its tax treatment is less favourable than debt and because of all the ancillary costs of providing a constant flow of information to shareholders. Senior managers, for example, must expect to field a steady stream of questions from investment analysts and must make presentations to institutional investors. Raising funds by issuing new shares is a highly complex and expensive exercise involving lawyers, accountants, merchant bankers, stockbrokers and underwriters. Finally, shares are an expensive form of finance because of the inefficiencies due to moral hazard and insider dealing. Most of these problems can be avoided in family companies whose shares are not traded on The Stock Exchange and where there is no split between ownership and management.

The stock market is ill-adapted to meet the needs of small companies. It is hard to keep track of what they are doing and there will not be a steady flow of trading in the shares. So UK companies, as a result of friendly or unfriendly amalgamations, have tended to grow large and diverse. The main activity at head office will be financial management; raising funds; preparing accounts and handling investor relations. The top managers will have a financial or accounting background. They may have little understanding of the technologies on which their manufacturing processes are based or the markets that they serve. They are therefore incapable of identifying new products or new manufacturing processes. In a changing world they are incapable of innovation. They preside over carefully audited decline.

The managers' reluctance to innovate is enhanced by the reward structure within which they operate. The greatest threat to their own careers is for their company to be taken over. Their primary objective is to avoid this. They must do what their shareholders want. They dare not use the forecasts of their own skilled and experienced staff to embark on a policy that goes against current conventional wisdom. Indeed they will be reluctant to adopt any policy that reduces next year's profits even if the long-run effect would be highly beneficial. Their management will be directed towards producing a steady upward trend in earnings per share, and creative accounting will be one of the main management skills required. Management will have a short-term perspective, looking towards the next half-yearly profit number. Long-term development of the business will have a lesser priority.

Takeovers are greatly overrated as a discipline for poor managers. They are public relations contests rather than genuine choices between different management policies. With most shareholders' real knowledge of the company based on nothing more than a few pages of accounts and some glossy photographs, it cannot be anything else. At least in Germany management changes are based on inside knowledge.

The takeover game is essentially run by and for the merchant banks. They act as advisers to aggressors and victims and, in exchange for large fees, orchestrate the whole show from just off-stage. A company which stays aloof from the process and refuses to pay tribute to the merchant banker is likely to be set up as a victim. The Guinness trial showed how large amounts of money could be offered to 'friends' and 'supporters' in a takeover battle in irregular and unauthorised ways which hovered on the margins of corruption. At the end of a lengthy trial the purpose and destination of some multi-million pound payments to Swiss bank accounts was still unclear.

Shareholders in the United Kingdom have a short-term outlook and view their shares as trading chips. They should accept that, as proprietors, they must take some responsibility for the long-term development of their companies.

4.5   Conclusion

There are strongly held views on both sides of the argument. Critics of the United Kingdom financial markets sound more convincing when detailing their charges than when proposing remedies. If United Kingdom shareholders are too quick to sell their shares to a takeover raider, how are they to be prevented or dissuaded from doing so? Would it help if shareholders were refused voting rights until they had held their shares for six months? Could more non-executive directors help bridge the information gap between companies and their shareholders? Or are both these ideas mere tinkering?

The arguments for and against the present structure of the UK financial markets may seem closely balanced. But surely the greatest handicap from which they have suffered has been inflation. It is inflation that has damaged the banking system and artificially stimulated stock market activity. It is also inflation that stokes the takeover market. The great wave in takeover activity towards the end of the 1980s was fuelled by an increase in the money supply which left banks with a surplus of money to lend. The merchant banks were quick to conjure up takeover deals which helped them to solve their problem.

If the fundamental problem of inflation can be solved, as a result of the Exchange Rate Mechanism of the European Monetary System or, perhaps, eventually, through a single European currency, the United Kingdom could have the best of all worlds as far as its financial markets are concerned. An efficient, well regulated stock exchange; fixed interest finance available to companies at reasonable rates and for reasonable terms; and an overall cost of capital for industrial and commercial companies that will help them to compete successfully on a global basis.

Questions for discussion

1. Will the system of corporate finance in Britain come to model itself on continental Europe, or will continental Europe move in the direction of the United Kingdom?
2. Would you agree that in the United Kingdom shareholders have more powers than they can properly use?
3. In view of the difficulty in controlling insider trading, should directors and managers be prohibited from buying, selling or owning shares in their companies?
4. Does Britain need a state-controlled investment bank?
5. If inflation damages financial markets, why have successive British governments not controlled inflation more effectively?
6. Should company managements have greater protection against takeover bids?
7. Does Britain's large expenditure on Foreign Direct Investment weaken the British economy?

Suggestions for further reading

A good survey of the financial system in the United Kingdom is:
Peasnell, K. W. and C. W. R. Ward (1985), *British Financial Markets and Institutions*, London: Prentice Hall.
Domestic and international functions of the London markets are described in:
Clarke, W. M. (1991), *How the City of London works: an introduction to its financial markets*, London: Waterlow.

A comparison between the UK and German systems of corporate finance, at a more advanced level, can be found in:

Mayer, C. and I. Alexander (1990), 'Banks and securities markets: Corporate financing in Germany and the United Kingdom', *Journal of the Japanese and International Economies*, December, pp. 450–75.

The charge that the UK financial system prevents company managers from taking a long term view is discussed in:

'Creative tension', *National Association of Pension Funds*, London, 1990.

The restructuring of The Stock Exchange is discussed in:

Thomas, W. A. (1986), *The Big Bang*, Oxford: Philip Allan

and the new regulatory structure is criticised in:

Seldon, A. (ed.) (1988), *Financial Regulation – or Over-regulation?*, London: Institute of Economic Affairs.

Finally, a regular flow of short articles discussing developments in the UK financial markets can be found in the *Bank of England Quarterly Bulletin*.

Chapter 5

Unemployment

PRABIR BHATTACHARYA

5.1 Definition and measurement

Unemployment is usually defined as the difference between the number of people willing and able to work at prevailing wage rates, and those who actually have jobs. The unemployment rate is the number unemployed expressed as a percentage of the labour force.

Unemployment in Britain has traditionally been measured as the number of people registered as unemployed at job centres on a particular day each month; since 1982 the measure used has been the number of people claiming Unemployment Benefit each month. There are a number of problems with this measure. First, it fails to take account of those who are registered as unemployed but are not eligible, or choose not to apply, for benefit. Second, the new, like the old, method of counting fails to take account of workers out of work and seeking a job and hence economically active, but who choose not to register as unemployed. Third, there is a large number of workers (especially women) who are discouraged from entering the labour force because of the depressed labour market conditions. Since these individuals are *willing* to work at current real wages and job conditions but are deterred from doing so by the prospects of unsuccessful job search, they should be included in the total of those unemployed. In a more buoyant labour market this group of workers would be economically active and appear generally in the stock of unregistered unemployed.

As against these, however, the stock of claimants does include groups of workers who are not available for work and these should be excluded from the total. The 1983 Labour Force Survey, for example, showed that those who did not want to work for family or other reasons amounted to 6.1 per cent of the claimant total. Indeed by 1985 the benefit count was actually giving higher readings than labour-force surveys showing who was actively seeking work. Some benefit claimants were long-term unemployed discouraged from seeking work; others were doing part-time or even full-time jobs in the black economy. Not surprisingly these difficulties in obtaining precise estimates have encouraged commentators to exercise considerable latitude in their own calculations. Those horrified at the scale of unemployment in Britain inevitably publish estimates much higher than the official figures while those more sanguine about the problem do the opposite.

Having indicated how unemployment is measured one might expect that we should regard full employment quite simply as that state of the economy where measured unemployment is zero (making suitable allowance both for those who do not register and for those not available for work). To do so, however, would be incorrect. Ours is a dynamic and mobile economy. Individuals quit jobs to look for better positions or to retrain for more attractive occupations. These phenomena, and many more, produce some minimal amount of unemployment. Economists call this the level of *frictional unemployment*. Frictional unemployment includes people who are temporarily between jobs because they are moving or changing occupations, or because their old firm went out of business, or for other similar reasons. A second type of unemployment – often difficult to distinguish from frictional unemployment – is called *structural unemployment*. This refers to situations where workers have lost their jobs because they have been displaced by automation, or because their skills are no longer in demand, or for other similar reasons. When the only unemployment is frictional and structural, the economy is said to be at full employment, and the measured unemployment rate is then called the *natural rate of unemployment*. In much of the macroeconomics literature the term 'natural rate' is used interchangeably with the 'non-accelerating inflation rate of unemployment', where the rate of unemployment is compatible with a stable rate of inflation (see Parkin and King, 1992, Ch. 31).

5.2   Costs of unemployment

When the level of employment is below the full employment level (i.e. the unemployment rate is above the natural rate), actual output will be below the economy's potential output, so that there is an economic cost of unemployment in terms of lost output. The relationship between output and employment is complex, so that a 1 per cent reduction in employment is not necessarily associated with a 1 per cent reduction in output. Indeed, if actual employment is 1 per cent below the full employment level, then output may well be below potential output by 2 per cent or more. This is because firms are likely to respond to a slump in orders (i.e. a fall in demand for their products) in other ways besides reducing employment.

For instance, when output is reduced by, say, 2 per cent, firms may accomplish some part of this, say 1 per cent, by abolishing overtime and cutting back the number of hours worked by employees. In that case, a drop in output of 2 per cent is accompanied by a fall in employment of only 1 per cent.

In other words, a given change in the level of unemployment might indicate a much greater change in the level of output. The American economist Arthur Okun suggested a one-to-three ratio for the United States (i.e. a 1 percentage point rise in the unemployment rate indicating a 3 per cent fall in gross national product (GNP)) and formulated this into what became known as Okun's Law. Earlier, Godley and Shepherd had suggested the one-to-two ratio used above for the United Kingdom. It is of course difficult to estimate the true ratio and this may change over time, but it is clear that the value of output lost in periods when unemployment is well above the natural rate can be very large indeed.

However, there are other economists who think that the cost of unemployment in terms of lost output is not so high. They believe that the natural rate of unemployment itself varies (see section 5.4). Thus if rapid technological advances in a particular period lead to the growth of new industries (e.g. high-technology, computer-oriented industries) and the decline of some old industries, then there would be a higher than normal amount of labour turnover. Unemployment would temporarily rise as many people lose their jobs in old industries. Lowering the unemployment rate in this case would prevent the necessary reallocation of labour. To reap the full advantage of the new technologies, workers need to relocate to new industries. If they do not, then both output and income would be lower than that which the new technologies could otherwise have achieved.

Apart from the lost-output cost of high unemployment, there are obvious and potentially substantial social costs. We live in a work-oriented society. A worker forced into idleness by a recession endures a psychological cost that is no less real for our inability to quantify it. High unemployment breeds mental anxiety and ill health and leads to a higher incidence of divorces, suicides and the like. There is also growing evidence that high unemployment leads to increased crime and social disruption.

Another important cost of unemployment is the erosion of human capital that it causes. Accumulated work experience is a valuable asset. Those forced into idleness by unemployment not only cease accumulating experience, but lengthy periods of unemployment have adverse effects on work habits, make workers 'rusty' and thus less productive when they are re-employed. Lengthy periods of unemployment also undermine the enthusiasm for training or relocation where that is a possibility. Short periods of unemployment exact different kinds of costs. A record of regular employment is important in applying for a new job. And a person who has frequently been laid off will lack this record of reliability.

5.3 The unemployment record

The unemployment record in the United Kingdom is set out in Figure 5.1. Unemployment, it will be noted, was extremely high during the inter-war years, the worst period being the Great Depression of the early 1930s, when over 20 per cent of the labour force was unemployed. By comparison, the post-war unemployment rate was very low until the late 1970s. By the early 1980s it was starting to get back to prewar levels and in 1985 and 1986 over 3 million people were seeking jobs. This basic pattern applies in many other industrialised countries. However, the United Kingdom was more successful than other countries, especially in Western Europe, in bringing unemployment down in the late 1980s, as indicated in Table 5.1.[1] Since late 1990, however, unemployment has started to rise again in the United Kingdom and the figure could once again approach 3 million by the end of 1992.

It must be stressed that the United Kingdom unemployment rates for the years 1855–1990 illustrated in Figure 5.1 are not wholly comparable. There have been changes from time to time in the way the numbers unemployed are counted, with several changes occurring in the 1980s. Before 1986, the unemployment rate referred to the percentage of the civilian labour force who were unemployed as a percentage of the total number of civilians employed plus the number regarded as unemployed. Since 1986, however, the unemployment rate refers to the number of people regarded as unemployed as a percentage of the total labour force

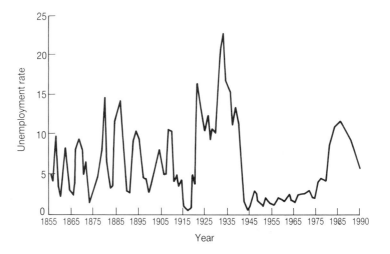

Figure 5.1 UK unemployment (%). (*Sources:* B. R. Mitchell, *Abstract of British Historical Statistics*, Cambridge: Cambridge University Press; CSO, *Economic Trends*)

Table 5.1 OECD standardised unemployment rates

Country	1979	1983	1985	1986	1987	1988	1989
United States	5.8	9.5	7.1	6.9	6.1	5.4	5.2
Japan	2.1	2.6	2.6	2.8	2.8	2.5	2.3
United Kingdom	5.0	12.4	11.2	11.2	10.3	8.5	6.9
Italy	7.5	8.8	9.6	10.5	10.9	11.0	10.9
France	5.9	8.3	10.2	10.4	10.5	10.0	9.6
Germany	3.2	8.0	7.2	6.4	6.2	6.2	5.5
EC average	5.6	10.4	10.8	10.8	10.5	9.8	8.9

Sources: OECD Economic Outlook, OECD Labour Force Statistics.

which includes not only the number of people employed and unemployed but also the self-employed and HM forces. The post-1986 approach reduces the measured unemployment rate since the number of people regarded as unemployed is divided by a larger number. It is difficult to be precise about the effects of these changes, but it has been suggested that the figures for the later years are probably at least 2 percentage points below what they would have been if the changes had not been made.

5.4 Labour market and unemployment

What explains the fluctuations in the rate of unemployment? What policies are needed to deal with high unemployment? How effective have the policies of the government been in dealing with high unemployment? Before we can answer these questions, it is first necessary to consider briefly the working of the labour market.

There are two leading theories of labour market equilibrium, one based on the assumption that money wages are flexible and the other based on the assumption that they are sticky (the former is often referred to as the 'neoclassical' view, the latter 'Keynesian'). Under the flexible money wage theory, the real wage rate (i.e. the money wage divided by an index of consumer prices) adjusts to ensure that the quantity of labour supplied equals the quantity demanded. The theory is illustrated in Figure 5.2. The demand for labour curve is LD and the supply of labour curve is LS. This market determines an equilibrium real wage rate of £6.00 an hour and a quantity of labour employed of 10 billion hours. If the real wage rate is below this equilibrium level, the quantity of labour demanded exceeds the quantity supplied. In such a situation, given the price index, the money wage rate will rise since firms are willing to offer higher money wage rates in order to overcome their labour shortages. Consequently, the real wage rate will rise until it reaches £6.00 an hour, at which point there will be no shortage of labour.

Conversely, if the real wage is higher than its equilibrium level of £6.00 an hour, the quantity of labour supplied exceeds the quantity demanded. In this situation, firms will have an incentive to cut the money wage rate and households will accept the lower money wage to get a job. Given the price index, the real wage rate will fall until it reaches £6.00 an hour, at which point every household will be satisfied with the quantity of labour that it is supplying. Under the flexible money wage rate theory, changes in the money wage rate cause the real wage rate to adjust, ensuring that the quantity of labour supplied equals the quantity demanded.

According to the flexible money wage theory, the unemployment rate is always equal to the natural rate of unemployment. There is a balance between the quantity of labour demanded and the quantity of labour supplied. But the quantity of labour supplied is the number of hours of labour available for work at a given time without further search for a better job. The quantity of labour demanded is the number of hours of labour that firms wish to hire at a given time, given their knowledge of the individual skills and talents available. Households supply hours for work as well as time for job search. Those people who devote no time to working and specialise in job search are the ones who are unemployed. Additionally, unemployment may exist if the real wage rate is deliberately maintained above the level at which the labour supply and labour demand schedules intersect. It can be caused either by the exercise of trade union power or by minimum wage legislation which enforces a real wage rate in excess of the equilibrium real wage rate. Unemployment thus caused is known as

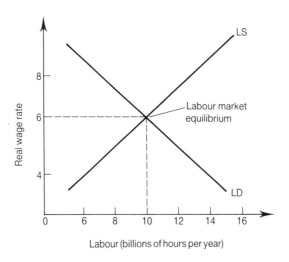

Figure 5.2 Equilibrium with flexible money wages

classical unemployment and is usually included as part of the natural rate of unemployment. (The natural rate of unemployment, in other words, strictly includes frictional, structural and classical unemployment.)

In contrast to the flexible wage model, the sticky wage theory of the labour market emphasises that money wage rates are fixed by wage contracts for a year or more ahead and that they do not adjust freely minute by minute to enable changes in the real wage rate to maintain a balance between aggregate quantity of labour demanded and supplied. Real wage rates change more frequently than do money wage rates because of changes in the price level, but not with sufficient flexibility to achieve continuous full employment. In such a situation how is the wage determined? The money wage rate is set in the expectation or belief that, on the average, the quantity of labour demanded will equal the quantity supplied. However, when firms and workers agree to a money wage rate for a future contract, they do not know what the price level is going to be. All they can do is base the contract on their best forecast of future prices. If the price level turns out to be the same as expected, then the real wage rate is the same as in the flexible wage case and employment will also be the same. However, many other outcomes are possible. Consider what would happen to employment if the price level turns out to be different from what was expected.

The sticky wage theory assumes that it is the quantity of labour demanded which determines employment. Thus if the money wage rate is fixed and the price level turns out to be lower than what was expected, the real wage rate will be higher than the equilibrium real wage. Firms will, therefore, demand less labour than households wish to supply and employment will be below the labour market equilibrium. Conversely, when the money wage rate is fixed and the price level turns out to be higher than what was expected, the real wage rate will be lower, firms will demand more labour and employment will be higher.

According to the sticky wage theory, fluctuations in unemployment arise primarily from the mechanism just described, with the real wage deviating from its equilibrium level. Those economists who emphasise the role of sticky wages in causing fluctuations in unemployment commonly regard the natural rate of unemployment as constant – or slowly changing. Fluctuations in the actual unemployment rate are fluctuations around the natural rate. This interpretation of fluctuations in unemployment, it will be noted, contrasts sharply with that of the flexible money wage theory. The flexible money wage rate theory predicts that *all* changes in unemployment are fluctuations in the natural rate of unemployment.

This debate among economists about the causes of unemployment is not just of academic interest and importance. It is critical for the design and conduct of macroeconomic stabilisation policy. If most of the fluctuations in unemployment do arise from sticky money wage rates, aggregate demand management can moderate the size of fluctuations in unemployment. By keeping aggregate demand (i.e. the sum of consumption, government expenditure and investment) steady so that the price level stays close to its expected level, the economy can be kept close to full employment. If, however, real wages are flexible enough to ensure that all unemployment is 'natural unemployment' and fluctuations in actual unemployment are fluctuations in natural unemployment, then aggregate demand policy has no role to play. Attempts by government to reduce unemployment below this natural rate by expansionary macro policies would then cause excess demand. This excess demand will lead to increases in wage and price inflation. In the short run workers are 'fooled' by the increase in money wages into believing that real wages have risen, and hence into supplying more labour, with less time being devoted to search and leisure activities. Consequently, unemployment falls. However, this deviation is only a short-run experience. In the long run workers realise that real wages have not risen, and their supply of labour therefore falls back again. As no government could contemplate a sustained acceleration in the rates of wage and price inflation, unemployment could not be permanently reduced below the natural rate. According to the flexible money wage rate model, to reduce the natural rate of unemployment permanently, the labour market has to be made more competitive and hence microeconomic policies (supply-side measures) are required. These may include the removal of labour market constraints caused by trade unions, minimum wages or wages councils (see Chapter 11), which maintain the real wage rate above its equilibrium level. Alternatively, reductions in marginal income tax rates (if not offset by higher indirect taxes – see Chapters 13 and 14) may provide the incentive for an increase in labour supply, whilst an increase in labour productivity would raise the demand for labour (SL and/or DL in Figure 5.2 would shift to the right).

5.5   Accounting for the rise in British unemployment

Economists remain a long way from agreement about the causes of unemployment and the reasons for its sometimes high and constantly fluctuating rate. In practice, however, Keynesian and neoclassical approaches to the determination of unemployment need not be mutually exclusive. A period of persistent high unemployment may reflect both unemployment above the natural rate and an increase in the rate over time. Thus all the recent attempts to estimate the natural rate for the United Kingdom suggest an upward trend over most of the last twenty years. Layard and Nickell (1985) have suggested that the natural rate of unemployment for male workers was around 2 per cent between 1955 and 1966, and then doubled by 1967–74 and doubled again between 1975 and

1979 to around 7.8 per cent. The rate then rose to 10.7 per cent by 1980–3. Davies' (1985) summary of three recent studies similarly suggests a rise of around 2–4 per cent between the late 1970s and the mid-1980s, that is about half the actual rise in unemployment. This rise in the natural rate, it has been suggested, has been caused, among other things, by increases in trade union power, by the unemployed becoming less available for work due to higher replacement ratios (when unemployment benefit rises relative to wages from working, we say the replacement ratio has risen), by reduced pressure from benefit offices on recipients to find work and due to a general weakening of the work ethic.

The striking fact that estimates of the natural rate have moved up with the actual rate of unemployment suggests some form of 'hysteresis'. Pure hysteresis means that the current value of a variable depends upon history, the variable having no tendency to move towards any particular level. So there is hysteresis in unemployment if the natural rate of unemployment this year is affected by the unemployment level in previous years. Jenkinson (1987) investigates several possibilities for this influence and particularly important in this context appears to be the behaviour of the long-term unemployed. The long-term unemployed tend to become discouraged, they are not very active in looking for work and their loss of skills makes them less attractive to employers. They stop being part of the effective supply of labour and they therefore have little downward impact on wage pressure. The natural rate will increase as the proportion of long-term unemployed rises; support for this proposition has come from a wide range of models. Higher unemployment may also reduce labour market efficiency as on-the-job search is reduced and this results in lower labour market mobility among employed workers and increases mismatch between workers and jobs.

Any empirical investigation of the post-1979 unemployment experience must allow for both Keynesian and neoclassical mechanisms to operate. A good example is Layard and Nickell (1985, 1987). Results from their work suggest that demand factors played very little role in the growth of male unemployment (data on male unemployment are more comprehensively and reliably documented than data on the unemployment of women) in the 1960s and early 1970s, where union militancy and in the 1970s the rise in real import prices appear to be the dominant causes of that growth. The picture dramatically changes when we consider the rise in male unemployment in the late 1970s where contraction of aggregate demand alone accounted for 85 per cent of the rapid rise in male unemployment. Layard and Nickell conclude that although the influence of unions and replacement ratios may have caused an increase in unemployment in the 1960s and early 1970s, it is the contraction of aggregate demand which was mainly responsible for increases in subsequent years. McCallum (1986) reaches similar conclusions about the importance of restrictive fiscal and monetary policy, as does Pissarides (1986). It would thus appear that the increase in United Kingdom unemployment in the 1960s and 1970s can almost entirely be explained by forces that had increased the natural rate. The story, however, was very different in the late 1970s and the first half of the 1980s. Although the natural rate continued to increase, a substantial bout of Keynesian recession or deficient demand was overlaid. That is why unemployment rose so sharply.

Conversely, UK unemployment fell rapidly in the late 1980s partly because the natural rate of unemployment fell due to supply-side measures of the government and partly because of a strong expansion of aggregate demand. Conditions for receiving Unemployment Benefit were made more stringent in 1986 under the Restart Programme and there was a crackdown on those registering for benefit. The dramatic fall in British unemployment after 1986 was partially due to these measures, which increased the effective labour supply so that, when demand surged ahead, there was initially only a limited increase in wage inflation.

The strong expansion of aggregate demand in the late 1980s was caused both by the fiscal stimulus of tax cuts and because the financial revolution (see Chapter 4) made available consumer credit to an extent never previously encountered. The growth of demand, which was initially hailed as a successful conclusion to the recession, eventually got out of hand because the government failed to appreciate its strength and did not believe in using fiscal policy to control it. The government greatly underestimated the growth of real demand in 1987 and 1988. This was due partly to deficiencies in the official statistical system and partly to a deterioration in the Treasury's previously impressive forecasting record. Thus, whilst the Treasury forecast that domestic demand would rise by 4 per cent in 1988, the actual increase turned out to be 8 per cent – so the forecast was wrong by a margin of 100 per cent!

The government's supply-side policies of tax-cutting and de-regulation were not sufficient to stimulate the British economy to expand supply by as much as they stimulated demand. Inflation, which had come down in the mid-1980s, began to climb again, soon returning to double-digit rates. The government was forced to raise interest rates substantially. However, the use of interest rates rather than fiscal policy to control inflation slowed the growth of the economy and bore heavily on home-owners in spite of massive mortgage subsidies. The 1987–9 boom gave way to slump in 1991–2. Unemployment, which had started to rise in 1990, is now expected to reach the 3 million figure once again by the end of 1992. The latest statistics (July 1992) show that long-term unemployment is at its worst for three-and-a-half years. By its failure to manage demand properly, the government thus threw away its achievements in reducing unemployment – a self-inflicted defeat that could have been avoided by a more cautious management of demand.

5.6   Government policies on unemployment

In the last twelve years there has been a remarkable turnabout in policies to deal with unemployment. During the Conservative government of Edward Heath in the early 1970s the then high levels of unemployment of 1971 and 1972 were greatly reduced in 1973 by a major increase in the aggregate demand for goods. Taxes were cut, public investment increased and there was a large expansion in the money supply. These were the instruments of the so-called 'Barber boom' which assumed that since unemployment was largely Keynesian in nature, such an expansion was all that was necessary. The only significant feature of policy that departed from this diagnosis was the emphasis placed on regional incentives to reduce 'structural' unemployment in certain regions in the country.

Since then much has changed and during the Callaghan government of the late 1970s, the need to control the public sector borrowing requirement and the money supply became important objectives of economic policy. However, it was the Thatcher government after 1979 which became particularly identified with the re-emergence of Conservative macroeconomics in Britain. In general, the government rejected the notion that a reflation of demand via increases in current public spending or public investment is a viable solution to high unemployment, and cuts in public investment and public spending programmes for a time reduced the PSBR as a share of GDP to one of the lowest in the industrial world (see Chapter 2). Instead the government has concentrated upon failures in the operation of the labour market and attempted to reduce wage pressure by various supply-side measures. The causes of unemployment, the government consistently argued, were high union density, an excessive ratio of benefits to wages and too much taxation of both employers and employees. Trade union reform, the reduction of earnings-related benefit, the crackdown on fraudulent benefit claimants, the abolition of the National Insurance Surcharge on employers and income-tax cuts all became parts of a supply-side package for reducing it.

Other aspects of government policy also confirm this broadly classical perspective. The emphasis on the quality of the labour force, especially as far as education and training are concerned, and the degree to which this determines the speed with which workers and employers adapt to 'new products and processes and new competitive pressures which offer new challenges and opportunities' indicate this. The government believes that this adaptability has not been characteristic of the British labour market and that this has lowered the natural rates of output and employment.

With its emphasis on policies to reduce the natural rate of unemployment and its assertion that too high a level of real wages rather than a shortage of aggregate demand is the primary cause of unemployment above the natural rate, the government has clearly identified itself with the classical view of unemployment. Critics of the government position, however, would argue that demand management policies are not impotent and that the impact of the government's deflationary policy since 1979 confirms this conclusion. Given the rigidity of prices and wages in the short run, contractions of aggregate demand initially lead to reductions in levels of output and employment and cause unemployment to rise above the natural rate. Estimates from the models discussed above suggest that about a quarter of unemployment in 1985, and almost half of the rise in unemployment during the period 1979–85, were due to contractionary macroeconomic policies. When aggregate demand increased in 1987, unemployment too declined. It is the government's failure in managing this demand properly that subsequently led to demand expanding faster than output and to the problems of high and rising inflation. It is also important in this context to remark that if sterling had entered the Exchange Rate Mechanism (see Chapter 7) in 1985 as advocated by the then chancellor and foreign secretary (but vetoed by Mrs Thatcher), it would have done so at a relatively high rate which could have been maintained only in the context of a more cautious economic policy than the one which actually ensued. The United Kingdom eventually joined the ERM in 1990 in the hope that financial discipline would be increased and inflation rates reduced. Indeed, the more firmly the government seems committed to maintaining a fixed exchange rate, the more pressure the United Kingdom firms are likely to be under to restrain costs in order to remain competitive with other EC countries.

One major aspect of government policy has been ignored so far and that is the use of special measures to reduce unemployment and to assist the unemployed. Certain types of unemployment and certain groups of unemployed people have been particularly selected for attention and various training programmes and work-sharing measures have been put into effect. In total there have been about twenty different, often short-lived, schemes. A brief outline of some of the more important of these schemes is presented below and their effectiveness examined.

5.6.1 Special employment measures

The first of the special measures was the introduction in 1975 of the Temporary Employment Subsidy and the Job Creation Programme. At its peak in May 1977, the Temporary Employment Subsidy (TES) covered about 200,000 workers, providing employers with a subsidy (£20 per week) to postpone redundancies. Although not directly targeted, TES was highly concentrated in manufacturing, with 90 per cent of the jobs covered being in this sector, and half of these jobs being in the clothing and footwear industries. The scheme, however, fell foul of an EC ban on this kind of subsidy and was abandoned in 1979. It was replaced by the Temporary

Short-Time Working Compensation Scheme (TSTWCS), a subsidy aimed at inducing employers to substitute work-sharing for redundancies; at its peak in March 1981, it covered nearly a million workers. Once again it was in practice highly selective, with 95 per cent of workers covered being in manufacturing. This scheme was abandoned in 1984. More recently, the Enterprise Allowance Scheme (EAS) provided a subsidy for unemployed workers to start up their own businesses; it covered an estimated 80,000 workers in 1986/7. Overall the Department of Employment estimated that the special measures reduced unemployment by about 450,000 in the middle of the 1980s.

An alternative to supporting employment levels in the private sector is to introduce 'public works' schemes to provide public sector employment opportunities for unemployed workers. The Community Programme (CP) was of this kind, the jobs being largely organised by public bodies and voluntary organisations. In October 1987 about 230,000 long-term unemployed adults were covered by this scheme, working on projects that promote general community interests, such as environmental or educational facilities' improvements. Although the scheme was open to all long-term unemployed over eighteen years of age, its flat-rate pay provided no incentives for those over the age of twenty-five to participate; from 1988, it was replaced by the Employment Training Programme, with trainees paid on a 'benefit-plus' basis which made it less attractive to young single workers but more attractive to family men.

The Community Programme did little to improve the supply side of the labour market. More serious efforts at improving the quality of the labour force were made with the Youth Training Scheme (YTS) for school leavers and the Technical and Vocational Educational Initiative for 14–18 year olds, starting in 1983 and 1984. The official inspectors of YTS found 'a high and growing proportion of schemes offering nationally recognised qualifications', but against this they also found that 'many trainers lacked the levels of knowledge and skill needed to guide trainees towards recognised qualifications or credits towards them' (*Employment Gazette*, July 1990). In 1988, the Manpower Services Commission (MSC) was redesignated the Training Commission and given the responsibility for running a single unified programme, Employment Training (ET). This took the place of the Community Programme and the YTS.

The final type of scheme used is work-sharing, though such schemes have been rather less important in the United Kingdom than those just outlined. The Job Release Scheme, begun in 1977, provides a financial incentive for older workers to retire early and release their jobs to unemployed people. The scheme peaked at 95,000 jobs and was withdrawn at the beginning of 1988; a short-lived version for part-time workers was introduced in 1983. Also in 1983 a Job Splitting Scheme was introduced and in 1987 extended as Jobshare; this provides employers with a grant to split a full-time job into two part-time ones or consolidate regular overtime hours into part-time employment. The long-term effects of all these schemes must be to reduce the size of the workforce and so permanently lower output.

To conclude, special employment measures would appear to be no more than a short-term palliative, providing only temporary relief for particular unemployment-prone groups. Since they do not affect the long-term re-employment probabilities of these groups they do not provide a long-run solution for participating individuals. It has also been argued that the deadweight loss of special measures is unacceptably high. The deadweight loss is the result of payments or expenditure to bring about an increase in jobs or prevent a reduction that would have happened anyway. The apparent success of the special measures would thus appear to be in terms of reducing official unemployment figures and there is no evidence that they represent an efficient response to improving the utilisation and allocation of labour.

5.7 Conclusion

Unemployment is an enormously costly economic and social problem. To reduce unemployment it is necessary to reduce wage pressure by supply-side policies while at the same time raising the level of real aggregate demand. If the stimulus to aggregate demand can be directed towards high-unemployment groups, then the inflation costs of raising employment can be reduced. In particular, expansion should be concentrated on producing job opportunities for long-term unemployed. Emphasis also needs to be placed on training and improvement in the supply of skills. The better the workers are trained, the better the outlook in the long term. Meanwhile, the retraining of workers in the middle age group, who become redundant, or who have left the labour market and wish to return, assumes greater urgency.

Questions for discussion

1. Do you think that the Department of Employment overestimates or under-estimates the number of people who are unemployed? Why?
2. What are the costs of unemployment?
3. 'The natural rate of unemployment will increase as the proportion of long-term unemployed rises.' Discuss.
4. How would the high unemployment in the 1980s be explained by (a) a Keynesian, (b) a classical economist?
5. What effect do special employment measures have on the rate of unemployment?

6. What should the links be between special employment measures on the one hand and the education system on the other?

Note

1. International comparisons of unemployment rates are fraught with difficulties. In Table 5.1, unemployment rates in selected countries are presented on the OECD standard basis using labour force surveys which define unemployment in terms of seeking work.

References and suggestions for further reading

Ashton, D. (1986), *Unemployment Under Capitalism*, Hemel Hempstead: Harvester Wheatsheaf.

Davies, G. (1985), *Government Can Affect Unemployment*, London: Employment Institute.

Jahoda, M. (1982), *Employment and Unemployment: A social–psychological analysis*, Cambridge: Cambridge University Press.

Jenkinson, T. (1987), 'The natural rate of unemployment: Does it exist?', *Oxford Review of Economic Policy*, 3, pp. 20–6.

Johnson, C. (1988), *Measuring the Economy*, London: Penguin.

Knight, K. (1987), *Unemployment: An economic analysis*, London: Croom Helm.

Layard, R. (1986), *How to Beat Unemployment?*, Oxford: Oxford University Press.

Layard, R. and S. Nickell (1985), 'The causes of British unemployment', *Economica (Supplement)*, 210, pp. S121–70.

Layard, R. and S. Nickell (1987), 'The performance of the British labour market', in R. Dornbusch and R. Layard (eds), *The Performance of the British Economy*, Oxford: Oxford University Press.

Lindbeck, A. and D. Snower (1986), 'Explanations of unemployment', *Oxford Review of Economic Policy*, 1(2), pp. 34–59.

McCallum, J. (1986), 'Unemployment in OECD countries', *Economic Journal*, 96, pp. 942–60.

Minford, A. P. L. (1983), *Unemployment: Cause and cure*, Oxford: Martin Robertson; 2nd ed, Oxford: Blackwell, 1985.

Parkin, M. and D. King (1992), *Economics*, Woking: Addison-Wesley.

Pissarides, C. (1986), 'Unemployment and vacancies in Britain', *Economic Policy*, 3, pp. 499–541.

Trinder, C. (1988), 'Special employment measures and employment', *National Institute Economic Review*, February, pp. 17–19.

Chapter 6

The UK external sector

HUGH FLEMING

6.1   Introduction

As with all modern developed economies international transactions are of great significance to the United Kingdom economy and any analysis of the economy must necessarily deal with developments in the balance of payments (and its component parts) and the role played by the exchange rate for the currency. In relating these to government policy it is probably not an overstatement to say that over the decade of the 1980s there is little evidence of any policies being directed towards the balance of payments position, although, as we shall see, changes in the balance of payments position can be heavily influenced by government policy in other areas of the economy. On the other hand there is clear evidence that at various times government was concerned about developments in the path taken by the exchange rate, and adapted its policy stance accordingly. In general terms government appeared to adopt a rather passive approach to the balance of payments position and an active approach to the exchange rate. The balance of payments position was seen as a reflection of the competitive position of British industry and the prevailing philosophy was essentially that industry 'put its own house in order'. The exchange rate was seen as being important in terms of domestic inflation and, therefore, a proper concern for government.

It is true of course that changes in the balance of payments necessarily impact on the exchange rate, and vice versa, so we cannot totally separate them in our analysis. Nevertheless for purposes of exposition it is useful to look at them separately in the first instance. Accordingly, the second section of this chapter will deal with the balance of payments, the third with the exchange rate and the two will be brought together in the conclusion.

6.2   The external account

The United Kingdom is an extremely open economy. Exports of goods and services account for around 28 per cent of gross domestic product and imports of goods and services account for almost 30 per cent of all domestic expenditure. In addition to transactions in goods and services, the world economy is increasingly characterised, indeed dominated, by massive flows of international capital in which the United Kingdom is a significant participant.

The balance of payments is a statement of the totality of economic transactions between the United Kingdom and the rest of the world. This accounting statement is conventionally divided into the balance on current account (to which most attention is typically directed) and the balance on capital account. The current account is itself divided into the visible balance – exports and imports of goods – and the invisible balance – trade in services, payment and receipt of interest, profits, dividends and transfers. The current account is inextricably linked with conditions in the domestic economy.

Export demand represents expenditure by non-residents on a country's domestic output of goods and services while imports represent an addition to domestic output, increasing the available supply of goods and services. The relevant balance – in this instance the relationship between exports and imports – is linked to the national income and product accounts of the economy. Aggregate expenditure may be written as:

$$E = C + I + G + X \tag{1}$$

while the available supply may be written as:

$$Y + Z \tag{2}$$

where E =   aggregate expenditure
C =   total consumption expenditure
I =   investment expenditure
G =   government expenditure on goods and services
X =   level of exports
Y =   value of domestic output (income)
Z =   level of imports

In equilibrium, with aggregate supply matched with aggregate demand, we have:

$$Y + Z = C + I + G + X \tag{3}$$

which is more conventionally written as:

$$Y = C + I + G + (X - Z) \tag{4}$$

If we consider income, it can of course be spent on consumption, it can be saved or it can be taken by government in terms of taxes (net of government transfer payments). Thus, we have:

$$Y = C + S + T \tag{5}$$

Combining equations (4) and (5) gives the equation:

$$C + I + G + (X - Z) = C + S + T \tag{6}$$

Since C appears on both sides of the equation it may be cancelled out, and rearranging the other terms gives us:

$$(X - Z) = (S - I) + (T - G) \tag{7}$$

On the right hand side we have the financial position (surplus/deficit) of the private sector and the financial position (surplus/deficit) of the government. Clearly the external balance $(X - Z)$ is determined by the respective financial positions of the private sector and the government, and if the right-hand side of the equation is negative, we necessarily have an external deficit.

With respect to the intersectoral financial flows, a deficit in one sector necessarily means that another sector has a surplus. This can sometimes cause confusion. In equation (7) we have three sectors, the private sector, the public sector and the external sector. The last is referred to as the overseas sector in official statistics. If the private sector and the public sector, taken together, has a deficit then the overseas sector must be in surplus. What this means is that the rest of the world has a surplus in its economic transactions with the United Kingdom. A positive figure for the overseas sector means that the United Kingdom is running a deficit, a negative figure means the United Kingdom has a surplus.

In the light of this analysis, the dramatic deterioration in the UK external account in 1988, 1989 and 1990 can now be readily understood. Table 6.1 presents data on the financial position of the private sector and the public sector, with the consequent outcome for the overseas sector. (Remember that a positive figure for the overseas sector represents a United Kingdom current account deficit.) As can be seen from column 5 of Table 6.1, the United Kingdom external position deteriorated steadily from 1981 to 1987 (there was a short-lived improvement in 1985). While the deterioration on the external account had been an ongoing feature of the 1980s, the position changed spectacularly in 1988 and 1989 with deficits which were, respectively, four times and five times greater than that of 1987. Looking back to equation (7) and considering the data in Table 6.1, it is clear that the massive deficit was a direct result of the financial position of the private sector. It is useful to break down the private sector into its constituent parts to explain further the developments on current account.

If we look at the personal sector we can clearly see a steady reduction in the sector's financial surplus, moving into deficit in 1987, with a huge increase in its deficit in 1988. From 1980 to 1984 the ratio of personal

Table 6.1   Sectoral financial positions (£ billion). (Discrepancies between the combined private sector/public sector figure and the overseas sector figure are reflected in the official statistics by the balancing item (errors and omissions) which have not been included here.)

Year	Personal sector (A)	Company sector (B)	Private sector (A + B)	Public sector	Overseas sector
1980	12.2	−0.6	11.6	−10.3	−2.8
1981	12.6	−0.2	12.4	−7.8	−6.6
1982	10.3	1.3	11.6	−7.6	−4.6
1983	6.9	6.7	13.6	−10.3	−3.7
1984	8.8	5.4	14.2	−12.9	−1.8
1985	7.2	5.5	12.7	−9.6	−3.2
1986	1.7	6.4	8.1	−7.8	0.6
1987	−5.3	7.4	2.1	−4.8	3.6
1988	−14.3	−3.6	−17.9	5.2	14.6
1989	−5.8	−19.1	−24.9	6.5	19.8
1990	7.2	−22.3	−15.1	0.5	13.8

Source: Economic Trends.

savings out of income fell each year – from 13.1 per cent in 1980 to 10.5 per cent in 1984. This decline speeded up thereafter, so that by 1988 the personal savings ratio had fallen to 5.4 per cent. This decline in the proportion of income saved coincides with a period of sustained increases in real disposable income. (While real disposable income fell at the beginning of the decade, it increased continually from 1982, and quite rapidly from 1985.) It was also a period of sustained increases in personal borrowing, particularly in the period up to and including 1988.

The decline in the proportion of (rising) income saved and the increase in personal borrowing resulted in private consumer demand (approximately 60 per cent of total domestic demand) rising faster than GDP. Measured at constant (1985) market prices, consumer expenditure increased in 1988 by 7.2 per cent against growth in GDP of 4.3 per cent. The gap between a more rapidly growing demand relative to domestic supply can only be filled by foreign supply, and imports of goods and services increased by 12.7 per cent. In a year in which there was negligible change in the exports of goods and services (0.02 per cent), the marked deterioration in the external balance which we have identified is inescapable. In keeping with an essentially 'hands-off' approach, the worsening external position was not viewed by government as a problem for government. In 1985 the House of Lords Committee on Overseas Trade had expressed concern about the future prospects for trade in manufactured products and called for a range of policies in support of competitiveness in manufacturing industry. This

Table 6.2 Personal sector (£ billion)

	Real disposable income	% change	Savings ratio	Consumer credit[1]	% change
1980	225.5	0.1	13.1	11.6	
1981	223.9	−0.7	12.5	14.1	21.5
1982	223.4	0	11.4	16	13.5
1983	229.6	2.8	9.8	18.9	18.1
1984	235.2	2.4	10.5	22.3	18
1985	241.3	2.6	9.7	26.1	17
1986	252.3	4.5	8.2	30.8	18
1987	261.3	3.5	6.6	36.1	17.2
1988	276.6	5.8	5.4	42.5	17.7
1989	291.2	5.3	7.1	48.4	13.9
1990	300.9	3.3	9.2	52.9	9.3

Note: [1] Amount outstanding at year end, excluding mortgage borrowing.
Sources: Blue Book; CSO Financial Statistics.

was dismissed by the chancellor (Mr Lawson) as a 'cocoon of subsidies'. He put forward the view that 'it is industry's job to make itself competitive'. In his 1985 Mansion House address he gave his reaction to the Select Committee's views: 'The government ... wholly rejects the mixture of special pleading dressed up as analysis and assertion masquerading as evidence which leads the Committee to its doom-laden conclusion' (Johnson, 1991, p. 207). The current account in 1985 was still in surplus to the tune of some £3.2 billion. By 1988 it had moved to a deficit of over £14 billion. The Committee's conclusion might well have been thought 'doom-laden' by the chancellor in 1985, yet it turned out remarkably prophetic.

Even this dramatic turn of events was not considered a cause for concern by the chancellor. As we have argued, the 1988 current account position predominantly reflects the behaviour of the personal sector. For the chancellor there was still no case for government reaction. The chancellor stated his position to the International Monetary Fund (IMF) in Berlin in September 1988: 'Private-sector behaviour is by its nature self-correcting over time ... there is a limit to the amount of debt which the private sector will be willing – or can afford – to undertake. Once that limit has been reached, the savings ratio will rise again' (Johnson, 1991, p. 206).

The chancellor's arguments can be seen to be valid in relation to the personal sector (consider the eventual increase in the savings ratio and the slowdown in the growth of personal borrowing at the end of the period (Table 6.2)) but they ignore the costs imposed on the company sector. For the personal sector, the financial deficit fell to around £6 billion in 1989 (from a 1988 high of around £14 billion) and moved to a surplus of some £7 billion in 1990. The personal savings ratio rose from a low of 5.4 per cent in 1988 to 7.1 per cent in 1989 and 9.2 per cent in 1990. If we look back to equation (7), this might suggest that the term $(S - I)$ had become positive by 1990 and, with a positive figure for the government sector (there was a budget surplus of £0.5 billion), the external account would move into surplus. The term $(S - I)$, however, relates to the whole of the private sector and can be broken down as

$$(S - I) = (S - I)_p + (S - I)_c$$

where the subscripts p and c refer to the personal sector and the company sector respectively.

The benefits to the external account associated with the changed position of the personal sector were negated by the changed circumstances in the company sector. Despite the substantial fall in the personal sector deficit in 1989, the current external deficit widened to almost £20 billion. Even with the personal sector in financial surplus in 1990 the United Kingdom economy still experienced a current account deficit of some £14 billion. While the root cause of the 1988 deficit lies in the behaviour of the personal sector, it is to the company sector that we must look for the explanation of the continuing problems of the current account. As we can see from Table 6.1, the company sector moved from surplus to (modest) deficit in 1988 and then to record deficits in 1989 and 1990. Several factors contributed to this turnaround.

Firstly, from around 1984–5 to 1988 the company sector was also characterised by relatively buoyant levels of investment. In addition to new investment the company sector was characterised by very high levels of expenditure on mergers and acquisitions. Prior to the stock market crash of 1987 a great deal of this acquisition activity was financed by borrowing. In 1988 acquisitions reached record levels, but following the 1987 crash much of this expenditure on acquisitions was cash-based, involving a significant outflow of funds from the company sector. By 1989 we have a company sector with high levels of borrowing and much depleted liquidity.

Secondly, we have the impact of higher rates of interest. In May 1988 the London clearing banks' base lending rate stood at 7.5 per cent, the lowest rate of the decade. Interest rates had in fact been coming down over a number of years and the fall was reinforced by the 'easy' money policy which was followed by government in response to the stock market crash of 1987. The consumer boom of 1988 (remember from Table 6.1 that the personal sector was £14 billion in deficit) not only generated a massive current account deficit, but also fuelled fears of rising domestic inflation. The government relied on one policy instrument, the rate of interest, to deal with the twin problems. In November 1988 base lending rate rose to 13 per cent. In October 1989 it stood at 15 per cent, a level which was unchanged for some twelve months. It is only in 1991 that we begin to see steady reductions in interest rates. Thus the company sector, with its high levels of borrowing and depleted liquidity, now faced significant cost increases in terms of much higher debt-service charges.

Thirdly, the downturn in the economy had inevitable consequences for company revenues, so that we witnessed increasing cash-flow problems in circumstances where companies lacked the cushion of adequate reserves. Such financial difficulties must force adjustment and indeed by the end of 1991 the company sector had moved back to surplus. The adjustment was of course to be found largely in the dramatic rise of liquidations.

What, if anything, might the experience of the last decade suggest about the course of the external sector over the foreseeable future? Two factors lead to a somewhat pessimistic view. At the time of writing, the government projects public sector deficits of well over £30 billion for each of the next two years. Given our sectoral analysis, an improved external outcome necessitates a much greater move into surplus on the part of the overall private sector than is so far evident. Secondly, the government and opposition parties emphasise the need for increased confidence as a prerequisite for an upturn in consumer spending. The experience of the 1988 consumer spending boom points to a significant proportion of any increased spending being directed towards foreign products. While imports account for around 30 per cent of domestic expenditure, the marginal propensity to import is certainly much higher. One of the widely accepted reasons for the 1988 experience was supply constraints in the domestic economy, i.e. the loss of manufacturing capacity in the early 1980s resulted in an inability of domestic industry to meet rising consumer demand.

The further loss of capacity during the current recession suggests that a consumer-led recovery will lead to major problems for the United Kingdom current account. A final conclusion on this possibility must also reflect the influence of the exchange rate, to which we now turn.

6.3   The exchange rate

As we mentioned at the outset, while the UK government appeared to take a rather passive approach to the balance of payments position, it did appear to pay close attention to what was happening with regard to the exchange rate. The exchange rate is simply the price of one currency in terms of another. Why should attention have been directed towards the exchange rate?

Before we consider detailed reasons for this attention, it is worth making three general points about attitudes to the sterling exchange rate over the period. At the start of the decade the UK government had decided not to join the Exchange Rate Mechanism of the European Monetary System. It was a decision which undoubtedly reflected both political and economic factors. In economic terms it was argued that sterling was subject to influences which did not affect other European currencies (the petrocurrency argument, for instance), that United Kingdom inflation was still too high relative to Europe and so on. Whatever the reasons, it is probably true to say that the primary focus remained on the exchange rate between sterling and the US dollar.

By the second half of the decade it was clear that the sterling–Deutschmark exchange rate was seen as more relevant, culminating in Chancellor Lawson's 'shadowing' of the Deutschmark in 1987–9, a policy which became the subject of fierce debate within the government. Finally we have the decision to join the Exchange Rate Mechanism, taken in October 1990. The change in emphasis can be seen even in everyday terms. In reporting the day's developments on the foreign exchange markets television newscasters now give the sterling–Deutschmark rate first and the sterling–dollar rate second! While we will refer in our analysis to one or two specific developments, the overall course of the exchange rate is set out in Table 6.3. As already noted, the exchange rate is simply the price of one currency in terms of another and, as with all prices (in the absence of direct controls), the exchange rate is determined by the forces of supply and demand. There are two approaches which government may adopt to influence the rate, both of which have been utilised by the UK government. It may itself deal in the foreign exchange market buying or selling foreign currency in exchange for domestic currency. Alternatively it may seek to influence supply and demand by affecting inflows and outflows of capital by varying the interest rate.

We can consider the possibilities in terms of a simple supply and demand analysis of the foreign exchange market. Figure 6.1 shows the supply of and demand for sterling. In the absence of government intervention the demand for sterling is a reflection of the rest of the world's demand for our products (UK exports) and the rest of the world's demand for UK assets, e.g. foreign wealth holders may wish to move funds into the UK to take advantage of high UK interest rates. Equally the supply of sterling reflects our purchases of foreign products (UK imports) and any desired movement of funds out of the United Kingdom to take advantage of better returns, say, in the United States. In the absence of intervention the market-determined exchange rate in Figure 6.1 is £1 = $1.75.

In considering the options open to the government we can look at the case of a rise in US interest rates. A rise in American interest rates means that funds held on deposit in New York now earn a (relatively) higher return than was previously the case. Other things being equal, there is now an incentive to move funds from London to New York. The supply curve in Figure 6.1 shifts out to the right as wealth holders supply sterling in exchange for dollars to place on deposit in New York. With the new

Table 6.3　Dollar/pound and Deutschmark/pound exchange rates

	$	DM		$	DM
1980.1	2.25	3.99	1986.1	1.44	3.38
2	2.28	4.13	2	1.51	3.38
3	2.38	4.22	3	1.49	3.11
4	2.38	4.55	4	1.43	2.87
1981.1	2.31	4.81	1987.1	1.54	2.83
2	2.97	4.73	2	1.64	2.96
3	1.83	4.47	3	1.62	2.97
4	1.88	4.22	4	1.75	2.99
1982.1	1.84	4.33	1988.1	1.79	3.01
2	1.77	4.23	2	1.84	3.14
3	1.72	4.28	3	1.69	3.16
4	1.65	4.13	4	1.79	3.17
1983.1	1.53	3.68	1989.1	1.74	3.23
2	1.55	3.86	2	1.63	3.14
3	1.51	3.99	3	1.59	3.07
4	1.47	3.93	4	1.58	2.87
1984.1	1.43	3.87	1990.1	1.65	2.80
2	1.39	3.78	2	1.67	2.81
3	1.29	3.78	3	1.86	2.96
4	1.21	3.71	4	1.94	2.92
1985.1	1.11	3.63			
2	1.25	3.88			
3	1.37	3.92			
4	1.43	3.71			

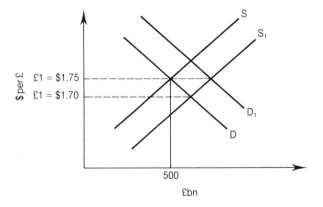

Figure 6.1　Exchange rate determination

supply curve S_1 the market-determined exchange rate falls to £1 = $1.70. Suppose the UK government would like to see the exchange rate stable at £1 = $1.75. This can be achieved if it can shift the demand curve to D_1. As we have indicated, the government may itself deal in the foreign exchange market. It may enter the marketplace as a purchaser buying up its own currency, using its holdings of foreign currency reserves to finance the purchase. Of course its ability to do this depends on its official reserve holdings which necessarily diminish in time with purchasing. Alternatively it may stimulate increased demand for sterling by raising UK interest rates so that the incentive to move funds to New York is removed.

Government interest in the exchange rate has been evident both in terms of the actual level of the exchange rate and the speed and direction of changes in the exchange rate. The first aspect reflects concern about inflation, while the second reflects a view of the exchange rate as a monetary variable. This dichotomy is somewhat artificial, since the two aspects are closely linked, but nevertheless we will deal with each in turn. The level of the exchange rate has been viewed as a key factor in UK anti-inflationary policy. This is primarily a reflection of the fact that imports constitute around 30 per cent of total domestic expenditure, though it is also accepted that many UK imports may be price inelastic. A fall in the exchange rate is a fall in the value of sterling, hence foreign products become more expensive. In the UK case such a fall, an exchange rate depreciation, means higher prices for those goods and services which make up 30 per cent of our expenditure. Such an outcome clearly has significant implications for the overall level of domestic inflation. Manipulating the exchange rate would allow us to influence the price of a major element of expenditure. It may be an exaggeration to state that the government followed a policy of cheap imports during the 1980s but, nevertheless, maintaining a high value for the exchange rate – or at least preventing it falling too far – was clearly seen as an important anti-inflationary policy instrument.

A review of the first half of the decade in terms of the sterling–dollar exchange rate provides evidence for our argument. As we see from Figure 6.2 the exchange rate was moving close to £1 = $2.40 during the second half of 1980, the highest level since the second quarter of 1973. Thereafter it steadily declined until the first quarter of 1985 when that downward trend was abruptly reversed. Why was the exchange rate initially so high? What was the nature of the fall? What explains the sudden reversal?

A key in the answer to all three questions is the rate of interest, or more particularly the UK rate of interest compared to that in the United States. At the start of the period the UK base interest rate was over 17 per cent, but more particularly it was some 6 per cent higher than the United States'. The differential provided a strong incentive to hold funds in London, hence a strong demand for pounds and a high price. From this initial 'high' there was a sustained fall until the first quarter of 1985. The fall in the exchange rate reflected developments in the United States such that the difference in interest rates progressively narrowed. From the initial position of a high demand for sterling there was now a high demand for dollars. The consequent fall in the sterling exchange rate was, however, accompanied by continuous falls in UK official reserve holdings. This suggests that the authorities sought to moderate the decline. Finally we have the sudden reversal. It is clear that at the beginning of 1985 the exchange rate was considered to have fallen too far. The reversal was engineered quite simply by a sharp increase in interest rates. The difference between interest rates in the United States and the United Kingdom widened from around 1 per cent to 5 per cent in January/February 1985. Thus the evidence of the first half of the 1980s suggests that both the level and the rate of change of the exchange rate were seen as matters of concern for the government.

The second aspect of the government's view of the exchange rate is to be found in the idea that the exchange rate, or more particularly changes in the exchange rate, can serve as an indicator of monetary conditions in the economy. The basic aim of policy remains the control of inflation, and in particular to bring inflation into line with major, low-inflation, competitors. In practice the German rate of inflation was the principal target. The essence of the exchange rate argument is that a depreciating exchange rate is indicative of monetary conditions which are, in relative terms, too easy. A depreciating exchange rate is taken to reflect expectations that future domestic inflation is going to be higher than competitors' and that monetary policy should therefore be tightened. Implicit in the argument is that UK monetary policy be kept in line with German monetary policy.

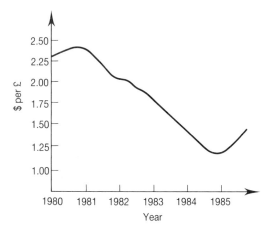

Figure 6.2 Dollar/pound exchange rate

This view of the exchange rate as a monetary indicator is one reason for the policy of 'shadowing' the Deutschmark, i.e. trying to keep the sterling–Deutschmark exchange rate relatively stable. A second reason was undoubtedly a preparatory move towards eventual membership of the ERM, though those two reasons are closely interlinked.

When we look at the sterling–Deutschmark exchange rate (Figure 6.3) we find a prolonged, albeit gradual, sterling depreciation. From mid-1987, Chancellor Lawson began the policy of stabilising the exchange rate, targeting a rate of around £1 = DM3. The policy gave rise to considerable controversy and debate (much of it political); nevertheless, considerable stability was achieved from the outset of the policy until its abandonment in late 1989 following the resignation of the chancellor, who spoke in the Commons of a long and bitter debate over exchange rate policy. The abandonment of the policy saw a resumption of the downward movement of sterling. It can certainly be debated whether or not £1 = DM3 was a wise choice of exchange rate target, but the episode (lasting some two-and-a-half years) clearly demonstrated that the exchange rate could be successfully managed.

The final phase of exchange rate policy comes with the decision to enter the Exchange Rate Mechanism of the European Monetary System in October 1990. Joining the ERM involved setting a central rate for the currency against a basket of other currencies in the system, around which there was a permitted band of variation (6 per cent in the case of the United Kingdom). The commitment to a fixed exchange rate imposed a constraint on domestic macroeconomic policy, particularly monetary policy. The attraction of such a commitment has come to be seen as giving credibility to

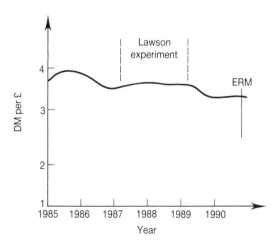

Figure 6.3 Deutschmark/pound exchange rate

policy-makers with regard to controlling inflation. A fixed exchange rate cannot be sustained over time if a country's rate of inflation is seriously out of line with rates of inflation in other countries. The constraint on monetary policy is to be found in the reduced room for manœuvre on interest rates.

A simple adaptation of Figure 6.1 allows us to examine the arguments (Figure 6.4). As with Figure 6.1 we have an initial exchange rate (ER_0) reflecting the interaction of supply and demand. Membership of the exchange rate mechanism commits a country to maintaining the exchange rate within a permitted band of variation. In effect we have a price floor and a price ceiling. Looking at the inflation argument first, we can characterise it in terms of a shift in both supply and demand curves. If the United Kingdom rate of inflation is markedly higher than its major trading partners' then United Kingdom products become less competitive and we may expect to export less (the demand curve shifts to the left from D to D_1) and we may expect to import more (the supply curve moves to the right to S_1). The effect is to push the exchange rate to the floor (A), and the authorities are obliged to take action to prevent any further fall. They can of course boost demand for the currency by raising interest rates, though this has implications for domestic economic activity.

Secondly, we can consider the reduced room for manœuvre with respect to domestic interest rates. As implied above, there is no problem in regard to raising interest rates, but this is not necessarily the case with regard to cutting interest rates or indeed keeping them constant. A cut in UK interest rates or a rise in, say, German interest rates reduces the attractiveness of holding funds in London rather than Frankfurt. The outcome is a flow of funds out of the United Kingdom. From our initial

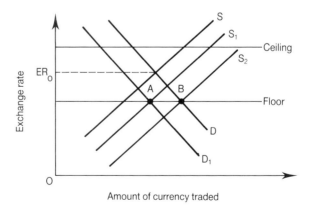

Figure 6.4 Exchange rate determination in the ERM

exchange rate (ER_0) there is a shift in the supply curve from S to S_2 and the exchange rate is again pushed to the floor (B).

While the interests of the domestic economy may be best served by reduced interest rates, such a reduction may lead to a capital outflow, and put serious pressure on the exchange rate. Given the commitment to a fixed exchange rate, a reduction in interest rates (though desirable) may have to be foregone, or postponed until conditions in other member countries change. There is reduced autonomy in macroeconomic policy. When sterling entered the mechanism the effective rate against the Deutschmark was £1 = DM2.95, around which there was permitted variation. Rising interest rates in Germany in 1991 and 1992 have clearly limited the extent to which the United Kingdom could reduce its own interest rates. In a world of free capital movements a substantial cut in UK interest rates would lead to an outflow of funds from the United Kingdom to Germany which might push the exchange rate below the permitted limit. Avoidance of this would almost certainly require that the cut in interest rates be reversed.

6.4 Conclusions

We earlier expressed some pessimism about the future prospects for the United Kingdom's external account and the question arises whether these prospects are likely to be improved through the Exchange Rate Mechanism. The Deutschmark/sterling exchange rate became the key exchange rate for the United Kingdom. The United Kingdom entered the ERM at a rate of £1 = DM2.95, a rate at which the UK economy was clearly uncompetitive internationally – we examined the external position in section 6.2. The sterling exchange rate quickly fell below DM2.95 and while it stayed within the permitted band of variation it has consistently been a 'weak' currency in the European Monetary System. Of course a relatively high exchange rate helps to dampen inflation but a sustained long-term improvement in the external account requires not merely that inflation be brought into line with inflation in major trading partners, but also that there is increased investment to improve productivity.

When we discussed the foreign exchange market (Figure 6.1) we argued that the government might influence the exchange rate by using interest rate policy or by direct intervention, using foreign exchange reserves. We also made the point that the ability to intervene depended on the level of foreign exchange reserves.

While sterling had for some time been a weak currency in the system, the position deteriorated in August and early September 1992, as sterling moved to the floor of the permitted band of variation. While there were repeated statements that the government would defend the exchange rate, market participants clearly believed that the government would find the cost too high. The cost is the economic impact of higher rates on an already depressed economy. By mid-September there was massive speculative selling of sterling. Both approaches to supporting the exchange rate were utilised. On 16 September the government, in an unprecedented move, increased interest rates twice, first by 2 per cent then by 3 per cent. There was also heavy intervention by the Bank of England and the Bundesbank. The interest rate increases did not change the views of the market and it was clear that the reserves would quickly run out. Intervention to support the exchange rate could not work. On 17 September sterling was taken out of the Exchange Rate Mechanism and allowed to float, while the interest rate increases (the 3 per cent, while announced, was not actually implemented) were reversed. The outcome was a significant devaluation of sterling. Against the previous central rate of £1 = DM2.95, sterling quickly fell to around £1 = DM2.50, a devaluation of some 15 per cent.

There is nothing wrong *per se* with a commitment to a fixed exchange rate; indeed there is much to be said in favour. The proviso of course is that the fixed rate should be a realistic rate. Twice before in this century – under the Gold Standard in the late 1920s, and again in the 1960s – UK governments tried to defend an overvalued exchange rate at considerable cost to the domestic economy. Twice before they also failed.

Questions for discussion

1. If the private sector is in surplus does it matter if the government has a budget deficit?
2. 'The UK external deficit reflects private sector decisions with the government taking a passive role.' Should the government take an active role? If so, how?
3. Why is the rate of interest important?
4. Membership of the ERM may impose constraints on domestic macroeconomic policy. What do you consider to be the economic advantages and disadvantages of such constraints?
5. This chapter concludes that a devaluation of sterling is desirable. What are the arguments for and against?

Suggestions for further reading

Curwen, P. (1992), *Understanding the UK Economy*, 2nd edn, London: Macmillan (Chs. 6–7).
Johnson, C. (1991), *The Economy under Mrs Thatcher*, London: Penguin.
Keegan, V. (1989), *Mr Lawson's Gamble*, London: Hodder and Stoughton.
Sloman, J. (1991), *Economics*, Hemel Hempstead: Harvester Wheatsheaf (esp. Ch. 22).
Walters, A. (1990), *Sterling in Danger*, London: Fontana.

Chapter 7

The European Community's impact on UK economic policy

ANDREW SCOTT

7.1 Introduction

After two unsuccessful applications during the 1960s, Britain (along with Ireland and Denmark) finally became a member of the European Community on 1 January 1973. This was the first enlargement of the European Community which, until then, included only the six founder member countries of France, West Germany, Italy, Belgium, the Netherlands and Luxembourg. In 1981 Greece became the tenth member of the European Community, while in 1986 the accession of Spain and Portugal took Community membership to the current situation of twelve member countries. It is highly probable that the 1990s will see a further enlargement of the Community with the accession of the European Free Trade Area (EFTA) countries, while the eventual accession of some of the former, centrally planned, East European states certainly cannot be ruled out.

In this chapter we examine the structure and economic policies of the European Community. In section 7.2 we set out the basic analytical framework used by economists to examine the economic effect of international integration. In section 7.3 we examine the development of Community economic policy and the manner in which this has impacted on the British economy. In section 7.4 we consider the future development of the Community and in section 7.5 we offer some concluding thoughts.

7.2 International economic integration

7.2.1 Basic concepts

The European Community is first and foremost an economic arrangement. It is based on the creation of a *common market* (Treaty of Rome, Article 3).

A common market is an area in which all goods, services, capital and labour that originate in one participating (or member) country shall enjoy unfettered access to all other participating (or member) countries. Economic integration occurs as a consequence of the removal of those barriers that presently segment both national product (goods and services) markets and national factor (labour and capital) markets. As we now see, a common market is one of four distinct stages, or levels, of international economic integration.

Free trade area: A free trade area describes a situation in which all physical barriers to trade (in both goods and services) between member countries are removed. Thus tariff barriers and import quotas are eliminated and consumers throughout the area are able to buy products from the lowest cost supplier inside the area. However, in the free trade area each country continues to have complete freedom to determine trade policy towards non-participating countries. This means that customs posts between members of the free trade area must be retained to ensure that products originating in non-participating countries are not 'deflected' to one country through a partner country which has a less restrictive external trade policy.

Economic theory tells us that the process of commodity arbitrage will ensure that an immediate impact of participation in a free trade area will be the removal of all national price differences for identical goods – that is, the 'law of one price' for traded goods and services will pertain within the area. However, because countries retain national control over trade policy with non-participating countries, the law of one price will not extend to imports originating outside the area.

Customs union: A customs union is a free trade area which also provides for a *common external tariff* with respect to trade with non-participating countries. Because the customs union is characterised by a single, common, external trade policy, imports to the customs union are subject to identical treatment regardless of the country through which these enter the union. Consequently, all internal economic frontiers in the customs union can be completely dismantled. In a customs union the law of one price will, in principle, also apply to imports originating outside the union.

Common market: A common market is a customs union with the additional provision that labour and capital (factors of production) are free to move within the area. The common market represents a higher stage in the process of economic integration as not only are national product markets integrated, as is the case with the customs union, but so too are national factor markets.

An important economic consequence of the shift from a customs union to a common market is that the law of one price that hitherto has applied only to trade products should now operate with equal force in factor markets.

This suggests that in a common market there will be a tendency towards the equalisation of factor returns; that is, national differences in both wage rates and interest payments on capital invested will be removed as both labour and capital move within the common market to take advantage of the highest returns available.

Economic and monetary union: An economic and monetary union is a common market in which national monetary and fiscal policies are unified. Essentially the members of an economic and monetary union surrender autonomy over virtually all the instruments of national economic (monetary and fiscal) policy. National economies effectively vanish to be replaced by one super-economy in which countries become constituent states or regions. An economic and monetary union combines all of the characteristics of a common market, but goes further. Monetary union means that national currencies disappear, to be replaced by a single, common, currency. Consequently, national central banks are replaced by a union-wide central bank which alone determines the monetary policy for the union as a whole.

7.2.2   Integration and economic efficiency

The static effects

The economic effects of integration are analysed using a framework developed by Professor Jacob Viner during the 1950s and universally referred to as 'customs union theory'. Before Viner's contribution, the dominant view was that integration must raise economic welfare among the participating countries as it involved the dismantling of trade barriers and was thus a step in the direction of universal free trade. In short, integration would *always* benefit the participating countries as they would be able to exploit the classical gains from trade. Viner suggested that this view was incorrect. This somewhat paradoxical conclusion emerges from the distinction Viner drew between 'trade creation' and 'trade diversion'.

Trade creation refers to additional (or new) trade that is created between partners in the customs union following the removal of trade barriers. Thereafter, consumers throughout the union have access to the lowest cost supplier and inefficient producers – those who previously survived only by virtue of protection from external competition – are forced out of business. The result is an improvement in the efficiency of resource allocation throughout the union and a corresponding increase in consumer welfare. The extent to which trade-creating gains are available to a potential member of a customs union will be a key factor in determining the merits of membership.

Trade diversion, which is welfare reducing for the union as a whole, occurs when membership of a customs union results in consumers switching from a low-cost supplier outside the union to a higher-cost source of supply inside the union. Trade diversion occurs because all tariffs on imports from the partner countries are removed whereas the tariff continues to apply to imports originating outside the union. The import tax has two effects: first, it protects national suppliers from more efficient external suppliers; and second, it redistributes income from consumers to beneficiaries of subsequent higher public spending or lower taxes (see Sloman, 1991, Ch. 21).

In practice membership of a customs union is likely to involve elements of trade creation and trade diversion. As we will see, this was certainly true when Britain joined the European Community. The extent to which welfare-enhancing trade creation or welfare-reducing trade diversion dominates will depend very much on the specific characteristics of the countries forming the union. However we can make some general observations on the basis of Viner's two welfare effects:

1. Trade creation will be greater the more intense is the degree of competition in the industrial structures of the countries forming the customs union. This conclusion follows from the fact that a greater share of high-cost production will be displaced when the removal of trade barriers is between economies which have competitive rather than complementary production structures.
2. The extent to which trade diversion occurs will depend upon the height of the tariff imposed for the union as a whole. The higher the external tariff protecting the union as a whole then the greater is the likelihood that trade diversion will occur. This conclusion can be most easily understood if one remembers that a customs union which has a zero external tariff is in fact satisfying the condition of universal free trade.
3. The larger the size of the union – in terms of number of countries participating – then the less likely is trade diversion. Again in the extreme case in which every country is a member of the union we would effectively have a situation of universal free trade. On the other hand, trade diversion is more likely where only a few countries are involved as this restricts the opportunity for a re-location of production and consumption.

In practice economists have found the magnitudes of these static effects to be extremely small. In the most studied case, that of the European Community, trade creation has been estimated at less than 1 per cent of Community GDP while the magnitude of measured trade diversion has been significantly below this. So although the European Community has been found to be net trade creating, and therefore has raised welfare to consumers, the extent of the gain has been very small. Furthermore, it is widely acknowledged that the static effects of international integration will almost certainly be exceeded by the dynamic effects. These dynamic effects are *not* captured in Viner's comparative static framework.

The dynamic effects

A common criticism of Viner's contribution to the theory of international economic integration is that although he did clarify conditions under which integration would reduce economic efficiency, his analysis focuses exclusively on the static or *impact* effects of the customs union. And by so doing, a number of sources of potential economic gain, which together would be likely to exceed trade-diverting losses, were ignored. These are the *dynamic* effects of integration. In theory, dynamic effects refer to the consequences of international integration that directly influence the rate of economic growth of the members of the union over time. It is commonly assumed that these dynamic effects are positive in that together they will raise the rate of growth for the union as a whole above the rate which would otherwise be expected. There are two principal sources of dynamic gain from international integration.

The first is *scale economies* in production. Economies of scale refer to the reduction in the unit costs of production that occurs with an increase in the scale of production. After the union has been formed, producers in individual member states will be able to export freely to partner country markets. As a result output will increase and unit costs will fall. The central point is that scale economies provide an added source of consumer gains from international integration. The rate of economic growth is improved as economies of scale release resources to be used in the production of other goods and services. Further, economies of scale may generate additional gains through *external trade creation*, which occurs when the cost savings in production allow producers to increase their share of non-union member markets. This increases further the union-wide rate of economic growth.

The second dynamic gain commonly associated with a customs union derives from the intensification of competition that results as barriers to trade are removed. With the removal of barriers, domestic firms now find that their hitherto protected domestic market is being contested by foreign rivals. This forces management to improve its performance in controlling production and administrative costs.

Together economies of scale and competitive effects constitute the main sources of dynamic gains from economic integration. This does not, however, exhaust all the possible dynamic gains. For example, it is possible that membership of a customs union will cause an acceleration in the pace of technological development if the growth in firm size associated with servicing a larger market increases the earnings available for corporate research and development. Further, servicing a larger market means that the risks associated with research and development can be spread over a higher number of consumers. A conclusion from the analysis of dynamic effects arising from international integration is that even where membership of a customs union results in a measure of trade diversion adversely affecting economic welfare in one country, this might be more than compensated for by the dynamic gains from integration.

7.3 The economics of the European Community

7.3.1 The foundations of the common market

The European Community is first and foremost an economic arrangement based on the principles of a common market. Consequently the Treaty of Rome establishing the European Economic Community (as it was called at that time), provides for the elimination of all barriers to the free internal movement of goods, services, capital and labour and the adoption of a common external policy concerning trade between member and non-member countries. It also seeks to ensure that this liberalisation of intra-Community trade would result in greater competition within the Community, leading to gains in consumer welfare, by setting out the basic principles of a common competition policy to apply in all member countries.

It was realised from the outset that establishing a common market would be a lengthy process. Not only would this involve the abolition of a large number of formal impediments to implementing the 'four freedoms' (i.e. the free movement of goods, services, capital and labour), there was also a wide range of technical obstacles in the form of national laws and regulations that would have to be harmonised before a common market could become a reality. This too would take time. However, in order that the foundation of the common market could be speedily put in place, the Treaty of Rome set out a twelve-year timetable during which the minimum steps of eliminating all formal barriers (i.e. tariffs and quotas) to intra-Community trade would take place. In practice, this was achieved by July 1968, some eighteen months ahead of schedule. The same timetable was successfully applied to the introduction of a common external tariff. Of course the common external tariff did not mean that all elements in the external economic policy of member countries were harmonised and determined at the Community level. Non-tariff barriers to trade remained firmly under the control of individual member countries and these were used, in part at least, to compensate for the loss of national sovereignty over formal trade policies.

In addition to establishing the free trade basis of the common market, the Treaty of Rome called for the introduction of a common agricultural policy and a common transport policy. Although a common transport policy never materialised, the CAP was in place by the mid-1960s. Thereafter, all aspects relating to agricultural policy in Community countries were determined exclusively at the Community level. The two key objectives of the CAP were to provide a fair income to farmers and to ensure that consumers had reliable access to foodstuffs at reasonable prices. The former would be secured through the principle of intervention buying or selling by Community agencies with a view to ensuring that market prices never differ significantly from a predetermined 'target' price. This target price is fixed by agreement between the agricultural ministers from the member countries, and should reflect the interests of consumers as well as those of producers. In practice, however, the interests of consumers have been secondary to the political need to fix the target price at that level that ensures a reasonable income is received by the least efficient farmer. The result has been that efficient producers have tended to increase production as much as possible in order to take advantage of the relatively high (compared to world market) Community prices thereby creating the massive agricultural surpluses that have become such a feature of Community farming.

Finally, under the Treaty of Rome a European Social Fund (ESF) and a European Investment Bank (EIB) were established. Both agencies were intended to facilitate the transition to a common market. The ESF would assist by providing finance for retraining and resettling unemployed labour, while the EIB was to contribute to the 'balanced and steady development of the common market' by providing investment funds for the purpose of aiding the development of backward regions, modernising undertakings or financing schemes of interest to more than one member country.

Initially the Community's economic and social policies were financed from a common budget to which member countries directly contributed revenues. However, from 1980 the Community's budget has been financed by so-called *own resources*. Under this arrangement revenues accruing from the operation of the common external tariff, the agricultural levy, a share of VAT collected in each member state and (from 1988) a contribution based on national GNP are designated as Community revenues to be assigned to the common budget.

By the end of the 1960s, therefore, the Community had successfully laid the foundation of a common market. The intra-Community movement of goods had been freed from all tariff restraints, a common external tariff had been introduced, the CAP was in place, a common indirect taxation system (VAT) had been agreed upon, and limited progress had been made in removing the barriers to the free internal movement of both labour and capital. Despite this, however, significant obstacles to the creation of a 'common market' remained.

The free movement of goods remained an unfulfilled objective due to the plethora of non-tariff barriers (NTBs) to trade that extended over a vast range of consumer and capital goods and which continued to segment national markets and, consequently, undermine competition. Consequently, consumers throughout the Community were failing to enjoy the full benefits of integration as domestic producers remained relatively immune from competition in these (still protected) markets. Many of these NTBs were technical in nature, and took the form of minimum product standards justified on the basis of health and safety. And although Article 100 of the Rome Treaty did empower the Commission to issue proposals for harmonising standards where necessary for the functioning of the common market, these proposals had to have the unanimuous support of the Council of Ministers. Elsewhere, other NTBs continued to distort trade: preferential public procurement, state subsidies to domestic industry and administrative barriers constituted deliberate attempts by national authorities to undermine competition in the Community.

Little progress had been made in achieving free trade in services. On the one hand for those services purchased by government there was clear national favouritism. This continued throughout the 1970s despite the publication of Commission Directives in 1974 and 1976 outlawing this practice. For financial services (banking, insurance, etc.), on the other hand, there were two problems. First, there was an analogous 'health and safety' problem to that preventing comprehensive product market integration, i.e. consumers might find it difficult to take legal action against a services supplier located in a different country. Second, for trade in *financial* services to be genuinely free, there would have to be no restrictions on the free movement of capital between member states. The objective of free movement of capital (Articles 67–73) was far from being achieved because member states were simply unwilling to relinquish capital (exchange) controls as an instrument of macroeconomic policy.

Finally, although the free movement of labour had become a reality in 1968, when the principle of national priority was abandoned, this did not require member states to recognise professional standards and qualifications awarded elsewhere in the Community. Consequently, the free movement of labour was effectively restricted to a very small sub-set of the labour supply.

7.3.2 British membership of the European Community

Britain's membership of the Community coincided with attempts to accelerate the process of economic integration. In 1969 the heads of government of the six founder members had set themselves the target of achieving full economic and monetary union by 1980. In addition, moves would be made to build upon the successes of the 1960s by deepening the degree of integration in both product and factor markets by further measures of both negative and positive integration.

In practice, however, the 1970s turned out to be a disappointing decade for the Community. Rather than building on the successes of the 1960s, the 1970s saw a 'turning-inwards' of national economic policies throughout the Community such that by the end of the decade the process of economic integration had been thrown into reverse. The global recession that was triggered by the oil price rise in 1973 intensified the pressure on governments to protect national producers from foreign competition. In the Community this resulted in an increase in the incidence of non-tariff barriers to trade and not the progressive dismantling of these measures of hidden protectionism that had been planned. At the same time the exchange rate stability that had been a feature of the 1950s and 1960s gave way to a period of considerable volatility with the demise of the Bretton Woods regime in the early 1970s. Finally, rather than removing barriers to the free movement of capital, member countries tended to raise these barriers to even greater heights during the 1970s in an attempt to insulate domestic monetary policy from external forces.

Britain's relations with the Community deteriorated alarmingly during the second half of the 1970s. Despite the result of the consultative referendum conducted in 1975, at which two-thirds of those voting approved of membership of the European Community on the renegotiated terms secured by the Labour government, opinion polls soon began to record public disapproval of British membership. There were three main reasons for this change in public opinion.

First, the operation of the CAP manifestly ran counter to the interests of British consumers. In order to protect Community farmers from imports, foodstuffs originating outside the Community were subject to a levy that raised their selling price to slightly above the minimum price which Community farmers were guaranteed. Because world prices were almost always below EC intervention prices, consumers of non-Community foodstuffs bore the full force of this protection. And because the lion's share of the United Kingdom's substantial food imports did come from countries outside the Community, British consumers found themselves disadvantaged by the CAP as food prices increased significantly after membership.

A second problem related to the net contribution that the British government was making by the end of the 1970s. The CAP was by far the single biggest element of Community expenditure – accounting for up to 75 per cent of total expenditure from the common Community budget. As a net importer of foodstuffs, Britain did not benefit from CAP spending. Instead, as food imported from non-EC countries attracted a levy under the rules of the CAP, Britain made a comparatively high gross contribution to the common budget. Even though Britain was a net beneficiary from other aspects of Community policy, most notably the European Regional Development Fund (ERDF), the final result was that Britain was making a net contribution to the Community by 1979 of approximately £1 billion.

Not only was this widely held to be unfair given the United Kingdom's relatively low share of Community GDP, but it was also seen to be linked to an agricultural policy that was capable only of generating enormous surpluses of unwanted foodstuffs.

Finally, Community membership was regarded by many as being partly responsible for the erosion of Britain's manufacturing industry and the associated rise in unemployment. There were two elements to this view. The first concerned the impact of exposing a weakened industry in Britain to the full force of continental competition – especially from Germany. Whilst the proponents of British membership of the Community had steadfastly maintained that greater competition was necessary to shock Britain's industry out of its complacency, critics insisted that this would result in the further decline of manufacturing and, by extension, Britain's already weak balance of payments position. Certainly the evidence by the late 1970s seemed to support the anti-common market lobby. A second adverse consequence of EC membership identified mainly by left-wing critics was that the free market basis on which the European Community was founded would impose severe constraints on the conduct of national industrial policy in Britain, particularly trade controls and industrial interventionism.

Even with the benefit of hindsight it is difficult to assess whether, on balance, membership of the European Community contributed significantly to the economic problems that Britain experienced during the 1970s. Certainly there is no doubt that the CAP operated to the detriment both of economic efficiency and the British consumer. Not only were consumers required to pay higher prices for foodstuffs after EC membership, but the protectionist element of the CAP encouraged an increase in output from Community farmers when lower cost supplies were available outside the Community. Moreover, the CAP did lead to the emergence of an unacceptable outcome with regard to Britain's contribution to the Community budget. On the other hand, however, it is very difficult to attribute the problems of British manufacturing industry during the 1970s to membership of the European Community. There is ample evidence that by the time Britain joined the Community its manufacturing industry was already displaying symptoms of long-term decline. And although the exposure to greater competition from other EC partners might well have added to these problems, almost certainly membership did not of itself create any fundamentally new problems.

7.3.3 Economic integration during the 1980s

By the end of the 1970s the progress in European economic integration had come virtually to a standstill. Moreover, a political crisis raged over Britain's insistence that both the Community budget and the CAP be fundamentally reformed. This political crisis reached its zenith in the early 1980s when the combative and nationalistic negotiating stance adopted by the new British premier, Margaret Thatcher, replaced the low-key approach preferred by the previous Labour administration. Mrs Thatcher's demands for an immediate reduction in Britain's net contribution to the EC budget were speedily rewarded with temporary rebates over the period 1980–3. In 1984 a 'permanent' solution was found in the form of the British abatement whereby Britain was entitled to claim a rebate from the budget of up to two-thirds of the difference between its share of VAT contributions to the common budget and payments received from that budget.

Britain's aloof stance from the Community increased during this period. In 1979 the European Monetary System was introduced as a mechanism for creating a 'zone of monetary stability' in the Community in an attempt to overcome the economic problems that had come to be associated with exchange rate volatility. The demise of the Bretton Woods exchange rate regime in 1973 had ushered in a period of floating exchange rates. Contrary to initial expectations, both exchange rate volatility and the average Community rate of inflation increased dramatically thereafter. Thus by 1978 it was clear that if the process of economic integration was to recover its momentum both problems needed to be addressed. The EMS was a response to this. By locking member countries' currencies together within a fixed exchange rate system, all members would be forced to reduce their inflation rate to that recorded by the lowest inflation country. Otherwise they would lose exports and suffer an increase in imports as their relatively high rate of inflation undermined the competitive position of home producers. This discipline would be provided by the Exchange Rate Mechanism which defined a maximum permissible deviation for each currency of ± 2.25 per cent (± 6 per cent for the lira) from a central rate against the ECU – this being a weighted basket of all other currencies in the arrangement. When a currency reached either limit in this range, a combination of domestic policy changes and diversified intervention would be used to stabilise the currency.

Although Britain did formally become a member of the EMS, the government initially opted not to participate in the ERM. The main reason for this was that domestic economic policy at that time was based on control of the money supply. Had Britain become a member of the ERM then monetary policy, including interest rate policy, would have to reflect the needs of the exchange rate and not the needs of the domestic economy. It is, of course, arguable that an exchange rate target would have resulted in a poorer record with respect to inflation and unemployment over the 1980s than that recorded. Critics of the government's stance on the ERM point to the lower unemployment recorded by members of the mechanism over the decade while supporters of the government insist that Britain's record on productivity and the control of inflation surpassed that for ERM members. Eventually, in October 1990, Britain opted to join the ERM. However, this decision has to be seen in the context of the economic issue that dominated the European Community over the 1980s.

The Single European Market

The idea of 'completing the internal market' was initially advanced as a means of overcoming the apparently deep-seated economic difficulties that confronted the member states of the European Community in the early 1980s. In what was described at the time, somewhat inelegantly, as 'Euro-sclerosis', each of the EC economies was characterised by a low (sometimes negative) rate of economic growth co-existing with an historically high level of inflation and unemployment. A substantial part of the cause of this problem was attributed to the failure of Europe's industries to compete on a global basis, and part of the blame for this was, in turn, attributed to the fragmented nature of the Community's internal market. In short, fragmentation was rendering Europe's industries uncompetitive at a global level.

The 'idea' of completing the internal market was transformed into a practical objective with the publication of the Commission's White Paper in June 1985. This is usually referred to as the 'Cockfield' paper, after Lord Cockfield, the senior British Commissioner who was charged with the task of preparing the White Paper. The Paper listed almost 300 measures that were needed for a wholly unified European market. A timetable for the introduction of the appropriate Directive was presented opposite each measure, and 31 December 1992 was identified as the date by which the entire process of creating a Single European Market (SEM) had to be completed. The White Paper identified three categories of barrier that had to be swept away:

1. *Physical barriers* in the shape of border formalities that presently disrupt the internal movement of goods and persons inside the European Community. The removal of physical barriers will reduce the costs of moving goods around the Community, and lessen the inconvenience to individuals as they travel between individual member states.
2. *Technical barriers* of four types; (a) technical barriers to trade in products; (b) preferential public procurement; (c) restraints to free trade in services; and (d) measures that restrict cross-border movement of capital. The removal of technical barriers to trade is being achieved by a combination of 'mutual recognition' of technical standards, technical regulations and certification procedures prevailing in individual member states and, where necessary, common minimum standards

being defined by the Community's standards authorities (CEN and CENELEC). It is generally acknowledged that this 'new approach' has been successful in removing barriers to intra-EC trade. Note that the 'new approach' replaces the old method whereby *common* minimum standards had to be agreed upon before market integration could be effected. In the area of public procurement, almost all the legislation required to open public markets throughout the Community to competition is now in place. In services, two areas will be most affected by the SEM: transport and the financial services sectors. In transport, the major proposals relate to the de-regulation of road haulage, scheduled to be completed by 1993.

3. *Fiscal barriers* will be removed by securing a broad uniformity in VAT rates and excise duties throughout the European Community. Unless this is achieved, border posts will need to be retained to ensure that differential VAT rates do not distort trade flows inside the European Community.

The benefits (and costs) of the SEM

In 1988, the European Commission published the results of a major research exercise (the Cecchini Report) in which authoritative estimates of the economic benefits that would accrue to the Community as a whole as a direct result of completing the SEM were presented. The figures presented in the Cecchini Report were indeed impressive. It was estimated that, at 1986 prices, the total (once-and-for-all) gains available from the SEM project amounted to between 170 and 250 billion ECU, representing something like 4.5 per cent to 6.5 per cent of Community GDP. Moreover, the Commission confidently asserted that completion of the SEM would create almost 2 million new jobs over a decade. Conveniently, the Commission distinguished between four independent sources of economic gain. Firstly, there are benefits, estimated at 8–9 billion ECU, associated with the *removal of physical barriers to trade*. This refers to the added costs producers have to absorb as a result of delays in shipping goods across the European Community caused principally by customs formalities.

Secondly, there are considerable cost savings (57–71 billion ECU) on offer by removing *barriers that affect overall production*, i.e. measures that restrict or limit competition in national markets. A principal source of economic gain within this category is the abandoning of preferential public procurement policies, thereby ensuring that taxpayers got the best 'value for money'. Significant consumer savings would also accrue directly as a result of increased competition across the range of product and service markets that would necessarily follow once technical barriers to trade were removed.

Thirdly, the study estimated cost savings of 61 billion ECU as a consequence of firms *exploiting economies of large-scale production*. As individual Community markets became more competitive, industrial re-structuring will necessarily follow. Inefficient plants will close down, and as output from the efficient plants increases, economies of scale will be realised and, consequently, unit costs of production will fall.

Finally, the Cecchini study suggested that savings of the order of 46 billion ECU would accrue as a consequence of *greater competition forcing improvements in managerial practices* – reducing overstaffing, managing inventories, etc. – and eliminating excess profit margins that are protected by barriers to competition. Economists tend to refer to this as removing X-inefficiencies.

The SEM can therefore be regarded as an attempt to increase the role that the free operation of market forces has in determining economic performance. It is a supply-side solution to Europe's economic 'sclerosis'. The underlying argument is that national intervention has produced a situation in which the internal EC market is fragmented, and that this, in turn, has seriously damaged the Community's economic dynamism and, in turn, its relative economic performance. The economic gains that are expected to accrue will result directly from the improved efficiency of markets, which will lead to an improvement in the allocation of resources across the Community, and a commensurate reduction in the influence of public policy. The eventual outcome will be a renaissance for the Community's economy, with Europe's producers re-capturing the markets that it lost to its American and Japanese rivals during the 1970s and early 1980s.

7.4   Present developments in the European Community

Much of the agenda that the Community is presently following is a direct product of the programme to complete the SEM. This programme has spilled-over into two important internal economic policy areas – regional policy and monetary policy. Elsewhere the work of the Commission of the European Community is dominated by external matters, particularly enlargement.

7.4.1   Regional policy

It is generally agreed that completion of the internal market is likely to be accompanied by an increase in the extent of regional economic disparities inside the Community. Of course, regional economic disparity in the European Community is not a new phenomenon. Substantial divergence in regional economic development was evident in the original community of six member countries. However, the three enlargements that have occurred since 1973 have seen the accession of countries characterised by a considerably lower level of economic development than the Community average: Portugal, Greece, Ireland and Spain fall into this category. Regional economic backwardness is not the only regional problem afflicting the Community. There are a number of areas in the Community which are suffering problems of declining economic activity. These are areas that previously relied on industries such as steel making, shipbuilding, coal mining, textiles and heavy engineering for employment and income. As these industries have gone into seemingly terminal decline large tracts of the Community have come to be scarred with the twin problems of mass unemployment and extensive poverty.

The case for a common regional policy rests on two, closely related, propositions. The first is explicitly political, and simply says that if the process of economic and political integration is to continue, then gaps in the material conditions between the rich and the poor regions in the Community must be narrowed. In short, each country must be able to demonstrate that Community membership is doing no net harm to their economy, or that any damage that is being done is more fully compensated than would otherwise be the case. This argument is particularly forceful when applied to the four countries in which economic development is lagging the Community average.

The second justification for a common regional policy flows from the fact that the process of economic integration may create new, or exacerbate existing, regional problems in some member states. This can easily be demonstrated in the context of the Single European Market. Much of the gains from the SEM arise due to the cost savings that will result from the rationalisation of industry. Inefficient firms will close down and the efficient firms will expand. Further gains are available if economies of large-scale production are exploited. But if these static and dynamic benefits from economic integration are unevenly divided, some countries or regions stand to lose. Regional economic policy is intended to assist these areas in developing new economic activity, thereby ensuring that the economic resources of the Community as a whole are fully employed.

Although the Community has had a regional development policy in place since 1975, it was not until the reforms implemented in January 1989 that this policy began to make a real contribution to resolving the regional problem in the Community. Prior to this, Community spending on regional assistance had suffered from an inadequacy of resources being spread too thinly over too wide an area. It was also the case that some governments considered that all financial flows from the Community budget should be treated as general Exchequer revenue and not ear-marked for regional economic policy. In those cases Community policy had no impact whatsoever.

The 1989 reforms do appear to be making a genuine contribution to closing the economic gap between the poorest and the richest of the Community's regions. The basis of these reforms is to be found in the Single European Act that Community heads of government signed in 1986. This commits the Community collectively to 'reducing disparities between the various regions and the backwardness of the least-favoured regions' (Article 130A). There are two key elements to the 1989 reforms. The first is the rationalisation of all aspects of Community economic policy which have a bearing on economic and social cohesion. Thus the operation of the European Regional Development Fund, the European Social Fund, the European Investment Bank and the structural aspects of the CAP were to be brought together under the general title of 'structural policy' in order to ensure that each was contributing to a set of mutually reinforcing objectives. The second element of the reform was to increase and to concentrate the resources devoted to these structural policies. In 1987 only some 17 per cent of spending from the Community budget was allocated to structural policy. Under the reforms, the share devoted to regional policy has risen to 27 per cent by 1992 and is expected to increase to 34 per cent by 1997. Moreover spending is now more concentrated than previously was the case. Approximately 80 per cent of Community spending from the structural funds is targeted at the lagging regions where per capita GDP is less than 75 per cent of the Community average (mainly in Portugal, Greece, Ireland, Spain and Italy). Most of the remaining funds are allocated to converting regions seriously affected by industrial decline, where unemployment is above the Community average (mainly in Britain, France, Belgium, Spain and Italy).

There is evidence that the concentration of assistance and the significant increase in resources devoted to structural policy is assisting the lagging regions in particular. If so, this would mark the first occasion in which Community regional policy is having a discernible impact in narrowing economic disparities between the regions of the Community. However, this regional effort has to be seen against a backdrop of further economic integration in the Community. In particular, the role played by regional policy will have to increase if the current moves to intensify EC monetary integration are to be successful.

7.4.2 Monetary union

The Maastricht Summit of the twelve Community heads of government concluded with a commitment being made to introducing a single currency by 1 January 1999 at the latest. With the introduction of a single currency, the Community will have effected the transition from a common market to a monetary union. Monetary union requires that two conditions be met:

1. Each country must undertake to maintain complete convertibility of its currency with respect to other union currencies, without restriction either on current account or capital account transactions.
2. The rate of exchange between the currencies of the union must be fixed within extremely narrow margins of permissible fluctuation, although the exchange rate between union countries and non-union countries can be left free to move according to market forces. In theory, at least, there is no difference between a monetary union with a *single* currency, and one characterised by *irrevocably* fixed exchange rates between a number of currencies (as, for example, is the case between England and Scotland).

The first condition implies that all exchange controls have to be dismantled as countries move towards a monetary union. Historically, a number of EC countries have used controls on capital movements as a means of assisting them to conform to a predetermined exchange rate target, or of protecting domestic economic policy from the vagaries of, sometimes dramatic, exchange rate movements. Current account restrictions, on the other hand, are rare, as a common market simply could not function with controls on convertibility for the purposes of intra-area trade.

The second condition implies that monetary policy between member states has to be comprehensively harmonised and this, as we discuss later, will certainly involve aspects of fiscal policy harmonisation. It is easy to show why this is necessary. If each country was able to follow its own monetary policy, the convertibility requirement under item 1 above would enable any individual country to create as much domestic credit as it wanted and to exchange this for real goods and services originating in partner countries. The consequence would be to increase the inflationary pressures in the union as a whole. Consequently, a necessary condition for monetary union is either that national authorities engage in close, and binding, co-operation in the area of monetary policy, or that all national monetary policies are 'pooled' by the introduction of a single currency which is thereafter controlled by a single, union-wide, central bank.

When these two conditions are examined together, the practical implications of monetary union from the perspective of the individual country become clear. Members of a monetary union lose autonomy over all aspects of domestic monetary policy. The rate of increase of the money supply will be jointly determined, implying a common rate of inflation for the union as a whole. National budget deficits cannot be monetised and instead will have to be financed from borrowing on the common capital market at the common rate of interest. Individual countries will no longer have recourse to the exchange rate as an instrument of policy. Any initial divergence between national inflation rates will manifest itself by falling output and employment in the high-inflation economies, and this will persist until inflation rates throughout the union converge to the lowest country level. Precisely how long this convergence in national inflation rates takes depends on the inflationary process in the particular member states.

The benefits and costs of monetary union were the subject of a major investigation by the European Commission. The results were published in November 1990, and include the following:

1. *Efficiency and growth:* the introduction of a single currency for the Community would completely eliminate the transactions costs of exchanging Community currencies. Moreover, movement to a single EC currency would eliminate exchange rate uncertainty, thereby encouraging businesses to invest for export without fears that a future exchange rate change will undermine the competitiveness of their products in other member states.
2. *Price stability:* the introduction of a single currency would force inflation in the European Community to converge to the lowest rate. This would benefit the European Community as price stability is itself advantageous for efficient resource allocation.
3. *Public finance:* because national budget deficits can no longer be financed by an expansion in the domestic money supply, governments will be forced to discipline their borrowing, thus leading to lower interest rates.
4. *External gains:* the EC single currency (ECU) would be a major player in the global economy. The Commission insists that this will further benefit the Community by leading to lower costs in international trade, ensuring that there are more ECU denominated financial issues managed by European banks, implying smaller needs for holding (costly) reserves of foreign currencies, and also producing some financial gains via seigniorage.

These gains from introducing a single currency have to be offset against potential costs. It is generally agreed that the main cost from monetary union is that it significantly erodes the macroeconomic competence of a government. This is most clearly seen with respect to monetary policy. With the advent of a single currency and a single central bank, national authorities necessarily lose control over domestic money supply, interest rates and the exchange rate. Although economists tend to argue that exchange rate changes are not able to affect permanently the competitiveness of a country's exports – with the influence of higher import costs and rising global demand for now cheaper exports ('law of one price') soon restoring the initial relative conditions – some economists remain convinced that exchange rate adjustments continue, in practice, to provide temporary relief from external crises which can be used to implement policies that will attack the underlying problem of excessive inflation.

However, it is not only monetary policy that is affected in a monetary union. Fiscal policy too becomes subject to greater formal or informal discipline. As governments are no longer able to finance their spending plans by increasing the domestic money supply, recourse must be taken to borrowing from the private sector. However, this will require interest rates to rise in order to persuade individuals to accept government debt. If the market operates perfectly then it is unlikely that excessive public borrowing would be a problem. However for a number of reasons the market for government debt is unlikely to discount this debt at the appropriate rate. A consequence is that individual governments might be able to raise considerable funds on the private financial market dealing in the single currency in order to fund national public spending plans. There is a danger that this will be inflationary for the area as a whole. Consequently, although 'regional' fiscal independence theoretically is permissible inside a monetary union, a minimum degree of constraint in the conduct of regional fiscal policy is certain to exist in practice.

Whether the benefits of a monetary union outweigh the costs is extremely difficult to determine. Essentially the problem is one of comparing microeconomic benefits with potential macroeconomic costs; similar to the problem of comparing apples to oranges. None the less the Community is committed to moving fairly speedily in the direction of monetary union. Between now and 1996 the member country governments are obliged to set in place the institutional changes necessary for a transfer of monetary responsibility away from national bodies to the Community Central Bank. At the same time domestic monetary and fiscal policies have to be designed with a view to achieving economic convergence within the Community. Formal constraints on national fiscal policies have been agreed which prevent national authorities from incurring excessive budgetary deficits in the run-up to the single currency.

Finally it should be noted that of the twelve EC member countries Britain uniquely secured an exclusion from automatic transition to the single currency area. Although Britain is a signatory to the Maastricht Treaty on Economic and Monetary Union, Prime Minister John Major insisted that what has come to be known as the 'opt-out' clause was included. Under this clause, although Britain is bound to proceed towards monetary union, and implement those institutional and economic policy measures necessary for achieving this, it is not bound to accept the single currency. Essentially the opt-out clause guarantees that the British parliament will have the right to vote on this final step before it is taken, with the government of the day having the right to veto the introduction of single currency should this be the decision of parliament.

7.4.3   External economic policy

The Community's external economic agenda is dominated by two issues: enlargement of the Community to include the countries of the European Free Trade Area; and economic relations with the emerging East European countries. We will review each of these in turn.

The Community enjoys close economic links with the seven countries that make up the EFTA namely, Norway, Sweden, Finland, Iceland, Austria, Switzerland and Liechenstein. Since 1973, the Community and the EFTA countries have together constituted a free trade area in industrial products, although the Community reserves the right to restrict imports from EFTA countries should these threaten the interests of Community producers. Limited concessions have also been granted on fisheries products. Further, the agreements bind the EFTA countries to observe particular rules on the granting of state aid to industry and other potentially uncompetitive practices in so far as they affect EC–EFTA trade, which would otherwise give EFTA firms an unfair advantage in Community product markets. The EC–EFTA agreements have been administered by a joint committee.

In practice, the relationship between EFTA and the European Community has become increasingly unequal, in favour of the Community, since the Single European Market programme was introduced in 1985. As the entire range of intra-Community barriers to the free movement of goods, services, capital and labour was to be abolished by 1992, the margin of disadvantage confronting even the closest Community partners in the EFTA countries was bound to widen as that deadline approached. Through the 1980s discussions were held between the Community and the EFTA countries with a view to creating a common European Economic Space (EES) or Area (EEA) within which the EFTA countries would be allowed access to the Community's single market on identical terms to Community members. In return, of course, the EFTA countries would reciprocate and desist from any practice that discriminated against EC countries. However, to ensure that the EFTA countries enjoyed no unfair advantages in the SEM, and to protect Community enterprises from discrimination, the Commission insisted that EFTA countries must accept all Community economic legislation, including policy with respect to market competition, the environment, state assistance to industry, harmonised EC standards and preferential public procurement. But although the EFTA countries would need to accept EC policy, those countries would have no input to the formal decision-making process from which EC economic legislation emerged. Nor would these countries, as non-member countries, have access to the redistributive facilities of the Community – regional and social policy.

The upshot is that the EFTA countries are required to obey Community rules on matters relating to economic policy but have no formal influence in making or implementing these same rules. In the light of what we might refer to as this 'democratic deficit', it is hardly surprising that the EFTA countries have now, separately, begun to apply for full membership of the Community. Already applications from Austria, Finland and Sweden have been tabled, and it is certain that the remaining EFTA countries will table membership applications within the next couple of years.

Whereas it has been a renewal of the Community's internal economic dynamic that forced the pace of EC discussions with the EFTA countries, it was geo-political developments of the most dramatic type that have been responsible for present Community policy with regard to East European countries. With the ending of the cold war and the ensuing collapse of the economies of the East European states, the Community has been in the vanguard of providing economic assistance to Poland, Hungary, Czechoslovakia and the newly independent states of the former Soviet Union. The former German Democratic Republic became a part of the Community as a result of German unification in November 1990.

During the past two years, the Community has broadened and intensified the preferential economic treatment that it offers these countries. In addition, the Community is at the forefront of international initiatives to provide economic aid in the form of financial and technical assistance measures to these countries. As the painful economic reforms that are necessary to effect the transition to a market-oriented system have proceeded in the countries of East Europe, it has become clear that membership of the European Community is their medium-term objective. Thus far the Community has avoided making any commitment concerning this, although it will be difficult for the Community to ignore their aspirations over the longer term.

7.5 Conclusions

In this chapter we have investigated the evolution of the economic policies of the European Community. It is clear that the European Community has, progressively, come to occupy a more important position with respect to the economic function of the British government, as it has with respect to economic policy in all twelve member countries. Moreover there is little doubt that this process will accelerate in the next decade. If the Community does – as seems to be likely – complete the single European market more or less on schedule, and if the agreements reached during the Maastricht Summit in December 1991 are indeed implemented, then the next ten years will mark a change in the economy of Western Europe that simply is without parallel in modern times. The economic function of each member country will inevitably be weakened, with the Commission enjoying a substantial increase in economic competences. It is clear, therefore, that British domestic economic policy henceforth is set to diminish in both scope and potency. It is, of course, much too early to say whether the aspirations of the Community heads of government will be met on schedule. Already there are some indications that a transition to full monetary union is no longer as popular with the most important member countries as it was at Maastricht.

If internal policy developments are somewhat difficult to predict, there can be little doubt that external economic policy will gain in significance over the next few years. There is a real prospect that the seven EFTA countries will be full members of the European Community by the mid-1990s. Elsewhere the countries of East Europe have indicated their desire to join the European Community; however, it is much too soon to predict developments in this area. Finally, it is worth stressing that both the deepening and the widening of the Community are bound to change the part played by the Community on the global economic stage.

Questions for discussion

1. What is the difference between a free trade area and a common market?
2. Define the conditions necessary for an economic union to be realised. What are the implications of such a union for the conduct of economic policy in the participating countries?
3. What do you understand by the terms *trade creation* and *trade diversion*? What insights does this give in respect of a country's membership of a customs union?
4. What do you understand by the expression *completing the internal market*? How is this likely to improve consumer welfare in the European Community?
5. Why is regional policy an important aspect of the European Community's economic policies?
6. What are the costs and benefits of a monetary union?

Suggestions for further reading

Bulmer, S., S. George and A. Scott (1992), *The United Kingdom and EC Membership Evaluated*, London: Frances Pinter.
El-Agraa, A. (1990), *The Economics of the European Community*, Hemel Hempstead: Philip Allan.
Hitiris, T. (1991), *European Community Economics*, Hemel Hempstead: Harvester Wheatsheaf.
Pinder, J. (1991), *European Community: The building of a union*, Oxford: Oxford University Press.
Sloman, J. (1991), *Economics*, Hemel Hempstead: Harvester Wheatsheaf.
Swann, D. (1992), *The Economics of the Common Market*, Harmondsworth: Penguin.
Tsoukalis, L. (1991), *The New European Economy*, Oxford: Oxford University Press.

Part II

Microeconomic issues

Chapter 8

Industrial economic policy

PETER CLARKE

8.1 Introduction

In this chapter I maintain that those who argue for the exclusion of government from industrial policy have not taken into account the policies employed by international competitors in the global market. I conclude that there is a substantial role for government, not only in contributing to the creation of a competitive domestic environment, but also in matching competitors' government support in international markets. In coming to this conclusion I emphasise the process of decision-making as well as the implementation of the policies themselves.

The next section identifies the potential content of industrial policy. This is followed by a consideration of the problem or problems which industrial policy has to tackle, with some discussion of how these problems arose. The identification of the problems and their causes are essential steps in understanding the process of policy determination. The chapter proceeds with a discussion of the constraints within which policy is determined, and continues with an examination of the rationale for the different theoretical approaches to industrial policy. There is then a description of the current policy framework followed by a presentation of the policies adopted by the United Kingdom government since 1979 and an evaluation of their success. EC policy and its effects on the United Kingdom policy-makers provide the final stage of the discussion before the concluding section.

8.2 What is industrial policy?

Industrial policy can involve a wide range of policy instruments. Generally, it includes any policy implemented by government which is directed towards a particular industry with the objective of improving that industry's competitive position. Policy can be directed, for example, at an infant industry in order to protect its development, or at a mature industry in order to facilitate rationalisation or regeneration. Industrial policy may be conveniently divided into four main policy areas: competition, regional, research and development, and international trade. Each area can involve a number of individual policies, some of which are effective in more than one policy area. The list below presents a sample of the policies that are in common use:

1. Protectionism.
2. Export subsidies.
3. Financial assistance to displaced workers.
4. Subsidies for R&D.
5. Education and training.
6. Antitrust policies.
7. Infrastructure support.
8. Direct loans to reduce risk.
9. Tax policy to encourage investment.
10. Procurement policy of the government.

This list gives an indication of the scope that governments have in aiding industry, and almost all governments use some combination of the measures listed above and more, either explicitly or covertly (OECD, 1990).

8.3   What is the problem to be solved?

Industrial policy is not formulated for its own sake, but to solve a particular problem or problems. The initial stage is to identify the problem, and the second is to set a policy objective with the aim of solving it. There has been a great debate about the extent and significance of Britain's industrial decline. There are those who argue that the structural changes that have taken place in the United Kingdom should be expected in a mature economy and that there is no problem. On the other hand the opposition makes statements to the contrary. One incontestable observation is the decline in the United Kingdom's international competitive position. There has been, over the last four decades, a decline in the United Kingdom's relative importance in world trade (Foreman-Peck, 1991). Data to support this development can be found in the decline in the United Kingdom share of world trade, the change from surplus to deficit in the United Kingdom balance of trade and the degree of import penetration (see Tables 8.1 and 8.2).

These two trends in the international trade statistics are mutually supportive in providing evidence of the United Kingdom's decline. In a dynamic world economy with many newly industrialised countries, it could

Table 8.1 Share of world merchandise
trade for the United Kingdom (calculated
from IMF International Financial Statistics)

1950	1960	1970	1980	1990
10.8%	9.1%	6.9%	5.9%	5.5%

be expected that the United Kingdom's share of world trade would fall. However, this is no reason why, if it is maintaining its relative competitive position, a long-term manufacturing trade surplus should turn into a deficit. In 1983 Britain had an overall deficit on trade in manufactured goods for the first time. This situation has persisted even in the current long recession, when it could be expected that there would be a significant reduction in imports.

Further supporting evidence of the decline in the United Kingdom's relative competitiveness is the difference in productivity between the United Kingdom and its major competitors. Statistics show that over the last twenty years it has lagged significantly behind many of its major competitors in productivity growth; this is despite the improvement in the United Kingdom's productivity since 1979, primarily due to restructuring during the 1980–2 recession. One consequence of this is that in 1991 an industrial worker in the United Kingdom produced only 65 per cent of the output of an equivalent German worker.

In addition the United Kingdom has lagged seriously behind its major competitors in manufacturing growth. Further OECD data shows that UK manufacturing growth in output since 1979 has been lower than any of the other OECD countries apart from Greece. The decline in the international competitiveness of the United Kingdom has had repercussions for the economy. The unemployment rate has increased for all the industrialised countries over the last three decades, the EC average increasing from 4.4 per cent in the 1970s to 9.8 per cent in the 1980s. The UK figure has increased by a larger percentage from 3.9 to 9.8 per cent. Lastly, the United Kingdom has experienced rapid decline in its manufacturing base, has had relatively slow growth over the whole period, and has experienced declining investment in research and development. These changes in the circumstances of the United Kingdom economy are all part of the main problem, the decline in international competitiveness.

8.4 The reasons for the loss of international competitiveness

If the main industrial problem of the United Kingdom has been correctly identified, the next stage is to diagnose the cause or causes of the problem. Only when this stage has been completed is it possible to look for policy

Peter Clarke

Table 8.2 UK visible trade and import penetration

	1979	1980	1981	1982	1983	1984	1985	1986	1987	1988	1989	1990
Value (£ million)												
Exports	40 471	47 149	50 668	55 331	60 700	70 265	77 991	72 656	79 446	80 776	92 792	102 038
Imports (fob)	43 814	45 792	47 416	53 421	62 237	75 601	81 336	82 141	90 669	101 854	116 632	120 713
Visible balance	−3 343	+1 357	+3 252	+1 910	−1 537	−3 336	−3 345	−9 485	−11 223	−21 078	−23 840	−18 675
Import penetration												
Ratio imports/ home demand	26.9	26.2	27.8	29.0	31.1	33.4	34.3	34.3	35.2	35.6	36.7	

Source: Central Statistical Office.

options. There is no simple, all-embracing explanation of the United Kingdom's decline in international competitiveness. Parts of the problem may be found in non-economic explanations which lie beyond the scope of this chapter. The economic explanations refer to several levels. At the highest level are those which contribute to the creation of the overall economic environment, while those at the lower levels work within that environment. The following contribute to a greater or lesser extent to the United Kingdom's decline in international competitiveness:

- First, it has failed to accept that to take part in the world market firms and governments must adopt a global perspective. Most of the growth markets are global markets with fierce international corporate competition often supported domestically by an active government industrial policy.
- Second, firms in the United Kingdom have a tendency to concentrate on short-term objectives and policies, while the main competitors, Germany and Japan, adopt much longer time horizons. The pressures on corporate management from the financial sector to adopt short-term objectives constrain their ability to take the long-term view required, for example, in investment and in research and development.
- Third, structural economic relations do not appear to be appropriate for improving international competitiveness. The relationship between the financial and product markets is an example of the many features of the British economy which differ significantly from those existing in competitor economies. Thus, the UK financial sector, though regarded by many as one of the most efficient and competitive in the world, contributes little to funding real investment in the manufacturing sector. The role of German and Japanese banks in providing the main source of corporate finance in their respective countries contrasts significantly with the United Kingdom's.

The above explanations of the United Kingdom's problem manifest themselves in lower operational explanations of the problem. These include the following: de-industrialisation, low growth rates, low investment in new plant and machinery and infrastructure, low expenditure on R&D, and a poor record in industrial training and education.

Although these explanations for Britain's industrial problems are not exhaustive, they provide much of the background in which past and current, corporate and government policy has been enacted. They represent fundamental characteristics and trends of the UK economy. This does not mean they cannot be altered, as they have been in the past. But it does imply that current policies can either be directed to altering the overall economic environment or attempting to work within it. The former requires a long-term perspective, while the latter may generate little success if the overall economic environment is inappropriate.

8.5 Significant industrial policy interdependencies

It is important to understand the overall economic policy environment in which industrial policy is expected to work. Industrial policy is not determined in a vacuum, and there are important interdependencies between policy domains:

1. *Macroeconomic and microeconomic policy.* The fiscal and monetary policies employed by government have a significant and a continued influence on industrial success. The difficulty arises because macro-policies, implemented to meet macro-objectives such as inflation control, can and do have serious implications for firms' success, especially in a recession. Industrial policy cannot be insulated from the effects of the relatively short-term, political cycle. For example, the effect of any industrial policy to stimulate investment in plant and machinery or in research and development expenditure, may be more than offset by restraining macroeconomic policies.

2. *Governments' and corporations' objectives for industry.* Because firms and governments do not always represent the same interest groups in society they are likely to have different objectives. Firms in a recession may have as their sole objectives the wish to survive. Therefore they will concentrate on preserving their cash flow by resisting long-term commitments. Governments on the other hand may be more interested in stimulating investment in productive capacity to contribute to the climb out of the recession.

3. *The governments' and corporations' industrial strategies.* Even if firms and governments agree on a particular objective, such as the maximisation of long-term profits, they may perceive the achievement of that objective by different and sometimes conflicting means. Corporate managers may state that they believe in market competition but many of their actions are an attempt to develop their own market niche or dominant firm position.

4. *The governments' policies in different areas of industrial policy.* Because of the range of industrial policy areas and the policies which can be used in them, there is the possibility that a specific policy which contributes to one objective will be counter-productive in respect to another. The conflict between the use of the patent system and dominant firm policy is an obvious example.

5. *The United Kingdom's and rival countries' industrial policy.* Lastly, a country involved in international competition cannot determine its industrial policy in ignorance of the actions of its competitors' government. Policies which exclude government intervention at a domestic level will fail to improve international competitiveness if other countries' governments are successfully intervening (Audretsch, 1989). The US anti-trust legislation is primarily directed at the limitation of

economic power in any market. It does not provide for a case-by-case investigation as to whether a monopoly could be the best way to achieve economic efficiency. Competition is not only king, irrespective of the costs, but it is also all-pervasive. Japan in contrast adopts a different attitude. The Japanese have a more receptive policy towards cartels. This incorporates a view of fair trade which assigns priority to international competitiveness over their domestic dominant firm policy. They will also encourage consortia of corporations to undertake R&D jointly.

Many of the criticisms directed at government industrial policy arise because of a failure to understand these relationships. Often policies exacerbate rather than contribute to the solution of problems. It is only when the relationships are fully understood, especially the last, that appropriate policies can be correctly determined and efficiently implemented. Any failure in this respect may not only mean the lack of a level playing field for UK companies, it would imply that their international competitors are playing at a much higher altitude.

8.6   Philosophical rationale of policies

In the field of industrial policy, and particularly in the area of competition policy, there are two main views which are diametrically opposed to each other. One argues for a strong interventionist policy, based on neoclassical economics; the other for a non-interventionist, *laissez-faire* policy based on the Austrian School (Hay and Morris, 1991).

The neoclassical school focuses on the characteristics of markets and particularly on market failure. Although there are a number of market failures, much criticism has been directed at dominant firms and their capacity, by increasing price and reducing output, to reduce economic welfare. This has led to the structure–conduct–performance approach, which emphasises the causal relationship between these three elements. The argument is that once the market structure has been determined then the conduct of the firms in the market, and their economic performance, can be predicted. In a competitive market, market pressures lead to long-term normal profits and any long-term dominant firm profits which exist are interpreted as the result of the abuse of market power. Competition policy underpinned by this approach emphasises the creation of the appropriate competitive market structure. It takes the position that monopolies, or markets with high concentration, will not lead to the efficient allocation of resources and therefore a policy which will reduce the level of concentration should be implemented.

The Austrian School attempts to embody a much more complex and dynamic conception of the market environment. It takes the position that as long as market entry is not artificially restricted, long-run allocative and cost efficiency are generated. Entry or even potential entry ensure that firms are always vulnerable to competitive pressures. Large profits, as may be generated by a dominant firm, are viewed as a reward for entrepreneurship and greater efficiency, and a vital element in an active and dynamic economy. Investment in both product and process innovation are seen as responses to the existence of large profits which attract resources to compete for them and may ultimately lead to lower long-run costs.

Policy recommendations based on this school of thought consequently take a much more relaxed attitude to dominant firms and industries with high concentration ratios. It has provided the basis for a *laissez-faire*, non-interventionist posture by government in respect to industrial policy. It has also led to the de-regulation of a number of industries, for example, the bus industry in the United Kingdom and the airline industry in the United States.

Adherents to the structure–conduct–performance rationale can adopt a dogmatic approach to competition policy, as in the United States, and automatically restructure markets characterised by a dominant firm. An alternative application involves comparison of the costs and benefits of a dominant firm. Each case is individually investigated to assess whether it does generate net benefits. The Austrian School in its extreme form recommends no government intervention at all, as unconstrained markets in any current guise represent the most efficient means of resource allocation. In its qualified form it acknowledges that governments can contribute to the creation of the appropriate competitive economic environment. For example, it can legislate against price fixing and horizontal mergers.

Though both theoretical approaches have some degree of credibility, there is a difficulty associated with the uncritical acceptance of either as the basis for industrial policy. Neither is appropriate, given the complexity of the economic environment in which industrial policy must work. Both approaches provide some insights to the problem and possible solutions. But they cannot cope with the whole picture. Particularly, they are unable to accommodate fully the inter-relationships described above, especially that between different countries' industrial policies.

An extension of the neoclassical model acknowledges that firms work in an internationally imperfect market and that a significant part of trade nowadays is between industrialised countries and on an intra-industry basis. These two trends have become so important in the last two decades that it has led to the introduction of a 'new trade theory'. The policy implications of this theoretical development have been to reinforce the case for government intervention especially in the case of subsidies and taxes affecting trade.

In the current world market it is Japan that is the current 'winner' in the international market. It would then seem sensible to understand the basis on which it sets its industrial policy. Japanese policy reflects elements of both the theoretical extremes portrayed above. It has neither adopted nor rejected either of them exclusively. This has led to the introduction of the concept of the development state or managed economy. In this approach, the government actively participates in forming the appropriate domestic market structure. In Japan overall policy determination is managed by the Ministry of International Trade and Industry (MITI), and includes representation from all sections of the interest groups involved in the industrial sector.

8.7 The current industrial policy framework in the United Kingdom

Some elements of current industrial policy originated over four decades ago. Development was initially slow but developed more rapidly in the 1960s and 1970s (Office of Fair Trading (OFT), 1990). The present framework for the four areas referred to in section 8.2 is presented below.

8.7.1 Competition policy

This is the area of industrial policy which has in the past attracted most attention. It is the responsibility of the secretary of state for trade and industry (president of the Board of Trade) and involves dominant firms (monopolies), mergers and takeovers, restrictive practices, and anti-competitive practices. One of the more controversial elements of policy over the last decade has been privatisation of public sector organisations. As this topic is dealt with fully in Chapter 10, the only reference to it here concerns its implications for market behaviour where there is a dominant firm. Competition policy is governed by four Acts of Parliament:

1. The Fair Trading Act 1973.
2. The Restrictive Practices Act 1976.
3. The Resale Prices Act 1976.
4. The Competition Act 1980.

Each Act is directed primarily at a particular aspect of competition policy, the first dealing with mergers, takeovers and monopolies, the second with agreements in restraint of trade, the third with minimum price setting and the last with anti-competitive practices. The above legislation is implemented through two bodies: the Monopolies and Mergers Commission (MMC) and the OFT, headed by the director general (DGFT). The Restrictive Practices Court provides the legal decisions in the area of restrictive agreements or minimum resale prices. The OFT oversees the overall state of competition and initiates action when necessary, it reports its findings to the secretary of state, and implements policy. Final decisions rest with the secretary of state or, within its jurisdiction, with the Restrictive Practices Court.

Dominant firm (monopoly) policy

This area of policy is more commonly known as monopoly policy, but the main focus is not on monopolies, as there are only a few of them in the United Kingdom, but on firms or a group of firms which have a significantly large market share of a good or service. The large market share generates market power and therefore provides firms with the potential to act as if they were monopolies. For at least four decades, until the mid-1980s, the increase in the size of firms had led to increased market concentration in industry in the United Kingdom. In the 1980s there was a halt to this trend, but because of a surge of mergers in the last part of the decade, it is likely to have proved only temporary.

In the United Kingdom under current legislation a monopoly position is considered to exist when a company supplies or purchases at least 25 per cent of United Kingdom total market supply. In addition, for the purposes of the Act, monopolies are also said to exist when a group of companies with 25 per cent or more of the market act so as to affect competition. The secretary of state for trade and industry or the director general of fair trading have the right to refer any such company or companies to the MMC. It investigates the company and reports back, intimating whether a monopoly exists, and if it is working against the public interest. The point to note is that it is not the existence of the monopoly that causes concern but that it may be working against the 'public interest'. If the MMC decides that a monopoly exists and that it is acting against the public interest, the secretary of state can take any of the following courses of action:

1. Ask the firm to cease the activities which have given the cause for concern.
2. Order the firm to cease its unacceptable activity.
3. Reject the advice of the MMC and leave the firm to continue as it has in the past.

There are two main difficulties in the application of this policy. The first is the difficulty of defining what is meant by public interest. Although the Fair Trading Act sets out criteria which provide the ground rules for determining what is in the public interest, the MMC has considerable discretion in determining whether or not a firm is acting against the public interest.

The second difficulty is that in many industries the minimum efficient scale of production (MES) is greater than the size of the domestic market. Government policy to promote domestic competition will therefore lead to higher unit costs. This leads to pressure on governments to accept a wider view of a firm's market than the domestic one.

Mergers and takeovers

Mergers and takeovers affect the level of competitive activity and may have repercussions for the degree of market concentration in the economy. The legislation requires investigation of mergers or takeovers which lead to a merged firm having over 25 per cent of a market, or where the companies involved have gross assets above some minimum level. This minimum level has increased over the years and since 1984 has been £30 million. Meeting one or both of the above criteria can lead to reference to the MMC.

There are three categories of merger or takeover: horizontal, vertical and conglomerate. Each represents a different strategic response to the conditions in which a corporation works. The first has a direct effect on industry concentration but both of the others can lead to restrictions on competition in the marketplace. Over the years the relative importance of different types of merger has changed, partly as a response to government legislation. It has been directed primarily at the concentration problem and has led to fewer horizontal and more conglomerate mergers and takeovers.

Once a merger has been brought to the notice of the DGFT, he or she initially carries out a preliminary inquiry. If the inquiry finds that there are grounds to believe that the public interest will be detrimentally affected, the DGFT then advises that the secretary of state should refer the merger to the MMC. It is not an automatic referral as the secretary has discretion over the decision. If, after its investigation, the MMC concludes that the merger is against the public interest, it will recommend how the position can be resolved. This may involve rejecting the merger outright or a restructuring of the merger. The final decisions as to whether a merger should be referred to the MMC and whether a merger should be allowed to go ahead, are left to the secretary of state.

Once again there is little consistency in the decisions of what is in the public interest. In addition, due to the need for speed there is little time to undertake a thorough investigation as to the relative merits of each proposed merger. Yet one of the major criticisms of this policy concerns the time taken to investigate mergers and takeovers. Although the speed of the average investigation has been reduced from six to three months, this is still a long time in financial sector terms, particularly if the delay puts one firm at a disadvantage. This is the case if there is competitive bidding and one firm's bid is not referred to the MMC while the other or others are. Lastly, the role of the secretary of state, with the power of veto on referral to the MMC and the right to reject the MMC's recommendation, means that politics are always an influence on a decision (Peacock and Bannock, 1991).

Restrictive trade practices

The Restrictive Trade Practices Act 1976 covers any agreements between firms in respect to prices, market share, terms and conditions of contracts of supply and distribution, etc. These agreements between firms are viewed as possibly reducing the level of competition, and the Act has jurisdiction over all forms of contracts whether explicit or informal, written or verbal. Under the Act, the agreements must be presented for registration with the DGFT. The DGFT decides whether the agreement has to be registered and, if that is the case, then refers it to the Restrictive Practices Court. It is the Court which decides whether the practice is in the public interest. Such agreements are assumed to be against the public interest until the firms involved can prove otherwise. In order to do so they must show that the advantages of the agreement's existence outweigh the costs. If an agreement is found not to be in the public interest, an order is passed for it to be struck down. There are very few agreements which have been held to work in the public interest.

Resale price maintenance

The imposition by any supplier of a minimum resale price is known as resale price maintenance (RPM), and is prohibited by the Resale Prices Act of 1976. The Act has banned RPM from all markets except those for books and pharmaceutical products. These two exceptions have been granted on public interest grounds. It is the responsibility of the DGFT to respond to any complaints of price fixing. Normally the DGFT will obtain an agreement from the firm to desist from the action. If it will not desist, the DGFT can apply for a court injunction to prohibit any minimum price agreement. The Office of Fair Trading deals with an average of thirty claims a year, and in recent years these have resulted in four or five firms being requested to stop resale price maintenance. The activity is more prevalent than the above numbers suggest as it is common practice for firms to recommend prices which by 'convention' are accepted by the trade.

Anti-competitive practices

The passing of the Competition Act 1980 reflected the, at least publicly proclaimed, pro-competitive attitude of the Conservative government. The Act identified the existence of 'anti-competitive practices', as policies which provide firms with advantages over their competitors which are not based on efficiency. The Act empowers the DGFT to investigate a firm which is believed to employ such anti-competitive practices. If evidence is found to support the belief, the DGFT can secure an agreement with the firm to cease the activity. If no such agreement can be obtained, then the case is referred to the MMC to determine whether the anti-competitive practice is against the public interest. A report is forwarded to the secretary of state, who is empowered,'if there is a case, to direct the company to stop the practice. Just as in dominant firm policy, there is a problem of definition as to what constitutes an anti-competitive practice. So far, cases have included predatory pricing, refusal to supply and particular types of discount. Although it would appear at first sight that there would be numerous cases to be investigated, few cases have actually been proposed for examination. To date, the Act has had little effect on firm practices.

8.7.2 Regional policy

The alleviation of disparities in the distribution of prosperity throughout the United Kingdom has provided a rationale for regional policy. In the United Kingdom, such policy has primarily assumed the form of financial support, specifically investment grants, subsidies and tax concessions, as well as constraints on the expansion of firms in prosperous areas of the United Kingdom. There are two stages in policy implementation: first, the identification of the areas of need; and secondly, the determination of the appropriate form of aid.

8.7.3 Research and development

Government participation in R&D has been both direct and indirect. As in all industrial countries the United Kingdom government has provided a legal framework to protect the intellectual property rights of inventors, i.e. the patent system. The patent system enables inventors to generate a return on their investment in R&D and therefore encourages firms to enter new markets or introduce new products or processes. On the other hand patents often lead to a market dominated by one firm because of the existence of barriers to entry as the result of the patent. The UK government also intervenes directly in R&D by spending large amounts to fund research projects, in both the defence and the civilian sectors.

8.7.4 International trade

The protection of domestic industries from foreign competition has often played a critical role in industrial policy. The main instruments of trade policy have been quotas, tariffs, selective assistance to industries and non-tariff barriers. Examples of the latter are the setting of standards, such as lawn-mower noise levels, and market sharing agreements. The development of the European Community with its restrictions on the use of quotas and tariffs, and other trade agreements which have a similar effect, have led to a decline in the importance of quotas and tariffs and an increase in the use of non-tariff barriers and market sharing agreements. These should end as a result of the Single European Act (see Chapter 7).

8.8   Policies of the Conservative government since 1979

The incoming government of 1979 was convinced that the United Kingdom's poor international competitive position was primarily due to the intervention of government in the industrial sector. As a consequence, the decade that followed saw a significant reduction in the role of the Department of Trade and Industry (DTI) in the determination of industrial policy (Johnson, 1991). The DTI's decline in importance was reflected in the number of ministers appointed to the post (thirteen in thirteen years), resulting in a lack of consistency in approach and policy. The first of these DTI ministers, Sir Keith Joseph, set the tone for the others to follow in arguing for de-regulation and the removal of many of the restrictions on industry. However, during the years that followed, there have been periods when the government has adopted an active role, for example in the information technology industry.

One significant measure of the reduction of government influence in this sector has been the decline in the percentage of government expenditure going to industry, energy, trade and employment. This figure was 5 per cent in 1979–80 and, despite attempts to reduce it by Keith Joseph, it was still the same figure in 1982–3. However, by 1986–7 it had been reduced to 4.2 per cent and to 4.0 per cent in 1990–1.

8.8.1   Competition policy

The main aim of UK competition policy has been to encourage and enhance the competitive process. Competition provides a critical element in ensuring efficient markets. The generation of efficient markets in the United Kingdom, it was argued, would produce a leaner and more active industrial sector which would compete more effectively in international markets. Despite these strong views, policy has not reflected a total commitment to competition. It has continued with the pragmatic approach which is accommodated in the legislation. The process of a case-by-case examination meant that any action by firms which reduced competition was not automatically banned; only when a form of market behaviour was found to be, or was likely to be, against the 'public interest' was it prohibited.

Dominant firm policy

The main legislative change, in the 1980 Competition Act, has been to bring nationalised industries under the monopolies legislation. Sixteen investigations have followed from this change, with over 600 recommendations to increase efficiency. However, in regard to its stated main objective, the MMC has been found to have little effect on maintaining or improving the competitive process. It is difficult to assess what contribution has been made to the improvement of the United Kingdom's competitiveness by current dominant firm policy. However, it is unlikely to have been a major one.

The reduction of government involvement in industry led to a radical review of direct government ownership in industry. The transfer of industries from public to private ownership, privatisation, occurred in the traditional industries, the car industry, steel and shipbuilding, as well as in the high-technology industries such as telecommunications (see Chapter 10 for further discussion). A number of these private corporations transferred were, and remain, monopolies. This is clearly a lapse from the government's commitment to competitive markets, since the transfer of ownership to the private sector did not change the market structure or the competitive environment and reveals the consequences of a conflict of policy objectives.

Merger policy

Under the Competition Act of 1980 the guidance for decisions on mergers and takeovers placed the emphasis on whether the merger or any other action was anti-competitive. An investigation into a merger to determine whether there would be anti-competitive consequences was broadened to take into account domestic and foreign suppliers in both the domestic and overseas markets.

In a period during which there was a great deal of merger activity, very few mergers were referred to the MMC. Thus in the years 1965–78 about 2.5 per cent of proposed mergers were referred to the MMC for investigation, the rest being unopposed. In the years 1979–87 of 2070 mergers only 64 were referred to the MMC, amounting to a little over 3 per cent of the total. In the years 1979–87, of the 64 mergers referred, 19 were declared against the public interest, 29 were declared as not against the public interest and 16 were abandoned by the firms involved before the MMC reported, and the referral was withdrawn.

A criticism of current merger policy is the role played by competition issues to the near exclusion of other aims of industrial policy. Since merger policy can have enormous effects in other policy areas, such as regional policy, these effects should also be taken into account in the decision. This is an area of potential conflict between the secretary of state and the MMC. The former is obliged to take the wider view, while the latter may have the narrower focus of competition. The decisions that have been taken still do not provide a clear set of criteria for the interested parties. There has been a continued lack of consistency in both the referrals to the MMC and in the decisions taken by the MMC and the secretary of state.

The effectiveness of merger policy should not just be assessed in terms of the numbers of cases investigated. Firms, for example, have moved away from horizontal mergers as a strategic option because of the policy towards them. However, the time and resources required to carry out an investigation will always provide a constraint on the number that can be considered, regardless of the cases that in principle should be referred to the MMC. The large number of mergers which took place through the 1980s, and their effect on industrial concentration, does not in itself mean that they affected the degree of competition and were against the public interest. However, it is difficult to obtain systematic information on what consequences they did have for competitive behaviour.

If the effect of merger policy on competition is difficult to identify it is even more difficult to assess its contribution to the improvement in the United Kingdom's international competitiveness. The small numbers investigated suggest that at best it can only be small. However, there are two reasons to suggest that merger policy may even exacerbate the United Kingdom's international position. The first reason is that the more sympathetic approach to mergers and takeovers has led to senior managers spending much of their time involved in this activity. They are either searching for victim companies to contribute to their own rapid growth, or are defending their company from predators. The opportunity cost is that management has been diverted away from building long-term viable companies capable of competing in global markets. The second reason is that if UK companies are not to be put in a disadvantaged position compared to their international competitors, they should be dealt with in the same way by United Kingdom policy as their competitors are treated by their own merger legislation.

Restrictive practices policy

By the end of 1991 over 5000 agreements had been registered. Over 50 per cent had been abandoned and approximately 1000 had all restrictions removed. The processing of this large number of cases was facilitated by a number of key cases which set the criteria for rejection of many others. Whether the abandoned agreements were really abandoned or merely replaced by informal arrangements remains a point of conjecture.

In 1976 the Restrictive Practices Act was modified to include services in addition to goods. This change was to generate one of the most important industrial developments of the 1980s, that of the de-regulation of the financial sector, with the reorganisation of The Stock Exchange through the 'Big Bang' in 1986 (see Chapter 4 for details). Government action in this area was prompted by a referral of The Stock Exchange restrictive practices to the Court. A deal was made between the government and The Stock Exchange whereby legislation exempted the latter from the Restrictive Practices Acts in return for a number of changes in practice, for example, the discarding of restrictive labour practices and the minimum commission rates.

The effectiveness of this policy is both difficult to assess and all too easy to overstate. The public abandonment of many agreements may have resulted in their materialising as covert agreements out of the public gaze. In addition, there have been doubts placed on the appropriateness of the role of the Court in making judgements on economic issues. What criteria do they use to ensure consistency towards the policy objectives and between cases?

This policy, too, could be considered relatively successful, and to have made a contribution to increases in allocative and cost efficiency, though at best its contribution to United Kingdom competitiveness was probably quite modest. Through an indirect effect, the de-regulation of the financial sector, it is even possible that it has had a negative effect on industrial competitiveness.

Anti-competitive practices

The 1980 Act reflected a strong commitment to erase anti-competitive forces, but the fact that there have been so few investigations, only an average of fewer than four a year, suggests window dressing rather than an active policy. It is difficult to see that, to date, this policy has contributed significantly to any industrial policy objective.

An overall assessment of the role played by the United Kingdom's competition policy in improving international competitiveness must conclude that it makes, at best, a marginal contribution. Despite the resources directed towards it, its effect on the lower-level operational objective of increasing the efficiency of resource allocation in the United Kingdom is also very small. Within industrial policy as a whole, one could argue that competition policy has received too much attention in the

United Kingdom, to the detriment of other, possibly more constructive, policies.

8.8.2   Regional policy

There have been significant changes in this area of industrial policy during the 1980s. In the early 1980s duty-free 'freeports' were introduced along with the creation of 'enterprise zones' which were exempt from local rates. In the mid-1980s, the Regional Development Grants system, which subsidised investment in particular areas of the country, was curtailed and, though its scope was widened to include services, in 1988 it was replaced by Regional Selective Assistance. The main thrust of policy has been to give more support to firms in the regions, particularly to aid small and medium-sized firms. In addition there has been a move from automatic to discretionary aid. Regional Selective Assistance helps projects which maintain employment or create additional jobs by providing the minimum resources to encourage supported firms to continue operations in the local area. The areas which qualify for aid have been reduced significantly and as a consequence there has been a large reduction in expenditure, as revealed in Table 8.3.

Some regional policy spending has received EC support, though this has

Table 8.3   Government expenditure on regional preferential assistance to industry

	1983–4	1984–5	1985–6	1986–7	1987–8	1988–9	1989–90	1990–1
Great Britain	648.9	636.8	584.1	746.2	556.2	615.7	540.1	497.2
North	130.2	125.5	96.6	137.3	109.3	134.1	117.0	85.0
Yorkshire and Humberside	36.3	44.3	36.4	41.9	38.8	50.2	32.4	29.4
East Midlands	17.5	11.4	8.8	10.7	9.4	8.8	9.5	5.5
East Anglia	0.0	0.0	0.0	0.0	0.0	0.0	0.0	0.0
South East	0.0	0.0	0.0	0.0	0.0	0.0	0.0	0.0
South West	12.1	14.6	12.3	23.0	14.8	14.7	10.7	9.0
West Midlands[1]	0.0	0.0	7.1	10.6	19.3	26.2	19.9	18.0
North West	104.2	106.4	87.5	129.6	79.0	82.3	74.3	57.5
England	300.3	302.2	248.7	353.1	270.6	316.3	263.8	204.4
Wales	120.0	147.5	138.4	150.7	132.4	148.2	131.7	133.7
Scotland	228.6	187.1	197.0	242.4	153.2	151.2	144.6	159.1

Note: [1] Certain Travel to Work Areas in the West Midlands attained assisted area status on 29 November 1984.
Source: Department of Trade and Industry.

given rise to controversy over the issue of 'additionality', namely whether the UK can use EC money to *supplement* or *substitute* for its own spending.

It is difficult to judge the effects of the change in regional policy either on regional employment or regional income levels. Previous policies were not considered to be a success as they often only attracted marginal firms or projects which were only viable with assistance and were highly vulnerable in times of recession. The foreign investments that have been attracted into areas of deprivation were more likely to be persuaded by a large, cheap and relatively skilled labour force than some marginal financing. Also, even though such incomers as the Japanese car firms must be of benefit to our balance of trade, they will eventually lead to a decline in the invisibles balance as profits are returned to Japan (see Chapter 6 for relevant definitions). As indicated, current regional policy is more selective and less well funded than in the past. Interestingly, some regions in the United Kingdom, such as Scotland, are coping with the present recession more successfully than the traditionally more bouyant areas like London and the South East. Regional policy may have made a modest contribution to this relative improvement.

8.8.3 Research and development

There has been a continuation of the long-term decline in the United Kingdom's private and public expenditure on R&D, and the overall expenditure has continued to be low by international comparisons. The low figure is a product of the short time horizons adopted in the private sector and the attribution process in the public sector. This is the situation where programmes funded by the European Community are attributed to specific government departments and are included as part of their public expenditure calculations. Despite this latter policy, government has continued to make a substantial contribution to R&D, but half of its expenditure has been on defence-related projects. These projects are generally large and are concentrated on a few defence contractors. Although these projects are currently important in the world defence market, evidence now confirms that there is little technological transfer between defence and civil sectors.

Government support in the civil sector includes the funding of projects in a particular industry or firm and the support of collaborative projects. The former has been used to fund projects which have widespread potential, such as software development and fibre optics. The objective of the most important collaborative project, the ALVEY project, was to promote research in the information technology industry over an extensive range of key technologies by promoting collaborative projects involving firms and the universities. This entailed a shift in the balance of funds from single-firm projects to joint research between companies and research units like the universities. Increasingly, the private sector was relied upon to finance near-market research, the amount of business enterprise R&D supported by the government falling from 30 per cent in 1981 to 19.4 per cent in 1987, while the government funded the more basic research. Many of the government's programmes in the mid-1980s were introduced when Kenneth Baker was secretary of state. It involved targeting a number of what were thought to be critical technological projects. Because it is often difficult to determine all the direct and indirect effects of R&D, even those projects targeted which failed, such as cable networks and the provision of financial services in the home, may eventually be seen to have made a contribution to technological progress.

Research and development is one of the most important elements of a successful modern economy. In many world markets corporations compete not with price but through product and process innovation. The fall in the proportion of world patents taken out by UK companies and the large increase recorded by Japanese and other rivals' companies is likely to anticipate a further reduction in the competitive capabilities of the United Kingdom (HMSO, 1992). Unlike the other areas of industrial policy, this area can have a more clearly specified objective, the increase in the number of world patents which, allowing for the time lag, is strongly related to international competitiveness.

The failure of UK policy on R&D to reverse the declining patent record of United Kingdom companies does not necessarily mean that the projects were not successful. If they had not been undertaken, the United Kingdom's current position might be even worse.

8.8.4   International trade policy

The development of the European Community and the progress made by the General Agreement on Tariffs and Trade treaty has limited the scope for the United Kingdom in this area of industrial policy. Policy can be divided into three areas: namely, policy within the European Community; policy governed by GATT; and lastly that area which does not come under the restriction of any international trade agreement. However, with the growth of intra-industry trade it is the first policy area which is most important.

Membership of the European Community and the development of an integrated market has led to policies to remove any constraints to trade within the Community, while at the same time imposing barriers to any suppliers outside it. The reduction of trade barriers between the member countries of the European Community stimulated UK imports and exports within the Community, reinforcing a pre-existing trend. At the same time, the existence of the Community's Common External Tariff discriminated against goods from countries outside it, especially, in Britain's case, against countries in the Commonwealth.

Given the import penetration experienced in nearly all United Kingdom markets, it is difficult to argue that trade policy has been conspicuously successful. It may be the case, however, that if some form of trade policy had not been in place the current situation might be still worse.

8.9 The European Community

The United Kingdom's membership of the European Community and the industrial policy adopted by the Community introduce a number of interesting points of discussion. It also creates an environment for potential conflict between the governments of the member states themselves and between the individual states and the European Commission.

EC industrial policy has slowly developed since the Treaty of Rome but with the creation of the internal market there is a more urgent requirement for a Community industrial policy to ensure consistent policies for all member states. A number of EC policies mirror those of the member countries, but EC policy objectives are set at a different level from those of the member nations which can generate policy conflicts (Bayliss and El-Agraa, 1990).

The Treaty of Rome (Articles 85, 86 and 92) provides the basis for the Community policy in this area. They prohibit and declare void agreements and concerted practices that have the object or the effect of preventing, restricting, or distorting competition within the European Community, and which affect trade between member states. They also constrain the member states from resourcing or helping in any way their own domestically located producers. These Articles provide the guidelines for policy but leave some leeway for interpretation. The rationale of EC competition policy, for example, is to foster competitive markets, but it is recognised that unconstrained market activity does not necessarily generate efficient and equitable solutions. Therefore the role of competition policy is to ensure that competitive markets can function.

The overall objective of the Commission's policy is to enable EC producers to compete successfully in global markets. This objective is to be achieved by maintaining a favourable business environment, by implementing a positive approach to adjustment and, lastly, by keeping an open approach to markets.

Though it is relatively early to assess the effectiveness of Community industrial policy, there have been a number of clashes between member states and the Commission. One area where a difference of view arises is that of merger decisions. A 1990 EC directive empowered the Commission to monitor all proposed mergers resulting in a combined worldwide turnover of over 5 billion ECU (the European Community's currency unit;

see Chapter 7), with at least two of the firms having a turnover of 250 million ECU in the European Community, unless two-thirds of either was in a member state. The problem arises because of differences of opinion over the definition of a market. Does the existence of the Single Market imply that what would have been treated as a monopolistic merger within a member state would be treated differently in the larger EC market? There is nothing new about this problem, but it is exacerbated by the frequent existence of conflicts of interest between the Commission and the member states involved. This is the case in respect of the targeting of industries to create Euro-champions, where the Commission tends to adopt a sympathetic position while the United Kingdom takes a strongly adverse stance.

One obvious area of difficulty for the United Kingdom is that the EC industrial policy should apply uniformly to all member states. Implicitly it is assumed that all members are faced by the same set of industrial problems, but there are strong arguments to suggest that the United Kingdom and Germany face quite different problems.

EC policy has already had and will continue to have important implications for each member state's industrial policy. However, the complexities of industrial economic problems for both the member states and the Commission have not and are unlikely to lead to a clear, unambiguous policy framework. The commitment to market forces will often be set aside and government intervention will take place at both a member state and at the Community level.

8.10   Conclusion

It is only necessary to undertake a brief investigation in order to conclude that all governments of industrialised countries employ some form of industrial policy, for even a consistent *laissez-faire* stance is a type of industrial policy. Of course it is, but no government actually adopts such a policy, despite declarations to the contrary.

During the 1980s, the Conservative government argued that the United Kingdom's past poor industrial record was partly due to the intervention of government. They therefore argued, for example, for a reduction in the role of the Department of Trade and Industry. But at the same they criticised other governments for adopting a more active role towards their industrial sectors. If government industrial policy only operated to the detriment of any country's industrial sector, why should their competitors be concerned about it? Clearly this is not the case. The question is, then, what form should policy take?

There are no quick and easy answers. The decline of the United Kingdom's international competitive position has occurred over many years and the road to recovery will be long. The length of the decline suggests that fundamental changes are required in the economic environment within which traditional industrial policy is determined. For example, the relationship between the financial and the industrial sectors might be restructured in a similar form to that in Japan and Germany. Re-industrialisation, which is what is needed, demands a more actively managed economy, requires an active government role and should involve more co-operation and co-ordination between those firms operating in the sector. This implies that neither the neo-classical nor the Austrian schools should exclusively provide the basis for policy, and that it should be a product of pragmatism not dogmatism. Pragmatism combined with a clear set of objectives should ensure a consistency of policy, together with the necessary flexibility required in a rapidly changing world economy.

If the necessary structural changes to the overall economic environment are made, the policies adopted in the traditional areas of industrial policy are less critical. For it is not clear that competition and regional policy have ever made significant contributions to the United Kingdom's international competitiveness. Also, membership of the European Community and the GATT will increasingly restrict the scope for any United Kingdom government to employ nurturing or protective policies towards its domestic industries. Lastly, the one policy area which can contribute to a long-run improvement in international competitiveness, if the regulatory framework allows, is that of promotion of R&D. This may require the adoption of a supportive policy to all R&D, in the form of tax concessions, grants, loans or the purchase of equity capital, or a change in patent law, or could involve the targeting of specific industries which are judged by all participants in the industrial sector to be the future global growth markets.

In conclusion, industrial policy should take cognisance of the relationships set out in section 8.4, and should comprise a set of non-conflicting policies which are a response to a clear and consistent set of objectives, of which the most important should be the improvement of the United Kingdom's international competitive position.

Questions for discussion

1. What is industrial policy? Describe the main areas of policy and a number of specific policies used within each of those areas.
2. Does the United Kingdom have an international competitiveness problem? If so, what are its causes?
3. What are the problems to be encountered in the determination and the implementation of an effective industrial policy?
4. Outline the principal elements of UK competition policy.
5. Describe the two main theoretical approaches to industrial policy.
6. How effective has industrial policy been over the last decade?

References and suggestions for further reading

Audretsch, D. B. (1989), *The Market and the State*, Hemel Hempstead: Harvester Wheatsheaf.

Bayliss, B. T. and A. M. El-Agraa (1990), 'Competition and industrial policies with emphasis on competition policy', in A. M. El-Agraa (ed.), *Economics of the European Community*, Hemel Hempstead: Philip Allan.

Curzon Price, V. (1990), 'Competition and industrial policies with emphasis on industrial policy', in A. M. El-Agraa (ed.), *Economics of the European Community*, Hemel Hempstead: Philip Allan.

Foreman-Peck, J. (1991), 'Trade and the balance of payments', in N. F. R. Crafts and N. Woodward (eds), *British Economy since 1945*, Oxford: Oxford University Press.

Hartley, K. and N. Hooper (1990), 'Industry and policy', in P. Curwen (ed.), *Understanding the UK Economy*, Basingstoke: Macmillan.

Hay, D. A. and D. J. Morris (1991), *Industrial Economics and Organization: Theory and evidence*, Oxford: Oxford University Press.

HMSO (1992), *Science and Technology Issues, A Review by ACOST*, London.

Johnson, C. (1991), *The Economy under Mrs. Thatcher 1979–1990*, Harmondsworth: Penguin.

OECD (1990), *Industrial Policy in OECD Countries*, Paris: Organisation for Economic Co-operation and Development.

Office of Fair Trading (1990), *An Outline of United Kingdom Competition Policy*, London: HMSO.

Peacock, A. and G. Bannock (1991), *Corporate Takeovers and the Public Interest*, Aberdeen: Aberdeen University Press.

Walshe, J. G. (1991), 'Industrial organization and competition policy', in N. F. R. Crafts and N. Woodward (eds), *The British Economy since 1945*, Oxford: Clarendon Press.

Chapter 9

The role of services in the economy

PATRICK O'FARRELL

9.1 Introduction

Services are embodied in all products of an economy, whether these supply the needs of producers or, as they ultimately must, of consumers. Service activities are implicated in every process of economic change whether of restructuring, growth or decline, at local, national and international level; yet they have been seriously neglected by economists. This is partly because many economists treat services as a residual, analogous to the 'non-production' functions of extractive and manufacturing firms. Such a view of services is misleading, since many are involved with material processing and the quality of such services directly influences the competitiveness of production (Marshall, 1988; O'Farrell and Hitchens, 1990). Any satisfactory definition must illuminate the economic role of all services, whether they are producer- or consumer-oriented, in the private or public sector, or concerned with handling information or materials (Wood, 1990, p. 4).

The chapter will review alternative classification schemes for service activities, including the economics approach and the market-based approach. The basic characteristics of services – intangibility, durability, interchangeability and interaction between customer and supplier – which are alleged to differentiate them from manufactured goods, are then outlined. The chapter then considers the fundamental issue of whether services are a prime mover in economic growth, whether they can exist without prior goods production, or whether services must always be dependent upon goods production. Subsequently we examine the problem of measuring service productivity; technology and restructuring in services, the empirical evidence on growth and decline of services in the United Kingdom and the location of business service growth. Finally the policy response to the growth of service activities is considered.

9.2 Alternative taxonomies of services

While there is not a complete consensus on the definition of services, most authorities consider the services sector to include all economic activities whose output (a) is not a product or construction; (b) is generally consumed at the time it is produced; and (c) provides added value in forms (such as convenience, assurance, comfort, knowledge or health) that are essentially intangible concerns of the purchaser. A key characteristic of services is that they offer the expertise necessary to support other economic activities. This expertise may take a wide variety of forms: knowledge of financial markets, research and development in manufacturing, maintenance and repair services, marketing skills, provision for leisure or support for educational and health needs. This view of services is demand-oriented, stressing the worth of materials handling or information services to other production or consumption activities (Marshall *et al.*, 1987).

However, in order to analyse services in a meaningful way it is useful to distinguish between different categories of services. One important category is those service activities which primarily handle information or data, e.g. research and development, management consultancy or marketing. Another important distinction is between the two main types of function that services perform. These are: producer (or intermediate) services which provide output which is consumed or used by other industries, e.g. accountancy or market research; and consumer services which produce output direct to consumers or households, e.g. retailing, hotels, cinemas, etc. A further distinction is between basic and non-basic (induced) services. Basic services are oriented to national and international markets and may provide a substantial net balance of payments contribution to a region or country. They are also able to generate self-sustaining growth independent of a particular locality and to yield significant multiplier effects. Other bipolar classifications which may be made between services are privately and publicly provided services and, related to this, marketed and non-marketed services.

9.2.1 The economics approach

The notion that the service sector is primarily dependent upon the demands of the 'wealth'-creating manufacturing goods sector for its prosperity, and that it is the non-basic component of the national or regional economy incapable of autonomous growth, dates from the thinking of Adam Smith. He distinguished between 'productive' and 'unproductive' labour: 'the labour of a manufacturer adds generally to the value of the materials which he works upon. ... The labour of a menial servant, on the other hand, adds to the value of nothing' (Smith, 1776 [1970], p. 430). In Smith's classification, not only menial servants were unproductive but also the sovereign, the army and navy, churchmen, lawyers, physicians and men of letters of all kinds. 'Like the declamation of the actor, the harangue of the orator, or the tune of the musicians, the work of all of them perishes in the instant of its production' (*ibid.*, p. 431). Hence, Smith made tangibility, with its associated quality of durability of the economic activity, the criterion of productiveness (O'Farrell and Hitchens, 1990, p. 164). It was Smith's disciple, J. B. Say, who realised Smith's error and who accepted that 'the professor, the doctor and the actor had claims to be regarded as producers' (Gide and Rist, 1948, p. 35). Despite Alfred Marshall's (1961, p. ix) dictum to the effect that 'there is not in real life a clear line of division between labour that is or is not productive', much of the conventional thinking on the subject of goods and services is based on the assumption of a clear-cut distinction between the two.

The taxonomy most widely used by economists and statisticians is reflected in the Standard Industrial Classification (SIC) (revised 1980) which classifies services by exclusion; they are not agriculture, mining, manufacturing or construction (see Table 9.1). Such an approach to taxonomy has severe limitations and inevitably throws up anomalies: e.g. there is no logical rationale for the inclusion of printing within manufacturing and computer software within services. Part of the confusion arises from the practice of defining services by listing industries rather than by trying to articulate the essence of service activity that all such industries still share.

The SIC classifies employment by industrial sector – i.e. the eventual product – irrespective of the nature of the particular job. The industrial classification of mechanical engineering, therefore, includes lawyers, typists and accountants. Indeed more than one-third of those employed in manufacturing industries are in service occupations, while almost one-fifth of those employed in service industries hold manual jobs. Conventional economic explanations of the rise of service employment (Clark, 1940) draw to a large degree on the 'sector theories' of economic development which explain the growing prominence of service sector employment in terms of changes in business demand and labour productivity. In this view, as consumer incomes rise, more discretionary spending occurs on higher-value goods and quasi-luxury consumer services. Production becomes more technically and organisationally complex to service these needs, and depends critically on high quality research and development and more advanced educational and training programmes (Greeenfield, 1966; Gershuny and Miles, 1983). The proportion of workers employed in the actual process of material transformation declines, however, as more capital-intensive methods are introduced, while the share of employment in services increases, not only because of increased demand, but also because their 'personal' character limits the application of capital equipment. These

Table 9.1 Employees in employment in Great Britain, 1981 and 1991 (thousands)

Industry	Division Class Group	1981	1991	Percentage change 1981–91
Distribution, hotels and catering; repairs	6	4113	4578	11.3
Wholesale distribution	61	840	918.7	9.4
Retail distribution	64/65	2060	2191.9	6.4
Hotels and catering	66	938	1199.7	27.9
Repair of consumer goods and vehicles	67	238	213	−10.5
Transport and communication	7	1406	1322.8	−5.9
Banking, finance and insurance, etc.	8	1724	2625.0	52.3
Banking and finance	81	478	615	28.7
Insurance, except social security	82	225	268.6	19.4
Business services	83	831	1488.9	79.2
Renting of movables	84	91	120.1	33.1
Owning and dealing in real estate	85	98	132.5	35.2
Other services	9	5846	6695.7	14.5
Public administration and defence	91	1505	1527.3	1.5
Sanitary services	92	280	375.4	34.1
Education	93	1492	1740.8	16.7
Research and development	94	121	93.3	−22.9
Medical and other health services	95	1285	1421.5	10.6
Other services	96	552	888.5	60.9
Recreational and cultural services	97	430	454.7	5.7
Personal services	98	180	194.2	7.9
Agricultural, forestry and fishing	0	370	260.4	−29.6
Energy and water supply	1	682	440.3	−35.4
Manufacturing industries	2–4	5932	4845.6	−18.3
Construction	5	1074	989.4	−7.9
All industries and services	0–9	21 148	21 764	2.9
All service industries	6–9	13 090	15 228.3	16.3

Source: Employment Gazette, December 1983 and October 1991.

trends and a world expansion of markets are accompanied by an increasing domination of business by large, frequently multi-national firms.

9.2.2 Market-based approaches

The sectoral definitions widely employed by economists do not take account of the different markets served by service industries (Marshall *et al.* 1987, p. 577). Services may be distinguished not only on the basis of their ownership (public or private), markets (final consumers or producers) and product characteristics (material or ephemeral) but also in terms of their commodification (market or non-market provision), the function performed (services for people, goods or money), and the quality of the exchange. However, focusing solely upon service industries plays down the extent to which services and other sectors are interdependent and the fact that many occupations within production perform service functions. The distinction between goods and services is not primarily a matter of the nature of the product, nor even the type of expertise offered; the main economic distinctions that separate different services are concerned with the types of markets served (Marshall *et al.*, 1987, p. 578).

9.2.3   The nature of services

An alternative approach to the definitional problems of services is to categorise services according to several characteristics which are alleged to differentiate them from manufactured goods: intangibility, durability, interchangeability and interaction between customer and supplier.

Tangibility. Many authors argue that intangibility is both the only characteristic common to all services and the factor that best distinguishes them from immaterial goods. What is immaterial in services is the performance of the service itself as opposed to the person doing it, any materials used or the good to which a service is attached. There is limited usefulness in distinguishing between companies according to whether they produce goods or services; it may be more useful to distinguish between tangibles and intangibles (Levitt, 1981). All products, whether they are manufactured goods or services, possess some degree of intangibility. Hence, it is useful to define a continuum of intangibility ranging from highly intangible products such as films, insurance or travel at one end to highly tangible ones such as cars, milling machines or face cream at the other (O'Farrell and Hitchens, 1990, p. 166). However, even the apparently most tangible products, such as a lathe or a washing machine, possess intangible features such as delivering it on time, installation, training in correct operation, servicing, repair and maintenance work, which are crucial to the product's successful operation. This emphasises the inability to measure properly the service content of the final output of manufactured goods.

Durability. Durability is a characteristic which has been used to distinguish goods from services; but, as in the case of tangibility, it does not clearly discriminate between them. Much depends on the time span used as the demarcation between perishable, semi-durable and durable. Routine office cleaning, for example, may be classified as a perishable producer service since the premises must be recleaned within a short space of time.

In the semi-durable category, Greenfield (1966, p. 9) placed advertising services concerned with sales promotion; and among durable producer services he classified services concerned with the strategic direction of the firm, such as those provided by management consultancy firms and R&D projects. A strategic business plan, market research report, computer software, the contract of a solicitor or the music written by a composer may all have much longer lives than many so-called durable manufactured goods. Hence the concept of durability is not confined to services and is not a valid discriminator between services and manufactured goods.

Interchangeability of goods and services. Services are directly interchangeable with manufactures in a variety of situations. Few customers care whether a refrigerator manufacturer implements a particular feature through a hardware circuit or by internal software. New computer-aided design can substitute for design equipment; while improved transportation or distribution services can lower a manufacturer's costs as effectively as cutting direct labour or material inputs. Even more fundamentally, products themselves are only physical embodiments of the services they deliver (Quinn, 1988, p. 20). A disk delivers a software program or data set; a car delivers a service, transport; electrical appliances deliver entertainment, dishwashing, clothes washing and drying, cooking and food storage – all services. Most products, therefore, provide a convenient or less costly form in which to purchase services.

Interaction. A fundamental weakness of many studies in the past is that they have assumed that services perform separate functions from production and consumption. Yet the distinguishing characteristic of service output is that it is primarily a process or activity that produces changes in persons or the goods they possess (Riddle, 1986, p. 11). A primary feature of service production is the complexity of the relationship that exists between the producer and the customer, of which there are three general types: (1) the producer may provide services in isolation from the customer, as is the case in many professional services; (2) the customer may self-serve, using equipment and/or procedures arranged and maintained by the producer (e.g. leasing a photocopying machine); and (3) the producer and the customer may produce the service in interaction with one another so that the latter affects its performance and quality. Frequently the buyer and seller have to come together to create the service, as in the cases of a haircut, medical consultation, dental treatment or installation of a quality control (QC) system in a manufacturing company. In such instances the quality of the QC system will be greatly facilitated by a clear definition of needs by the firm's management. Therefore, the quality of many services depends not only upon the performance of the supplier, but also on how well the customer performs in interaction with the supplier (O'Farrell and Moffat, 1991). This highlights another important difference between services and manufacturing: namely that the service product is not considered to be output unless it is sold; in other words there must be consumer participation and, inevitably, simultaneity of supply and demand.

9.3   The primacy of goods production or a key role for producer services?

9.3.1   The role of services in development

Does the apparent increased domination by services of employment in late twentieth-century developed economies imply that services are less capable of triggering productivity gains, technological advances, tradable exports and inter-industry multipliers than are manufacturing industries? Can services be considered 'basic', to be a prime mover and exist without prior goods production, or must services always follow and be dependent upon goods production? Do services play a peripheral, or supportive, role *vis-à-vis* goods production, or do they lie at the heart of any economy and provide the facilitative milieu in which other, especially market-oriented, production activities, become possible? We shall consider this question by examining the role of services in production and then the issue of productivity in services.

First, many services, such as medical, legal, entertainment, banking, consultancy and education do not necessitate prior goods production. Such service activities require that there be income for individuals to buy the services; the source of that income can be either a goods or a services producing industry, or other income such as rent, interest, savings or dividends. Second, the status of many services as intermediate inputs into industrial production has long been recognised. A substantial proportion of what is characterised as the service sector – distribution, transport, utilities, business or producer and many government services – is linked to an evolving division of labour within primary and secondary industries. Data for the United Kingdom, Australia, Canada and the United States in the 1970s showed that one-third (22–38 per cent) of tertiary sector output (share of GDP) took the form of intermediate services to the 'productive' sectors (Gershuny and Miles, 1983, p. 30). More recently, the OECD analysed GDP data for eight member countries by classifying services (i.e. excluding 'goods' and 'government') into those 'directly linked to goods production', those which 'are a necessary adjunct to the process of producing goods', and 'free-standing services' which are 'bought by households in their capacity as final consumers' (Blade, 1987, pp. 164–5). It was found that on average production-related services contributed 25 per cent of GDP and 'free-standing services' 20 per cent. Another analysis of input–output data from seven OECD countries showed that over 50 per cent of output, on average, of transport, communications, banking and insurance, and 'services to firms' industries goes to intermediate consumption, that is to enterprises, as does 25 per cent of distribution and 'various' other services output.

Other studies have also demonstrated the vital function of services within manufacturing: approximately 75 per cent of the total value added in the US goods sector is created by service activities within that sector (Quinn and Gagnon, 1986, p. 101). About 25 per cent of US GNP was accounted for (in 1980) by services used as inputs by goods-producing industries – more than the total value added to GNP by the manufacturing sector (Riddle, 1986, p. 21). Indeed service occupations have been expanding within manufacturing industry as part of ever-lengthening production sequences necessary to conceive, plan, enable, supervise, produce and maintain the production and distribution of goods. The ability to compete for many firms – both manufacturing and service – is increasingly dependent on the quality of knowledge (information services) at the disposal of management. There has been a rapid increase in demand for advice and information on merger and takeover options, portfolio investments, product design, computer-aided manufacturing systems, quality control, commercial and international law, market research, corporate strategy and advertising. To an increasing degree, therefore, it is the services end of the production chain – design, research, quality, style, marketing, delivery, packaging, and advertising – which determines the competitiveness of agricultural and manufacturing investment. Services are responsible for a growing share of value added to products. Such service provision may be organised and supplied hierarchically from within the firm, as inputs purchased externally on the market, or as downstream external services once the product leaves the factory. Furthermore, government funding of transport, communications and utilities infrastructure, advisory and trade promotion organisations, regional development agencies and training are evidence of the critical role of the state in supplying support services to production. All the evidence therefore points to manufacturing, other service firms and the public sector being important sources of demand for service inputs.

There are two patterns which appear at odds with the notion of services being intermediate inputs to goods production: first, all service groups serve both intermediate and final demand markets: second, a substantial volume of transactions is generated within and between service industries themselves such as links between financial institutions and legal and accountancy services, or between advertising agencies, market consultants and other service firms. In the United Kingdom more of the output from producer service industries goes to other services (22 per cent) than to manufacturing (18 per cent) (Marshall et al., 1987 p. 588). This reinforces the point that some components of producer services have market outlets that either are independent of manufacturing, or embrace both the producer and consumer service sectors (e.g. hotel, travel, banking, legal, consultancy and insurance service companies). Hence, the diversity of services has led to an awareness that the role and contribution of services to production is both more extensive and more complex than previously supposed.

The traditional relationship of manufacturing 'demand' determining service 'supply' is no longer applicable for important parts of the two sectors because of various interdependencies between them. Furthermore, there are circumstances where the demand from services had led manufacturing investment. Many goods-producing industries manufacture items such as printing, computer systems and information technology (IT) that are inputs to service industries, i.e. services are the prime movers. Also technological breakthroughs in certain services have stimulated the expansion of important manufacturing industries, as for example with research and development (scientific instruments), health care (medical equipment) and information processing (typewriters, photocopiers, computers). Similarly the transformation of the form of provision and consumption of some services has led to major surges in demand for a variety of goods such as household appliances, leisure equipment and home improvement supplies. This reflects a move towards the self-service economy where rising costs of labour services have encouraged households to substitute goods for paid services. There is no basis for the belief that goods production is more necessary to an economy, more income-generating, or more wealth-enhancing than services. Therefore, it is argued that the conventional economist's sectoral view of the economy needs to be rethought because it encourages an artificial distinction between goods and services.

Producer services are at the leading edge of the growth in service employment, and are central to the economic base of a nation. The key to the dynamics of service growth and uneven spatial development lies in growing intermediate demands for services, frequently operating at an international scale. Indeed, services can be an important element of international trade. First, manufactured exports contain a high proportion of value added due to service inputs, although the service is classified to the manufacturing sector. Second, analysis of input–output data for OECD countries by Petit (1986, p. 123) revealed that direct foreign trade accounts on average for 8 per cent of service output. Although trade in services is very difficult to measure accurately, most experts agree that the total volume of services trade is underestimated. One feature of services trade is that most of the facilities and jobs created by services exports are in the user country, e.g. banks, hotels, retail stores, consultancy firms, advertising agencies. Unlike manufacturers, fewer services are produced in the parent country and exported across borders. In contrast to manufacturing exports, services trade data frequently recognise only the fees or profit margins that services companies can repatriate – a small fraction of their total transactions value.

9.3.2 Productivity

Productivity in services is notoriously difficult to measure because of the problems of defining output units and quality differences in services. For example, how does one evaluate the productivity of a medical surgeon who increases the number of operations performed per day from six to twelve but with substantially increased risk to the health of patients? Is the number of letters delivered per postal worker a meaningful productivity measure if more letters are late or lost? Can a university professor be assumed to have enhanced productivity if he or she has increased the number of research papers published per annum but at a cost in terms of quality? What use are standard economic productivity measures which assume that output value is only equal to its cost?

Investment in new technology by many services has grown markedly with financial services, retailers, distribution and the health sector among the leaders. As workers master new technologies they frequently discover new applications not envisaged in the original investment. Barras (1986) showed services sector productivity in the British economy growing at 2.9 per cent annually (based on the real value of output per employee) from 1960 to 1981, whereas manufacturing productivity grew at less than 1 per cent on the same basis. The primary causes of this phenomenon were (a) the continued demand growth in services, which led to (b) both capital deepening in services and improved capital quality (output gain per unit of invested capital) within services. The analysis of Barras (1986) suggests that the shift to services has not been an important factor in the slowdown of British national productivity growth.

When services are delivered to manufacturing or other service clients by a business service firm such as a management consultant, how should productivity be evaluated? First, it could be measured according to the number and quality of reports produced per annum; or, second, by the number of clients served. Third, we argue that their economic contribution, at any stage of production, can be measured only in relation to the benefits they bestow, directly or indirectly, on these other activities. The value of service inputs to customers depends on how these are combined with other inputs. This requires a 'total factor productivity' approach to assessing the economic contribution of services to other sectors. This might be assessed by the impact of the service delivered upon the productivity and competitiveness of the client organisations (O'Farrell and Hitchens, 1990, p. 168). This latter is the more meaningful criterion, that is in terms of the effectiveness of the service as viewed from the perspective of the client. In this light the notion of a distinct 'service sector' is misleading as is that of a manufacturing sector (Wood, 1990 p. 5). Any understanding of services must be based on the reality of economic interdependence.

9.4   Technology and restructuring in services

New technologies have substantially improved performance in many service industries. Jet aircraft made long-haul passage and freight movement efficient. New diagnostics, life support systems and surgical procedures have revolutionised medical practice. New loading, refriger-ation and handling techniques have facilitated an expansion of inter-national trade. Electronics information and communication technologies have been widely adopted in the retailing and wholesale trade, engineering design, financial services, communications and entertainment. Such new technologies permit firms to realise new economies of scale and scope. Thus banks, airlines and retailers use their networks to extend into a range of new activities.

The advent of new technology, the internationalisation of markets, increasing cost pressures and trends towards growing concentration via mergers and acquisitions mean that many service sectors are experiencing the type of major restructuring that manufacturing has undergone since the late 1960s. The conventional view of services is that, in contrast to most sectors of modern manufacturing, many parts have until recently been characterised by low concentration ratios due to the ease of entry, which leads to the domination of the industry by large numbers of very small enterprises. This is particularly the case in retailing and other consumer and personal services. But this situation is changing: such evidence as exists appears to show that in most service sectors the concentration ratios are steadily rising (Howells and Green, 1986). In fact, many of the world's largest companies are service enterprises – in hotels, leisure, retailing and financial services, for example. Service multi-nationals with interests in different service sectors have emerged, as well as companies involved in both manufacturing and services. In fact, the growth of multi-site and multi-national service enterprises is helping – along with the similar trends that occur in other sectors of the economy – to integrate regional and sub-regional economies increasingly into the world economic system.

Accountancy provides an example of a business service sector which has undergone substantial organisational change. Twenty years of rapid structural change following the Second World War, largely involving mergers and acquisition, has resulted in a polarisation of the industry between a very small number of large companies and a vast number of very small practices, with medium-size operations being squeezed out. Internationalisation of the profession over this period has resulted in both the United Kingdom and world markets being dominated by 'the big six' firms which in 1981 audited 493 of the world's top 500 companies.

Retailing is another sector in which concentration is rising and technical changes, combined with cost and competitive pressures, are leading to locational changes. Many of the most famous high-street names are now international operators subject to the great competitive pressures that entails. Large multiple retailers now account for over 50 per cent of retail sales in the United Kingdom, while single-outlet retailers have around 30 per cent of the market (Howells and Green, 1986). The market share of the multiples continues to rise both in the United Kingdom and other EC countries. Among the multiple chains there is a move towards non-central stores with greater floorspace, with adverse effects on the 'corner shop'. New technology is providing major opportunities for increased productivity, both in terms of the automation of the check-out operation and the way in which this is linked to improved stock control. The move towards greater sensitivity to consumer demand which this allows is accompanied by a centralisation of distribution facilities which would be impossible without computerisation.

9.5 Growth and decline in the service sector

9.5.1 Sectoral divisions

Growing labour market imbalances, which became apparent in the mid-1970s and which have persisted during the 1980s, have resulted in considerable interest in recent years by politicians, policy-makers and academic researchers in the nature of the job generation process. Attention is turning to the service sector as the major source of new jobs and the only one which appears to offer large-scale employment growth potential. The data in Table 9.1 show that overall employment in Great Britain expanded by 2.9 per cent between 1981 and 1991 but that there were considerable between-sector differences in employment change. Manufacturing employment fell by 18 per cent (1 086 000 jobs) while agricultural employment declined by 30 per cent, construction by 8 per cent and energy and water supply by 35 per cent. Within the major service industry divisions, transport and communications employment fell by 6 per cent but all other groups expanded: distribution, hotels and catering by 11 per cent; banking, finance and insurance by 52 per cent; and other services by 15 per cent. All services (divisions 6–9) created 2.138 million net new jobs between 1981 and 1991, and the proportion of people employed in services rose from 62 per cent to 70 per cent. Within services the greatest growth was recorded by business services with a net increase of 79 per cent or 658 000 jobs between 1981 and 1991. Other service industries recording high rates of employment growth between 1981 and 1991 include owning and dealing in real estate (35 per cent), renting of movables (33 per cent), sanitary services (34 per cent), banking and finance (29 per cent) and insurance (19 per cent).

9.5.2 The location of business services

Business services perform a crucial function as inputs to other industries in order to improve their competitiveness. Since many of these services must be performed in interaction with the clients, their location is important. The 'other business services' activity heading (8395) is an extremely dynamic sector in which employment expanded dramatically by 171 per cent between 1981 and 1989, a net increase of 228 428 jobs (Table 9.2). This SIC heading covers management consultants, market research and public relations consultants, document copying, duplicating and tabulating services, and other services 'primarily engaged in providing services to other enterprises' such as employment agencies, security services, debt collection, press agencies, freelance journalists, translators and typing services.

The most striking feature of Table 9.2 is of course the remarkable

Table 9.2 The regional distribution of other business service employment in the United Kingdom, 1981–9

| | Employment in other business services (8395) | | | | | |
| | 1981 | | 1989 | | Change 1981–9 | |
Region	No.	%	No.	%	No.	%
Greater London	54 477	40.9	133 940	37.0	+79 463	+146
Rest of South East	23 832	17.9	78 634	21.8	+54 802	+230
East Anglia	2 156	1.6	7 557	2.1	+5 401	+251
South West	5 621	4.2	20 132	5.6	+14 511	+258
East Midlands	4 151	3.1	13 639	3.8	+9 488	+229
West Midlands	11 299	8.5	23 630	6.5	+12 331	+109
North West	10 619	8.0	29 479	8.2	+18 860	+178
Yorkshire and Humberside	5 514	4.1	17 852	4.9	+12 338	+224
North	3 181	2.4	7 251	2.0	+4 070	+128
Wales	2 473	1.9	6 323	1.7	+3 850	+156
Scotland	8 269	6.2	20 289	5.6	+12 020	+145
Northern Ireland	1 630	1.2	2 924	0.8	+1 294	+79
United Kingdom	133 222	100.0	361 650	100.0	+228 428	+171

Note: Employment is in full-time equivalents, with part-time staff treated as 0.5 of full-time.
Source: Bryson *et al.*, 1991.

dominance of Greater London as far and away the greatest centre of information-based business service activity in the United Kingdom. By 1989, firms operating in London employed 134 000 workers, or 37 per cent of the national total (Bryson *et al.*, 1991, p. 11). No other city or county approached this concentration of activity. The next largest centre, Greater Manchester, accounted for only 17 000 jobs, one-eighth of London's total, with the West Midlands conurbation third with 15 000 (Bryson *et al.*, 1991, p. 14). Regionally, however, South East England outside London contains the second largest cluster of other business service employment, with nearly 80 000 jobs in 1989. The South East as a whole thus accounts for no less than 59 per cent of total United Kingdom employment in this sector. The very clear focus of information-based business services in Britain upon southern England is further highlighted by the fact that by 1989, South West England accounted for nearly as many jobs as Scotland, and substantially more than Wales, northern England and Northern Ireland combined. Trends in the growth of this sector during the 1980s have further reinforced this pattern. Thus Table 9.2 shows that between 1981 and 1989, the four fastest-growing regions were all in southern England (South West, East Anglia, Rest of South East and the East Midlands).

Conversely most northern and western regions – Scotland (+145 per cent), Wales (+156 per cent), the North (+128 per cent) and Northern Ireland (+79 per cent) – recorded growth rates below the national average (+171 per cent). In volume terms, too, the South East dominated the national growth map, with an extra 134 000 jobs, or 59 per cent of the net national growth. Hence, the north–south divide in other business services widened appreciably between 1981 and 1989. However, the rate of employment growth in London was actually below the national average, while that in two northern regions – the North West and Yorkshire and Humberside – was above it. This is partly due to a relative de-centralisation of business service firms from London into the South East, with relative (but not absolute) losses in London and relative (and absolute) gains in the South East outside London (O'Farrell and Hitchens, 1990, p. 146).

The concentration of business services in major metropolitan regions is related both to the international operation of many service activities, their customers, and the positive impact of associated corporate head offices on a network of related specialist suppliers of expertise. Other parts of the country, however, rely heavily upon the contracting-out of service activities by a manufacturing sector facing stiff international competition. Not surprisingly, the restructuring of service companies in response to such shifts in demand, including diversification into new growing markets and strategies of specialisation on core businesses, seem to favour metropolitan regions, with the resulting growth of high-income professional occupations supporting a range of leisure, recreation and retail services.

9.5.3   Towards a service economy?

Since 70 per cent of British employment in 1991 is in services, this raises the question as to whether government should intervene to dampen the trend towards a services economy. Frequently concern is expressed about the decline of the manufacturing sector in the United Kingdom, that the economy cannot endure as just a services producing economy and that only manufacturing represents the creation of 'real' wealth. Those who advocate policies to counter the process of 'de-industrialisation' have in mind a scenario of high-productivity factory workers being replaced by low-productivity fast-food restaurant employees, based on the simplistic notion that manufacturing creates more wealth than services. More generally the reasoning for this seems to be as follows: (a) the production of goods generates more income than the production of services; (b) the production of services can take place only after the demands for goods have been satisfied; and (c) the country cannot survive – especially in international trade – by producing only services. Is the economy better off because a consumer spends £100 on golf clubs rather than £100 on green fees – the former being goods, the latter services? This seems doubtful since the goods purchased are less likely to be 100 per cent domestic value added than the service.

The notion that goods production is more income generating than services may be linked to the presumption that investment may be more wealth enhancing than current consumption. This would be true of buildings, machine tools or construction machinery – investment goods that can be more wealth-enhancing to the economy than can the production of many specific services. However, many other goods (e.g. processed foods, newspapers, soft drinks, ice cream) are current consumption items. By contrast, education – a major service industry – enjoys the greatest long-term, wealth-producing potential of any industry. An economy could survive and prosper, in theory, producing only services – if that economy's competitive advantages were in the production of services. Hence, the arguments typically advanced for considering service industries as inferior to goods-producing industries seem to have little validity. Yet the concern over the declining manufacturing base in the United Kingdom cannot be dissociated from the apprehension about the rise of services. There is no case for advocating a stronger shift to services or for retarding that shift in some arbitrary way. Government policy should aim at raising productivity throughout the economy, no less in services than in manufacturing. However, as we shall see in the next section, UK industrial policy is predicated on the assumption that goods production is more important than services.

9.6 Services policy

9.6.1 Office dispersal

The response of industrial policy to the growth of service activities has been limited. Policy-makers have largely ignored the potential contribution of the sector to economic development due to a perception of services being dependent upon manufacturing. Regional policy has been in operation since 1934 yet only in the last twenty years has the government introduced measures for services. Regional policy was based on influencing the inter-regional movement of mobile manufacturing industry through provision of factories, industrial estates and later loans and grants in the Development Areas, and through floorspace controls in the congested areas, particularly the South East and Midlands.

In the early 1960s the first policy measures towards service activities were introduced – Office Development Permits (ODP) and the formation of the Location of Offices Bureau (LOB) in 1964 – initiatives prompted as much by increasing congestion in central London as the needs of the regions for office employment (McCrone, 1968). The Office Industry Development Act applied initially to London and the West Midlands conurbation and required all office developments over 3000 square feet to apply for an ODP. Permits were only granted where it could be demonstrated that there was a need for a central area location, that no other suitable accommodation was available and that the development was 'in the public interest'. In 1966 the controls were extended to the whole of the South East, the West Midlands, the East Midlands and East Anglia; but after 1969 the exemption limit was raised to 10 000 square feet (Marshall, 1988, p. 206). The Conservative government in 1979 abolished both the ODP system and the LOB.

The implementation of the office dispersal policy was not very successful since it was based on a considerable overestimate of the growth of office employment in central London. From 1965 to 1976, almost 28 million square feet of office floorspace was prohibited in central London under the ODP system, approximately 30 per cent of the floorspace applied for (Alexander, 1979). Nevertheless between 1966 and 1977 some 145 000 private sector jobs were diverted out of central London (Alexander, 1979). Much of this movement took place over short distances, usually to other parts of the South East. Of the 70 000 jobs de-centralised between 1963 and 1970, only about 1 per cent actually moved to the Development Areas.

9.6.2   Government office relocation

In parallel with the government's policy to redistribute private sector office employment, attempts were made to relocate public administration from London. Between 1963 and 1972 some 23 500 civil service jobs were dispersed from central London (Marshall, 1988, p. 208). This policy was more beneficial to Assisted Areas than the de-centralisation of private sector office jobs, since over 50 per cent were moved to problem regions, notably Scotland, Wales, the North, and the North West. Much of the relocation undertaken involved clerical back-office jobs; the high-quality headquarter posts remained in London.

   In a new phase of relocation policy, the government decided in 1974 to relocate 31 000 civil service jobs outside London over a decade. Some 90 per cent of these jobs were to go to the Assisted Areas: Glasgow, Cardiff, Newport, Mersey and Teeside were the major beneficiaries. Although this programme still continues, a reduction in the projected number of relocated jobs, cutbacks in public expenditure since 1979 and opposition from civil service unions have all reduced the scale of the programme (Marshall, 1988, p. 205). Consequently, while almost 31 000 civil service jobs were dispersed from London between 1963 and 1983, more than one-third of civil service employment is still concentrated in the South East.

9.6.3   Policy instruments

In 1973 the government introduced special incentives – the Service Industry Removal Grants – which provided employee transfer grants of £800 in addition to grants providing rent relief for up to five years or to facilitate the purchase of premises (HMSO, 1974). Aid, however, was restricted to mobile projects (those with a choice of location) and those which created a minimum of ten jobs for transferred firms and twenty-five jobs for new start-ups in the Assisted Areas. Assistance for local services was excluded. Later a job creation grant was introduced providing £1500 per job in Special Development Areas and £1000 per job in Development Areas (HMSO, 1977). A final increase in the maximum levels for the job creation and employee removal grants to £8 000 and £2 000, respectively, took place in 1981. The policy was discontinued in 1984 and the job creation element of the scheme incorporated into the more general Regional Selective Assistance programmes, but the employee transfer grants were abolished. The number of awards made was relatively low and the assistance constituted only 1 per cent of regional aid in 1977 (Daniels, 1982). Since 1984 the pressures for de-centralisation have diminished and the concentration of business services, financial services, and information technology in London and the South East has increased.

9.6.4   Current policy

The election of a Conservative government in 1979 brought an immediate commitment to review the system of regional incentives. Following a series of spatial cutbacks in the extent of the Assisted Areas, a White Paper in 1983 proposed, *inter-alia*, 'less discrimination against service industries' (HMSO, 1983). A new regional policy was introduced in November 1984 involving a two-tier structure, a redrawn map of Assisted Areas, a new regional development grant (RDG) scheme placing more emphasis upon job creation, a cutback in expenditure and an extension of the eligibility of the service sector. Services qualified for the first time for automatic regional assistance and the eligibility criteria were broadened considerably to include a wide range of service activities (Table 9.3). In selecting the services for assistance the Department of Trade and Industry targeted 'industries with a choice of location', those which were of 'regional importance' and those which would have little displacement effect (i.e. which would not replace existing jobs). In the first year following the 1984 review, aid to services accounted for one-third of new RDG approved expenditure; but since then the scale of assistance to services has declined (Marshall, 1988, p. 213). Services were also eligible for aid under the Regional Selective Assistance (RSA) scheme assuming they satisfied the criteria of viability, proof of need, efficiency, employment benefit, own contribution to costs and exporting beyond the local area.

The most recent revision to regional policy occurred in March 1988, when the automatic RDG scheme was discontinued. The discretionary RSA scheme continues to be available in development areas and intermediate areas for both manufacturing and qualifying service projects. The changes also included an expansion of government assisted business advisory services available to both manufacturing and service companies which have fewer than 500 employees and wish to use private services in design, quality, marketing, manufacturing systems, business planning and financial and information systems. This Enterprise Initiative scheme involves subsidising the costs of consultancy services of between five and fifteen working days, with two-thirds of the cost paid for firms in assisted areas and half in non-assisted locations.

Regional aid is but one component of government assistance to industry which also incorporates nationalised industry support, competition policy, employment measures, innovation policy and sector-specific measures. Few schemes are specifically designed for services, the major exception being the computer services field. There is also a variety of schemes which

Table 9.3 The eligibility for regional policy assistance of producer services: 1984 scheme

Scheme	Service eligibility
Regional development grant	Data processing and software development
	Technical design, testing analysis, etc.
	Business services
	Management consultants
	Market research and public relations
	Exhibition contracting and organising
	Industrial research and development services
	Administration, headquarters
	Advertising agencies
	Industrial photographic services
	Venture capital providers
	Credit card companies
	Export houses
	Repair (except for consumer goods and vehicle repair)
	Value added network services
	Cable television
	Mail order houses and similar services provided direct to the public, e.g. football pools
	Freight forwarders
Regional Selective Assistance RSA grant Training in support of RSA Exchange risk cover	All producer services, unless more specific forms of assistance are available, e.g. for R&D projects
Government factories	All producer services, although eligibility is subject to job density minima per 1000 sq. ft (apart from Northern Ireland)

Source: Marshall (1988).

are not restricted to specific sectors; most of these are in the employment and training, export promotion and general business investment field.

9.6.5 The European Community and services policy

Thirty years after the enactment of the Treaty of Rome, barriers to intra-EC trade in services have finally begun to fall. The fragmentation of markets for services has been the result of a combination of two factors: the intrinsic nature of services and government regulations. Regulation plays a dominant role in most service industries. In the presence of market failures, regulation may be justified on grounds of efficiency. Three types of failures are relevant to service industries. First, imperfect competition prevails in many services: some industries are natural and/or public monopolies (e.g. the railways) and regulation may be required to prevent monopolistic abuse. Others tend to be oligopolistic (e.g. the banks). Second, the problem of imperfect information pervades many services, inviting government intervention in the form of occupational licensing and certification (e.g. accountancy, law and medicine). Third, negative externalities arise in certain service industries because of asymmetric information such as in financial services where failure of one institution may cause problems to others. This situation calls for regulation through licensing and certification.

In recent years government regulations have come under severe attack. It was argued that regulation, rather than acting in the public interest, tends to be captured by special groups seeking monopoly rents; and doubts were raised about the effectiveness of regulation as an instrument for correcting market failure. These criticisms contributed to the de-regulation movement which spread to Britain and throughout Europe in the 1980s. The attempts to open up service markets in Europe go back to the origin of the Community. The Treaty of Rome calls for 'restrictions on freedom to provide services within the Community [to] be progressively abolished during the transitional period' (Article 59) and for 'restrictions on the freedom of establishment . . . [to] be abolished by progressive stages in the course of the transitional period' (Article 52). Liberalisation of trade in services made no significant progress until the mid-1980s because of the high degree of government regulation and the disparity in regulatory regimes between member states. The 1985 Commission White Paper on Completing the Internal Market called for the principle of mutual recognition to be used as a lever for liberalising services trade. The decision to liberalise intra-EC services trade by 1992 was motivated by technological changes, regulatory changes in the United States and the worldwide efforts to liberalise services trade launched as part of the Uruguay Round of GATT negotiations.

Intensifying competition has been the key component of policy pursued by the Commission for completing the Internal Market in services. So far the emphasis has been upon de-regulation, i.e. introducing competition in markets hitherto subject to government regulation. As integration in service markets proceeds, another aspect of competition policy will become important: namely, tackling barriers to competition erected by companies themselves. Any regulation requires a careful prior assessment of the nature and degree of market failure. As a corollary, there is no single optimal degree of regulation that applies to all sectors. Furthermore, is the appropriate level of regulation local, national or Community-wide? The Commission tends only to assume regulatory responsibility at the EC level when it cannot be handled nationally, which raises questions about the appropriate division of regulatory power between the Community and its member states (an issue discussed in Chapter 7). Also, the issue of the balance between de-regulation to make EC markets more competitive and industrial policy to promote the competitiveness of EC firms did not arise in services until recently. The major emphasis has been upon a strict application of the rules of competition in order to eliminate barriers to intra-EC trade in services. Regulatory barriers to world trade have insulated EC firms from foreign corporations and thereby marginalised the question of competitiveness. There is a possible trade-off between competition and competitiveness. The creation of larger service firms through mergers or growth may be important in order to compete against US multinationals in some industries (e.g. air travel) but this would simultaneously stifle competition within the Community. The direction of future EC services policy remains uncertain.

9.7 Conclusions

There is growing evidence that some convergence between manufactured goods and services is taking place; products are ultimately the physical embodiments of the services they supply. The trends towards smaller batch sizes in manufacturing and increased customisation of products are features which make manufacturing more like services. Simultaneously some services (such as fast-food outlets and shuttle air services) are taking on production line characteristics and are, therefore, becoming more like manufacturing.

Economists have traditionally classified services by industry and occupation. The standard industrial classification, however, is flawed because it is not founded upon a satisfactory conceptualisation of the nature of service activities but is based upon the eventual product. It is important to note that the distinction between goods and services is not primarily a matter of the nature of the product, nor even the type of expertise offered; the main economic distinctions that separate different services are concerned with the types of markets served.

An alternative approach to the taxonomic problem of services is to categorise them according to several characteristics which are alleged to differentiate them from manufactured goods: tangibility, durability and interaction between supplier and customer. We have argued that intangibility is inadequate as a definition of services; it is preferable to classify goods and services according to a continuum of relative intangibility. Similarly durability does not clearly discriminate between goods and services; different degrees of perishability exist amongst both manufactured goods and services. The nature of the customer–seller interaction represents a more meaningful discriminator: the quality of many services depends not only on the performance of the supplier but also upon how well the consumer performs in interaction with the supplier. The definitional problems of services differ only in degree from those of manufacturing as a whole or for economic market states such as monopoly or market competition.

Productivity in services is notoriously difficult to measure because of the difficulty of defining output and quality differences. Barras (1986) demonstrated that services sector productivity in Britain grew at 2.9 per cent per annum from 1960 to 1981, whereas manufacturing productivity grew at less than 1 per cent. In the case of producer services which satisfy intermediate demand, we argue that productivity should be assessed by the impact of the service delivered upon the competitiveness of the client organisations.

The service sector (divisions 6–9) created 2.138 million net new jobs between 1981 and 1991 and the proportion of the United Kingdom population employed in services rose from 62 per cent to 70 per cent. Over the same period manufacturing employment declined by 1.086 million jobs (18 per cent). Within services the greatest increase was recorded by business services with a net increase of 79 per cent or 658 000 jobs between 1981 and 1991.

The long history of British government intervention in industry indicates a consistent bias towards the manufacturing sector. Financial incentives for services were not introduced until the 1960s, involved little job creation and a small share of regional aid. Moreover expenditure on regional policy has been substantially reduced. The major thrust of EC policy on services has been upon de-regulation, by introducing competition in markets hitherto subject to government regulation in order to eliminate barriers to intra-EC trade.

What about the longer-term prospects for growth based upon services? Because the utility of all products and services is created in the mind (i.e. a diamond, a Mozart opera, a Mercedes Benz, a Shakespeare play, a holiday in Italy, or a stylish hat may have little functional value relative to its high price) the growth of the services economy is limited only by the capacity of the mind to conceive of activities as having high utility (Quinn, 1988, p. 25). A safer, healthier, better-educated society may be considered to have higher welfare than one with more physical goods. Services such as education, art, music, literature, public health levels, scientific know-how, represent critical investments, yielding higher productivity and living standards both in the present and future.

Questions for discussion

1. Review the weaknesses of the Standard Industrial Classification as a system for classifying services.

2. Outline the major factors responsible for the rapid growth in service employment during the past twenty years.
3. Discuss the extent to which services may be conceptualised as a fundamental part of the 'wealth'-creating sector of the economy.
4. Should policy-makers be concerned about the increasing proportion of jobs in service industries and the simultaneous decline of manufacturing employment?

References and suggestions for further reading

Alexander, I. (1979), *Office Location and Public Policy*, London: Longman.

Barras, R. (1986), 'A comparison of embodied technical change in services and manufacturing industry', *Applied Economics*, 18, pp. 941–58.

Blade, D. (1987), *Goods and Services in OECD Economies*, Paris: OECD.

Bryson, J., D. E. Keeble and P. E. Wood (1991), 'The rise of small business service firms and regional development in the United Kingdom: some empirical findings and theoretical issues', paper presented to RESER Conference, Lyon, September.

Clark, C. A. (1940), *The Conditions of Economic Progress*, London: Macmillan.

Daniels, P. W. (1982), *Service Industries*, Cambridge: Cambridge University Press.

Daniels, P. W. (1989), 'Some perspectives on the geography of services', *Progress in Human Geography*, 13(3), pp. 427–33.

Gershuny, J. and I. D. Miles (1983), *The Service Economy: The transformation of employment in industrial societies*, New York: Praeger.

Gide, G. and C. Rist (1948), *A History of Economic Doctrines*, London: Harrap.

Greenfield, H. I. (1966), *Manpower and the Growth of Producer Services*, New York: Columbia University Press.

Guile, B. R. and J. B. Quinn (eds) (1988), *Technology in Services: Policies for growth, trade and employment*, Washington: National Academy Press.

HMSO (1974), *Industry Act 1972, Annual Report 1973–74*, London.

HMSO (1977), *Industry Act 1972, Annual Report 1976–77*, London

HMSO (1983), *Regional Industrial Development*, Cmnd 9111, London.

Howells, J. and A. E. Green (1986), 'Location technology and industrial organization in UK Services', *Progress in Planning*, 26, pp. 83–184.

Levitt, T. (1981), 'Marketing intangible products and product intangibles', *Harvard Business Review*, 59, pp. 54–102.

McCrone, G. (1968), *Regional Policy in Britain*, London: George Allen & Unwin.

Marshall, A. (1961), *Principles of Economics*, 9th edn, London: Macmillan.

Marshall, J. N. (ed.) (1988), *Services and Uneven Development*, Oxford: Oxford University Press.

Marshall, J. N., P. Damesick and P. Wood (1987), 'Understanding the location and role of producer services in the United Kingdom', *Environment and Planning A*, 19, pp. 575–93.

O'Farrell, P. N. and D. M. Hitchens (1990), 'Producer services and regional development: key conceptual issues of taxonomy and quality measurement', *Regional Studies*, 24, pp. 163–71.

O'Farrell, P. N. and L. A. R. Moffat (1991), 'An interaction model of business service production and consumption', *British Journal of Management*, 2, pp. 205–221.

Petit, P. (1986), *Slow Growth and the Service Economy*, New York: St Martins Press.

Quinn, J. B. (1988), 'Technology in services: past myths and future challenges', in
B. R. Guile and J. B. Quinn (eds), *Technology in Services: Past myths and future
challenges*, Washington: National Academy Press.

Quinn, J. B. and C. E. Gagnon (1986), 'Will services follow manufacturing into
decline?', *Harvard Business Review*, 86(6), pp. 95–106.

Riddle, D. I. (1986), *Service Led Growth: The role of the service sector in world
development*, New York: Praeger.

Smith, A. (1976 [1970]), *The Wealth of Nations*, edited by A. Skinner, Harmondsworth, Middlesex: Penguin.

Wood, P. (1990), 'An integrated view of the role of services', in R. Teare, L. Moutino
and N. Morgan (eds), *Managing and Marketing Services in the 1990s*, London:
Cassell Education.

Chapter 10

Privatisation

PAUL HARE

10.1 Introduction

Industries and enterprises in the United Kingdom were mainly national-ised in two waves. The first wave occurred in the late 1940s under the post-war Labour government, and most of the businesses nationalised then belonged to the public utilities: coal, electricity, public transport, gas. These were added to activities already in the public sector, such as the Post Office. The second wave of nationalisation also occurred under a Labour government, this time in the 1970s, and included a number of industrial firms which were considered important for the country's economy, but which for various reasons were failing to compete effectively in the domestic and external markets: among these were British Aerospace, British Shipbuilders, British Leyland (now, in its privatised form, the Rover Group) and the computer firm ICL. The industry with the most chequered history in this period was steel: for it was nationalised in the late 1940s, de-nationalised (we would now say 'privatised') in the 1950s and re-nationalised in the 1960s, only to be privatised once again in the 1980s.

In practically all these cases, nationalisation was seen as a solution to a problem. In the first wave of nationalisations, the problem usually had to do with the consequences of years of underinvestment and neglect, sometimes exacerbated by the controls which had been in force during the Second World War (1939–45). Later on, it appeared that the issue had more to do with the failure to compete successfully, associated with low innovation, cautious management and more aggressive marketing by firms in other countries. In any case, government ministers undoubtedly hoped that once they had brought certain firms into public ownership, and established new management structures for them, they would not be troubled further. As it turned out, this was a vain hope. There were several reasons for this, which need to be understood in order to appreciate the pressures which had built up by 1980 to put the whole process into reverse and embark on an increasingly ambitious programme of privatisation. Thus the reasons included the following:

1. The newly nationalised businesses required large amounts of investment for their modernisation, and had to compete for resources with other parts of the public sector.
2. The managers of the nationalised firms were not presented with clear commercial objectives.
3. The pressures to improve efficiency were sometimes very weak, due to the lack of effective competition and to the knowledge that bankruptcy would not be permitted even if financial performance was very poor.

These factors led to a number of attempts in the 1960s and 1970s to improve the management framework and financial accountability of the nationalised industries; and when these efforts were perceived to have failed, they contributed to the shift of opinion towards privatisation.

In the next section, I briefly review the attempts to establish a satisfactory management framework for the nationalised industries and look at some evidence on nationalised industry economic performance. Then section 10.3 surveys the 1980s privatisation programme, both in terms of what actually happened, and in terms of the new forms of competition and/or regulation which emerged. This provides the background to the final section, 10.4, which considers what remains to be privatised, remarks on some of the lessons from the 1980s experience and considers privatisation policy options for the 1990s.

10.2 Management of nationalised industries and firms

Most state sector businesses in the United Kingdom were set up as public corporations.[1] Organisationally, these were joint stock companies with the state (in the form of the Treasury) being the sole (or in a few instances such as BP, the majority) shareholder. Each business had a responsible minister through whom reports to parliament would be made, and from whom came various directives and advice about the running of the firm or industry. In theory, the boards of the individual nationalised firms could decide on all operational matters for themselves, while they had to seek ministerial permission for strategic decisions concerning major investments. This 'division of labour' looks quite neat on paper, but worked badly in practice: the result was that ministers found themselves 'interfering' in many aspects of their firms' affairs, resulting in blurred responsibility for their ultimate performance.

A further complication was the lack of clear objectives for nationalised firms in the relevant statutes. Often they were enjoined to cover costs 'taking one year with another', or to pay attention to certain social objectives, while general commercial criteria (such as seeking higher profits) or efficiency goals (like raising productivity in a given period) received less emphasis. Moreover, in the public mind many of the nationalised industries were perceived as providing an essential service, in which profit-making was popularly regarded as undesirable. One consequence of this attitude, apparent in much of the popular reporting about present and former nationalised industries and firms, is that they could expect to be criticised more or less whatever their financial performance. If they made losses, this represented an unacceptable drain on the public purse, while if they made significant profits they were considered to be profiteering (even when the net return on capital employed was rather low compared to the private sector norms).

To establish some sort of order in the relationships between nationalised industries and firms and their supervising ministries, the government published White Papers on the topic in 1961, 1967 and finally in 1978 (HM Treasury, 1961, 1967, 1978). These had to deal with three tasks: establishing a proper financial framework for the sector, and making recommendations about both pricing rules and investment criteria. In the theoretical literature on public sector production the latter two concerns have attracted most of the attention, with well-known arguments for marginal cost pricing, and for investment based on the net present value approach using a discount rate suitable for public sector projects (see Webb, 1973).

Given their importance, these arguments are worth reviewing briefly,

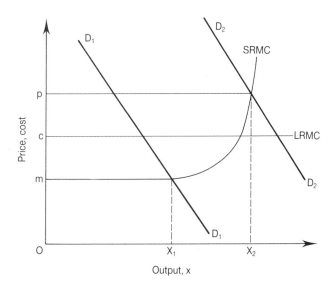

Figure 10.1 Pricing and investment in nationalised industries

which we do with the help of Figure 10.1. The horizontal axis shows the output level of a typical nationalised firm, the vertical axis shows price or cost as appropriate. The short-run marginal cost curve, corresponding to a given capital stock, is labelled SRMC. The long-run marginal cost curve, which takes account of the incremental capital costs (amortisation plus a normal rate of return on capital) associated with raising output is LRMC; this is drawn horizontal for simplicity, implying constant returns to scale, but other assumptions are easily incorporated.

In any given period, the best policy is to use the existing capital stock as efficiently as possible. If demand is low, corresponding to the demand curve D_1, this implies that the optimal price, $p_1 = m$ (= SRMC, for output below full capacity), and the level of output will be x_1. Under these conditions, since $p_1 < c$ (LRMC), it is not profitable to undertake further investment. If demand is high, corresponding to the demand curve D_2, the optimal price, $p_2 = p$ (= SRMC, for full capacity output), and the level of output will be x_2. In this case, since $p_2 > c$, new investment will yield more than enough additional revenue to cover the normal return on capital; consequently, new investment is justified.

These basic ideas about pricing can easily be modified to allow for situations where the demand fluctuates considerably (like electricity over a day, and over the year; or telephone services), or where the pricing structure incorporates a fixed element as well as a price per unit of product consumed. But the formal analysis required to deal with these cases is beyond the scope of this chapter.

Aside from these important allocative issues, the government became increasingly concerned to strengthen financial controls, and the 1978 White Paper therefore introduced a system of short-term financial targets (external financing limits, or EFLs) associated with attempts to determine suitable medium-term financial goals for each firm/industry. The aims were to reduce the burden on the Exchequer of loss-making state firms, and to bring the whole sector closer to self-financing.

Under the various policy 'regimes', how did public sector firms perform? Fortunately, several studies have been carried out, covering the 1960s, the 1970s and the first half of the 1980s (see Pryke, 1971, 1981, 1982; also Molyneux and Thompson, 1987). The third of these studies made comparisons between similar public sector and private sector activities, while the most recent one was able to compare firms still in public ownership with those recently privatised. The results make interesting reading. In the 1960s, it seems that the nationalised industries performed quite well compared to the rest of the economy – in terms of productivity, pricing and profitability; but in the 1970s the situation was far less rosy, with the further enlarged public sector lagging well behind the private sector in terms of productivity improvements, profitability and employment. This is the background against which public opinion gradually shifted to favour privatisation, supported by further critical studies of the nationalised industries, such as Redwood (1980), Redwood and Hatch (1982). Nevertheless, the most recent study of efficiency shows that performance has been better in the 1980s *both* in the recently privatised firms *and* in those remaining in state hands. This suggests that ownership is not the only issue relevant to performance, a point we return to below.

10.3 Privatisation in the 1980s

When the Conservative government came to power in 1979, privatisation was not a central part of its initial programme, though it did speak in general terms about the need to reduce the state's role in the economy. However, it soon started to prepare plans for the privatisation of certain state-owned firms, and for the de-regulation of others. The programme which gradually evolved began quite slowly and accelerated through the decade, until by 1990 the share of nationalised industries in the GDP had fallen from 10 per cent in 1979 to well under 5 per cent. Moreover, the programme was not confined to the nationalised industries, since it also included publicly owned housing and, increasingly, a wide range of services provided by local authorities and other public bodies (see LeGrand and Robinson, 1984).

In the United Kingdom context, therefore, privatisation has to be understood in very broad terms. It includes the following:

1. The sale of all or part of an existing public company, by public offering or by negotiation with a single buyer.
2. The conversion of part of a public company into a distinct business unit, and its separate sale.
3. The de-regulation of a given public company (possibly combined with partial or complete sale).
4. The subsidised sale of council houses to their tenants.
5. The compulsory competitive tendering of local authority services.
6. The introduction of market-type mechanisms into the health service, education and other spheres of public provision (e.g. contracting out, formation of hospital trusts, etc.).

From this list it is apparent that privatisation includes measures to strengthen the scope for competition in areas where it was formerly restricted by statutory monopoly or other constraints. As was implied at the end of the last section, ownership change is only part of the story, albeit an important part.

Such a wide-ranging programme of privatisation inevitably had many goals, the balance between which varied somewhat over time. The most important goal, though not always the most prominent, was that of improving the efficiency of the firms and services concerned. But others included raising revenue for the Treasury, creating a 'share-owning democracy', facilitating competition between alternative suppliers and encouraging wider home-ownership (see Kay *et al.*, 1986).

Not surprisingly, these goals were not always compatible. For instance, raising revenue for the Treasury requires the share price of a given state-owned firm to be as high as possible, while making such shares attractive to the general public sometimes favoured a rather lower price. Also, selling off a natural monopoly usually contributed little to fostering competition, and even required new regulatory bodies to be established to restrain the exploitation of monopoly power. Breaking up the firms into smaller units in order to enhance competition would only have been possible at the cost of a lower selling price and hence less revenue for the Treasury.

Despite these and other complications, privatisation in the United Kingdom made remarkable progress in the 1980s. In terms of the assets transferred into private hands, housing privatisation clearly made the largest single contribution, with over 1.5 million local authority and new-town tenants buying their houses during the 1980s. These tenants received discounts which were initially set at 50 per cent (of a notional market price), later increased to 60 per cent and then 70 per cent for those with at least three years of a tenancy (see *Social Trends* 22 (1992), HMSO). Sales of the nationalised industries taken together contributed about £42 billion to the Treasury during the period 1979/80 to 1991/2 (Source: *Autumn Statement*, HM Treasury, various years). In terms of shareholding, there were several million new shareholders in the United Kingdom as a result of privatisation offerings to the market, though most of the new shareholders only held one or two privatisation stocks and tended not to be active traders. Many of them sold their privatisation stock quite quickly, in order to benefit from an immediate capital gain.

Focusing on the privatisation of the nationalised industries, the public corporations, Table 10.1 indicates that several methods of privatisation were employed. Some companies, such as the Rover Group (formerly British Leyland), were sold to single buyers; these were typically cases where the government believed, probably correctly, that there would be limited interest among the general population in buying the shares. In other cases, non-core parts of the business were formed into separate companies and then privatised: an example here is the hotels formerly owned (and badly managed) by British Rail. Then with firms like British Petroleum (BP) (in which the government initially held a 51 per cent stake), and British Telecom (BT; initially wholly state-owned, but privatised in stages), shares were sold by public offering while still leaving the government with a significant shareholding. Finally, some firms were privatised completely by means of a single public offering.

For some of the most complex cases, a good deal of restructuring preceded the actual privatisation, at times accompanied by considerable

Table 10.1   UK privatisation – progress in the 1980s. (The table shows a selection of the major privatisation 'events' during the last decade; it is not a complete listing.)

Name of firm (current)*	Date of privatisation	Method of privatisation
British Aerospace	1981	Share issues, 1981, 1985
British Airways	1986	Public sale of shares
British Coal	None	Privatisation expected in mid-1990s
British Gas	1986	Share issues, 1986, 1988; new regulatory body
British Petroleum	1981	Share sales 1979, 1981, 1983, 1987
British Rail	None	White Paper on rail privatisation published summer 1992. Non-rail assets (hotels, other property, etc.) sold in 1980s
British Steel	1984	Share issues 1984/5 and 1988
British Telecom	1984	Public sale of shares; regulatory body
Electricity Industry	1990	In England and Wales, twelve distribution companies and two generating companies (PowerGen and National Power) privatised by public share offer. Distribution companies jointly own National Grid company. Government retains Nuclear Electric. In Scotland, Scottish Power and Scottish Hydro-Electric privatised by public share offer. New regulatory body.
Jaguar Cars	1984	Public sale of shares; company subsequently purchased by the Ford Motor Company
National Bus Company	1980–8	De-regulation, 1980; split into separate, mainly regional, companies; majority sold to management by 1988
Regional Water Authorities	1989/90	Public offering of shares; regulatory body
Rover Group	1987	Formerly part of British Leyland. 'Sold' to British Aerospace under favourable conditions which attracted some EC criticism

Note: * In many instances, firms changed their name upon privatisation, sometimes also at other times; the table shows the most recent name.
Sources: P. Hare and J. Dunkerley, 'Nationalized industries', Ch. 12 in Crafts and Woodward (1991); White Papers and press reports – various.

controversy. This was most evident for the electricity supply industry, where two large producers were established in England and Wales[2] (PowerGen and National Power), together with a separate company managing the national grid, jointly owned by the twelve regionally based distribution companies. In addition, after much debate it was finally accepted by the government that the country's nuclear power stations could not be included in the privatisation as originally envisaged.

Table 10.2 New regulatory bodies established in the United Kingdom

Name	Full name	Activities
OFTEL	Office of Telecommunications	Established 1984. Regulates BT – inland calls, line rentals, international calls; provides conditions for new entrants like Mercury; regulates the equipment market; licenses new forms of telecommunications service.
OFGAS	Office of Gas Supply	Established 1986. Regulates gas supplies to domestic users – average price per therm; industrial gas supplies, connections charges, etc. not regulated. Changes in cost of gas to British Gas can be passed forward into prices.
OFWAT	Office of Water Services	Established 1989. Regulates standard domestic and non-domestic supply by thirty-four water and sewerage companies. Limits price of unmeasured water per customer, and measured water per unit of water.
OFFER	Office of Electricity Regulation	Established 1990. Regulates prices for transmission, distribution and supply by the twelve regional electricity companies, overall electricity costs for smaller customers. Generation business is not regulated.

Source: C. Veljanovski (ed.), *Regulators and the market*, London: Institute of Economic Affairs, 1991.

Accordingly, a separate state-owned company, Nuclear Electric, was formed to manage these assets.[3]

Although in relatively limited spheres it was possible to foster competition in the public utilities, in practice it was expected that they would retain substantial monopoly power in their principal markets. For this reason, new regulatory bodies were established to supervise the industries concerned; the bodies formed up to mid-1992 are listed in Table 10.2, together with their main roles.

It can be seen that the new regulators usually have a very broad remit. In the case of the Office of Telecommunications (OFTEL), for instance, it not only includes the regulation of BT itself, but also extends to the promotion of competition in the telecommunications market as a whole by creating conditions in which new entrants like Mercury can survive and prosper, and in which other entrants can get established (this includes conditions for access by other providers to the BT network). There are also powers to monitor customer satisfaction with telecommunications services, and to demand that specified standards be attained by the providers. Finally, OFTEL has powers to regulate new telecommunications services.

As far as BT itself is concerned, OFTEL can impose restraints on pricing policy (including network access charges to other suppliers), and it can impose service quality standards. Clearly, since these controls affect the future profitability of BT, it is important to maintain a reasonably stable, predictable regulatory environment. At the time of privatisation itself, it was also important for investors to know what the initial regulatory regime would be like, so that the share price could be set properly.[4]

On the pricing of telecommunications services, OFTEL determines guidelines for BT periodically (initially for five years, subsequently for three-year periods), based on the so-called (RPI – X) formula. In this formula, RPI stands for the annual rate of increase in the retail price index (in per cent), while X denotes a required annual rate of improvement in productivity (also in per cent). Then in setting its prices for a specified basket of services, BT would be allowed to raise its average price by (RPI – X) per cent, with much less (if any) restriction on changes in the relative prices within the basket. For its first five years, X was set at 3 per cent, so that BT could raise prices by at most 3 per cent less than the prevailing rate of inflation; then in 1988 X was raised to 4.5 per cent, and in the most recent review it rose further to 6.25 per cent, which means that BT is expected to improve its productivity even more rapidly than before. However, the evidence of its profitability, together with cost and price information about telephone companies in other countries suggest that this should be manageable.

For each firm (or group of related firms) being privatised in the United Kingdom, a separate Act of Parliament has to be passed, this Act covering the structure of the new firm or industry, specifying the private sector firms that will result from the privatisation and including as necessary the regulatory issues of the sort just discussed above. Thus to implement a programme on the scale of that seen in the United Kingdom in the last decade or so, very large amounts of parliamentary time have been required, sometimes to the detriment of legislation in other areas. One wonders whether it might not have been possible to arrange for a general enabling law to be passed, which ministers could then use to make specific arrangements to privatise firms in their respective domains. This would, however, have considerably diluted the extent of parliamentary supervision over the privatisation process.

Two broad sectors were largely state-owned at the start of the United Kingdom's privatisation programme; namely, energy and transport. In the former, gas, coal and electricity were all in public ownership, being joined in the 1970s by a state-owned oil company, British National Oil Corporation (BNOC, later Britoil); the government also held a substantial shareholding in BP. One of the original arguments for bringing most of the energy sector into public ownership was the view that its different components could benefit from some co-ordination of investment across the sector, on the basis of agreed projections for the growth of the economy. Typically, energy investments are very costly, take many years to plan and implement, and have long lives. Hence the social costs of mistakes in the sector are likely to be very high. Nevertheless, early post-war attempts to plan the sector largely failed. It became apparent that the government was unable to plan the development of the sector any better than the private sector could do; moreover, the private sector proved increasingly willing to supply the large amounts of capital required to develop energy supplies, as was evident during the 1970s and 1980s as investment in the North Sea (oil and gas) enjoyed an extended boom.

In the case of transport, the principal airlines, the railways, much passenger shipping and the freight sector of road transport as well as the buses were mainly in state hands. The growth of private car ownership, and competition from private firms in other parts of the transport sector, adversely affected the economic conditions of the state-owned firms. It is possible that with better management, and more sustained attempts to plan the relative rates of development of different types of transport, superior outcomes might have been achieved. But in practice, co-ordination was no more effective than in the energy sector, except sometimes at the very local level. Again, therefore, the failure of the state to manage its assets effectively helped to undermine much of the resistance to privatisation that remained.

As the Conservative government's privatisation programme took shape, and it became clear that virtually everything that could be privatised would be, state firms in the 'queue' to be sold off started to prepare themselves for life in the private sector. They did so partly by lobbying government to maintain their existing organisational forms (or to make as little change as possible), hence preserving much of their monopoly power. In this, most firms were remarkably successful. They also took steps to cut costs and rationalise production with much more determination than nationalised industry managers had usually exhibited in the past. This is probably one reason why the most recent study of privatised and state industry performance, reported in the last section, was unable to find significant differences between the two groups of firms.

Another reason has to do with the types of firm likely to 'benefit' from privatisation. Those firms with the greatest potential for cost reduction and/or quality improvement are not the large public utilities whose extensive networks inevitably confer monopoly power, but those in which there is greater scope for competition through new entry or through breaking up the original state-owned firm. Also, firms which have recently reduced costs sharply may have exhausted most of the available opportunities for a time, and may not therefore be able to cut costs much further after privatisation. Now in the United Kingdom, those firms privatised first were not, on the whole, those whose privatisation would have been expected *a priori* to yield the greatest benefits according to these criteria.

A final theme to emphasise here is the relative importance of ownership and competition in the different forms of privatisation. For the standard nationalised industries/firms, the balance is most influenced by the underlying technology of the firms concerned. Thus in the bus industry, deregulation and the promotion of competition came first, followed by the completion of privatisation through ownership change (often by means of management buyouts). The former is generally considered to have exerted the greater impact upon quality of service, consumer choice and prices. In that situation, privatisation merely allows the formerly state-owned parts of the industry to compete more effectively against new private sector rivals. In the case of the telecommunications industry, the combination of regulation of BT's core business by OFTEL and its promotion of competition in the sector wherever it was feasible probably did more to improve the performance of the sector than the relatively straightforward ownership change. Hence in most instances it is not easy to see why an ownership change alone would exert a dramatic effect on an industry's performance within the context of a predominantly market-type economy like the United Kingdom's.[5]

10.4 Privatisation: issues for the 1990s

As we have seen, very little remains in the traditional state-owned sector in the United Kingdom following a decade of privatisation. Those businesses which are still state-owned, such as British Coal and British Rail, did not appear to be promising prospects for privatisation in the 1980s, though possible schemes were considered from time to time and this decade is likely to witness major changes in these industries. The newly re-elected Conservative government has already made clear that it envisages rapid progress here, and a White Paper on rail privatisation has already been published.

At the same time, attention has turned towards other areas of the public sector, such as the provision of local authority services, the health service and parts of the education system. In addition, existing policies to privatise much of the housing stock held by local authorities and various public sector housing agencies (such as Scottish Homes) can be expected to continue.

In local authorities, not only are there increasingly tough requirements on them to put services which they would previously have supplied themselves, such as street cleaning, repair and maintenance of buildings, etc., out to competitive tender, but some of their major areas of responsibility are being transformed. The most notable instance so far concerns the provision of primary and secondary education, where schools are now able to opt out of local authority control and become self-governing bodies. Their budget then comes directly from the Department of Education, and the only controls over an opted-out school are the requirement to follow the National Curriculum and the liability to regular inspections by the Schools Inspectorate (which has itself been privatised).

In the health service, National Health Service (NHS) hospitals can now become self-governing trusts, financing their activities by selling their services to other parts of the health service, including directly to private patients. GPs (general practitioners) can also operate more independently of their local health board by becoming budget-holders: using their assigned budget, and knowing the costs of different forms of treatment, they can then provide what they judge to be the most appropriate services to different patients. Since these reforms, as well as those affecting schools mentioned above, are both new and only partly implemented, it is too early to assess their impact on the efficiency of resource allocation in these areas. It is important to emphasise, however, that their aim is to make fuller use of market-like mechanisms in health and education; to date, there has been no formal change of ownership over the assets employed to provide health and education services.

What has been learnt from over a decade of privatisation in the United Kingdom, and how far will it affect the development of policy in the 1990s? First, it turned out that privatisation was feasible in much of the state-owned sector, that in most cases it was popular (no doubt partly because of the inducements of low-priced share issues) and that the programme could be designed to satisfy several aims: improving efficiency, widening share-ownership, yielding revenue for the Treasury. Second, many of the firms/industries privatised were able to resist attempts to restructure them to foster greater competition, and in some cases this required new regulatory bodies to be established to restrict the exploitation of monopoly power after privatisation.

Third, it was nevertheless clear that improvements in overall performance were most likely to occur in those areas where individual incentives would be strongly influenced by privatisation and/or where competition was strengthened. The former was most noticeable in the area of housing privatisation, where in most cases the new private owners were more inclined to spend money on maintaining and improving their property than the former local authority landlords had been. On the other hand, housing privatisation selectively removed from the public sector housing stock many of the better properties, little of the revenues from privatisation could be used to build new public sector houses (because of restrictions imposed by central government) and the ability of local authorities to meet housing needs in their areas was severely undermined. At the same time, some of the new owners experienced financial difficulties due to the combination of high interest rates and deepening recession, and were sometimes unable to retain their new properties. Hence the substantial benefits (both private and social) of much of the housing privatisation must be offset by these negative factors.

Increases in competition were most striking in the aftermath of bus deregulation in the early 1980s, and although many of the companies were eventually fully privatised (often by management buyout, as noted above) it was the competitive environment which did most to stimulate change. Moreover, the change was not confined to the buses, since British Rail was obliged to respond with revised prices and conditions for young travellers and other groups whose cross-price elasticity of demand was relatively high.

Fourth, it now seems very likely that the remaining public sector firms will be privatised in the coming decade, whether or not they meet any or all of the conditions for privatisation to improve performance. The idea seems to be, quite simply, that the government is unwilling to continue present subsidies, and that it is increasingly prepared to contemplate virtually any degree of contraction or re-organisation as the 'price' for getting these firms out of state hands. In the context of areas of policy such as transport, or energy, where there are important actual and potential interactions between different sub-sectors of the industry (as noted above), as well as with the users/customers, such an ideologically based approach to further privatisation has little to recommend it. Nevertheless, the apparent (or perceived) success of privatisation elsewhere is likely to maintain substantial momentum in favour of privatisation under the present government.

Finally, in areas other than housing and the conventional nationalised industry sector, the 'competition' rather than 'ownership' aspect of privatisation will predominate, with an increasing separation between the public financing of various activities and the actual delivery of services. Sometimes, as in competitive tendering of local authority services, bids can come both from either the original local authority providers or from private firms. Presumably, when the latter are successful the local authority would have to declare some of its existing staff redundant (some of whom might then be taken on by the new supplier). On the other hand, experience indicates that with outside sourcing of services the monitoring and supervision costs can rise quite sharply, so that the net financial benefits from such provision can be less than anticipated.

In other cases, such as in the recent attempt to induce universities to 'bid' for students from the Universities Funding Council (UFC), there is no question (yet?) of new private 'producers' entering the market, but the intention was to stimulate increased competition among existing institutions. In the event, this first attempt largely failed, since over 90 per cent of the bids were at or close to the guide prices which had been announced at the start of the process. Despite this, there is little doubt that the environment within which universities operate – for both teaching and research – will gradually become more competitive and will be increasingly influenced by prices rather than by direct controls over volumes. Specifically, this means that student number targets and mainly centralised, block-grant funding will gradually be replaced by a more de-centralised system in which student fees and research costs play a much more important role.

Overall, one must judge the results of the United Kingdom's privatisation policy as mixed. Many former public sector businesses and organisations have been transformed, with new management structures, a tougher competitive environment and regulation where appropriate. But economic units still in the public sector have undergone roughly parallel changes, so that it is not always evident that privatisation *per se* is what made the difference. Similarly, outside the conventional nationalised industries there has been considerable development of competitive structures and new arrangements to stimulate individual incentives. Much of this is beneficial in that it forces organisations which were otherwise not compelled to think in terms of cutting costs or improving performance to do so, though sometimes (as we noted above) at a cost in terms of their ability to fulfil broader social objectives.

Questions for discussion

1. Did nationalised industries fail? If so, why? If not, in what respects did they succeed?
2. Discuss the advantages and disadvantages of different methods of privatisation.
3. Are there any industries or firms which should *not* be privatised?
4. Discuss the relative importance of 'ownership' and 'competition' as factors influencing the results of a privatisation. Give examples to illustrate your answer.
5. What were the main aims of privatisation in the United Kingdom during the 1980s, and how far were they achieved?
6. How far would you expect United Kingdom privatisation in the 1990s to diverge from the 1980s experience?

Notes

1. The most prominent exception being the Post Office, which was run as part of the civil service until 1961. In that year, however, it became a public corporation, which was later split into two public corporations in 1981, when British Telecom was formed.
2. In Scotland, the situation was different. Two firms emerged from the

privatisation there, Scottish Power and Scottish Hydro-Electric, both of which are engaged in the production and distribution of electricity.
3. This problem arose because of doubts about the economic viability of these power stations, and uncertainty about the costs of de-commissioning them at the end of their useful lives. PowerGen and National Power were required to purchase specified amounts of their electricity supplies from Nuclear Electric.
4. There is obviously a trade-off between the tightness of regulation and the share price, tougher regulation depressing the share price since it lowers potential profits.
5. The situation would, of course, be rather different in the case of the formerly planned economies of Eastern Europe.

References and suggestions for further reading

Crafts, N. F. R. and N. Woodward (1991), *The British Economy since 1945*, Oxford: Oxford University Press (esp. Ch. 12).

HM Treasury (1961), *Financial and Economic Obligations of the Nationalised Industries*, Cmnd 1337, London: HMSO.

HM Treasury (1967), *Nationalised Industries: A review of economic and financial objectives*, Cmnd 3437, London: HMSO.

HM Treasury (1978), *The Nationalised Industries*, Cmnd 7131, London: HMSO.

Kay, J. A., C. Mayer and D. Thompson (eds) (1986), *Privatisation and Regulation – The UK Experience*, Oxford: Oxford University Press.

LeGrand, J. and R. Robinson (eds) (1984), *Privatisation and the Welfare State*, London: Allen & Unwin.

Molyneux, R. and D. Thompson (1987), 'Nationalised industry performance: Still third rate?', *Fiscal Studies*, 8(1), pp. 48–82.

Pryke, R. (1971), *Public Enterprise in Practice*, London: MacGibbon & Kee.

Pryke, R. (1981), *The Nationalised Industries: Policies and performance since 1968*, Oxford: Martin Robertson.

Pryke, R. (1982), 'The comparative performance of public and private enterprise', *Fiscal Studies*, 3(2), pp. 68–81.

Redwood, J. (1980), *Public Enterprise in Crisis: The future of the nationalised industries*, Oxford: Basil Blackwell.

Redwood, J. and J. Hatch (1982), *Controlling Public Industries*, Oxford: Basil Blackwell.

Stevens, B. (1992), 'Prospects for privatisation in OECD countries', *National Westminster Bank Quarterly Review*, August, pp. 2–22.

Webb, M. G. (1973), *The Economics of Nationalized Industries*, London: Nelson.

Chapter 11

Trade unions and industrial relations

IAN PATERSON and LESLIE SIMPSON

11.1 Introduction

Industrial relations legislation has undergone significant change in the period since 1979. Measures taken to limit the powers of trade unions formed part of supply-side economic policy. The government argued that trade unions had become too powerful and had used their powers in ways which pushed up labour costs, restricted productivity improvements and increased the level of unemployment. As Table 11.1 shows, trade union membership had grown rapidly from 10.2 million in 1968 to 13.3 million in 1979, an increase of over 30 per cent. Coupled with this, trade unions had acquired increasing political and economic influence. In part, this was the result of legislation introduced during the 1970s which increased trade union powers at the expense of employers. It was also a consequence of the growth of formal closed shop arrangements. Dunn and Gennard (1984) have shown that by 1978 closed shop arrangements affected at least 5.2 million people, 23 per cent of the labour force.

The government also put considerable emphasis on the conviction that inflexible pay arrangements were a barrier to creating new jobs. It argued that national pay agreements restricted labour flexibility and discouraged the growth of employment opportunities. Employers were therefore urged to de-centralise their pay bargaining arrangements. Attention was also given to the role of wages councils, bodies which fix legal minimum wages in certain industries where collective bargaining arrangements are inadequate. The government argued that wages councils contributed to unemployment and that the national rates they set were inconsistent with the need for flexible pay determination. It introduced legislation to curtail their powers and now intends to abolish them altogether.

Table 11.1 Trade union membership and density in the
United Kingdom; selected years 1968–89

Year	Union membership ('000s)	Potential union membership ('000s)	Union density (%)
1968	10 200	23 203	44.0
1970	11 187	23 050	48.5
1975	12 026	23 548	51.1
1979	13 289	24 393	54.5
1980	12 947	24 485	52.9
1981	12 106	24 265	49.9
1983	11 236	24 134	46.6
1986	10 539	24 807	42.5
1987	10 475	24 707	42.4
1989	10 158	24 404	41.6

Sources: Various issues of the *Employment Gazette* and its
occasional Historical Supplements. The potential union
membership data represent employees in employment with the
addition of the unemployed, at June of each year.

11.2 The effects of trade unions

The impact of trade unions on the level of wages and employment can be
analysed by making use of microeconomic models of the labour market.
Two possibilities are considered, the first where there is a perfectly
competitive labour market and the second where a monopsonist has the
power to influence wage rates.

In the perfectly competitive model, it is assumed that all workers have
the same skill level and perfect information, and will seek employment
where wage rates are highest. The case is illustrated in Figure 11.1, where
SL is the labour market supply curve. Individual employees will balance
the opportunity cost of work – forgone leisure opportunities – against the
wage rate to be paid. Assuming prices are constant, the higher the wage
rate the greater will be the supply of labour. The labour market demand
curve, DL, is the horizontal summation of the labour demand curves of
individual firms. All firms are profit maximisers and will increase their
demand for labour up to the point where the marginal cost of labour – the
wage rate under perfect competition – equals the marginal revenue
product of labour. Diminishing marginal returns will cause the marginal
revenue product of labour to fall in the short run as firms employ more
labour. Consequently, the demand for labour will be higher the lower is the
wage rate. In this model the labour market is in equilibrium when the
wage rate is equal to WE and the level of employment is NE.

Powerful trade unions may be able to secure wages which are above the

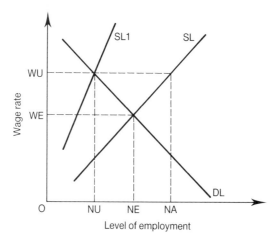

Figure 11.1 Perfect competition model

equilibrium level. The consequence will be a reduction in the demand for labour and an increase in the supply of labour, causing involuntary unemployment. The amount of unemployment which results depends on how far the wage rate is pushed above the equilibrium level, and also on the wage elasticity of the labour market demand and supply schedules. If a trade union negotiated a wage rate of WU in Figure 11.1, the demand for labour would fall from NE to NU and the supply of labour would rise from NE to NA. This would give an excess supply of labour of NA–NU. A national minimum wage fixed at WU would have the same consequences. If the trade union was further able to insist that firms maintain the equilibrium level of employment, NE, this would result in overstaffing, reduced competitiveness and profitability, and might force some firms out of business.

Alternatively, trade unions may be able to raise the equilibrium wage rate by restricting the supply of labour. This could be achieved by controlling employee training or restricting access to jobs by imposing a closed shop. At each wage rate the supply of labour will be reduced so that the labour market supply curve moves to the left. This is indicated in Figure 11.1, with a move to SL1. The result is that the wage rate rises to WU, and the equilibrium level of employment falls to NU. Two types of closed shop arrangement may exist. A pre-entry closed shop requires membership of the union prior to employment and is associated with restricting entry. A post-entry closed shop exists where employees must join the union within a short period of being employed.

The case of the monopsonist arises where one employer, or a group of employers acting together, can dominate a labour market. In either case, employment decisions directly affect wage rates. Figure 11.2 demonstrates the extreme case of a single profit maximising monopsonist. The labour market supply schedule SL, shows how much labour will be supplied at each wage rate. In order to employ more labour the firm must raise the wage rate. Unlike the perfectly competitive model, the marginal cost of labour is greater than the wage rate. (If a monopsonist employing fifty workers at a wage rate of £300 per week increases the wage rate to £301 per week to attract an additional employee, the marginal cost of labour will be £301 + (50 × £1) = £351). This is illustrated by schedule MCL. The monopsonist's demand for labour schedule DL, shows the marginal revenue product of labour at each level of employment. At the level of employment NM, the marginal cost and marginal revenue product of labour will be equated. In order to employ NM workers the firm will only need to offer a wage rate equal to WM. Compared with the competitive model, the equilibrium wage rate and level of employment are lower. If as a result of trade union pressure (or the introduction of a national minimum wage) the wage rate is increased to WU, the level of employment will rise to NU. This is because the marginal cost of labour will now be equal to the negotiated (or minimum) wage rate WU. As the marginal revenue product of labour is greater than the marginal cost of employing additional units of labour for all employees willing to work at the wage rate WU, the level of employment will increase to NU. In Figure 11.2 the level of employment would continue to rise as the trade union negotiates higher wages (or minimum wages are increased) up to the competitive wage rate, WC. Although employment would start to fall if wages were pushed beyond WC, it would remain above NM until the wage rate reached WT.

In both models it has been implicitly assumed that changes in the wage rate do not affect the marginal revenue product of labour. However, it is possible that an increase in wage rates could have the effect of increasing worker productivity. This response to wage increases, known as the efficiency wage effect, is the result of higher wages providing an incentive for employees to work up to their full capabilities and, in addition, reducing labour turnover. A wage increase might also result in an improvement in management efficiency. Where management has relied on low wages in order to remain competitive, the shock of having to pay higher wages may encourage the use of more modern technology and efficient production processes. In both cases there would be an increase in the marginal revenue product of labour at each level of employment, resulting in a shift of the labour demand schedule to the right. It is possible, therefore, that an increase in wage rates might reduce, leave unchanged or even increase the level of employment depending on the structure of the labour market and the impact of the higher wage rate on labour productivity.

The overall effect of trade unions on productivity is not immediately obvious. Different attitudes towards flexibility and technological change

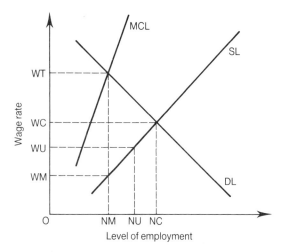

Figure 11.2 Monopsonist model

will result in different consequences for productivity, even when levels of unionisation are similar. In some cases the existence of trade unions may increase labour productivity. This is likely to be the case where good industrial relations exist and co-operation between employees and employers is encouraged. Unions may support management efforts to reduce inefficiency with resulting increases in output and productivity. Similarly, higher productivity may be expected when union activity keeps managers aware of, and alive to, what is happening around them. Freeman and Medoff (1984) have argued that by giving employees a 'collective voice' in the firm, trade unions improve communications between workers and management. This 'collective voice' contributes to increased productivity, in particular by reducing labour turnover and waste. However, when industrial relations are poor, with employees and employers in frequent conflict, productivity may suffer. Furthermore, by restricting technological change or maintaining restrictive practices unions may be responsible for low productivity levels. Restrictive practices may be the result of work rules or agreements on staffing levels negotiated between management and trade union representatives. Such agreements have been quite common in the manufacturing sector of British industry. Whilst a decline in agreements of this type was experienced in the early 1980s, Millward and Stevens (1986) found that in 1984, bargaining over staffing levels for manual workers still existed in 40 per cent of private manufacturing establishments which recognised trade unions. Overall, the effect of trade unions on productivity may be seen as the net effect of forces pulling in opposite directions. Establishing the outcome is an empirical issue.

11.3 Empirical studies

Studies of the impact of trade unions on wages in Britain clearly indicate a mark-up of union over non-union wages. The mark-up is largest where a closed shop operates, with pre-entry closed shops having the greatest impact on wages. Blanchflower and Oswald (1988) suggested that the average mark-up for union members was 10 per cent or just under, with the bulk of the premium associated with closed shops. The study undertaken by Stewart (1987) distinguished between skilled and semi-skilled manual workers. In the case of skilled workers, Stewart found that the average union mark-up was insignificant in the absence of a closed shop. However, where a pre-entry closed shop existed it rose to 7.5 per cent and in a minority of cases exceeded 25 per cent. For semi-skilled workers the union mark-up averaged 7.8 per cent, rising to 9 per cent in the case of a post-entry closed shop and 15 per cent where a pre-entry closed shop existed.

Conflicting arguments exist regarding the effect of the trade union legislation outlined in section 11.4 on the ability of unions to bid up wages. The survey undertaken by Brown and Wadhwani (1990) claimed that there was no evidence to suggest that the legislation reduced the capacity of trade unions to bid up wages during the 1980s. However, Layard and Nickell (1987) suggested that, whilst the trend in the union mark–up had been upward before 1982, a decline in union membership after 1979 and the impact of trade union legislation had caused the gap between union and non-union wages to narrow.

There is little evidence to support the argument that the relatively higher wages in unionised workplaces are obtained at the cost of lower employment levels. Nor is there any indication that employment in unionised plants has risen relative to that in non-unionised plants as a result of the recent industrial relations legislation. The study undertaken by Blanchflower and Millward (1988), which used data from the Workplace Industrial Relations Surveys of 1980 and 1984, suggested that the reverse had been the case. Their study classified private sector workplaces into three categories, (a) non-union, (b) weak union, (c) strong union (where a closed shop existed at least for some workers). They found that over the period 1980–4, 33 per cent of the establishments in the non-union category experienced more than 20 per cent employment growth. Only 18 per cent of the weak-union establishments and 9 per cent of the strong-union establishments achieved comparable results. Furthermore, whilst 37 per cent of strong-union workplaces and 27 per cent of weak-union establishments experienced a greater than 20 per cent reduction in employment, only 15 per cent of non-union private sector workplaces had a comparable fall. However, Blanchflower and Millward suggested that these findings should be treated with caution. Using multiple regression analysis, they discovered that establishment size was a major factor explaining changes in employment during this period. New small establishments, which tended to be non-union, accounted for the greater proportion of employment expansion, whilst large traditional establishments, which tended to be highly unionised, were in many cases in decline. Thus, subject to further research, they concluded that once other significant influences are accounted for, there is no strong statistical evidence of a relationship between employment change and trade union presence in the workplace.

Brown and Wadhwani (1990) suggested that the slower employment growth in unionised plants during this period may have been the result of an increase in productivity growth arising from changes in working practices. If trade union legislation, or some other influence, had resulted in unions giving up some of their restrictive practices, this could have explained the faster productivity growth and lower levels of employment.

Empirical studies of the impact of trade unions on productivity levels do not provide clear evidence to support the view that their presence is generally associated with lower productivity. Wilson (1987) studied fifty-two firms in the United Kingdom metal-working industry taking data over the period 1978–82. He found that in firms where the level of unionisation was less than 50 per cent, unions had negligible effects on productivity. Where the level of unionisation was between 50 per cent and 80 per cent, the effect was positive. For firms in which over 80 per cent of employees were union members, however, the impact on productivity was negative. Machin (1987) used the same data set as Wilson and found that unions had no damaging effects on productivity, except in large plants with more than a thousand employees.

Another study by Edwards (1987) examined manufacturing plants with more that 250 employees and came to the conclusion that unionisation had little or no effect on productivity levels. A more recent study undertaken by Nickell et al. (1989) investigated the impact of trade unions on total factor productivity growth. They used company accounts data in a survey of 127 manufacturing firms and found that on average unionised firms experienced faster productivity growth than non-unionised ones over the period 1980–4. Virtually no difference was found between the average rate of productivity growth of unionised and non-unionised firms for the succeeding two years. Ingram and Lindop (1990) used CBI databank information to examine productivity growth over the period 1987–9. They found that in a period of very rapid productivity growth in the manufacturing sector, non-unionised firms outperformed those that were unionised.

11.4   Industrial relations legislation

Between 1980 and 1990 the government introduced a series of statutes affecting British industrial relations. The main issues dealt with were strikes, the closed shop, trade union government, trade union recognition and minimum wage fixing.

It was the government's view that disruption to production should be minimised by reducing the capacity of unions to call strikes and make them effective. In Britain, unlike most other European countries, the right to strike is not laid down by statute. Instead, statute law has provided immunities from common law judgements concerning conspiracy and liability for damaging an employer's business through strike action – or some other kind of industrial action such as an overtime ban, a go slow or a work-to-rule. The legislation introduced after 1979 limited the extent of these immunities in various ways.

The Employment Act of 1980 restricted picketing to a person's own workplace, thus outlawing secondary picketing. Consequently, anyone picketing at locations other than their own place of employment became liable to action in the civil courts for interfering with commercial or employment contracts. This statute also restricted the legality of other types of secondary industrial action, such as the 'blacking' of goods. Such action had to be confined to a direct supplier or customer of the employer with whom the trade union was in dispute. The Employment Act of 1990 has since made all secondary industrial action unlawful by removing entirely a trade union's immunity from claims for damages when action is taken against a supplier or customer of the employer with whom the union is in dispute.

The Employment Act of 1982 had earlier abolished the special immunities that had prevented trade unions being sued in their own names. It stipulated that a union would be liable for unlawful industrial action if that action was authorised or endorsed by any committee or official with authority under the union's rules to call industrial action. Limits, however, were placed on the damages courts could award. Formerly, only union officers could be sued for organising unlawful industrial action on behalf of their union – the union's funds were safeguarded. The 1982 Act also attempted to prevent political strikes by requiring that a trade dispute, with its accompanying immunity from civil damages, must 'wholly or mainly' relate to employment matters rather than simply being 'connected with' such matters as was previously the case. The new definition of a trade dispute in the 1982 Act also excluded disputes between employees in an effort to prevent inter-union disputes.

Trade union immunity was further restricted by the Trade Union Act of 1984. This provided that if a union authorised or endorsed strike action without first securing majority support for it in a secret ballot, immunity would be lost. This provision also applied to any other form of industrial action which interfered with or broke employment contracts. The Employment Act of 1988 followed this up by giving union members the right to seek a court order restraining their union from organising industrial action if the ballot requirement had not been met. Moreover, it gave union members the right not to be disciplined by their union for refusing to take part in any form of industrial action.

The Employment Act of 1990 made trade unions legally responsible for unofficial strikes called by shop stewards or any lay officer. If industrial action is organised by any union official, the union concerned becomes legally liable unless either a secret ballot has been conducted approving the action or the action is repudiated in writing by the union's executive committee or chief officer. This Act also opened the way for employers selectively to dismiss employees taking unofficial industrial action.

The Conservative government's view of the closed shop was that it not only infringed individual liberty, but also caused economic damage by raising labour costs and encouraging inefficient working practices. Statutory support for the closed shop was thus gradually removed in an attempt to stifle it.

The government had inherited a situation in which employers could dismiss anyone for non-membership of a union where a closed shop agreement was in force, unless an employee had a genuine religious objection to union membership. The 1980 Employment Act widened this conscience clause and also sought to protect those already employed when a closed shop was established. Individuals with conscientious or deeply held personal reasons for not wishing to join a union, or who had been engaged before a closed shop agreement was concluded, were given the right not to be dismissed by their employer for non-membership of a union. In addition, the Act also tried to ensure that new closed shops could only be introduced if the great majority of the employees concerned were in favour. It laid down that, unless a new closed shop agreement had been approved by 80 per cent or more of those affected by it, the employer concerned could not legitimately dismiss anyone for not being a union member. A periodic review of existing closed shops was introduced by the 1982 Employment Act. This made dismissal for non-membership of a union unfair unless a closed shop agreement had been approved by 80 per cent of the workforce concerned within the previous five years.

Protection given to employers and employees against the operation of closed shops was widened by the 1988 Employment Act. The Act made dismissal for non-membership of a trade union automatically unfair by repealing the earlier legislative provisions that had allowed employers to dismiss individuals for not being union members where a closed shop had been approved by the required majority. It also removed all legal immunity for industrial action organised by a union to compel an employer to establish or maintain any kind of closed shop arrangement.

The 1990 Employment Act aimed to put an end to the pre-entry closed shop by making it unlawful to deny anyone a job because that person is not a union member. The Act also made it unlawful to refuse to employ someone because he or she is a member of a trade union. Complaints alleging either of these infringements can be made to an industrial tribunal, which has the power to award compensation if any such complaint is upheld.

The Conservative government also decided that statutory intervention was appropriate in the internal affairs of trade unions in order to ensure that union leaders were properly accountable to their members. The implication was that this would make union behaviour more responsive to the national economic interest. The Trade Union Act of 1984 required the members of the principal executive committee of a trade union to be elected by a secret ballot of all the union's members at least once every five years. Enforcement was left in the hands of ordinary union members, who were given the right to apply for a court order requiring their union to comply. The Employment Act of 1988 insisted on postal ballots in elections for union executives, thereby ruling out workplace ballots, and also required independent scrutiny of ballots.

Furthermore, the 1984 Act laid down that a secret ballot of the members must be held at least once every ten years if a union wished to use funds for political purposes. Ever since 1913 unions had had the right to maintain special political funds, separate from their general funds, but holding a ballot to establish such a political fund had been a once-for-all requirement. The 1988 Act provided for the appointment of a Commissioner for the Rights of Trade Union Members. The commissioner's job is to give advice and support to any union member who wishes to take action against his or her union for failing in its statutory obligations and who might otherwise be deterred because of the difficulty of pursuing a case through the courts.

The power of trade unions depends partly on whether or not employers are forced to recognise and bargain with them and, consequently, the early repeal of the previous Labour government's legislation on union recognition was highly significant. Part of the Employment Protection Act of 1975 empowered the Advisory, Conciliation and Arbitration Service (ACAS) to investigate and pronounce upon applications by unions that specific employers should negotiate with them. If an employer refused to comply with an ACAS recommendation in favour of union recognition, the union concerned could apply for a binding arbitration award on pay and conditions for the employees involved. These provisions were repealed by the Employment Act of 1980.

The Conservative government also decided to reduce the powers of wages councils. It took the view that the councils made the unemployment situation worse by fixing minimum wage rates above the levels at which people, especially young people, would be prepared to work. The Wages Act of 1986 therefore removed employees under the age of twenty-one from the protection of wages councils, so that employers could offer them jobs at lower wages to reflect their level of training and experience. The Act also

Table 11.2 Stoppages of work due to industrial disputes in the United Kingdom, 1965–89

Years	Average number of stoppages per year	Average number of working days lost per year
1965–9	2 380	3 929
1970–4	2 885	14 077
1975–9	2 310	11 663
1980–4	1 351	10 486
1985–9	881	3 940

Source: Calculated from annual data in various issues of the *Employment Gazette*.

limited the powers of the councils to setting a basic minimum hourly rate, an overtime rate and the point at which overtime should start. This limitation meant that the councils were no longer able to set different minimum rates for different grades of workers within an industry or to fix holiday entitlements.

11.5   Impact of the legislation

It is important to assess the effects that changes in the law relating to industrial relations matters have had. As far as strike activity is concerned, Table 11.2 shows that both the number of strikes and working days lost through strikes were much lower in the 1980s, particularly in the second half of the decade, than they had been during the 1970s. In part this can be explained by unemployment and structural changes in the economy, both of which had a dampening effect on strike activity. Furthermore, Britain's declining strike record after 1979 was part of an international trend.

Nevertheless, legislative changes appear to have had an influence on strike activity. The restrictions on what constitutes a trade dispute, on picketing and on secondary industrial action all had some impact, but the most significant change in the law was undoubtedly the strike ballot requirement introduced in 1984. Since then ballots have become an increasingly common feature of the negotiating process, with union members in general now regarding them as a prerequisite for industrial action. Indeed, ballots have sometimes been used to put pressure on an employer to make an improved offer which is then accepted. The use of ballots has thus reduced the number of strikes, not only by making it less likely that a stoppage will take place without the support of the majority of employees affected, but also because employers often respond to a positive ballot result by making further concessions which lead to a settlement of the dispute without a strike actually occurring.

The legislation dealing with the closed shop has helped to reduce its coverage significantly, although in the early 1980s, according to Millward and Stevens (1986), the number of employees in closed shops fell mainly because of job losses in establishments that had compulsory union membership arrangements. The introduction in 1982 of the five-year ballot for the maintenance of existing closed shops turned out to be very important. Relatively few employers and unions decided to hold ballots and a number of major employers either ended their closed shops or gave a commitment that nobody would be dismissed for non-membership of a union. By the end of 1986 ACAS estimated that no more than 30 000 employees were covered by legally approved closed shops. However, despite dismissal for non-membership of a union being made automatically unfair in 1988, some post-entry closed shops continued to operate on an informal basis. A National Opinion Poll (NOP) survey in 1989 suggested that the total number of people in closed shops of all kinds was still of the order of 2.5 million. Of these, 1.3 million workers were in jobs where they had to be union members before being considered for employment or before starting work, and this led the government to legislate against the pre-entry closed shop in 1990.

The legislative intervention in the internal government of trade unions did not cause them undue problems. Some unions did have to change their constitutions as a result of the ballot requirements for union executive committees, but many unions already elected such committees by a full ballot of the membership. Whether or not greater membership participation makes unions more responsive to external economic circumstances is, as Brown and Wadhwani (1990) have remarked, difficult to assess. They argue that direct election in unions whose membership is geographically dispersed tends to favour whichever faction within the union is the best organised, irrespective of its moderation or radical nature. Ironically, the legal requirement to hold a periodic 'political fund ballot' has resulted in more unions being entitled to spend money for political purposes than was the case ten years ago.

The repeal of the legislation on union recognition, along with other statutory restrictions on union activity (and the government's decision in 1984 to ban trade unions at Government Communications Headquarters (GCHQ) in Cheltenham), encouraged some employers to limit or push back union recognition. This may be significant in explaining why the membership of trade unions continued to fall after 1986, even though unemployment was also falling. There was an increase between 1987 and 1989 in the number of employers withdrawing union recognition for certain grades of staff, and this was sometimes accompanied by pressure from the employer for staff to drop their union membership. However, de-recognition of unions was not common and, overall, affected only a relatively small number of employees. It usually occurred in situations where, for whatever reason, union membership had fallen to relatively low levels. Nevertheless, there were some well-publicised exceptions, notably in the newspaper industry and the P&O Ferries dispute.

Finally, the changes made to the wages council legislation in 1986 have had two interesting effects. One of the reasons for limiting the powers of wages councils to setting a single minimum hourly rate was to make the orders issued by the councils easier for employers to understand. It was hoped that this would reduce the problem of underpayment which had become a serious one. There was, as Simpson and Paterson (1992) have shown, a substantial fall in both the number of workers underpaid and the number of establishments found to be underpaying after 1986. The removal of workers under the age of twenty-one from the wage-fixing powers of wages councils accounted, in part, for a fall in the gross pay of young people relative to adult pay.

11.6   EC directives

It is not surprising that a British government committed to greater labour market flexibility and reducing trade union power was unwilling to see that course of action obstructed by industrial relations policies at the EC level. As a result, Britain has blocked a number of proposals put forward by the European Commission. During the early 1980s, for example, a proposed directive granting part-time and temporary workers the same rights as full-time employees, and another dealing with parental leave for family reasons, were both vetoed by Britain in the Council of Ministers. Britain later blocked the so-called Fifth Directive on Company Law, which would have required transnational companies to establish one of three forms of employee participation as part of their decision-making processes. The Vredeling Directive was also obstructed by British opposition. This Directive would have required large companies to inform and consult employees on matters ranging from the company's structure and financial situation to its business developments and likely trends in investment and employment.

The British government has also been alone in voting against the European Commission's Charter of Fundamental Social Rights, which first appeared in 1989. The Social Charter, as it became known, was the culmination of the Commission's attempts to provide a social dimension for the European Community as it progressed towards the creation of a single internal market. The Charter listed a series of labour and social rights to be guaranteed across member states, addressing such issues as working conditions, freedom of movement of labour, fair remuneration, social welfare schemes, freedom of association and collective bargaining, vocational training, equal treatment for men and women, health and safety at work, child labour and information, consultation and participation. The follow-on development to the Charter was a legislative action programme for implementing most of its provisions. This programme contained forty-seven proposals, seventeen of which were draft directives – mostly in the area of health and safety. Key industrial relations issues, however, such as trade union recognition and the right to strike, were excluded from the action programme, partly because of their sensitive nature in certain countries.

At the Maastricht summit in December 1991 the twelve EC member states reached agreement on a European Union Treaty, but only after a so-called 'social chapter' was excluded from one of its two constituent parts – the Treaty of Political Union. The 'social chapter' provided, amongst other things, for a wider range of employment-related issues to require only a qualified majority vote in the Council of Ministers and the establishment of a mechanism that would enable European-level employers' organisations and trade unions to play a greater part in formulating and implementing Community social policy. The British government declined to sign any treaty containing provisions in these areas, maintaining that it would result in regulations being imposed on Britain which could harm its competitiveness and increase unemployment. De-regulation of employment and the decline in trade union influence in Britain would, the government claimed, be threatened by the proposed 'social chapter'. To enable the European Union Treaty to be signed by all EC member states, the 'social chapter' was dropped. Instead, a protocol was added to the treaty stating that all countries except Britain wished to proceed along the path laid down in the Social Charter of 1989 and had reached an agreement among themselves to this end. The protocol allows the eleven to establish common social legislation through EC procedures and mechanisms, but outside its legal framework. The European Union Treaty itself is subject to ratification.

However, the British government has been obliged to amend some employment legislation to bring it into line with EC directives, most notably in the area of equal opportunities. The Equal Pay Directive of 1975 provided for 'equal pay for work of equal value', a feature that had not been included in the British Equal Pay Act of 1970. Following a decision of the European Court of Justice in 1982, the right of men and women working for the same employer to 'equal pay for work of equal value' was added to British law. Further changes in British law have been made as a result of two other rulings by the European Court in connection with the Equal Treatment Directive of 1976. The Sex Discrimination (Amendment) Act of 1986 brought private households and firms with fewer than six employees within the scope of the law and, more significantly, prohibited retirement age discrimination so that an employer cannot require female employees to retire at an earlier age than male employees. Furthermore, as a consequence of the 1986 Single European Act, which was designed to remove remaining obstacles to the free movement of goods, services, capital and labour within the European Community, the British government may be required to accept changes in employment law in order to harmonise regulations affecting health and safety at work. This has resulted in the controversy over the proposal to restrict the length of the working week to a maximum of forty-eight hours.

11.7   Conclusion

Industrial relations legislation since 1979 has been a major plank of government economic and social policy. In addition, pay bargaining has become more de-centralised. Since the mid-1980s a growing number of industries have ceased participating in national pay bargaining. In some cases this has accompanied de-regulation or privatisation, for example in the water, electricity and bus industries. However, it has also occurred in industries that have historically been in the private sector, such as engineering and banking. These developments will have pleased the government, but the main driving force behind them may well have been competitive pressures rather than government encouragement.

Following its re-election in April 1992 the government announced its intention to introduce further legislation on industrial relations during the 1992–3 parliamentary session. Although the Queen's Speech mentioned only 'improvements' in the law, the government had indicated some three months before the election that it intended to press ahead with most of the changes set out in a Green Paper published in July 1991. With regard to strikes, the forthcoming legislation is expected to require pre-strike ballots to be fully postal, to insist on seven days' notice being given in writing to employers before industrial action takes place and to enable members of the public affected by unlawful industrial action in public services to obtain a preventive court order. It is also expected to give individuals the right to join the union of their choice, unrestrained by inter-union agreements on 'spheres of influence', even though this could undermine deals in which only one union is recognised to represent a company's workforce. Another anticipated change in the law concerns the 'check off' system, under which employers deduct union subscriptions from pay packets and transfer them in bulk to the union. This is likely to require the approval of individual union members once every three years.

There can be no doubt that the wide-ranging changes in industrial relations legislation since 1979 have had an impact on trade unions and the labour market. Whether or not this will translate into a lasting improvement in economic performance remains to be seen. The government seems set to continue its policy of trying to reduce the influence of trade unions, even though some of its supporters warn against tilting the balance too far against them. In any case, many observers have argued that economic conditions are at least as important as industrial relations legislation in influencing trade union power.

Questions for discussion

1. Why does employment fall when trade unions succeed in raising wages in a perfectly competitive market?
2. In what circumstances would a trade union be able to raise the wage rate of its members without reducing their employment prospects?
3. What does the empirical evidence tell us about the impact of trade unions on productivity, employment and wage rates?
4. What were the main objectives of the industrial relations legislation introduced between 1980 and 1990?
5. Assess the impact of the industrial relations legislation enacted since 1979.
6. Why did the British government oppose a number of draft Directives affecting industrial relations drawn up by the European Commission?

References and suggestions for further reading

Blanchflower, D. G. and N. Millward (1988), 'Trade union and employment change: An analysis of British establishment data', papers and proceedings of the Second Annual Congress of the European Economic Association, *European Economic Review*, 32 (2/3), pp. 717–26.
Blanchflower, D. G. and A. Oswald (1988), 'The economic effects of Britain's trade unions', London School of Economics, *Centre for Labour Economics*, Discussion Paper no. 324.
Bridgford, J. and J. Stirling (1991), 'Britain in a social Europe: Industrial relations and 1992', *Industrial Relations Journal*, 22 (4), pp. 263–72.
Brown, W. and S. Wadhwani (1990), 'The economic effects of industrial relations legislation since 1979', *National Institute Economic Review*, February, pp. 57–70.
Dunn, N. S. and J. Gennard (1984), *The Closed Shop in British Industry*, London: Macmillan.
Edwards, P. (1987), *Managing the Factory*, Oxford: Blackwell.
Freeman, R. and J. Medoff (1984), *What do Unions Do?*, New York: Basic Books.
HMSO (1981), *Trade Union Immunities*, Cmnd 8128, London.
HMSO (1983), *Democracy in Trade Unions*, Cmnd 8778, London.
HMSO (1987), *Trade Unions and their Members*, Cm 95, London.
HMSO (1989), *Unofficial Action and the Law*, Cm 821, London.
HMSO (1991), *Industrial Relations in the 1990s*, Cm 1602, London.
Ingram, P. and E. Lindop (1990), 'Can unions and productivity ever be compatible?', *Personnel Management*, July, pp. 32–5.
Layard, R. and S. Nickell (1987), 'The performance of the British labour market', in R. Dornbusch and R. Layard (eds), *The Performance of the British Economy*, Oxford: Oxford University Press.

Machin, S. (1987), 'The productivity effects of unionisation and firm size in British engineering firms', *Warwick Economic Research Papers*, no. 293.

Millward, N. and M. Stevens (1986), *British Workplace Industrial Relations 1980– 1984*, Aldershot: Gower.

Nickell, S., S. Wadhwani and M. Wall (1989), 'Unions and productivity growth in Britain, 1974–86', London School of Economics, *Centre for Labour Economics*, Discussion Paper no. 353.

Simpson, L. and I. Paterson (1992), 'A national minimum wage for Britain?', *Economics*, 28(1), no. 117, pp. 12–18.

Stewart, M. (1987), 'Collective bargaining arrangements, closed shops and relative pay', *Economic Journal*, 97 (March), pp. 140–56.

Wilson, N. (1987), 'Unionisation, wages and productivity, some British evidence', *University of Bradford Management Centre Discussion Paper*, February.

Chapter 12

Controlling environmental pollution

LESLIE SIMPSON

12.1   Introduction

The emission of waste products is a continuing source of environmental pollution. Although the environment has the ability to assimilate a certain level of waste, this is not unlimited. Where the assimilative capacity is exceeded pollution problems arise, resulting in a wide range of environmental damage. A paper mill may discharge waste products into a river and cause damage to fish stocks and hence losses to fishermen operating downstream. If the paper mill is not required to compensate the fishermen for their losses and no action is taken to control the firm's polluting activities, then the waste emissions will continue regardless of the damage done. Environmental pollution involves costs to society as a whole over and above the private costs of production and consumption of individuals and firms. Such costs are called external costs and occur when producers and consumers have free and unrestricted access to environmental resources for waste disposal purposes. Over time the damage will increase as air, water and land are degraded and depleted. In these circumstances there is clearly a need for government intervention to control pollution.

Every activity involves an opportunity cost. Pollution control is no exception to this and, whilst significant benefits may result from reducing the emission of waste products, control can only be achieved by incurring abatement costs. This is the basis of the pollution control controversy, for although many would argue that any action which reduces the level of environmental pollution is to be supported, others would argue that the benefits from a reduction in pollution damage must justify the costs incurred in achieving it.

12.2 The optimal level of pollution control

Figure 12.1 brings together the damage and abatement costs associated with different waste emission levels for two profit-maximising firms operating in a competitive economy. MDC is the marginal damage curve which measures the monetary value of the additional damage done by increasing waste emissions by one unit. Initially it is assumed that the assimilative capacity of the environment is able to cope with the discharges. When the total quantity of emissions discharged by the two firms exceeds Q1, however, pollution costs are incurred. As the amount of emissions rises, the harm done by each additional unit of waste increases. Hence the MDC schedule slopes upward as the quantity of emissions gets larger.

The marginal abatement cost schedule, MAC, shows the opportunity cost of reducing waste emissions by one unit. It is the horizontal summation of the marginal abatement cost schedules for two firms, MAC1 and MAC2. Initially, pollution abatement is relatively inexpensive. However, as the level of emissions is reduced the marginal abatement cost increases. The range of options for waste reduction available to the two firms may be quite extensive including a change of production process, technology or inputs, recycling, waste treatment and reduced output. In order to obtain the least cost combination of options for each successive reduction in the quantity of emissions, each firm must equate the marginal cost of all available pollution control strategies.

In the absence of any regulation or incentive for the firms to reduce waste disposal, the quantity of emissions will be at Q3 for firm 1 and Q6 for firm 2. For both firms marginal abatement cost will be zero. The total level

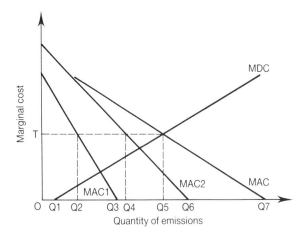

Figure 12.1 Optimal pollution control

of emissions will be Q7 (Q3 + Q6), where MAC is also equal to zero. However, this is very inefficient in terms of economic welfare. If the quantity of emissions was cut by one unit, society would gain more from the reduced environmental damage than it would lose from increased abatement costs. The optimal quantity of emissions is at Q5, where MAC and MDC are equal. Between Q7 and Q5 the marginal benefits from reduced environmental damage exceed the marginal costs for each unit reduction in emissions. However, reducing the quantity of emissions below Q5 would involve marginal costs in excess of marginal benefits.

How should a pollution control agency distribute the total reduction in emissions, Q7–Q5, between the two polluting firms? For any given quantity of emissions reduction, the agency should reduce the emissions of the polluter for whom the additional unit of emissions reduction adds least to the total abatement costs. This amounts to saying that the agency should distribute the emission reductions among the waste dischargers in such a way that the marginal abatement costs of each discharger is equal to the marginal abatement cost of all other dischargers. This will give the lowest possible monetary value of total abatement costs. In Figure 12.1 the most cost effective distribution of emission reductions will be Q3–Q2 for firm 1 and Q6–Q4 for firm 2. Firm 1 will continue to discharge Q2 units of waste and firm 2 will continue to discharge Q4 units of waste. The total quantity of emissions will be at the optimal level, Q5. With this distribution of emissions the marginal abatement costs are equal for both firms. If this condition did not hold, an increase in emission by the firm with the higher marginal abatement cost, matched by a reduction in emissions by the firm with the lower marginal abatement cost, would achieve the optimal quantity of emissions at a lower total abatement cost.

The model usefully highlights the economic principles involved in pollution control management and can be more generally applied to situations involving any number of polluters. However, establishing the optimal level of pollution control in practice will be extremely difficult. Where many firms are involved in contributing to the discharge of a pollutant, and each firm has a range of options available for reducing emissions, establishing the least cost combination of abatement alternatives at each emission level with any degree of accuracy raises many problems. The difficulties involved with measuring and evaluating the marginal damage associated with each level of emissions are even more daunting. These involve establishing the relationship between different emission levels and the harm done, and putting a monetary value on the damage. Estimating the monetary value of damage resulting from air pollution, for example, would involve calculating damages to health, property, agriculture and the natural environment. Although economists have made considerable advances in dealing with these issues, many gaps still remain.

In view of the major problems involved in determining the optimal level of pollution control, it is perhaps not surprising that the optimal approach to setting emission levels has not been adopted. In practice pollution control agencies in Britain have tended to use a pollution standards approach to policy-making. It is very unlikely that the resulting emission level would coincide with the optimal level of pollution control. Nevertheless, in the absence of an accurate knowledge of MAC and MDC, a pollution standards approach to environmental management can give rise to a net increase in economic welfare, as long as the total benefits arising from the implementation of the standards set exceed the total costs. For air pollution control this has involved a case-by-case specification of the production technology and pollution control equipment that is required. The emission level for each process is effectively determined by the production and abatement technology which is installed. An alternative approach, which has been used for water pollution control, concentrates on the benefits of emission reductions. Data relating the concentration of pollution in the environment to its physical effects are used to set a minimum ambient environmental quality objective. Appropriate action is then taken to reduce emission levels in order to achieve the standard set. Direct controls have been the most popular policy instruments for achieving environmental quality objectives in the past. These have included regulations limiting emission levels from individual firms and industries, and the specification of production processes and abatement technology as referred to above.

12.3   Economic incentives

In recent years there has been a growing awareness of the potential advantages of using economic incentives to achieve pollution control objectives. First, economic incentives achieve reductions in the emission of pollutants at the lowest possible total abatement cost. Secondly, whereas regulations may encourage only minimum compliance, economic incentives can provide a continuing inducement for dischargers of pollutants to find new and more cost-effective ways of reducing emission levels. Thirdly, economic incentives are perceived to be the most appropriate means of pollution prevention because they encourage the development of cleaner technology.

To achieve pollution control objectives at the lowest total cost, reduction in emission levels should be undertaken by those operators with the lowest marginal abatement cost. Consider the case in Figure 12.1 where MDC and MAC are known and the optimal quantity of emissions is Q5. If a pollution charge per unit of emission is introduced, equal to MDC at Q5, pollutant emissions will fall to Q5. When the charge, T, is introduced polluters have the option of reducing emissions or paying the pollution charge. Figure

12.1 shows that between Q3 and Q2 for firm 1, and between Q6 and Q4 for firm 2 the marginal abatement cost is less than the pollution charge. Firm 1 and firm 2 will reduce emissions to Q2 and Q4 respectively, to the point where the marginal abatement cost is equal to the pollution charge. Because both polluters are subject to the same pollution charge, it follows that their marginal abatement costs will be the same and that total abatement costs will be minimised. The total quantity of emissions will be at the optimal level Q5 (Q2 + Q4). The pollution charge could also be used to achieve a specified ambient environmental quality objective. Each polluter would have an incentive to reduce the amount of waste discharged until the marginal abatement cost had increased to the level of the pollution charge. By fixing the pollution charge at the appropriate level an environmental agency would be able to implement whatever degree of emission control it required at the lowest possible abatement cost. This contrasts with the regulatory approach, where only by chance could the environmental agency hope to achieve the most cost-effective allocation of emission quotas.

A pollution charge per unit of emissions may be impracticable where there are many sources of emissions with no obvious point where they can be monitored. In these circumstances an alternative would be to add a pollution tax to the price of materials used or products and services sold. This is done on the presumption that the environmental damage caused by the pollutant is proportional to the quantity of the good produced. The tax would raise the price of the final product, reducing the quantity demanded and hence reducing the level of pollution. In Figure 12.2, the industry demand curve, D, indicates the benefits consumers receive from a product in a perfectly competitive industry. S1 is the industry supply curve which shows the marginal cost of production at each level of output. The quantity of the product purchased will be Q2 and the price paid by consumers will be P1. By requiring the firms to include external costs in their costs of production the supply curve would move upwards, for example to S2. Equilibrium price would then rise to P2 and output fall to Q1. In terms of Figure 12.2, the ideal tax would be just enough to encourage producers to view their supply curve as S2 instead of S1. However, the size of the tax can be adjusted to achieve whatever level of pollution control is judged acceptable.

In 1985 member countries of the Organisation for Economic Co-operation and Development adopted the Declaration on Environmental Resources for the Future. By doing so they re-affirmed their acceptance of the Polluter Pays Principle (PPP[1]) first adopted in 1972, and undertook to introduce more flexible, efficient and cost-effective pollution control measures, through a consistent application of PPP and a more effective use of economic instruments. The PPP, as defined by OECD in 1972, simply requires that polluters should bear the costs of pollution prevention and

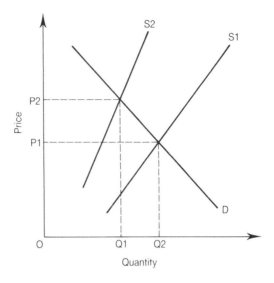

Figure 12.2 Pollution tax

control measures decided upon by public authorities to ensure that the environment is in an 'acceptable state'. It does not imply an acceptance of the pollution charge or tax approach described above, where polluters pay a charge on unabated pollution.

In accordance with PPP, pollution charges are used in Britain to recover the costs of services provided by pollution control authorities, and the treatment of industrial effluents at sewage works. However, the emphasis is on revenue collection rather than providing an incentive for pollution abatement. There are exceptions such as the tax differential designed to encourage consumers to switch to unleaded petrol. Nevertheless, despite the arguments supporting the use of economic incentives, such approaches to pollution control are seldom used. The emphasis is placed on the use of standards and regulations as discussed below in the cases of air and water pollution.

12.4 Air pollution

Responsibility for air pollution control in Britain has traditionally been shared between central and local government. Central government agencies, operating under the Alkali and Works Regulation Act 1906 and the Health and Safety Act 1974, have regulated 'scheduled' industrial processes and plant with the greatest pollution potential. Until 1987 'scheduled' processes in England and Wales were the responsibility of the Industrial Air Pollution Inspectorate. In 1987, control transferred to Her Majesty's Inspectorate of Pollution (HMIP) as part of a policy of integrated pollution control. In Scotland, Her Majesty's Industrial Pollution Inspectorate (HMIPI) has similar responsibilities.

The approach to pollution control adopted by these central government agencies is based on the specification of production and abatement technology. Prior approval is required from the Inspectorate before any new plant or process can be operated. Before the introduction of new legislation in 1990, operators and inspectors had a duty under the Health and Safety at Work Act 1974 to ensure that production processes made use of the best practicable means for preventing the escape of noxious or offensive gases and for rendering such gases where discharged harmless and inoffensive. Practicable was defined in the Control of Pollution Act 1974 as, 'reasonably practicable, having regard among other things to local conditions and circumstances, to the current state of technical knowledge and to the financial implications'. The approach to establishing best practicable means (BPM) was pragmatic and involved discussions between the inspectorate and the industry concerned. The conclusions were published in BPM notes which prescribed agreed production technology and abatement techniques and specified the emission limits achievable. Supporters of the BPM approach to environmental pollution control argued that its main advantage was its flexibility, and the opportunity it allowed for regulatory officials to take account of the varying circumstances of different plants. Furthermore, it was claimed that the process of negotiation between polluters and regulatory officials increased the likelihood of polluter compliance. However, critics argued that BPM was too flexible and that too much weight was given to the costs of pollution abatement and insufficient attention given to benefits from reduced environmental damage.

Local authority powers have been more limited. Under the provision of the Clean Air Acts of 1956 and 1968, it was possible for local authorities to require operators of non-scheduled combustion processes to adopt appropriate abatement equipment before commencement of operations. However, in the case of other processes local authorities were unable to take action until some offence had occurred, effectively precluding any application of BPM to most activities under local authority control.

The Environmental Protection Act 1990 introduced radical changes to the control of air pollution. This was the result of two important influences. First, Britain was required to implement the European Community Directive on Emissions from Industrial Plant. Secondly, the government decided in 1987 to introduce integrated pollution control. Under the 1990 Act all production processes which cause environmental damage are designated 'prescribed processes'. Each category of 'prescribed process' is divided into two parts. Part A covers plants with the potential for creating pollution damage in more than one environmental medium. They are subject to the control of central government agencies, HMIP in England and Wales and HMIPI or the River Purification Boards in Scotland. These agencies will be responsible for emissions to air, water and land, with the overall objective of minimising the pollution of the environment as a whole. Part B processes are controlled by local authorities for air pollution purposes only. For the first time, local authorities will give prior written authorisation for the prescribed processes under their care. Operators of all prescribed processes, are required to use 'best available techniques not entailing excessive cost' (BATNEEC) to prevent or minimise pollution. Processes under the control of central government agencies are also required to adopt the 'best practicable environmental option' (BPEO).

The Department of the Environment has issued guidance on the meaning of BATNEEC. 'Techniques' refers both to the process used and the way in which it is operated, 'available' refers to obtainable processes, and 'best' means the most effective for dealing with pollution. However, best available techniques need not be used if they involve excessive cost. For new processes, whether or not costs are excessive depends upon the environmental benefits that result, thus implying a balance of costs and benefits of pollution control. For existing plant, what is excessive depends on the particular operating circumstances of the plant. Plant inefficiency and financial exigency are not acceptable excessive cost arguments.

12.5   Water pollution

Before 1989, the principal legislation for the prevention of water pollution was Part II of the 1974 Control of Pollution Act. Under this legislation effluent discharges into rivers, estuaries and coastal waters in England and Wales were controlled by ten Regional Water Authorities (RWAs) as part of a programme of integrated river basin management. In addition to water quality management and conservation, RWAs were responsible for several related services, including the supply of water and the collection, treatment and disposal of sewage. The approach to water pollution control adopted by the RWAs was based on environmental quality objectives related to the assimilative capacity of the receiving waters. To achieve these objectives, emissions were regulated by consents issued by the RWAs. The RWAs issued their own consents for discharges from sewage treatment works. This conflict of interests between water quality management and sewage disposal led critics to argue that RWAs themselves were major water polluters who did not give sufficient priority to pollution control relative to their other responsibilities.

The 1989 Water Act separated sewage disposal and water quality management. Private water service companies, set up under the Act, were given responsibility for the provision of water supply and the collection, treatment and disposal of sewage. Overall responsibility for water quality management was given to a regulatory body called the National Rivers Authority (NRA). The government had initially planned to privatise the RWAs in their original form, making them responsible for water supply, sewage disposal and pollution control. However, EC intervention prevented this. It was pointed out that the EC Directive on the Discharge of Dangerous Substances to Water required a 'competent authority' to authorise the discharge and the question was asked whether a private company could act as a 'competent authority'. Under the new arrangements statutory water quality objectives will be set by the Secretary of State for the Environment on the advice of the NRA subject to meeting the quality standards required by EC water pollution Directives.

In Scotland seven mainland River Purification Boards and three Island Councils are responsible for controlling pollution of inland and coastal waters and conserving the water resources of their areas. They have the duty of ensuring that specified water quality objectives are achieved and issue consents for the discharge of trade and sewage effluent.

From April 1991, discharges to water from 'scheduled' industrial processes came under the control of HMIP in England and Wales and HMIPI or River Purification Boards in Scotland under the system of integrated pollution control introduced in the 1990 Environmental Protection Act. The most hazardous substances are subject to strict environmental quality objectives, and producers are required to adopt BATNEEC and BPEO. These developments represent a significant move in Britain's water pollution control policy towards the stricter, precautionary, EC approach to pollution standards.

12.6   EC directives

EC environmental legislation is now very extensive and covers a wide range of issues. Consequently it has had a significant impact on the environmental programmes of member states. The first action programme on the environment was adopted by the EC Council in 1973, the fifth will be implemented in 1993. Under the 1988 Single European Act 'environmental protection requirements shall be a component of the Community's other policies', thereby raising the profile of the environmental consequences of other EC programmes. These EC developments reflect the increasing public interest in the environment, and the recognition by member states that environmental issues are an important factor in EC development.

EC air pollution directives can usefully be divided into three categories. The first, aimed at avoiding non-tariff barriers to trade, include directives which set uniform pollution standards for products, such as those limiting the amount of sulphur in gas oil, lead in petrol and the emission of carbon monoxide, unburnt hydrocarbons and nitrogen oxides from vehicles. Secondly there is a set of directives controlling ground level air quality standards including smoke, sulphur dioxide, nitrogen dioxide and lead. In each case the primary objective has been to protect human health. The third category of directives sets emission standards for industrial plant. In 1987 the EC Council adopted a Framework Directive on Emissions from Industrial Plant. This was the first significant response of the European Community to the problem of acid rain. Member states must ensure that all plant causing air pollution obtains authorisation before commencing operations.

To date, by far the most interesting and important Daughter Directive, deals with power station emissions of sulphur dioxide, nitrogen oxide and dust. The Directive, adopted in November 1988, which is known as the Large Combustion Plant Directive, deals with combustion plant of over 50 megawatts. All new plant is required to incorporate BATNEEC and is subject to uniform emission limits. Existing plant must be modified to conform with the agreed overall national reductions in sulphur dioxide set out in the Directive. The British reductions are 20 per cent by 1993, 40 per cent by 1998 and 60 per cent by 2003 compared with 1980 emissions (see Table 12.1).

EC water pollution directives can similarly be divided into three categories. The first involves the implementation of exposure standards with the primary objective of protecting human health. The Directive on Drinking Water falls into this category. Secondly, there are several Directives which set quality objectives to protect public health and amenities. These include the Directives relating to bathing, fresh water fish and shellfish, and water from which drinking water is to be abstracted. The third category of Directives set emission limits for dangerous substances. The Framework Directive on Dangerous Substances in Water was adopted in 1976, but not without controversy.

A major policy problem affecting the EC environmental programme has been the long-running dispute between Britain and the other member states over the use of uniform emission limits for the control of water pollution. There has been general agreement that uniform pollution standards should be specified for products as part of product harmonisation – to avoid a situation where different national pollution standards might operate as non-tariff barriers to trade. However, there has not been comparable agreement over the wider use of uniform emission limits. The British position was that emission limits were the means of implementing environmental quality objectives and, as such, they should reflect local circumstances. It was quite logical, therefore, that emission limits would vary from place to place. Countries such as Britain with an extensive

Table 12.1 Ceilings and reduction targets for emission of SO_2 from existing plant (1000 tonnes)

	Emissions 1980	Emission ceilings			% reduction over 1980		
		1993	1998	2003	1993	1998	2003
Belgium	530	318	212	159	−40	−60	−70
Denmark	323	213	141	106	−34	−56	−67
Germany	2225	1335	890	668	−40	−60	−70
Greece	303	320	320	320	+6	+6	+6
Spain	2290	2290	1730	1440	0	−24	−37
France	1910	1146	764	573	−40	−60	−70
Ireland	99	124	124	124	+25	+25	+25
Italy	2450	1800	1500	900	−27	−39	−63
Luxembourg	3	1.8	1.5	1.5	−40	−50	−60
Netherlands	299	180	120	90	−40	−60	−70
Portugal	115	232	270	206	+102	+135	+79
United Kingdom	3883	3106	2330	1553	−20	−40	−60
European Community	14 430	11 065.8	8402.5	6140.5	−23	−42	−58

Source: Official Journal of the European Communities, L336, vol. 31, 7 December 1988.

coastline and fast-flowing rivers and estuaries would be in a position to achieve environmental quality objectives with higher pollutant emission levels than other countries lacking in such geographical advantages. Those member states which were supporting the use of uniform emission limits argued that if some countries had lower standards than others, this would result in unfair competition. Britain's response was that this was no more than an application of comparative advantage.

Under the Framework Directive two lists of substances have been compiled on the basis of their toxicity, persistence and bio-accumulation. For list 1, which includes such substances as mercury, cadmium and lindane, subsequent Daughter Directives are used to specify emission limits based on BATNEEC to which all dischargers must conform. Because of Britain's objection to this uniform emission limits approach, member states were given the option of choosing an alternative means of control based on environmental quality objectives. Under this arrangement it is possible to use different emission limits to reflect different environmental conditions as long as the environmental quality objectives are met. For list

2, which includes possibly less dangerous substances such as copper, lead, zinc and chromium, member states are required to organise pollution reduction programmes based on emission limits linked with environmental quality objectives.

The application of the Framework Directive, and the subsequent Daughter Directives on Dangerous Substances in Water, continues to be controversial. The majority of member states would like to extend the uniform emission limits approach to list 2 substances. Others, including Britain, prefer the environmental quality objectives approach. The recent developments in Britain where the Environmental Protection Act requires the use of BATNEEC coupled with environmental quality objectives can be seen as an attempt by Britain to come more into line with its EC partners.

12.7 Integrated pollution control

The case for integrated pollution control in Britain was first put forward in the Fifth Report of the Royal Commission on Environmental Pollution in 1976. The Commission argued that in view of the close connection between different types of industrial pollution, the lack of co-operation between pollution control authorities was unsatisfactory. It was evident to the Commission that pollution control in one medium was giving rise to increased pollution in another, with the possibility that the overall impact was worsened. The Royal Commission recommended an integrated approach to the most difficult pollution problems. The objective was to minimise the damage to the environment as a whole by selecting the best practicable environmental option. It was not until 1986 that the government announced that a new unified pollution inspectorate, Her Majesty's Inspectorate of Pollution, would be set up for England and Wales in 1987. The Environmental Protection Act 1990 established the legislative basis for HMIP and integrated pollution control. In Scotland responsibility will go either to HMIPI or to the River Purification Boards.

In 1988 the Royal Commission's Twelfth Report set out to define BPEO. The concept is concerned not only with the optimal combination of waste disposal methods in order to minimise environmental damage, but also incorporates production technology, operating procedures and control equipment. Paragraph 2.1 of the Twelfth Report states:

> A BPEO is the outcome of a systematic and consultative decision making procedure which emphasises the protection and conservation of the environment across land, air and water. The BPEO procedure establishes, for a given set of objectives, the option that provides the most benefit or least damage to the environment as a whole, at acceptable cost, in the long term as well as in the short term.

Establishing a BPEO will involve the identification, quantification and evaluation of the environmental impact of polluting processes, taking account of the alternative emission disposal options. Recognising this challenge, paragraph 3.20 of the Twelfth Report comments:

> The advice of experts may be sufficient to ensure that best results for the environment are secured. However, where trade-offs are difficult or controversial, the selection of a BPEO cannot be left to scientists, industrialists and regulatory experts alone. Public involvement is needed so that the public values underlying the choice of a BPEO are identified and clearly understood.

These developments in integrated pollution control represent major changes in Britain's pollution control policy. Recent announcements by the government envisage further developments. These will come in the form of two independent environmental protection agencies, one for England and Wales and the other for Scotland. In each case these new agencies will bring together the key pollution control functions affecting air, water and land under a single organisation.

There are several reasons cited for the proposals: first, the agencies will resolve the problems of overlap and potential conflict between pollution control authorities; second, they will be able to ensure that full consideration is given to achieving BPEO; third, environmental monitoring will be undertaken on a co-ordinated basis and finally, the new organisations will be independent. The precise role and functions of the proposed agencies are at present under consideration.

12.8 Conclusion

The development of integrated pollution control in Britain is based on the argument that there are important links between pollution in different media. In so far as these linkages exist, the proposed Environmental Agency for England and Wales, and the Scottish Environmental Protection Agency will be better placed than existing agencies to ensure that the social costs of environmental pollution are minimised. Nevertheless, it is not unreasonable to question the extent to which the new agencies will be in any better position to establish the relationship between the costs and benefits of pollution control, or to achieve pollution control objectives at the lowest cost. The White Paper, *This Common Inheritance* (1990), identifies two broad approaches to the future control of pollution in Britain. These are the use of regulation so that agreed standards can be applied and economic incentives including taxes and prices which can be used to influence producers and consumers.

Pollution control policies adopted in the United Kingdom during the next decade and beyond will be influenced by EC environmental legislation and the global policies emerging from the Earth Summit which took place in Brazil during June 1992. For example, Britain recently took a step towards the introduction of a pollution tax when the European Commission adopted proposals for introducing a European carbon-tax. The objective is to reduce the emissions of carbon dioxide as part of a programme of controlling greenhouse gas emissions to counter the problems of global warming. All EC member states have agreed to stabilise carbon dioxide emissions at 1990 levels by the year 2000. The proposed tax, which would be introduced in stages, combines a tax on the carbon content of fuels and a tax on all non-renewable forms of energy. It would encourage energy conservation and fuel substitution from carbon-intensive fuels to those which generate less carbon dioxide per unit of energy. Pearson and Smith (1991) suggest that there is considerable scope for fuel substitution in response to relative price changes. However, the low price elasticity of demand for energy means that relatively high taxes would be required in order to have any significant impact on the overall demand for energy. The main objection to this tax is that it would reduce competitiveness on a world-wide basis. Because of this objection the European Commission argues that the European Community should only implement the tax if its main industrial competitors act similarly. In view of the uncertainties associated with the problem of global warming it is still unclear whether the not inconsiderable cost of controlling greenhouse gas emissions would be justified by the benefits which might result.

The Earth Summit brought together political leaders from all over the world in an attempt to establish a global strategy for dealing with environmental issues such as the greenhouse effect, ozone holes and de-forestation. At the end of the Summit heads of government were invited to sign an Earth Charter establishing basic principles of sustainable development and a document called Agenda 21 setting out a list of objectives for the twenty-first century. Government leaders were also invited to sign two binding conventions on climate change and bio-diversity (Cockburn and Hecht, 1992; Pearce, 1992). The success of the Summit will depend on which and how many leaders sign the agreements and whether or not they are eventually ratified and implemented.

Questions for discussion

1. Explain the concept of an optimal level of pollution control.
2. How should pollution control authorities allocate the total reduction of emissions between polluting firms?
3. Compare the regulatory approach to air and water pollution control used in Britain. To what extent do these adopt the principles of pollution control advocated by economists?
4. Why do economists prefer economic incentives to regulatory controls?
5. Why does the Royal Commission on Environmental Pollution advocate the adoption of the Best Practicable Environmental Option?

6. In what circumstances might different national pollution standards operate as non-tariff barriers to trade?

Note

1. Not to be confused with the alternative meaning of PPP – purchasing power parity – discussed in Chapter 6.

References and suggestions for further reading

Cockburn, A. and S. Hecht (1992), 'Up a blind alley', *New Statesman*, 5 no. 204, (29 May), pp. 18–19.

Department of the Environment (1990), *This Common Inheritance: Britain's environmental strategy*, Cm 1200, London: HMSO.

Haigh, N. (1990), *EEC Environmental Policy and Britain*, Harlow: Longman.

Organisation for Economic Co-operation and Development (1989), *Economic Instruments for Environmental Protection*, Paris: OECD.

Owens, S. (1990), 'The unified pollution inspectorate and best practicable environmental option in the United Kingdom', in N. Haigh and F. Irwin (eds), *Integrated Pollution Control in Europe and North America*, London: Conservation Foundation, Institute for European Environmental Policy.

Pearce, D., A. Markandya and E. B. Barbier (1989), *Blueprint for a Green Economy*, London: Earthscan.

Pearce, F. (1992), 'Last chance to save the planet?', *New Scientist*, 134, no. 1823 (30 May), pp. 24–28.

Pearson, M. and S. Smith (1991), *The European Carbon Tax: An assessment of the European Commission's proposals*, London: Institute for Fiscal Studies.

Royal Commission on Environmental Pollution, Twelfth Report (1988), *Best Practicable Environmental Option*, London: HMSO.

Chapter 13

Public expenditure and taxation

PHILIP WELHAM

13.1 Introduction

Should governments intervene in markets at all? Adam Smith's 'invisible hand' suggests efficiency is maximised where people pursue their own interests. Consumers maximise utility, equating marginal utility with price by purchasing goods up to the point where the utility derived from the last unit consumed is just equal to the price paid. Firms maximise profits by equating marginal cost with marginal revenue which, under conditions of perfect competition, is the same as price. Thus the yardstick of economic efficiency is satisfied, namely the marginal utility that consumers derive from a good equals the marginal cost of providing it. However, this holds in perfectly competitive markets only and ignores problems of external costs such as pollution (see Chapter 12), problems of acquiring information and the unequal distribution of income and wealth (see Chapter 14). Whenever market failures occur governments may intervene in an attempt to improve the allocation of resources.

'Public goods' (goods that are indivisible and consumed by everyone, such as defence) cannot readily be supplied by private markets because consumers cannot be prevented from deriving the benefits of the good once it exists. The benefits from defence, public sanitation, prevention of spread of infectious diseases and policing, for example, accrue to society in general. If some people pay for these goods others (so-called *free riders*) derive benefits also and thus do not have to pay at all or can contribute less than the benefits they derive. The economic characteristics of public goods are developed more fully in the next section. Externalities (effects on the utility of people other than the producer or consumer of the good) are another area where market failure occurs. Whilst markets take into account the costs and benefits of the two parties to the transaction, buyer and seller, the benefits and costs to third parties, such as benefits from attractive landscaping or costs such as noise pollution or chemical waste damage caused by firms, are not taken account of by the market mechanism. Unless the state intervenes to legislate, tax or subsidise so that externalities do influence the output level of the industry, economic efficiency will not be achieved.

Market failure also occurs when information is less than perfect. Many people are likely to underestimate their needs in old age and make insufficient provision. Others cannot calculate their risks of being unemployed, or might prove to be bad risks for private insurance purposes. There is a general agreement, therefore, that the state should provide retirement and unemployment benefits as well as sickness, single-parent and other benefits. Lack of information, at least on one side of the market, also leads the state to regulate work conditions and quality of consumer products, together with requiring information about the nature and composition of many products. Finally, a category of goods called 'merit goods' (goods or services that society thinks everyone should consume) gives rise to state intervention not in order to deliver efficiency as it has so far been defined, but because the state wishes to 'improve on' consumer preferences. The state takes a paternalistic line and requires consumption of certain goods (e.g. education is compulsory up to the age of sixteen), or bans other goods (e.g. drugs). Other examples of merit goods are the provision of a universal health service and housing benefits for low-income groups.

The economics of public expenditure and taxation, or Public Finance as it is called, covers three main areas. The first area is macroeconomic, involving issues such as stabilisation and growth of the whole economy. This has been covered in Chapter 2. The second area involves equity. Taxes and expenditure affect the distribution of income and wealth. These issues are the subject of the next chapter. The final area concerns the allocation of resources. Public spending and taxation affect the efficient use of resources. In this chapter we shall be discussing the appropriate size of the public sector, the components of government expenditure and the way the tax base and tax rates affect firms' and households' decisions. We will cover central and local government together. The term General Government Expenditure (GGE) is used when central and local spending are jointly considered. Local government finance is covered in Chapter 15.

13.2   The public sector share of national income

To understand the economic ideas behind the division of national income into public and private sectors we present a two-person model of the economy to show how demands for public goods and private goods should be aggregated. In Figure 13.1 the demands of two individuals for public and private sector goods are shown. O is the origin for public goods and Y is the origin for private goods. OY (the horizontal axis) represents the

potential of the economy for producing public or private goods and is
equivalent to national income for our two-person economy. As the output of
public goods is increased, less resources are available to produce private
goods and consequently the output of private goods falls. Individual A's
demand for public sector goods is D_A and is shown as starting at P_2, the
maximum valuation A places on one unit of public goods. A's demand for
private goods is $D_A{}^1$ which slopes down to the left from P_5 and obeys the
normal properties of demand curves apart from being plotted to the left
from Y instead of to the right. Similarly B's demand for public goods is
shown as D_B, starting at P_3, and for private sector goods is $D_B{}^1$.

Since public goods are non-rival in consumption, i.e. A's consumption of
defence or the benefits of a lighthouse do not diminish the amount of the
good or service available for B, their two demand curves are summed
vertically, giving a joint demand for public goods D_{A+B} (note, therefore,
that $P_2 + P_3 = P_4$). Private goods are removed from the market when
purchased so a good consumed by A is not available to B. The two demands
for private goods have to be added horizontally giving $D_{A^1+B^1}$. The
opportunity cost of public sector goods is the foregone private sector
production and the value placed on the private goods by A and B. $D_{A^1+B^1}$ is
thus the marginal cost or supply curve for public goods as well as the
demand of the two individuals for private goods. Thus Figure 13.1 shows
the optimal division of national income into a public (OX) and private
sector (XY), with the marginal valuation of the last unit produced of public
goods OP_1 being equal to the value placed on the last unit produced of
private sector goods. Both A and B consume OX of public goods but A

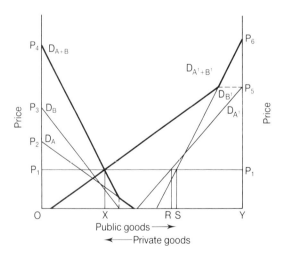

Figure 13.1 Demand for public and private goods

consumes YR and B consumes YS of private sector goods. This approach appears to provide a sound theoretical basis for dividing national income between private and public goods.

Unfortunately, though we can get good information for private sector demand, shown by the prices people are willing to pay, there is almost no good information about demand for public goods. People do not have to pay directly for public goods and even if they did the free rider problem would lead them to under-declare their preferences and hope that others would pay for the public good. The basic rule that public goods in total, and for each component of public spending, should be produced up to the point where marginal benefit equals marginal cost gives a broad goal but lack of adequate information means implementation in practice is highly unlikely. The rule does draw attention to the fact that utility is maximised when attention is paid to estimates of demand (benefits) as well as costs. It is not sufficient to consider costs only.

One of the major concerns of the government after 1979 was to control the growth of public expenditure, and it is of interest to look at the system of planning used. (For a fuller, year-by-year, account see Johnson, 1991.) The key issue is whether future plans for government expenditure are made in cash terms, that is the amount of money to be spent (cash limits), or in volume terms, that is expressed in current prices with future adjustments to be made to allow for any rise in prices. From 1961 to 1976 plans had been made in volume terms (also called 'survey prices' or, less reverently, 'funny money'). Between 1976 and 1982 plans were made in cash terms for one year and volume terms for three years. After 1982 spending was planned in cash terms only. Cash terms provide a better guide to the finances needed and for macroeconomic purposes. However, volume plans are necessary if efficiency objectives are important since they give a better guide to the real resources being provided.[1] Volume plans place greater emphasis on the needs for government spending. For instance, though an increase in student numbers needs greater finance in cash terms too, the cash figures do not look as sacrosanct as they would if they were framed in volume terms. Limiting the amount that could be spent in cash terms, i.e. cash limits, was not applied initially to demand-determined spending like social security payments but attempts were made in the late 1980s to make all spending subject to cash limits.

Turning to the path of actual government expenditure, we can see from Table 13.1 that GGE in cash terms grew from £75 billion in 1978/9 to £222 billion in 1990/1. The real change was from £190 billion for 1978/9 expressed in 1990/1 prices. The ratio of GGE (including transfer payments) to gross domestic product (GGE/GDP) showed an increase from 37 per cent in 1963 to 49 per cent by 1975 and a fall to 43 per cent in 1977 (data sources as for Table 13.1). The fall was partly accounted for by the exclusion of nationalised industries' investment after 1976 but also reflected a sharp

Table 13.1 General government expenditure, 1978/9 to 1990/1 (£ billion except for row 4)

	1978/9	1981/2	1984/5	1987/8	1990/1
1. GGE excluding privatisation proceeds of which:	75	121	153	178	222
2. GGE on services	65	103	132	155	195
3. debt interest	7	13	16	18	18
4. (1) as % of GDP[1]	44	47	47	42	40
5. GGE in real terms[2]	190	202	215	215	216
6. Privatisation proceeds	0	0.5	2	5	5

Notes:
[1] The figures for GDP have been adjusted (down by *c.* 1.8%) before 1990 to allow for the effects of the community charge.
[2] Cash figures adjusted to 1990 1 prices by the GDP deflator.
Note that row 5 figures have been reduced by privatisation proceeds.
Cash terms for rows 1, 2, 3, 6.
Sources: Cm 1920 *Public Expenditure Analyses to 1994–95*, HMSO, Tables 2.1, 2.2 and 2.3.

cut in public sector investment advised by the International Monetary Fund. In 1979, the incoming Conservative government set out to reduce GGE/GDP, but the opposite happened so the target was revised in 1980. Real government spending was planned to fall for the next four years. As can be seen from Table 13.1, this did not happen either. Real expenditure was roughly constant between 1984/5 and 1988/9 after which it started to rise again. GGE/GDP fell from 1983 to 1990, mainly reflecting the rise in gross domestic product. The fall in income in 1991, together with the rise in government expenditure, has halted the process. The United Kingdom was about at the OECD average in 1986 for the size of the public sector. However, it should be noted that almost half the expenditure is on transfer payments which influence spending decisions in the private sector. The absorption of factors of production into the public sector represents just over 20 per cent of gross domestic product.[2]

A very worrying aspect of the growth of GGE concerns the ratio of capital to current spending in the public sector. From 1974 to 1979 capital spending divided by GGE had fallen by 40 per cent. Gross domestic capital formation, before subtracting sales of assets, increased from £8 billion in 1980 to £12 billion in 1990 (figures in 1985 prices from the *Blue Book* (the United Kingdom's National Accounts), Table 9.3) but capital formation has still not got back to 1974 levels in real terms. Much of the public sector capital stock is in a bad state of repair. For example, a recent National Audit Office report (quoted in the *Observer* of 22 March 1992) said that £3 billion was needed for repairs to schools alone. This issue is not pursued further here, since it has already been referred to in Chapter 2.

13.3 Components of government expenditure

It is useful to distinguish four main reasons why an item of government spending might grow. The first is because of a demand for increased quality. The demands for health and education are thought to grow as income increases. There is some dispute about whether the income elasticity is above or below 1. Above 1 would indicate an increasing proportion of income going on that item. For health and education the income elasticity of demand is certainly greater than zero, indicating increased real expenditure through time to satisfy the demand for increased quality of service. Examples of increased quality would be a larger proportion of an age group staying on for tertiary education, lower pupil to teacher ratios, improved forms of treatment for medical conditions and longer patient time with doctors. The second reason for growth of expenditure is also connected with demand: namely, to satisfy an increased need due to a structural change in the economy. An ageing population means that the demands on the health service increase and more pensions have to be paid. Similarly a rise in the birth rate would in five years give rise to a need for more primary school places and teachers. Though each pensioner or pupil would be getting the same quality of service as before, the increased numbers push up government spending.

On the cost side we get the other two reasons for an increase in GGE – increases in the costs of inputs and increases in the prices of inputs. A good example of the former comes from defence. External defence is regarded as successful if potential aggressors can be deterred. Increasing sophistication of military equipment drives up the cost of achieving external defence without deriving any extra benefits (ignoring spill-over effects of research for non-military purposes). The price of inputs increases whenever salaries rise relative to productivity and, as many forms of government spending are labour-intensive, the scope for productivity gains is often less than in industries that set the lead in wage bargaining. The price of inputs also rises if bureaucratic factors expand the personnel employed in producing a given public service without giving an increased output.

In the 1980s government White Papers on expenditure put much more emphasis on restraining costs than on estimating the needs for government services. Formally the objectives of the Financial Management Initiative (FMI) that was introduced in 1982 covered assessment of outputs and performance in relation to objectives, which would involve demand assessment. But the White Papers seemed to stress the other objectives of FMI: namely, making the best use of resources ('value for money') and acquiring information, particularly about costs. Costing of programmes had been done on a regular basis since 1961 under the Public Expenditure Survey Committee (PESC) system which provides the basis for the public expenditure White Papers. Demand studies had been conducted under Programme Analysis and Review (PAR) though the information was never published. The Heath government introduced PAR in 1970 but it was abandoned in 1980 – which suggested the emphasis that was going to be placed on costs and the introduction of market system influences into the public sector. In addition the National Audit Office was set up in 1984 to provide independent advice and suggestions for improving efficiency and effectiveness.

It is extremely difficult to define and measure efficiency in most areas of public spending. The level of health or education of the nation cannot be measured directly and evaluation of the benefits from health and education is problematical, therefore. Some benefits, like those from defence, are impossible to assess in a monetary sense and thus the value of benefits cannot be equated with costs. To try to deal with these difficulties performance indicators were developed in the 1980s. Targets for output, costs and dates for achieving programmes were set. Performance indicators rarely involve a final output measure. Various alternatives are used, such as intermediate output or the gap between supply and demand or input use. The difficulty with intermediate and input yardsticks is that when a change in output is linked to a single input change the effect may have been caused by substitution of extra inputs of some other factor or efficiency gains from all inputs together. The scope for performance indicator gains can be pushed too far if other measures are not used to check reliability. For example, gains from hospital bed turnover could be offset by re-entry of newly discharged patients.

Better information about demands and needs would help analysis about what are reasonable levels of public provision of a good or service. Some areas obviously should not have queues forming, examples being emergency medical treatment or response of a fire engine. But how many emergencies should it be possible to deal with simultaneously? There cannot be provision for all eventualities. Costs of provision are positive but a zero price charged to users means no demand gets choked off by the price mechanism. Thus in some situations economic efficiency requires that not all demand be satisfied and possibly queues form. Not satisfying demand and long waiting times can be carried too far; for instance, there would be no point in a one-year waiting list for abortions.

Government expenditure is made up of the items shown in Table 13.2 together with interest payments on the National Debt, which are shown in Table 13.1. Debt interest has been approximately 10 per cent of total GGE in the 1980s. Apart from debt interest the main components of GGE are social security payments, the NHS, education and defence. The largest fall in Table 13.2 occurred for housing. The fall was not quite as dramatic as it

Table 13.2 General government expenditure on
services (% of total)

	1978/9	1984/5	1990/1
Defence	11.5	13.0	11.2
Trade and industry	4.7	3.9	2.3
Employment and training	1.7	2.3	1.5
Transport	4.6	4.3	4.1
Housing	7.0	3.7	2.5
Other environmental services	3.8	3.0	3.7
Law and order	3.9	4.7	5.8
Education and science	14.0	13.3	14.5
Health	12.0	12.7	14.2
Social security	26.0	30.2	30.1
Other	9.8	8.9	10.1
Total	100.0	100.0	100.0

Notes:
[1] The share of housing is reduced by sales of dwellings
being subtracted from the actual expenditure for 1984/5 and
1990/1.
[2] The table excludes debt interest.
Source: Cm 1920 Public Expenditure Analyses to 1994/95,
HMSO, Table 2.4.

appears since the value of house sales is subtracted from the expenditure
figures. The other area to show a significant fall was trade and industry.
Defence increased its share of GGE in the early 1980s. The government
objective had been for a real rate of growth for defence of 3 per cent per
annum but this objective was dropped in the late 1980s and the share of
defence fell back again. In the 1990s defence expenditure may decline
further if the 'peace dividend' materialises. However, careful planning is
needed if benefits are to ensue – with unemployment already high, a large
reduction in defence personnel would not yield immediate dividends.
Education formed a marginally smaller proportion of total spending in
1990/1 than it did in 1978/9.

Social security had the largest increase, mainly in the earlier part of the
period. The change was due to an increase in the number of pensioners (not
the value of the basic pension, though outgoings on the State Earnings-
Related Pension increased) and to an increase in the number of people
unemployed. The increase in the number of low-income households led to
greater spending on housing and supplementary benefits (see the next
chapter for a fuller discussion of social security issues). Government
expenditure on the NHS increased as a proportion of the total, as is shown
in Table 13.2, and it increased in real terms from £20 billion in 1978/9 to

£28 billion in 1990/1 (figures in 1990/1 prices). But such figures do not tell enough about the true trends in health expenditure since relative price effects (RPE) are excluded (see note 1). Nor do they tell us about the demand for health provision.

Total spending in real terms (based on interpolating data in the government White Paper – Cm 1920) increased by 8 per cent for defence, 25 per cent for health and 30 per cent for education between 1980 and 1990. These figures can be compared with information from Table 9.3 of the 1991 *Blue Book* which gives changes in real terms adjusted for the RPE. On this basis, the volume of real spending for the same period increased by 2 per cent for defence, 1.5 per cent for education and 14 per cent for health. The figures are for final consumption only but this was the major component of expenditure. (Gross domestic capital formation divided by current expenditure in 1990 was 3 per cent for defence and 6 per cent for both health and education – data from the *Blue Book*, Table 9.4.)

Unfortunately a more complete picture of the volume of real spending is not provided in official sources. Patchy information is given in the White Papers but a systematic examination of the volume of spending and the need for it is not provided. Specific research enquiries are needed to get a better picture. One such study is provided by le Grand *et al.* (1990). They point out that not all spending on health is funded by the government. Private health spending was equivalent to 3 per cent of NHS expenditure in the late 1980s and prescription charges were about 3 per cent. Also patients bear indirect costs of travel and waiting time. But government expenditure is still the main component of health spending. Le Grand *et al.* compare the annual growth rates for the NHS for the period 1973/4–1978/9 with the period 1978/9 to 1987/8. For the latter period the annual rate of growth in real terms was 2.8 per cent and in volume terms, i.e. allowing for the RPE, it was 0.9 per cent, while need grew at 0.8 per cent. (The earlier period figures were volume growth of 4.4 per cent against need of 0.2 per cent.) These figures ignore any change in demand, as opposed to need, and also any efficiency gains – which are estimated by le Grand *et al.* to be about 2 per cent of the budget in the late 1980s. The probability is, however, that demand was outstripping provision in the 1980s. Spending on the NHS has increased since 1990 in connection with the market-style changes that have been introduced but it is too early yet to judge how significant the changes have been. Market-style reforms may improve efficiency and lead to a greater awareness of consumer preferences but le Grand *et al.* (1990) argue that the cost savings claimed for the introduction of quasi-markets into the public sector may not materialise. Higher administrative costs may result from the procedures, and higher labour costs may occur if unions bargain with smaller units instead of a large monopsonist.

GGE on housing consists mainly of new house building and subsidies to tenants. The figures are usually presented net of privatisation proceeds so appear to be lower than a comparison with, say, the 1970s would indicate (since no privatisation was going on then). A dramatic fall took place in capital formation. Public sector completions in Great Britain were 131 000 in 1978 (stock was 6.5 million) and 31 000 in 1990 (stock was 5.1 million). In that time 1.7 million council houses were sold. Originally the sales were meant to provide funds for new building, but central government restrictions meant that new building in the public sector continued to decline throughout the 1980s. Private rented housing plus housing association stock fell by 0.5 million. The lack of sufficient rental accommodation developed into a more serious problem in the 1980s with increases in homelessness and people in temporary accommodation (see Hills and Mullings, 1990). Between 1978 and 1990 total housing stock increased by 2 million and owner–occupier stock by 4 million. Over-encouragement of the latter led in the 1991–2 recession to a large number of repossessions.

The subsidy component of local authorities' housing revenue account (HRA) expenditure (data from the *Blue Book*) was 58 per cent of the total in 1978 and 63 per cent in 1990. Rents were increased but there was a larger concentration of low-income tenants as only the better-off had been able to purchase their house. The form of the subsidy changed away from general contributions from central and local government to the HRA (which reduce rents on average) towards benefits for individual tenants. (Local authority subsidies, called 'Rate Fund Contribution', were stopped on central government instruction after 1990.) Rent rebates, re-named Housing Benefits after 1982, formed 12 per cent of HRA in 1978 and 40 per cent in 1990. Housing Benefits depend negatively on income and positively on rent paid. Thus the structure has good features but the benefit rates became less generous in the period under consideration. If we ignore ownership of dwellings as being of mainly political interest, and judge housing expenditure against the two objectives of increasing the number of dwellings and providing housing assistance to the poor, it can be seen that policy has been only partly successful. The number of public sector houses built (and the total for all sectors) has been very low by post-war standards but the subsidy system overall improved in that a greater proportion of the subsidies became progressive.

13.4 Taxation

The primary object of taxation is to raise revenue to finance government expenditure. So one criterion for a successful tax is whether it can yield a substantial revenue net of collection costs. Two main principles have been proposed to justify an individual's contribution; these are the ability to pay and benefits received. Ability to pay involves horizontal equity, namely that people in identical circumstances should pay the same amount of tax ('equal treatment of equals') and vertical equity, namely that people should pay according to their means ('the rich should pay more than the poor'). In the United Kingdom tax system, the ideas behind horizontal equity give rise to different allowances to reflect different family circumstances. When considering vertical equity it is useful to classify taxes into poll, regressive, proportional and progressive taxes. With a poll tax each person pays the same amount. A tax is regressive when the proportion of income paid in tax declines as income increases. A poll tax is the extreme form of regressive tax, other forms having the absolute amount paid in tax increasing as income increases. Under a progressive tax the proportion of income paid in tax increases as income increases. A regressive tax could, therefore, satisfy the criterion of 'the rich pay more than the poor', if the phrase is interpreted in an absolute sense. But usually ability to pay is equated with a progressive tax in the sense just defined.

The benefit principle tries to bring market ideas into the public sector. Under it people should pay taxes in accordance with the benefits they receive from public expenditure. The benefit principle appears to have a certain plausibility. However, as we saw in the previous section, it is almost impossible to establish just how much people value public goods and services. If it were the only guide for taxation, the benefit principle would deny a redistributive role for the government budget. In practice it provides justification for few of the UK taxes. The tax on petrol can be thought of as a tax on a complement in lieu of a user charge for roads. Employees' National Insurance contributions (NICs) can be regarded on average as paying for pensions (but other taxes also help the 'fund'). At the individual level, contributions do not match amounts received in pensions or unemployment benefits. Local rates provided a residue of the benefit principle in that taxes rose with the rental value of property, as did consumption of some but not all local services. The largest item of local expenditure is education, so the link behind the benefit principle relating to local rates is very tenuous.

Neither the benefit nor ability-to-pay approaches to taxation get us very far in examining economic issues. It is better to turn to the effects of taxes on the level of activity of the economy, the distribution of well-being and the allocation of resources. The first two areas are dealt with elsewhere (especially in Part I, and Chapter 14). This chapter concentrates on efficiency, though we need to bring in distributional aspects also.

Taxes affect three sets of choices in markets. Labour market effects are discussed in Chapter 2. Choices about which current goods or services to buy and hence the relative sizes of different industries and choices about whether to consume now or in the future are discussed here. Figure 13.2 shows two cases of the effect of a unit tax on a good. In case A, demand for the product is completely inelastic. Supply without the tax is S, giving equilibrium at P_1Q_1, and with the tax it is S + T, giving P_2Q_1. Revenue is the shaded area. In case B demand is more elastic and the effect of the tax is to reduce the amount traded from Q_2 to Q_3 and push up price from P_0 to P_2. (Tax revenue in case B is $(OP_2 - OP_1).OQ_3$.) In case A there is no loss of producer surplus and the loss of consumer surplus is equal to the tax revenue. In case B the combined loss of producer and consumer surplus is greater than tax revenue by area EFG, which is called an 'excess burden', a form of efficiency loss. Excess burdens increase as demand or supply becomes more elastic, as Figure 13.2 shows. Similar arguments hold for choices between goods now and goods in the future, i.e. for decisions about consumption or asset accumulation.

There are two types of taxes on commodities – unit taxes and *ad valorem* taxes. A unit tax is constant per unit of output and an *ad valorem* tax is proportional to the price or value of the commodity. Figure 13.2 shows the effect of a unit tax such as the United Kingdom excise duties. An *ad valorem* tax like value added tax is most conveniently shown in a diagram as downward movement of the demand curve in a wedge-shaped manner, the demand curves before and after tax coinciding at zero price, i.e. where value is zero. Subsidies can be dealt with as negative taxes and exemptions from any tax base act like subsidies.

Where resource allocation is originally efficient, taxes have harmful effects which are greater the higher the elasticities of supply and demand. If, however, there are existing inefficiencies in resource allocation, taxes may be used to counter the inefficiencies in market provision. The use of taxes to restrict output has been proposed to counteract too rapid a

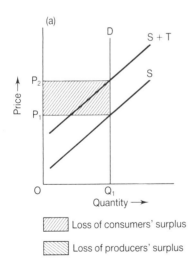
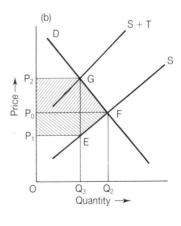

///// Loss of consumers' surplus

\\\\\ Loss of producers' surplus

Figure 13.2   Effect of a tax on a good

depletion of natural resources, e.g. fossil fuels. The argument that markets are inefficient rests on the view that people underestimate the benefits to themselves and future generations. Not all economists concur with this view. There is more general agreement that external costs can justify taxes since markets would otherwise be producing too much of that good (see Chapter 12). External costs to the health service could justify some taxation of alcohol and tobacco and pollution costs could justify taxes on petrol. Taxes have also been advocated for harmful products which would be an additional reason for taxing alcohol and tobacco. This paternalistic argument does not correspond to economic efficiency, as consumers' preferences would not be determining the optimal level of output. Nevertheless, many people would agree with taxes on betting, alcohol and tobacco on these grounds. Note that one argument for taxing tobacco, namely that demand is relatively inelastic, is inconsistent with the paternalistic argument. Also, because tobacco expenditure forms a high proportion of low-income budgets, there is an adverse effect on income distribution.

Taxes have effects in many areas simultaneously, hence it is worth looking at the trade-off between efficiency and equity. The standard argument is that the higher taxes needed to reduce higher incomes in order to improve equity lead to greater distortions in the market or reduced supply of resources and thus have greater efficiency costs. We look at exceptions to the standard rule in relation to the tax base and tax rates. Distortions to choices are introduced by exemptions from the tax base. If one form of income is taxed, there are stronger allocative effects than could occur if all income were taxed. Exemptions from income tax for superannuation contributions and Personal Equity Plans (PEPs) introduce distortions into the choices made about future income. Their removal would be a progressive measure since the benefits accrue primarily to higher income groups. The exemption of housing income and capital gains for owner–occupiers is a good example of a system which achieves neither of the two main objectives of successive governments' housing policy since 1945. The objectives were to provide more dwellings and to assist poorer households to get satisfactory accommodation. Rather than the provision of more units, tax relief for housing has encouraged the production of larger dwellings since the subsidy increases with the value of the dwelling. The largest subsidies accrue to higher-income ranges so the second objective is not achieved either. For further discussion of this issue, see Welham (1982).

Equity and efficiency do not necessarily conflict when the effect of a tax change is separated into average and marginal rate effects. The change in the average rate equates to the income effect of a price change and the marginal rate to the substitution effect. A higher average rate of tax on income makes people worse off and they take less leisure. A higher marginal rate reduces the reward for working an extra hour and people take more leisure. So if a progressive tax change increased the average rather than the marginal rate, there would be an increase in labour supply and a gain in equity.

Finally, before we look at the tax changes since 1979, let us look at the main base for tax purposes. Wealth could serve as a tax base but its role in the UK system has never been very important; however, it is discussed more fully in Chapter 14. The main base could be either income or expenditure. As we do not have a personal expenditure tax in the United Kingdom (i.e. a tax based on the aggregation of all of a person's expenditure in a period and possibly on a progressive scale), we will proceed on the assumption that a comprehensive measure of income is the appropriate yardstick for a neutral tax system. A neutral tax on either income or expenditure would treat all forms of saving equally (the former taxing all savings, the latter taxing none) and thus would not introduce distortions into capital markets. A comprehensive income tax (CIT) would tax all forms of real income equally. Any compensation for decline in real capital values due to inflation is not an appropriate part of the base. On the other hand, interest receipts should be included on a real not a nominal basis. Particular forms of income should not be exempt for tax purposes although personal exemptions can be justified for removing a subsistence element from income and for administrative convenience in removing very-low-income people from the tax net.

The total tax burden in the United Kingdom increased between 1979 and 1989 from 39 per cent to 43 per cent of gross national income at factor cost and the United Kingdom changed from ninth to tenth ranking out of sixteen OECD countries (source of data, *Economic Trends*, 1992). Thus there was no dramatic shift by international standards. The tax proportions of national income do not appear to tally with the fall in (GGE/GDP) from 44 per cent to 40 per cent, except that borrowing was significant in 1979 and negative in 1989.

Changes in the proportions of total revenue contributed by the main taxes in 1978 and 1990 are shown in Table 13.3. The taxes that showed the largest increase were VAT, up from 9 per cent to 17 per cent and corporation tax, up 5 per cent. Taxes that declined in relative importance were income tax (down 6 per cent), social security contributions and tobacco and alcohol duties. Taxes on capital and local taxes (discussed in Chapters 14 and 15 respectively) maintained constant shares. Petroleum revenue tax (PRT) appeared relatively small in 1978 and 1990 but contributed £7.4 billion in 1985. Overall, the table suggests a relatively stable tax structure, but this hides a large number of tax changes in budgets from July 1979 onwards.

The broad thrust of the Conservatives' strategy was to reduce the importance of income taxes because they believed income taxes had strong

Table 13.3 Government revenue from taxation

	1978		1990	
	£ billion	% of total	£ billion	% of total
1. Taxes on income	22	39	77	38
of which:				
income tax	19	33	55	27
corporation tax	3	5	21	10
petroleum revenue tax	0.2	–	1	–
2. Taxes on expenditure[1]	16	28	65	32
of which:				
VAT	5	9	35	17
tobacco	2	4	6	3
oil	2	4	9	4
alcohol	2	4	5	2
3. Taxes on capital	1	2	4	2
of which:				
death duties	0.3		1	
capital gains	0.5		3	
4. Social security contributions	12	21	35	17
5. Rates/community charge	6	11	23	11
Total	57	101	204	100

Note:
[1] excludes national insurance surcharge in 1978 – it is included in row 4 – and excludes business rates in 1990, which are included in row 5.
Sources: for 1990, *U.K. National Accounts 1991*, Tables 7.2, 8.1 and 9.6, for 1978, *National Income and Expenditure 1980*, Tables 7.2, 8.1 and 9.7.

disincentive effects. They also sought to reduce the tax burden on higher incomes. The resulting reduction in the redistributive power of the budget is discussed in Chapter 14. There is not space here to give all the tax changes after 1979 but some of the major changes are noted below (see Johnson, 1991, for fuller details).

Income is taxed in the following way. Most income is liable but some forms of income are not included on the tax forms, e.g. imputed rent, some interest on government securities and superannuation contributions. From income that is declared certain allowances, such as the single-person, married and age-related allowances, are offset to establish taxable income, which is then taxed at different rates. In 1991/2 the rates were 25 per cent on the first £23 700 of taxable income and 40 per cent on the rest. In 1978/9 the rates varied from 25 per cent on the first £750 of taxable income through 33 per cent of the next £7 250 and eight more intermediate steps until 83 per cent was paid on taxable income above £24 000. In addition, in 1978/9 there was an investment income surcharge of 10 per cent or 15 per cent with its own allowance. Investment income could thus be liable for a maximum rate of tax of 98 per cent. It can be seen that the income tax structure has been greatly simplified. The higher rates were removed in stages and the investment income surcharge was abolished in 1980.

Much of the simplification and the removal of the highest rates can be regarded as worthwhile. However a highest rate of 40 per cent is too low from an equity viewpoint and is low by international standards. The removal of the investment income surcharge leaves earned income paying a higher rate when the combined effects of income tax and NICs are taken into account. An investment income surcharge can be justified on the grounds that labour income lasts until retirement but asset income can run in perpetuity, and also on a second-best argument, namely as a proxy for a tax on wealth. The investment incomes of husband and wife were no longer aggregated for tax purposes after 1990 – a move that has mainly benefited higher-income couples. Separate taxation of husband and wife is to be welcomed in principle, though it has had little impact as yet, apart from the one mentioned.

Other income tax changes of note were the removal of mortgage interest deductions at the higher rate of relief in 1991 and holding the ceiling at £30 000 after 1983, thus reducing the real value of housing subsidies to the individual. Three changes shifted the income tax system in the direction of a CIT: namely, removing the relief for new life insurances premiums after 1984; increased taxation of fringe benefits; and the merging of capital gains tax (CGT) and income tax in 1988. (Features of CGT that do not conform to a CIT are the exemption of gains occurring before 1982; it is payable on realisation, not accrual, of gains; there are large allowances; and liability is removed on death.) However, there were moves away from a CIT, with increased exemptions for income tax and/or capital gains tax for the Business Expansion Scheme (1983), Personal Equity Plans (1986), Profit-related Pay (1987) and Tax Exempt Special Savings Accounts (1990). The new cost of these four items in 1991/2 is estimated at £450 million (data from Cm 1920, 1992, Table D.1). The same source gives tax relief for housing as £8 billion, for occupational pensions as £9 billion and personal allowances as £31 billion. Erosion of the tax base drives up the marginal rates of tax on what base is left and thus magnifies efficiency costs of taxation. Choices about which assets to save are strongly affected by the exemptions from the income tax system. The assets favoured include housing, pensions and schemes such as the formalised ones just mentioned. What is not subsidised is straightforward purchase of shares in companies.

NICs are paid by employers and employees. The employee rate used to have several bands but in 1991/2 there were two – a small 2 per cent band and 9 per cent for earnings up to £21 060 per annum. (A 7 per cent rate replaced the 9 per cent one for employees contributing to occupational pension schemes.) When income tax is combined with the standard NIC rates, an employee's marginal rate of tax varied from 0 per cent through 2 per cent, 9 per cent, 34 per cent, 25 per cent and finally 40 per cent. In other words, there was a dip in the marginal rate at the ceiling for NICs. The ceiling for employers' contributions was abolished in 1985. The maximum rate in 1991/2 was 10.45 per cent. Together, employer and employee NICs introduce a wedge of about 20 per cent between what a firm pays and what the employee receives in pre-income-tax earnings.

For low-income people, the combined effects of NICs, income tax and loss of social security benefits give rise to very high marginal rates of 'tax', sometimes over 100 per cent. The situation whereby a considerable increase in gross earned income leaves a person almost no better off or even worse off is called the *poverty trap*. The reductions in income tax rates after 1979 helped to lower the marginal rates but NICs were increased and this partially offset the income tax effect. In 1985 lower bands for NICs of 5 per cent and 7 per cent were brought in but at each new band the higher rate applied to all earnings, thus marginal rates were well over 100 per cent with NIC alone. This effect was broken in 1989 with a 2 per cent band that applied to everyone's earnings, and the other lower bands were removed. In the mid-1980s the effective marginal rate of tax was between 94 per cent and 127 per cent (comprising income tax, NICs, loss of Family Income Supplement (FIS) of 50 per cent and loss of Housing Benefits of 9–38 per cent). In 1985 a married couple with two children could not increase their net income despite a gross income increase from £60 to £140 per week.

In 1988 Family Credit replaced FIS and Housing Benefit was reformed. Anyone with measurable wealth greater than £6000 was ineligible. Tapers (the rate of benefit loss) of 70 per cent for Family Credit and 85 per cent for Housing Benefit applied after 1988 but they related to net income not gross income. The poverty trap rates could no longer be above 100 per cent. For the income range £60–120 the marginal rate was effectively 97 per cent in 1989/90 (made up of income tax 25 per cent, NIC 9 per cent, Family Credit loss 46.2 per cent and Housing Benefit loss 16.8 per cent; see Brown and Jackson, 1990, for fuller details). The worst features of the poverty trap had been reduced but there still remained a serious problem of marginal rates very near 100 per cent.

There are problems in trying to devise a scheme for reducing the poverty trap for working people with low incomes. To do so would mean creating a greater difference in net income between the bottom and the top of the trap. Lowering net income below the trap would reduce living standards for families already in poverty. This is the cheap but nasty way. However, it was the basis of the 1988 reform. Increasing net income at the top of the trap could be achieved by lowering either the rate of tax or the rate of benefit loss. Tax threshold increases tend to push the whole poverty trap higher up the income scale unless the threshold occurs in the trap. Tax changes apply to all taxpayers and cost too much unless offsetting 'tax increases are brought in higher up the income scale. Tax changes have relatively little effect on the poverty trap rates because benefit tapers now depend on net income. The 1992 Budget introduction of a 20 per cent income tax band for the first £2000 of taxable income reduced poverty trap marginal rates not by the 5 per cent drop in income tax rates but by 0.3 per cent. Even if taxes in the trap were zero, the current tapers combine to yield a marginal rate of 95.5 per cent! Thus reform needs to come on the benefit side if the trap is to be modified. But reducing benefit rate loss would be costly. It would increase the number of people eligible for benefits and would spread the poverty trap higher up the income scale.

A significant change in the taxation of corporate income started in 1984. Corporation tax had been 52 per cent (42 per cent for smaller companies) but many allowances existed, particularly for investment in plant and equipment. These investment allowances were scaled down drastically and the rate of tax was cut to 33 per cent (25 per cent for smaller firms). Thus over the period the base broadened and the rates were cut. Though this is generally a move in the right direction, there is dispute about whether investment allowances are important devices for encouraging growth of the economy.

The main tax increase in the period after 1979 was in VAT. The base remained broadly the same until 1989, when water, fuel and construction were included. The rate of tax, however, jumped from a range of 8–12.5 per cent to 15 per cent in 1979 and increased again in 1991 to 17.5 per cent. The moves could have been regarded as a move towards an expenditure tax system but both changes occurred in an attempt to find revenue to replace other taxes which were cut (income tax in 1979, Community Charge in 1991). Membership of the European Community imposed conditions on the VAT system but this has not had an undue effect on the United Kingdom government's strategy with regard to taxation. However, EC proposals for indirect taxes appeared at one stage to involve significant changes for the United Kingdom. Such items as food, transport, books and energy were to become liable for VAT instead of being zero-rated. The imposition of VAT on food would have an adverse effect on low-income families unless it was offset by an increase in benefits. The European Community's June 1991 position on tax harmonisation accepted zero rating for a limited range of goods and required a normal minimum of 15 per cent for VAT. These details and the EC harmonisation rates for excise duties have yet to be finalised.

Overall the tax changes of 1979–91 had a mixture of items of merit and of demerit from an efficiency point of view. Many tax changes are not desirable, especially if they are to be subsequently reversed. 'An old tax is no tax' is a saying which illustrates that adjustments occur after a new tax, which then become less noticed and sometimes less harmful. Changes in the system always impose adjustment costs, which depend on economic agents' expectations about the likely future course of tax policy. This issue of adjustment costs, however, is outside the scope of the present chapter.

13.5 Summary and future trends

The overall level of government expenditure is of less importance than getting the right level for the components. Almost certainly there has been too little spending in many areas, e.g. on education, health and housing. In particular, capital expenditure is far too low. Better information about the demand for, and benefits of, public expenditure should be provided. The benefits from public expenditure are the opportunity costs of tax cuts.

Despite the impression created by the switch away from the personal income tax towards indirect taxes, the overall burden of taxation increased in the 1980s. The 1990s are likely to reinforce this trend away from income taxes because of an ideological view that it would encourage incentives to work.

Changes in government expenditure and taxes in the next few years are likely to be dominated by the projected rise in government borrowing. Unfortunately the government appears more likely to cut expenditure rather than to increase taxes. Even if the political commitment to lowering – or at least not raising – income tax rates is kept, broadening the base to include items currently exempt, such as owner–occupier housing, superannuation payments and many savings schemes would provide revenue to reduce the amount of borrowing and increase efficiency by standardising the tax treatment of savings.

Questions for discussion

1. Which goods and services should the public sector provide? Are changes in GGE/GDP important?
2. How can the appropriate level of government expenditure on health be determined?
3. How do taxes impair economic efficiency? Under what circumstances can the allocative effects of taxes be justified?
4. Have the Conservative government's tax changes improved resource allocation?
5. Were government's housing objectives achieved in the 1980s?
6. What is the poverty trap? How can it be reduced?

Notes

1. Notice that these volume changes are not the same thing as the real GGE changes discussed later (Table 13.1) since the GDP deflator is used then. What is needed for volume planning is the appropriate price index for each spending

department which may be higher or lower than a general price index. The difference between the GDP deflator and the price index for a particular form of expenditure is called the 'relative price effect' (RPE).

2. In simple macroeconomic models, it is this which we usually refer to as G, rather than the broader conception of public spending used in this chapter.

References and suggestions for further reading

'Blue Book' (1991), *United Kingdom National Accounts*, London: HMSO.

Brown, C. V. and P. M. Jackson (1990), *Public Sector Economics*, 4th edn, Oxford: Blackwell.

Cm. 1920 (1992), *Public Expenditure Analyses to 1994–95*, London: HMSO.

Economic Trends (1992), 'International comparisons of taxes and social security contributions in 20 OECD Countries 1979–1989', London: HMSO, January.

Ermisch, J. (1991), 'Housing policy and resource allocation', *Oxford Review of Economic Policy*, Autumn, pp. 41–9.

Hills, J. (ed.) (1990), *The State of Welfare*, Oxford: Oxford University Press.

Hills, J. and B. Mullings (1990), 'Housing: a decent home for all at a price within their means', in J. Hills (ed.), *The State of Welfare*, Oxford: Oxford University Press.

Johnson, C. (1991), *The Economy under Mrs. Thatcher*, Harmondsworth: Penguin.

Keen, M. (1991), 'Tax reform', *Oxford Review of Economic Policy*, Autumn, pp. 50–67.

Le Grand, J., D. Winter and F. Woolley (1990), 'The National Health Service: safe in whose hands?', in J. Hills (ed.), *The State of Welfare*, Oxford: Oxford University Press.

Likierman, A. (1988), *Public Expenditure*, Harmondsworth: Penguin.

Welham, P. J. (1982), 'The tax treatment of owner–occupier housing in the UK', *Scottish Journal of Political Economy*, pp. 139–54.

Wilkinson, M. (1992), *Taxation*, London: Macmillan.

Chapter 14

<hr>

The distribution of income and wealth

PHILIP WELHAM

14.1 Introduction

Income in any period is the flow of earnings which results from the employment of a nation's factors of production. Wealth is a stock and is measured at a moment in time. Wealth is the value of two of the factors of production, namely land and capital. The relevant measure of wealth for our purposes is marketable wealth of the personal sector and corresponds to the nation's land and capital outside the government sector. Both income and wealth contribute to a person's welfare.

The welfare or well-being of an economy depends not just on total income or wealth but also on the distribution of income and wealth between different households or individuals. Welfare involves both efficiency and equity aspects. Economists agree that more income is preferable to less income and can thus study efficiency issues objectively. Equity is more difficult to assess since it involves comparisons between individuals and thus value judgements have to be made. Equity issues require decisions about whether welfare has increased when one person gains while another loses and hence whether more or less inequality is desirable. More equality usually, though not always, involves less efficiency. Economists rarely agree on what is a desirable degree of inequality. However, most would regard a move towards greater equality as being desirable provided the efficiency losses were not too severe. Most people would also accept the value judgement that households should have sufficient means to avoid poverty.

When we come to measure the distribution of income and wealth we meet the difficulty of trying to summarise a large number of observations by means of a single indicator, or a shortlist of statistical indicators. The usual ways in which distributions are shown in official studies are by means of a Lorenz curve, showing the percentage shares in income or wealth of different groups of the population, e.g. the top 1 per cent or 20 per cent, or by a Gini coefficient. The Lorenz curve (see Figure 14.1) plots the cumulative percentage of households (ranked usually from the lowest income to the highest) against the cumulative share of their income. If every household had the same income the bottom 20 per cent, say, would have 20 per cent of total income and the Lorenz curve would be the central diagonal of the diagram or the 'line of complete equality'. The further the Lorenz curve lies from this line, the greater is the degree of inequality. Lorenz curves can be regarded as showing greater or less equality in an unambiguous way provided that they do not intersect. If the Lorenz curves do intersect, part of the distributions reflects a move to greater inequality and the rest shows a move in the opposite direction.

The Gini coefficient appears to offer a solution to this problem. The Gini coefficient measures the degree of inequality by dividing the area between the Lorenz curve and the line of complete quality (area G in Figure 14.1 – the shaded area) by the total area under the line of complete equality (area OAB in the figure). A Gini value of zero means complete equality, a value of 1 means one household has all the income (sometimes the figures are expressed as percentages). The Gini coefficient provides a useful summary of degrees of inequality in general, though it has limitations even when the Lorenz curves do not intersect (see Atkinson, 1983, Chapter 3). Where the Lorenz curves do intersect it is important to know what has happened to different parts of the distributions and not to regard the Gini value as sufficient. The best way to proceed is by looking at estimates of several different quantile shares of the total. Quantiles, the generic term, can be examined for different sections of the population with, for example,

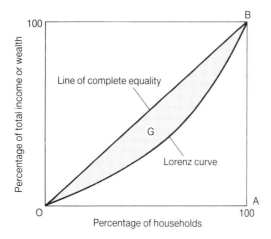

Figure 14.1 A Lorenz curve

quartiles showing the shares of the four quarters, quintiles each fifth, deciles each tenth.

The sequence in this chapter is as follows. Section 14.2 looks at the broad trends in the distribution of income; section 14.3 deals with the effect the government budget has on the distribution of income. Government expenditure yields benefits to households and taxes impose burdens so well-being between households is redistributed as a result of the budget. In section 14.4 changes in the patterns of wealth holdings are presented together with a brief discussion of policy measures that redistribute wealth. In section 14.5 poverty trends in recent years are discussed. Section 14.6 provides a summary and brief speculation about trends in the early 1990s.

14.2   The distribution of income

The most comprehensive measure of the distribution of income in the United Kingdom combines data from the Survey of Personal Income (SPI) based on Inland Revenue statistics together with Family Expenditure Survey (FES) information. Income includes transfer payments from the government as well as earned and investment income. The unit for this series is the family (a single person or a married couple). Data from selected years are presented in Table 14.1 to provide a broad picture of the trends in the distribution. Care must be taken in interpreting the trends as the data are not consistent. The years 1938/9 and 1948/9 are based on SPI data only. The exclusion of non-taxpayers leads to an underestimate of inequality as can be seen by the jump in the Gini coefficient in 1949 compared to 1948/9. For 1949 and 1964 mortgage interest tax relief is excluded from income – but it is included for 1978/9 and 1984/5; exclusion leads to underestimating income particularly in the top half of the distribution. It appears from the table, together with the above points about coverage, that inequality of incomes fell during the Second World War and, to a lesser degree, between 1949 and 1978/9 but increased after 1978/9. This finding holds for the Gini coefficient or the share of the top 1 per cent, 5 per cent or 10 per cent of the population. As can be seen from the share of the top 50 per cent, most of the gains from the trend towards greater equality were confined to this half of the distribution.

Unfortunately we do not have more recent data. The series was produced annually while the Royal Commission existed, but the incoming Conservative government abolished the Commission in 1979. The series on family incomes was then to have been produced on a three-year basis but it is now more than four years since anything was published (see *Economic Trends*, November 1987).

The data in Table 14.1 probably underestimate the degree of inequality. Inland Revenue data excluded income not declared for tax purposes, most

Table 14.1   Distribution of family income before tax

Shares of:	1938/9	1948/9	1949	1964	1978/9	1984/5
Top 1%	17	11	11	8	5	6
Top 5%	32	23	24	20	16	19
Top 10%	41	32	33	29	26	30
Top 50%	75	73	76	77	77	78
Gini coefficient	42	36	41	40	37	41

Notes:
[1] 1938/9 and 1948/9 from *Royal Commission on the Distribution of Income and Wealth* vol. 1, Table 10. Data based on SPI only (covers taxpayers only).
[2] 1949 and 1964, *ibid.*, Table 15. Based on SPI and FES (covers taxpayers and non-taxpayers). Data exclude mortgage interest tax relief.
[3] 1978/9 and 1984/5 from *Economic Trends*, November 1987. Data based on SPI and FES and include mortgage interest tax relief.

fringe benefits and capital gains. The FES is known to be unrepresentative of certain groups like the elderly, the self-employed, those on higher incomes, and it under-records casual earnings. We can bring part of the picture more up to date by looking at the distribution of earnings data provided by the New Earnings Survey given in *Social Trends* (1992). In 1981 the top decile of the male workforce earned 168 per cent of the median and the bottom decile earned 64 per cent. By 1990 the figures were 181 per cent and 58 per cent. A similar, though slightly less marked, pattern occurred for female workers. The pattern is thus one of a move to more unequal earnings.

More recent data on the distribution of income are also provided by the FES alone. The FES provides five different measures of income, corresponding to various stages in the redistribution of income which we will be looking at in the next section. The nearest to the measure given in Table 14.1 is 'gross income'. The Gini coefficient for gross income was 38 per cent in 1985 and 40 per cent in 1987 (see *Economic Trends*, 1990). Thus it can be seen that inequality has continued to increase in recent years.

This is also confirmed by an alternative measure used by the Central Statistical Office (CSO), namely equivalised income (equivalised income is income adjusted for household size). The Gini coefficient on this basis for gross income was 32 per cent in 1985 and 36 per cent in 1989 (see *Economic Trends*, 1992). The unit for the FES is the household, defined as one person living alone or a group of people living at the same address and having common needs. Both the 'household' and the 'family' suffer, therefore, in having varying numbers of people in a single unit. 'Equivalised income' attempts to get round this problem by weighting the income by a factor reflecting the different number of adults and different ages of children in an attempt to standardise for the size of the household (for details of weights see *Economic Trends*, 1992).

14.3   The redistribution of income

In order to assess the impact of the government's budget on the distribution of income, we need to compare the before and after situations. Ideally the comparison would be between the distribution of income as it would exist in the country without a government sector – the 'counter-factual' – and the actual distribution of income after adding the benefits households get from government expenditure and subtracting the burdens ('incidence') households suffer from taxes. We cannot estimate the counterfactual because the starting point or 'original income' as the CSO study calls it, has been affected by taxes and government benefits. There will have been, for example, effects of the budget on labour supply and on wage rates. Also, because unemployment and retirement benefits exist, households need to acquire less investment income. Original income therefore has to be the starting point.

The second set of difficulties lies in trying to assess the incidence of taxes and government expenditure. There are two types of problem: data availability and assessing economic incidence. Sufficient information on household incomes and expenditures is not available for a complete study. The FES provides the best data set available for the United Kingdom but it has limitations, some of which have been mentioned earlier in this chapter. Economic incidence issues concern just who loses from a particular tax and how much welfare is gained by a household from government expend-itures. Who gains most from defence expenditure? Is it mainly people with high income or large wealth or does everyone benefit equally? The difficulty of answering such questions has led the CSO to ignore defence expenditure in their analysis. Even for items which are included broad assumptions are made. The CSO attitude is that it will only include an item if there is a clear idea of where incidence lies. This is misleading because, as we shall see, we are also uncertain even about the items that are included. A better way to proceed would be to see how sensitive results are to alternative assumptions.

Figure 14.2 shows the effect of a tax on income under two different conditions of labour supply. The schedules labelled D in Figure 14.2 ((a) and (b)) show the quantities of labour that firms are willing to employ at each (pre-tax) wage rate. They correspond to the conventional demand for labour schedule. The schedules labelled D–T show the after-tax wages at each level of employment, as perceived by the workers, following the introduction of a progressive income tax.

In part (a) labour supply (S) is completely inelastic. Prior to the introduction of the income tax, the equilibrium wage is W_1 and the amount of labour employed is N_1. The effect of the progressive income tax is to reduce the net wage rate to W_2, the level of employment remaining at N_1. In this case, the full burden of the tax is borne by the employees in the form of reduced net wages. Employees' surplus is reduced by $ON_1.(W_1 - W_2)$, which is exactly the same as the tax revenue.

In part (b) the labour supply schedule is more elastic. Initially, the equilibrium is at W_1 and N_2. Following the introduction of the tax, however, both net wages and the level of employment fall, to W_2 and N_3 respectively. The pre-tax wage rate paid by the firms is driven up to W_3. In this case workers bear part of the burden of the tax, as do the owners of firms in the form of reduced employers' surplus. Employers' surplus is reduced by an amount equal to area W_1bcW_2 and employees' surplus is reduced by W_3abW_1. Tax revenue is just $ON_3.(W_3 - W_2)$. The two shaded triangles to the right of N_3 (area abc) represent an excess burden, i.e. a loss of surplus over and above the tax revenue. The two cases illustrate the importance of assumptions made about the incidence of taxes (similar arguments apply to taxes other than income tax). Empirical evidence suggests that the inelastic labour supply case is more likely in competitive markets and the CSO study makes this assumption for the incidence of all income taxes. In fact elasticity both of supply and of demand affect economic incidence. The burdens of taxation are assessed by allocating tax revenue to particular groups. The excess burdens are not included because of the difficulties of trying to measure them.

In the CSO study the burden of indirect taxes is allocated to consumers on the assumption that prices of products are raised by the amount of tax.

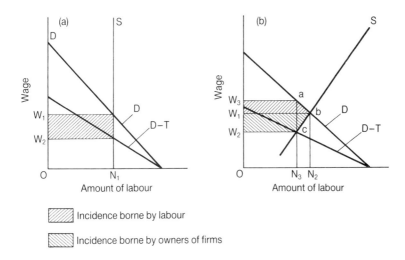

Figure 14.2 Incidence of a tax on income

To the extent that sales fall as a result of higher prices, owners of firms will get lower profits, but this possibility is not allowed for. The benefits from government transfer payments are attributed to the recipients and the benefits of health and education spending (measured as costs of providing the service) are allocated on a pattern-of-use basis. Some items, e.g. defence and debt interest, are not included, as indicated above. The CSO study allocates approximately half of total expenditure and two-thirds of taxes, so it can be seen to be an incomplete budget that is being examined. The main taxes missing are employers' National Insurance contributions, corporation taxes and business rates. One study, O'Higgins and Ruggles (1981), includes the missing items of the CSO budget and shows the effect of alternative assumptions about incidence of some of the key budget items.

The CSO study shows that the budget leads to a reduction in inequality in all years shown in Table 14.2. The effect can be seen when original income is compared with final income, e.g. in 1979 the Gini coefficient falling from 45 per cent to 32 per cent. Note that final income is not provided by the CSO for equivalised income, four stages only to post-tax income being given for 1989. Alternatively, the redistribution can be seen by the change in the share of the bottom quintile from 0.5 per cent of original income to 7 per cent of final income in 1979. Generally the bottom 40 per cent gains and the top 40 per cent loses as a result of the budget.

Other patterns that can be seen from Table 14.2 are that inequality of original income increased in the 1980s, as noted in section 14.2. Redistribution, measured as the change in the Gini coefficient between original and final, unadjusted income increased between 1979 and 1987. But the measure using equivalised income had the gap narrowing from a difference of 15 points between original and post-tax income in 1979 to 13 points in 1989. So the change over the period of the extent to which the budget reduces inequality is ambiguous. A large number of tax and benefit changes during the 1980s shifted the balance between rich and poor in favour of higher incomes (e.g. reduction in higher income tax rates, removal of investment income surcharge and increased investment income exemptions) and away from lower incomes (e.g. linking pensions to price changes rather than changes in average earnings). Thus one would expect the budget to play a somewhat less redistributive role in 1989 than it did in 1979 for a constant distribution of original income. The shifts towards less redistribution appear clear from the majority of changes made but it was not a publicly claimed policy by the government. Finally, Table 14.2 shows that income distribution net of taxes and benefits was more unequal in 1987 (or 1989) than it was in 1979.

The various stages in the process of redistributing income are shown in Table 14.3. Two years are shown but the pattern of change can be seen to

Table 14.2 Effects of taxes and benefits on the distribution of household income in the United Kingdom

Share of	Unadjusted income				Equivalised income			
	Original income		Final income		Original income		Post-tax income	
quintile group	1979	1987	1979	1987	1979	1989	1979	1989
Bottom	0.5	0.3	7	6	2.4	2.0	10	7
2nd	9	6	12	11	10	7	13	11
3rd	19	16	18	17	18	16	18	16
4th	27	27	24	24	27	26	23	23
Top	45	51	38	42	43	49	37	43
Gini coefficient								
(%)	45	52	32	36	44	50	29	37

Notes:
[1] Equivalised income attempts to standardise for different family size. See *Economic Trends*, January 1992 for weights.
[2] The income unit is the household.
Sources: 1979, 1987 unadjusted income, *Economic Trends*, May 1990, p. 118; 1979, 1989 equivalised income, *Economic Trends*, January 1992, pp. 164–5.

be in the same direction for both years. The major redistribution occurs between original and gross income. The adjustments made at this stage are to add in the benefits from government transfer payments, particularly the retirement pension. A further move towards greater equality occurs between gross and disposable income and is caused by allowing for the burdens of income tax, employees' National Insurance contributions and rates. (Rates had been included at the next stage in earlier editions of the CSO study.) Direct taxes on income are thus broadly progressive but indirect taxes, as can be seen by the difference between disposable and post-tax income, are regressive. The net effect of the tax system is to leave the Gini coefficient unaffected.

Economists writing on other issues usually assume that the UK tax system is progressive, presumably because they are thinking primarily of the effect of direct taxes. But Table 14.3 shows the same inequality measure for both gross and post-tax income. The tax system is proportional. The rich contribute the same proportion of their income as the poor to pay for public services. Other studies for other countries have reached the broad conclusion that their tax systems are neutral (i.e. roughly proportional). The final stage of the budget process – the allocation of benefits in kind such as health and education expenditure – leads to further redistribution to lower income groups. Overall, therefore, the budget does lead to a redistribution of income but it is due to the expenditure side of the budget not the tax side, with the major component of redistribution being the old age pension. O'Higgins and Ruggles (1981)

Table 14.3 Gini coefficients for the distribution of income at each stage of the tax benefit system

Gini coefficient (%)	1979	1987
Original income	45	52
Gross income	35	40
Disposable income	33	37
Post-tax income	35	40
Final income	32	36

Source: Economic Trends, May 1990, p. 118.

conclude that the CSO study overestimates the degree of redistribution somewhat but their overall conclusions were broadly similar.

An important point to consider, however, is the time scale. All the results so far derive from studies of the annual impact of the budget. The largest single contribution to redistribution comes from the retirement pension. Retired households are predominantly in the lower half of the income range in annual studies; but they would be randomly scattered through the income scale if lifetime income was considered. Pensions would then accrue not just to low income ranges but throughout the income scale, with a possible bias towards the higher end because richer people live longer. The budget redistributes, but over the life cycle rather than from rich to poor, as Welham (1990) argues.

Policy measures to reduce inequality of incomes can be separated into those that would reduce the spread of original income and changes that would increase redistribution through the budget. A minimum wage would cut off the tail of lower earned incomes but any increased unemployment that may result could offset the effect. Reduction in remuneration for high-income groups has been requested at times by governments with little apparent result. Incomes policies may temporarily achieve a narrowing of earnings but such policies do not usually last for long. Thus it is not easy to see how much could be done in the short run to reduce inequality of original income. In the longer term a change in social attitudes might narrow earnings differentials somewhat. But the change most likely to reduce inequality of original income would be a significant reduction in the level of unemployment.

Budget redistribution could be increased if the benefits from government expenditure accrued more to low-income groups and the burden of taxes fell more on higher incomes. Steps to increase the benefits to low income ranges involve increasing the benefit rate and indexing benefits to average earnings instead of retail prices. Increasing eligibility for Unemployment Benefits and stopping cash limits on Supplementary

Benefit payments would help but in a minor way. Measures to increase the tax burden on high-income groups include shifting the balance away from indirect taxes and towards income taxes, increasing the exemption limit for taxable income and increasing the higher rates of income tax.

Taxing investment income at the same or a higher rate than earned income (at present earned income is liable for income tax and National Insurance contributions) would hit higher-income groups and the elderly – the two main groups with investment income. When the investment income surcharge of 15 per cent was removed in 1984 it was on the grounds that the elderly would benefit. No mention was made of where the greatest part of the benefits would accrue. However, a better way of assisting the elderly would be to increase allowances for the over-65s either for all income or for investment income. Finally, measures to increase the tax base such as including imputed rent for owner–occupiers or not allowing deduction for superannuation payments, would be progressive.

14.4   The distribution of wealth

Marketable wealth, as can be seen from Table 14.4, is distributed much more unequally than is income. The information for wealth holdings comes from Inland Revenue estimates based on the value of estates at death. It is an imperfect measure because of the small sample of estates in certain categories, e.g. for young people or for estates below the exemption limit for tax purposes. Estimates for the total population are calculated by using mortality rates of different groups to get the value of estates for the living. Adjustments have to be made for types of assets that have been excluded, e.g. by being handed on in a manner that avoids tax liability. CSO estimates of the personal sector 'balance sheets' (i.e. aggregates of assets minus liabilities) are used to modify the Inland Revenue data. The revised estimates of the importance of these adjustments to wealth distributions since 1976 were issued in *Economic Trends* of October 1990. Previously the levelling off of the long-term trend to greater equality in wealth holdings was thought to start about 1980 but the date for levelling off is now given as 1976. The main causes of the revisions are reappraisals of the importance of joint property and new estimates of small estates.

The distribution of marketable wealth has had a Gini coefficient in the range 0.64 to 0.67 over the period 1976–89, showing a relatively stable distribution. The share of total wealth held by the top 1 per cent has declined slightly, from 21 per cent to 18 per cent but the share of the top 10 per cent has increased from 50 per cent to 53 per cent.

The long-term trend in the distribution of wealth is difficult to quantify due to changes in the data base, but Atkinson and Harrison (1978, Table 6.5) suggest that the share of the top 1 per cent fell from 61 per cent of total wealth in 1923 to 32 per cent in 1972. However, the share of the next 2–5

Table 14.4   The distribution of wealth. (Data refer to the adult population of the United Kingdom. The unit is the individual not the family. See text for discussion of the revisions to the data. The 'new series' was first published in 1990.)

| Share of wealth owners | Marketable wealth | | | | Marketable wealth plus pension rights |
| | Old series | New series | | | |
	1976	1976	1979	1989[1]	1989[1]
Top 1%	24	21	20	18	11
Top 5%	45	38	37	38	26
Top 10%	60	50	50	53	38
Top 25%	84	71	72	75	62
Top 50%	95	92	92	94	83
Gini coefficient	76	66	65	67	50

Note:
[1] Data provisional.
Sources: 1976 and 1979, *Economic Trends*, October 1990;
1989, *Economic Trends*, November 1991.

per cent increased slightly. The share of the top 10 per cent fell from 89 per cent to 70 per cent. Note that these figures are not compatible with those in Table 14.4 because they relate to England and Wales and do not cover property missing from the estate data, though allowance is made for the excluded population. The Royal Commission on the Distribution of Income and Wealth (1975) suggested that the contrary movements in shares of the top 5 per cent were due partly to attempts to avoid estate duty, and that the general levelling of the bottom 95 per cent was probably the outcome of increased standard of living and greater equality of incomes.

The composition of marketable wealth changes through time due to the relative growth of different items in absolute amounts together with different relative price movements. The main trend has been a growth in the share of dwellings (net of mortgage debt) from 23 per cent of net wealth of the personal sector in 1971 to 37 per cent in 1989 (see *Social Trends*, 1992, Table 5.20). In 1989 consumer durables were 7 per cent of net wealth, building society shares, bank deposits, cash and National Savings were 14 per cent and stocks and shares were 8 per cent.

There are interesting variations by size of estate. In 1986 the smallest estates (under £50 000) had almost half their net wealth in housing compared with only 20 per cent for the largest estates (over £300 000) (data derived from Stark, 1990, Table 38). Life insurance policies provided another 22 per cent for the smallest estates but only 9 per cent for the largest estates. Land and company shares, however, made up 46 per cent of the net wealth of the largest estates and only 2 per cent of the smallest estates. Mortgage debt as a proportion of gross wealth declined from 9 per cent for small estates to 2 per cent for larger estates but other debt increased from 4 per cent to 6 per cent. Total debt thus declines as the size of the estate increases.

Wider definitions of wealth would include the value of human capital (the present value of future earnings) and pension rights. There are no official estimates of the distribution of wealth including human capital but *Economic Trends* gives in addition to marketable wealth ('Series C'), marketable wealth plus occupational pensions ('Series D') and marketable wealth plus occupational and state pensions ('Series E'). The three series paint broadly the same picture for trends over the last fifteen years but the degree of inequality in any one year, as measured by the Gini coefficient, is reduced from 0.67 for series C down to 0.60 for series D and 0.50 for series E in 1989.

14.1.1 Redistribution of wealth

An individual's total wealth includes marketable assets together with the value, discounted back to the present, of future real income such as future earnings and pension entitlements. Proposed taxes on wealth, however, usually relate to marketable wealth only. A tax on wealth could be levied on an individual's stock of wealth but the UK system, at present, is to tax the transfer of wealth. It is easier administratively to tax once per lifetime than to have an annual wealth tax and it is normally easier for the individual to pay tax on inheritance than to have to sell off some of his or her own assets. Of the two main causes of wealth inequality – inheritance and accumulation of one's own savings – it is the former that is usually regarded as the least justified or 'deserved', and hence more appropriately taxed.

Taxation of wealth and the transfer of wealth can be justified on the grounds of ability to pay. Thus if two people have equal incomes, but one has much greater wealth, the wealth holder has the greater ability to pay taxes. Wealth confers power, prestige and influence which are not affected by income or expenditure taxes. Taxation is one of the main ways whereby existing inequalities of wealth holding could be reduced. However in the United Kingdom taxes on the transfer of wealth form a very small part of total tax revenue. Inheritance tax (IT) brought in 0.5 per cent of tax revenue in 1990 and Capital Transfer Tax (CTT), which it replaced in 1986, brought in about 0.5 per cent in 1980. Small as it is, the effect of taxes on the distribution of wealth has been reduced since 1986. CTT was levied on estates at death and on gifts between the living but IT removed the taxation of gifts between living people, and replaced a scale of ascending rates by a flat 40 per cent in 1988.

14.5   Poverty

There are severe problems involved in trying to define an absolute standard for poverty for the United Kingdom in the late twentieth century. The minimum food needed for existence depends on the type of work being done, e.g. a manual worker would need more food than an office worker. Dwellings in colder areas would require more heating. If an element is to be allowed for recreation, should it allow the purchase of a radio – or a black-and-white television – or even a colour television? Even if some minimum could be established for food, clothing, shelter and recreation, would the cost of, say, the calories and vitamins be priced at an expert's knowledge of nutritional values purchased at the cheapest retail outlet? These kinds of difficulties have led to poverty being studied in relative rather than absolute terms. Whilst there is no single or generally accepted measure of what constitutes poverty, the problem is often resolved by using the income level for government supplementary benefits or, more recently, 50 per cent of average earnings, as a yardstick.

Though there has been controversy over the issue, there appears to have been a fall in the real living standards of the poorest decile over the period 1979–88. Note that most measures rely on FES data which relate to households and exclude people in residential care and the homeless. The First Report of the Social Security Committee (1991) says that the median income of the poorest decile rose by 2 per cent after housing costs. A Written Answer in Hansard (23 July 1991) shows that eight of the nine lowest percentiles had falls in real income net of housing expenditure between 1979 and 1987. But these measures exclude living-expense changes other than housing costs. Barr and Coulter (1990) quote a calculation by Hills that allowed for indirect tax changes and concluded that the living standards of the bottom quintile fell by up to 8 per cent between 1979 and 1986.

Using a relative standard of poverty, the number of households below half average incomes changed from 3.75 million (or 7.1 per cent) of the total in 1979 to 9.13 million (16.8 per cent) in 1988 before housing costs. The increase was most marked for pensioners (1.7 million), the unemployed (1.2 million), full-time workers (1 million) and lone parents (0.7 million). After allowing for housing costs, the numbers were 4.93 million (9.4 per cent) in 1979 and 11.75 million (21.6 per cent) in 1988.

A combination of demographic trends and government policy caused the increase in low incomes. The ageing population led to more pensioners and the benefit levels were reduced relative to average incomes by being linked to the retail price index instead of average earnings. Unemployment levels were considerably higher in the 1980s, with government policy objectives emphasising inflation rather than unemployment. Also the value of benefits was eroded by the tightening of conditions of eligibility, the taxation of benefits and abandoning of statutory indexation. Social trends led to the increase in single-parent families. Government policy emphasising free market forces and reducing the role of wages councils contributed to the increased numbers of low-income earners.

The failure of private markets to provide adequate insurance for all contingencies is likely to require state provision of social security. Individuals are unlikely to purchase adequate insurance against unemployment even if they have entered the labour market, nor is everyone likely to purchase adequate pension arrangements for retirement. The growth of private occupational pensions may in time reduce the amounts that the state would need to provide; but many households are likely to need a state-provided safety net at some stage during their life cycle. As we have seen, the fall in levels of state provision contributed to increased poverty in the 1980s.

Government policy concentrated on incentive effects of benefits rather than the implications for household living standards. A reflection of this can be seen in the trend of replacement ratios – i.e. the ratio of income when unemployed to income when working. For a single person the figure was 22.3 per cent in 1974, 24 per cent in the later 1970s and 18.9 per cent by 1988. Similar patterns were displayed for other sizes of households. Barr and Coulter (1990) insist that the argument that higher replacement ratios lead to work disincentives is 'to put it no more strongly, not proven', nor is reducing the living standard of unemployed families a policy with which everyone agrees.

Perhaps the most serious aspect of the government's concentration on reducing spending rather than providing an adequate safety net can be seen in the arrangements introduced in 1988 through the Social Fund, which replaced the previous discretionary payments under Supplementary Benefits for certain specific expenses or debts of low-income households. Maternity payments for low-income mothers and funeral expenses remained as grants but other payments such as for a cooker, bed or pair of shoes were changed to a loan repayable from future benefits. Up to 40 per cent of a single person's benefit can be deducted (there is no overall limit but limits on individual items) to meet such expenses as poll tax, gas and electricity and water bills and now for mortgage interest payments. Two major problems are that the fund is cash-limited and there is no legal right of appeal against the decisions of the Social Fund officers. A National Audit Office report in February 1991 said that, in 1989/90, 780 000 or 34 per cent of applicants were turned down, 23 000 of whom were refused because the applicant was too poor (!) and 195 000 because there was insufficient money in the scheme.

Policy measures to reduce poverty involve reducing the incidence of particular events occurring or increasing the payments made to low-income households. We cannot, short of euthanasia, reduce the numbers of the elderly but the basic pension value can be increased. The rise in the number of single-parent families is the result of social trends but increased availability of part-time work together with crèche facilities could enable single parents to enter the labour market. Low incomes from earnings could be increased by expanding rather than contracting the role of wages councils. Perhaps the single most effective measure would be to reduce unemployment (as indicated above), but for those still without a job less restrictive rules for benefits and more generously funded training schemes would lower the incidence of poverty. In addition, attention needs to be paid to increasing the take-up rate for benefits.

14.6 Summary and future trends

From 1945 to 1979 there was a reduction in the inequality of income in the United Kingdom; but income inequality increased again in the 1980s. Continued emphasis on market forces and the increased level of unemployment are likely to increase income inequality further in the early 1990s. The tax system as a whole has little impact on the distribution of income but transfer payments redistribute annual income in favour of the poor. Redistribution is mainly over an individual's life cycle rather than from rich to poor (defined in terms of lifetime income). The distribution of income measured after taxes and benefits became more unequal in the 1980s and this trend is likely to continue into the 1990s. Poverty also increased in the 1980s and with the higher levels of unemployment in the early 1990s, is likely to continue to rise. The long-term reduction in wealth inequality ceased about 1976. Current taxation levels on wealth transfers are unlikely to cause significant redistribution of wealth and the best guess is that the stable wealth distribution since 1976 will continue.

Increased inequality of both pre- and post-budget income and the halting of the trend to lower inequality of wealth are bad news for people who desire a more egalitarian economy. What the government's attitude to inequality has been since 1979 can only be deduced from the accumulation of evidence on policy actions, since pronouncements on policy towards inequality have not been forthcoming. The likelihood is that, despite Mr Major's stated desire for a classless society, recent Conservative governments have not been unhappy with what has been happening to the distribution of income and wealth.

Questions for discussion

1. What have been the recent trends in the distribution of income and wealth? How reliable are the data?
2. How can we measure the extent to which the budget redistributes income?

3. What light does economic analysis throw on the question of who bears the burden of particular taxes?
4. 'Government expenditure has been paid for by income taxes raised from the rich.' Discuss.
5. Are taxes on wealth important in the United Kingdom? Should they be more important?
6. Is poverty a major problem in the United Kingdom? What can be done to reduce poverty?

References and suggestions for further reading

Atkinson, A. B. (1983), *The Economics of Inequality*, 2nd edn, Oxford: Oxford University Press.

Atkinson, A. B. and A. J. Harrison (1978), *Distribution of Personal Wealth in Britain*, Cambridge: Cambridge University Press.

Barr, N. and F. Coulter (1990), 'Social Security: solution or problem?', in J. Hills (ed.), *The State of Welfare*, Oxford: Oxford University Press.

Brown, C. V. and P. M. Jackson (1990), *Public Sector Economics*, 4th edn, Oxford: Blackwell.

Economic Trends (1987), 'The distribution of income in the United Kingdom 1984/5', November, London: HMSO.

Economic Trends (1990), 'The effects of taxes and benefits on household income 1987', May, London: HMSO.

Economic Trends (1990), 'Estimates of the distribution of personal wealth', October, London: HMSO.

Economic Trends (1991), 'Estimates of the distribution of personal wealth, II: Marketable wealth and pension rights of individuals 1976 to 1989', November, London: HMSO.

Economic Trends (1992), 'The effects of taxes and benefits on household income 1989', January, London: HMSO.

Hansard, Written Answer (23 July 1991), Columns 535–7.

Hills, J. (ed.) (1990), *The State of Welfare*, Oxford: Oxford University Press.

Higgins, M. and P. Ruggles, P. (1981), 'The distribution of public expenditure and taxes among households in the U.K.', *Review of Income and Wealth*, Series 27, pp. 298–326.

Pond, C. (1989) 'The changing distribution of income, wealth and poverty', in C. Hamnett, L. McDowell and P. Sarre (eds), *Restructuring Britain: The changing social structure*, London: Sage.

Royal Commission on the Distribution of Income and Wealth (1975), *Report no. 1*, Cmnd 6171, London: HMSO.

Social Security Committee (1991), *First Report, Low Income Statistics: Households below Average Income, Tables 1988*, House of Commons, London.

Social Trends (1992), London: HMSO.

Stark, T. (1990), *Income and Wealth in the 1980s* (Working Group Papers), 2nd edn, London: Fabian Society.

Welham, P. (1990), 'The impact of the budget on lifetime income: A survey', *Journal of Economic Studies*, 17, pp. 66–84.

Chapter 15

Local government finance

DOUGLAS MAIR

15.1 Introduction

The period since 1986 has been one of unprecedented change in local government finance in the United Kingdom. The system of property taxation, or rates, was abolished in 1990 and replaced by a Community Charge or poll tax. But within eighteen months, the poll tax in turn was replaced by a Council Tax scheduled to come into effect in financial year 1993–4. As well as replacing rates on domestic property, the government has also made important changes to the non-domestic rates paid by industry and commerce and to the system of Exchequer grants paid to local authorities. The introduction of the poll tax has proved to be one of the most unpopular tax reforms ever made by a British government and Mrs Thatcher's personal commitment to its retention was undoubtedly a factor leading to her replacement as prime minister in November 1991. One of her leading challengers, Mr Heseltine, made reform of the poll tax the major issue in his bid for the prime ministership. In the event he was beaten by Mr Major but Mr Heseltine's prize for coming second was his appointment as Secretary of State for the Environment, carrying with it the poisoned chalice of responsibility for coming up with an alternative to the poll tax.

In 1985, when it was deciding whether or not to replace rates, the government had to take into account many complex economic and political factors. It appointed four external assessors to advise it, of whom two, Professor T. Wilson and Sir Christopher Foster are economists. As we shall see, the government was strongly influenced by Foster, while Wilson has been much more critical of the decision to introduce the poll tax. In this chapter we shall concentrate mainly on the opposing arguments of these two men as both were closely involved in the discussions leading to the introduction of the poll tax and both have published their arguments for and against. Foster's arguments are set out in his 1980 book *Local Government Finance in a Unitary State* (Foster *et al.*, 1980), while Wilson has recently expressed his criticisms in *The Economic Journal* (Wilson, 1991).

15.2 Origins of reform

The introduction of the poll tax was proposed in a Green Paper (HMSO, 1986) entitled *Paying for Local Government* published in January 1986. In it the government stated that it had three main objectives: (a) to contain local government expenditure at 'affordable' levels; (b) to encourage local authorities to provide services more efficiently; and (c) to reduce detailed controls over local government.

Concern about the proper role for local authorities and their relationship to central government had apparently been resolved in the 1970s when, as a result of Royal Commissions in Scotland and in England and Wales, local authorities were reorganised into larger units. Both Labour and Conservative governments of that time wanted to enhance local democracy and ensure that the new larger local authorities should be more accountable to their electorates and less dependent on central government. Neither Royal Commission addressed the problem of whether local authorities had adequate local tax resources to fund their increased range of services. During the 1960s and 1970s the share of local government spending funded by central government grants had risen steeply and it was felt by both Labour and Conservative governments that this growing financial dependence on central government was not compatible with the greater local autonomy they were seeking to encourage.

In 1974, the Labour government appointed a Committee of Enquiry into Local Government Finance (HMSO, 1976) under the chairmanship of Mr Frank Layfield, to 'review the whole system of local government finance in England, Scotland and Wales and to make recommendations'. The basic principles on which the Layfield Committee concluded that the British system of local government finance should be based were accountability – that is, whoever is responsible for spending money should also be responsible for raising it so that the amount of expenditure is subject to democratic control; that the outcomes under the system should be fair both between individuals and between local authority areas; that the financial arrangements should make clear to decision-makers the economic implications of the choice between consumption and investment and should promote efficiency in the provision of services; and, finally, that the system should be stable, flexible and comprehensible.

Despite long-standing criticisms of rates as a local tax, the Layfield Committee felt that there was a good case in principle for retaining a local property tax, albeit with improvements to eliminate some of its inconsistencies and anomalies. No clear message emerged from the Layfield Committee that there was a single best alternative to local rates and public hostility to rates continued. The government reacted to this ongoing dissatisfaction with a Green Paper (HMSO, 1981), *Alternatives to Domestic Rates*. In this paper, the government put forward for consideration a number of possible alternative taxes, such as a local sales tax, a local income tax and a poll tax, along with an assessment of how well the government judged each tax performed in terms of certain criteria. Interestingly, a poll tax scored quite well in the government's view in terms of its perceptibility, accountability and predictability of yield, particularly as a supplement to other taxes.

In the light of public responses to the 1981 Green Paper, the government published in 1983 a White Paper (HMSO, 1983) in which it reaffirmed its commitment to rates as the main source of local revenue for local government for the foreseeable future. The government formally rejected the alternatives which had been considered in the 1981 Green Paper, particularly the poll tax, which was dismissed as being hard to enforce, expensive and complicated to administer and harshly regressive on people on low incomes without a rebate scheme.

The government's main concern in the 1983 White Paper was to acquire powers which would enable it to impose limits on the growth of local government expenditure. In the 1960s and 1970s, local government current expenditure had grown at about 3.5 per cent per annum, so that it had risen from about 5 per cent of all domestic expenditure in the early 1960s to over 8 per cent in the late 1970s. Since coming into power in 1979, the Conservative government had sought to reverse this apparently inexorable trend. It had reduced the percentage of planned expenditure met by Exchequer grants from 61 per cent in 1978–9 to 53 per cent in 1983–4 to make the cost of local services more apparent to local electors. But despite this and other measures, local government expenditure continued to grow. Between April 1979 and April 1983, domestic rates in England increased on average by 91 per cent while the Retail Price Index rose by only 55 per cent. While the government recognised that it had cut the Exchequer contribution to local authorities, its view was that the root cause of the large increase in rates had been the failure of local authorities to meet the government's expenditure plans. Had they done so, rates increases would have been below the rate of inflation. In the government's opinion, local authorities as a whole were continuing to spend more than the government believed the country could afford.

15.3   The 1986 Green Paper, *Paying for Local Government*

Until as late as 1983, the government had concluded that the rating system, warts and all, was still the best way to finance local government.

So what happened to change the government's mind? The issue came to a head in Scotland in 1985, where the system of local taxation is similar but not identical to that in England and Wales. One of the principal differences is that there is a statutory requirement on the secretary of state for Scotland to carry out a revaluation of property every five years. A revaluation was carried out in 1985 which had the effect of increasing the rateable values of all classes of property by a factor of 2.33 compared with the previous revaluation in 1978, but with domestic property bearing a significantly greater increase than industrial and commercial property. This provoked an outcry from domestic ratepayers, particularly in the dwindling number of predominantly middle-class constituencies still held by the Conservatives. Scottish local authorities took advantage of the revaluation to increase their spending by an average of 27 per cent, further compounding the outrage among Scottish ratepayers. The Scottish secretary made ineffectual attempts to stem the rising tide of protest. (See Bailey, 1986, for a good discussion of the events in Scotland.)

Faced with the prospect of further loss of electoral support in Scotland and the realisation that sooner or later it would have to carry out a property revaluation in England and Wales, where there had not been one since 1973, the government decided to bite the bullet. It got moral support from the influential right-wing think tank, the Adam Smith Institute, in the form of a pamphlet, *Revising the Rating System* (Adam Smith Institute, 1985). This pamphlet argued that 'the continuing and accelerating unfairness' of rates combined with the claim that 'they destroy jobs, put up prices and penalise improvement' meant that 'the time for talking is over' and 'future problems can be avoided if action is taken now' and that action should be that 'domestic rates should be replaced with a simple per capita tax on all adults over the age of eighteen' (ibid., p. 18). Never mind that the Adam Smith Institute did not provide any evidence to support its claims of the harmful effects of rates, this clarion call for a poll tax was music to the ears of a beleaguered government.

The main proposals of the 1986 Green Paper were the abolition of domestic rates and their replacement by a Community Charge (poll tax) payable by all residents over the age of eighteen with rebates for the unemployed, those on low incomes, students, etc., subject to everyone paying at least 20 per cent of the due poll tax. Responsibility for levying non-domestic rates was removed from local authorities and transferred to central government. National uniform business rates in the pound were set by central government for England and Scotland and index-linked to the Retail Price Index so that the rate burden on industry and commerce would not rise faster than the rate of inflation. The proceeds of the uniform business rate are now distributed back to local authorities on a per capita basis. The system of Exchequer grants was radically simplified to make it less complex and more stable. So let us now proceed to examine some of the main arguments underlying the reform.

15.4   The poll tax and public choice theory

The idea of the poll tax undoubtedly came from the Foster *et al.* book on local government finance, where they had written:

> an efficient local tax should fall on those who benefit from local government services. On these grounds we would prefer a poll tax, a local land tax or some form of housing tax . . . (because) local electors will have no incentive to be efficient unless they are substantially responsible for financing the services. Therefore, an efficient tax must fall on electors. (pp. 244–5)

The economic rationale underlying this argument can be found in the public choice theory approach to the study of politics which assumes that voters, politicians and bureaucrats engage in self-interested maximising behaviour in exactly the same way as consumers seek to maximise utility and firms to maximise profits. Much of this theory has been developed in the United States by Downs (1957), Buchanan and Tullock (1962) and Niskanen (1971) and its central idea is that political parties compete with each other for the support of the voters in the middle ground – the so-called median voter hypothesis. If a party can win the vote of the median voter it will win the election and form the next government. An important feature of this public choice approach is the argument that in a parliamentary democracy the restraint that politicians can exert over bureaucrats is relatively weak so that bureaucrats will to a large extent be able to pursue their own personal goals for income and power and consequently oversupply public goods. This public choice theory was undoubtedly influential in the 1980s amongst Mrs Thatcher's ministers and advisers.

In their book, Foster *et al.* argued that economic efficiency could only be achieved in local government when the median voter has to pay in terms of higher taxes the full marginal cost of the additional services from which he or she benefits. Also, they pointed to the failure of the Exchequer grant system of the time to reduce local expenditure because it took no account of the huge incentives generated by the prevailing grant system for local authorities to overspend. The 1986 Green Paper followed the Foster *et al.* argument closely and saw local overspending as a result of a mismatch between voting, benefiting and paying for local services and the opportunity for non-ratepayers to vote for higher services without having to pay for them. By making the rates paid by industry and commerce a national tax, introducing the poll tax and simplifying the Exchequer grant system, the government sought to improve accountability by creating a framework in which clear and comprehensible price signals were given to all local taxpayers.

The three key concepts which follow from the application of public choice theory and which underlay the poll tax reforms were the following:

1. Local elections are political markets in which voters exchange votes and taxes with politicians in return for public services.
2. Voters are concerned to maximise their utility, i.e. their consumption of public services at minimum cost.
3. Politicians are concerned mainly with their own re-election and seek to maximise votes by offering a supply of local public services at a tax price which matches the wishes of the median voter.

Midwinter (1989) is highly critical of this rationale and argues that it cannot be sustained on either theoretical or empirical grounds. He argues that the analogy with a conventional market situation is wholly misleading. In markets, consumers buy goods for personal consumption; in elections they vote for representatives on the basis of vague manifestos which have no price tags and no guarantees of implementation. Local authorities have no discretion over many of the services they provide because they are under a statutory obligation to do so imposed by central government. Nor does the empirical evidence support the Foster *et al.*/ Green Paper model. Indeed, it suggests that non-ratepayers are *less* likely to vote and there is no evidence of systematic bias in the pattern of voting of those who do vote. The Foster *et al.*/Green Paper model can be criticised for being a too simplistic and naive description of the behaviour of local voters which results from a much more complex amalgam of values, experience and perspectives of government performance.

15.5 Economic theory and poll taxes

Wilson expresses incredulity at the decision to make a poll tax the central feature of local taxation. A central proposition of welfare economics is that it is possible to define the conditions in which an optimal allocation of resources will occur – the so-called Pareto optimum – and any desired redistribution of income to achieve socially desired objectives can then be achieved by means of lump sum transfers of income in the form of taxes or subsidies. In such a theoretical and highly stylised framework, there is no conflict between efficiency and equity. But economists have long recognised the impossibility of gathering the information necessary to levy the optimal lump sum taxes, without these taxes ceasing to be lump sum. For economists, lump sum taxes are greatly to be desired because they do not distort consumers' preferences, with no misallocation of resources as a consequence; but economists have also learned that in an imperfect world they are seldom able to get everything (or, indeed, anything!) they would like. The only circumstance in which a lump sum tax like a poll tax would be optimal is if it charged to each household a sum just equal to the value of the benefits enjoyed by each household. In any other situation, inefficiency will occur. A good statement of the significance of lump sum taxes is by de Graaff (1987):

> Lump sum taxes are of some importance in theoretical work. But in the real world, poll taxes being their only viable form, they are rarely encountered precisely because they cannot in practice be matched to ability to pay or used to achieve a redistribution of income or wealth without ceasing to be lump sum. At most they are a bench mark against which the less than perfect taxes we normally encounter can be measured. (p. 252)

In its attempt to apply the argument that benefit taxation is the most appropriate basis for local taxation, the government made the unwarranted assumption that, in each local authority area, each poll tax payer received an equal amount of benefit from local public goods. This implies that, in the government's opinion, the income elasticity of demand for local public goods is zero – i.e. that people have the same demand irrespective of changes in their incomes. While it is difficult to estimate precisely what the income elasticity of demand is for local public goods, it is likely to be much closer to 1 than to zero – i.e. demand is likely to rise more or less in line with income.

15.6   Local government and crowding out

At the heart of the poll tax reform was the conviction of central government that, in total, local authorities were spending more than the country could 'afford' and that some large local authorities in particular were guilty of what the government described as 'excessive and unreasonable' expenditure. These authorities have had their spending capped by central government, that is, they have had limits imposed on them as to the amounts they are permitted to raise through rates or poll tax. In this section, we shall examine this 'overspending' argument more closely to establish just how much substance it has.

The standard public finance textbook approach to the functions of government is to split them into three branches – the allocative branch, concerned with achieving an efficient allocation of resources by correcting for market failure and externalities; the distributional branch, concerned with redistributing income in accord with accepted ideas of social justice; and the stabilisation branch, concerned with the use of fiscal and/or monetary policy to even out fluctuations in the level of activity in the economy. Government policy at any time will usually be a mix of all three and it is recognised that there are likely to be conflicts between them, particularly between stabilisation on the one hand and allocation and distribution on the other. In the literature on fiscal federalism, it is widely accepted that pursuit of stabilisation objectives is a function of central government as local governments do not have at their disposal the appropriate instruments of monetary or fiscal policy (see King, 1984, for a good discussion of this issue). Where there is argument, however, is over the extent to which, if at all, the activities of local government actually do frustrate the ability of central government to manage the economy. The 'Treasury view', as stated in the Layfield Report (HMSO, 1976, Appendix 1, pp. 277–8) and repeated in subsequent policy documents, is that because local authority spending and its financing has implications for the allocation of real resources within the economy as well as for prices and for monetary and financial conditions, it is central government's responsibility to relate local authority activities to the requirements of macroeconomic policy.

As we have seen earlier in this book, since the 1970s there has been a fundamental change in macroeconomic objectives and policy instruments. The objective of 'full employment' has been abandoned in favour of control of inflation, and monetary policy has been the principal policy instrument. Fiscal policy has been used to reduce the public sector deficit as a percentage of GDP (see Chapter 2). Central government's argument for controlling local authorities has been its contention that government deficits have been responsible for excessive growth in money supply and have contributed to inflation, high interest rates and crowding out of private sector expenditure.

Crowding out can take two forms – crowding out of real resources and crowding out of financial resources. The crowding out of real resources argument was first put forward in the 1970s by Bacon and Eltis (1978), who argued that the principal cause of Britain's continuing poor economic performance was that the demands of local and central government for resources resulted in a transfer of resources from the private to the public sector with a consequential loss of marketable output on which Britain's economic prosperity depends. The Bacon and Eltis thesis has been shown to be wrong or at least open to considerable doubt by a number of commentators, including Jackson (1980) and Newton and Karran (1985).

The financial crowding out argument is that private sector firms are unable to borrow, or can only borrow at higher interest rates, in capital markets because of excessive demands by local authorities. Meadows and Jackson (1986) dispose of this argument by demonstrating that up to the mid-1980s there is no evidence of an explosion in local government expenditures. Indeed, the share of GDP taken by local authorities both in terms of their total spending and particularly their exhaustive expenditure (that is, their total expenditure minus the transfer payments they make in the form of subsidies, pensions and debt interest payments which are not part of national income) has been falling since 1975. There has been a massive fall in the capital expenditure of local authorities so that the composition of their expenditure has changed substantially from capital account to current account items. Thus Meadows and Jackson find no evidence of crowding out by local authorities in capital markets. Equally, when one examines the labour market there is no conclusive evidence there that local authority pay scales have moved out of line with those of the labour market generally.

Have local rates added to inflation and, therefore, made central government's anti-inflation policies that much more draconian? Domestic rates had a weight of about 4 per cent in the Retail Price Index in the mid-1980s, but it is problematic whether rates should appear at all in the RPI which is, after all, intended to be a measure of the changes in the prices of goods and services people buy. Only if the rates paid by a household were an accurate measure of the value of the local public services enjoyed (which they were not) would it be legitimate to include rates in the RPI in the same way that it is legitimate to include the price of a pound of sausages. Then there is the problem of how to treat the rates paid by industry and commerce. The government's method is to treat business rates as an intermediate tax on production in the same way as it treats VAT, excise duties or employers' National Insurance contributions and assume that they are passed on in full to consumers in the form of higher prices. But this is only one possible way to treat business rates and it could equally be argued that they should be regarded as a profits tax and be paid out of firms' retained earnings. So, it is not at all clear that rates should be included as an item in the RPI and, therefore, contributing to inflation or, if included, whether it is appropriate to include all of rates or only a part.

At the very least, it is necessary to question the government's contention that the requirements of macroeconomic policy oblige it to exercise strict control over the spending and taxing of local authorities. On both theoretical and empirical grounds, there are reasons to doubt whether local authorities have been quite the villains they have been cast as.

15.7 Losers and gainers from the poll tax

For any change in government policy, there will be gainers and losers. The problem for government, therefore, is to come to a judgement whether the gains from a policy change are sufficiently large to offset any losses, so that society as a whole is better off. The government took the view that society would be better off as a result of the greater local accountability and greater equity it claimed for the poll tax. But these are rather nebulous concepts and difficult to measure. A more direct and tangible way of evaluating the gains and losses from the poll tax is to look at how many and what kinds of people will be paying less in poll tax than they would in rates and vice versa.

In the 1986 Green Paper, the government produced figures to show that of the 20 575 000 households in Great Britain, just over half (10 575 000) would be better off under the poll tax. Three-quarters of all households would be better off, or would lose less than £1 per week; 15 per cent of households would lose more than £2 a week and for 6 per cent of households the loss would amount to more than 2 per cent of net income. Not surprisingly, the big gainers would be single-adult households and the big losers large households with three or more adults.

The Green Paper estimates of gains and losses were rather crude and more detailed estimates have been produced by the Institute for Fiscal Studies (IFS, 1987, 1991). (See Smith in *The Economic Journal* (May, 1991) for a useful discussion of how the IFS produces its comparisons of the gains and losses from the poll tax.) Tables 15.1 and 15.2 show the estimates made by the IFS of the amounts paid in local taxes before and after receipt of rebates by decile of households ranged from the poorest 10 per cent to the richest 10 per cent. The local tax levels are calculated from a sample of 4530 households in England in 1986 from the Family Expenditure Survey. The figures in the tables reflect a revenue-neutral comparison of the two systems, i.e. local authorities are assumed to collect the same amount whether in rates or in poll tax. In comparing the burden of tax payments, household size (and hence the standard of living that can be achieved with any given level of household income) is important as well as household income. The IFS figures given in the tables have been adjusted to take account of family size and are expressed as *equivalent* income.

If we look first at the gross payments before rebates (Table 15.1), we see that both domestic rates and the poll tax are regressive taxes in the sense that the burden of tax falls as a percentage of household income among households with higher equivalent incomes. The distributional incidence of the two taxes is strikingly close, except that households with the highest levels of income pay somewhat less with the poll tax. When rebates are taken into account (Table 15.2), the picture changes substantially. More than a third of households are entitled to a rebate and the IFS assumes that all rebate entitlements are taken up. Under both systems, the third-poorest income group pays most in rates or poll tax (4.5 per cent of equivalent income) and the richest group pays least (2.1 per cent under rates and 1.6 per cent under the poll tax). Overall, the introduction of the poll tax has not significantly altered the burden of local taxes and the only groups to have shown any gains are those on highest household equivalent incomes.

As Table 15.2 shows, the transition to the poll tax *per se* did little to change the incidence of local taxes, although since 1986 there have been changes in the social security system, including an increase in benefits by an amount intended to compensate for the 20 per cent of the poll tax bill which all persons over eighteen are expected to pay. But whatever else it

Table 15.1 Gross local tax bills, England, 1986 price basis

	Households, by decile group of equivalent incomes										All
	Poorest	2	3	4	5	6	7	8	9	Richest	households
Domestic rates											
£ per week	5.90	5.92	6.34	6.58	6.40	7.51	7.84	8.35	8.69	10.83	7.44
as % of household income	14.1	8.8	6.9	4.9	3.7	3.3	2.9	2.6	2.5	2.1	5.2
Community Charge											
£ per week	5.92	5.99	6.28	7.46	7.69	8.14	8.29	8.19	8.13	8.48	7.44
as % of household income	13.6	7.9	6.1	5.0	3.9	3.4	2.8	2.4	2.2	1.6	4.9

Source: The Economic Journal, May 1991, p. 588.

Table 15.2 Local tax bills, net of rebates and rebate entitlements, England, 1986 price basis

	Households, by decile group of equivalent incomes										All
	Poorest	2	3	4	5	6	7	8	9	Richest	households
Domestic rates											
Net domestic rates											
£ per week	1.45	2.81	4.39	5.72	6.24	7.30	7.65	8.21	8.63	10.82	6.28
as % of household income	3.2	4.0	4.5	4.1	3.5	3.2	2.8	2.5	2.4	2.1	3.2
Rate rebate entitlement (£ per week)	4.45	3.11	1.95	0.86	0.36	0.21	0.19	0.14	0.06	0.01	1.15
Percentage entitled to rebates	99	84	53	22	10	6	5	3	2	0	29
Community Charge											
Net Community Charge											
£ per week	1.47	3.02	4.59	6.34	7.06	7.71	7.95	7.90	8.00	8.40	6.22
as % of household income	3.2	3.9	4.4	4.2	3.6	3.3	2.7	2.3	2.1	1.6	3.1
Community Charge rebate	4.45	2.98	1.69	1.12	0.63	0.43	0.34	0.28	0.13	0.08	1.28
Percentage entitled to rebates	99	88	52	29	21	17	14	11	7	4	35

Source: The Economic Journal, May 1991, p. 588.

may have achieved, the poll tax did little to redistribute the cost of local government services in a way which most people would have considered to be fairer.

15.8 The Council Tax

The poll tax has proved to be probably the most unpopular tax ever introduced. Local authorities have found it extremely difficult to enforce payment and at the time of writing some local authorities in Scotland had started bankruptcy proceedings against defaulters while some English local authorities were resorting to wheel-clamping. Mrs Thatcher saw the poll tax as the 'flagship' of her administration and, consequently, there was no prospect of its replacement while she still remained prime minister. Under Mr Major, the Conservatives acted quickly. In his March 1991 Budget, the Chancellor of the Exchequer, Mr Lamont, announced a major transfer of funding from local to central government to enable a reduction in poll tax bills of £140 per head, financed by an increase in VAT from 15 per cent to 17.5 per cent. The result is that the share of local government expenditure financed by local taxes has now fallen from 25 per cent to 14 per cent.

The 1991 Budget measures were followed in April 1991 by a Consultation Paper (HMSO, 1991) in which the government outlined its proposals for the replacement of the poll tax by a Council Tax. The government conceded that the public had not been persuaded that the poll tax reforms were fair and that a new scheme was necessary. It reiterated that the principles on which the Council Tax should be based were fundamentally those underpinning the poll tax, i.e. accountability, fairness, ease of collection, equitable distribution of the tax burden and restraint in local government spending. Thus, the government presented the Council Tax as a compromise between the need to maintain local accountability and the need to protect local taxpayers from excessive bills.

It is not easy to categorise the Council Tax. In operation, it is essentially a tax on domestic property – and in that sense marks a return to the former rating system – with one tax bill per dwelling. But, unlike the old rating system, the size of the bill will also depend on the number of adults in the dwelling. As a result of a property valuation carried out in 1991 and 1992, each dwelling is allocated to one of eight valuation bands, bands A–H, and Table 15.3 shows the bands for England. The valuation bands are being set by central government, and local authorities have no discretion over the intervals between the bands. Table 15.3 shows that there will not be a proportional relationship between the value of a property and the amount of the Council Tax bill. For example, the bill for a household living in a house valued at £200,000 (band G) will be 2.5 times (i.e. the ratio of the

Table 15.3 Valuation bands and tax ratios

Maximum value in band (£)	Band	Relative tax rate
40 000	A	6
52 000	B	7
68 000	C	8
88 000	D	9
120 000	E	11
160 000	F	13
320 000	G	15
Several million	H	18

Source: Department of the Environment.

relative tax rates, 15:6) as much as if that household lived in a house valued at £20,000 (Band A). The rationale underlying the relative tax bills is that property values give only a rough guide to ability to pay. Under the Council Tax, people in highly valued properties will pay more than those in lower valued properties, but the range over which the bills can vary is restricted.

The number of adult occupants will also determine the level of the Council Tax within any valuation band. With one adult resident, 75 per cent of the standard amount is payable and with two or more adult residents the full amount is payable. For Council Tax purposes, some classes of people, notably students, do not count as adults. Council Tax benefit will be payable to those on low incomes and for those on income support the whole of the Council Tax bill will be met by the benefit system so that the Council Tax will resemble an income tax for households with the lowest incomes.

Thus, the Council Tax is a lump sum tax but now with some degree of variability within any local authority area. It is a combination of a tax on property value, a residence tax and an income tax. To some extent, the Council Tax meets the criticism of the poll tax as a lump sum tax which we discussed in section 15.5 above. The implied income elasticity of demand for local public services is no longer assumed to be zero as it was under the poll tax. This is not to say that the Council Tax now fully satisfies the optimal conditions for a lump sum tax, but at least there is now some recognition that the benefits from local public services do vary with income. As the tax does not come into effect until 1993–4, it is too soon at the time of writing to come to any conclusion as to whether local taxpayers will accept it as fairer than the poll tax. Certainly, the Council Tax can easily be made more or less regressive by altering the relative tax rates, so that the present relative tax ratio of 18:6 (3:1) between bands H and A could be changed up or down and equally for other bands.

15.9 Conclusion

In a sense, it is difficult not to feel some sympathy for a government which was damned for keeping rates and damned for getting rid of them. Where one feels less sympathetic is over the government's use of some rather dubious economic theory and empirical evidence to justify policies which were introduced primarily for ideological reasons. Commenting on the 1981 Green Paper, *Alternatives to Domestic Rates*, the late Professor A. R. Prest (1982) of the London School of Economics was strongly critical of the poor level of its underlying economic analysis, accusing its authors of 'unpardonable ignorance of or contempt for intellectual developments' (p. 62) in the area of public finance. But, as we have seen in this chapter, in following the policy advice of one distinguished economist, Sir Christopher Foster, the government has brought on itself the obloquy of another equally distinguished economist, Professor T. Wilson. This highlights an issue which has appeared on a number of occasions in this book, namely the tension that can exist between economic theory and economic policy. Uncritical application of economic theory can lead to policy prescriptions which are either wrong or politically unacceptable. Economists can debate among themselves the merits of the theoretical arguments which underlay the introduction and demise of the poll tax; but in a democracy the ultimate test is acceptability to the electorate and on the issue of the poll tax the electorate has given a decisive answer.

As we saw above in section 15.6, the primary economic role of local government should be with the efficient allocation of resources. To achieve the goal of efficiency, ideally the charges made to citizens by local authorities for the services provided should equal the benefits enjoyed by citizens, otherwise the opportunity arises for misrepresentation of preferences. But as we have also seen, there are substantial informational problems associated with this approach which in practice are impossible to overcome. Now while in theory local taxation should only be concerned with issues of efficiency, the experience of the poll tax episode has shown clearly that for many people, equity is also an important consideration. No local tax which does not make some concession to ability to pay is likely to be acceptable to the electorate.

The new Council Tax can, therefore, be seen as an attempt by government to reconcile these conflicting objectives. By linking payment to the value of a property and to the number of residents (up to a maximum of two), the tax is an attempt at a user charge which recognises that the benefits received from local public services are both property- and person-related. While the Council Tax will be a rather rough and ready approximation to a user charge, it at least attempts to relate costs and benefits in a way that rates and the poll tax never did. Through its system of rebates, the Council Tax has some of the properties of an income tax, thereby acknowledging, if not fully satisfying, the wishes of the considerable number of people who would prefer a local income tax. Although the Council Tax may be regarded as something of a chimera, it is at least more defensible from an economic standpoint than rates or the poll tax ever were.

We now have a situation in the United Kingdom where only one pound in every seven that is spent by local authorities is raised from local taxpayers. This is despite the government's professed intention of increasing the accountability of local representatives to local voters. This is a situation which it is difficult to reconcile with effective local democracy. It may well be that as local voters become increasingly disenchanted at the attempts of central government to impose unpopular local taxes, we shall witness a growing movement for a system of local taxation which gives local authorities a tax base commensurate with the requirements of a genuine local democracy. The United Kingdom is almost unique in relying on a single local tax; most other countries use permutations of local income, sales, profits or property taxes. Also, as the United Kingdom moves further towards full economic and monetary union within the European Community, the scope for the British government to pursue an independent national monetary policy becomes increasingly limited. This further strengthens the argument for giving local authorities much larger local resources if we are to avoid a situation in which Brussels increasingly supersedes Westminster in the town halls of Britain.

Questions for discussion

1. What features of rates made them such an unpopular tax for ratepayers yet a tax which local authorities approved?
2. What are the arguments for and against stricter control of local government by central government?
3. To what extent was the opposition to the poll tax simply a predictable response by previous 'free riders', or a legitimate democratic expression of the view that ability to pay is a basic principle of local taxation?

References and suggestions for further reading

Adam Smith Institute (1985), *Revising the Rating System*, London.

Bacon, R. and W. Eltis (1978), *Britain's Economic Problem: Too few producers?*, 2nd edn, London: Macmillan.

Bailey, S. J. (1986), 'Rates reform: Lessons from the Scottish experience', *Local Government Studies*, 12(3), pp. 21–36.

Buchanan, J. M. and G. Tullock (1962), *The Calculus of Consent*, Ann Arbor: University of Michigan Press.

Downs, A. (1957), *An Economic Theory of Democracy*, New York: Harper & Row.

Foster C. D., M. Perlman and R. Jackman (1980), *Local Government Finance in a Unitary State*, London: Allen & Unwin.

Graaff, J. de V. (1987), 'Lump sum taxes', *New Palgrave Dictionary of Economics*, vol. 3, London: Macmillan.

HMSO (1976), *Local Government Finance: Report of the committee of enquiry*, Cmnd 6453, London.

HMSO (1981), *Alternatives to Domestic Rates*, Cmnd 8449, London.

HMSO (1983), *Rates: Proposals for rate limitation and reform of the rating system*, Cmnd 9008, London.

HMSO (1986), *Paying for Local Government*, Cmnd 9714, London.

HMSO (1991), *A New Tax for Local Government: A consultation paper*, London.

IFS (1987), *Local Taxes and Local Government*, Report Series no. 25, London: Institute for Fiscal Studies.

IFS (1991), *Local Taxation: The Options and the Arguments*, Report Series no. 38, London: Institute for Fiscal Studies.

Jackson, P. M. (1980), 'The public expenditure cuts', *Fiscal Studies*, 1(2), pp. 66–82.

King, D. (1984), *Fiscal Tiers: The economics of multi-level government*, London: Allen & Unwin.

Meadows, W. A. and P. M. Jackson (1986), 'UK local government: Alternative economic strategies', in M. Goldsmith (ed.), *New Research in Local–Central Relations*, Aldershot: Gower.

Midwinter, A. (1989), 'Economic theory, the poll tax and public spending', *Politics*, 9, pp. 9–15.

Newton, K. and T. J. Karran (1985), *The Politics of Local Expenditure*, London: Macmillan.

Niskanen, W. A., Jr (1971), *Bureaucracy and Representative Government*, Chicago: Aldine–Atherton.

Prest, A. R. (1982), 'Greener still, and greener', *Local Government Studies*, 8(3), pp. 61–74.

Smith, S. (1991), 'Distributional issues in local taxation', *The Economic Journal*, 101, (May), pp. 585–99.

Wilson, T. (1991), 'The poll tax – origin, errors and remedies', *The Economic Journal*, 101, (May), pp. 577–84.

Index

accountancy, 175–6
acquisitions and mergers, 107, 151–2
ad valorem taxes, 247
Adam Smith Institute, 275
additionality, 159
Advisory, Conciliation and Arbitration
    Service (ACAS), 213
aggregate demand and unemployment,
    93–4, 95, 96, 100
air pollution control, 224, 226–8, 229–30
ALVEY project, 159–60
anti-competitive practices, 152–3, 157–8
anti-trust legislation in United States, 146–7
asset prices, 47
asset sales, public sector, 24–5, 26, 28–9
assets, 72
Austrian School, 147–8
automatic stabilisers, 35, 40

balance of payments, 3, 15–16, 102, 103
bank(s),
    deposit accounts, 51, 52, 55
    and the EC, 62
    and financial markets, 67–8, 78–81, 83
    and liquidity, 67–8
    and technological development, 55
BATNEEC, 228, 229, 230, 231, 232
best practicable environmental option
    (BPEO), 228, 229, 232–3
best practicable means (BPM) approach to
    pollution control, 227
bonds, risk and real return for, 72
borrowing, personal, 105, 106
British Leyland, 194, 195
British National Oil Corporation, 197
British Petroleum (BP), 194, 195, 198, 201
British Rail, 199
British Telecom, 194, 195, 196, 197, 199

Britoil, 197
building societies,
    deposit accounts, 51, 52
business advisory services, 182
business cycles, political, 37
business rates, 275, 280
business services, 176, 177–9, 186

capital,
    human, 89
    marginal product of, 52
    mobility of, 118, 119, 124, 125
capital account, 103
capital controls, 7
capital gains tax, 251
capital transfer tax, 267
carbon tax, 234
Cecchini Report, 129–30
civil service office dispersal, 181
Clean Air Acts, 227
closed shops, 204, 206, 212, 215
Cockfield paper, 128–9
common agricultural policy (CAP), 122, 123,
    125, 126, 132
common external tariff, 118, 120, 122,
    160–1
common market, 117, 118–19
Community Charge, *see* poll tax
Community Programme (CP), 99
company gearing, 74–5
Company Securities (Insider Dealing) Act
    (1985), 61
competition, 121, 129, 130
Competition Act (1980), 149, 152, 155
competition policy, 16–17, 147–9, 149–53,
    154–8, 163
    and privatisation, 193, 199, 201
    and service industries, 184, 185, 186

competition policy (*continued*)
in the EC, 161, 184, 185, 186
in Japan, 147, 148–9
competitiveness, 142–5, 185
consumer price index (CPI), 46
consumer prices, 11, 14, 44, 45
consumer services, 166
consumer spending, 105, 108
consumption,
private sector, 11, 105
public sector, 11, 26
consumption smoothing, 33
Control of Pollution Act (1974), 227
corporate finance, 63–85 *passim*, 107–8, 145
corporation tax, 6, 249, 250, 253
cost push inflation, 51
Council Tax, 19, 272, 283–4, 285–6
crowding out and local government, 278–80
currency union, *see* monetary union
current account, 103
customs unions, 118, 119–22

de-regulation, 7, 129, 148, 157, 184, 193, 201
debt, government, *see* government debt
defence expenditure, 243, 244
deficit, public sector, 14, 23–41
deflation, 44
demand,
for labour, 91–4
for public and private sector goods, 237–9
see also aggregate demand
demand pull inflation, 51
development state, concept of, 149
diversification, risk, 65–6
dominant firm policy, 150–1, 155

Earth Summit (1992), 233, 234
Eastern Europe and the EC, 137, 138
economic development, sector theories of, 167
economic integration, international, 117–22
economic and monetary union, 119
economies of scale and international economic integration, 121, 130, 131
ECU (European Currency Unit), 127, 134
education expenditure, 243, 244
education policy, 6, 200, 201–2
efficiency and equity, 248–9, 256
efficiency wage effect, 207
EFTA (European Free Trade Area/ Association), 117, 136–7, 138
electricity supply industry, 195–6
employment,
and output, 88–9
and trade unions, 205–7, 209–10
and wages, 205–7, 209
full, 3, 88
in manufacturing, 176, 186

in services, 176–8, 186
employment legislation, 211–13, 217–18
see also industrial relations legislation
employment measures, 98–100
Employment Protection Act (1975), 213
employment smoothing, 34
Employment Training (ET), 99
energy sector,
privatisation of, 197–8
see also public utilities
Enterprise Allowance Scheme (EAS), 99
Enterprise Initiative, 182
enterprise zones, 158
environmental pollution, 18, 221–34
Environmental Protection Act (1990), 227–8
equal opportunities, 217
equities, 83
risk and real return for, 72
equity and efficiency, 248–9, 256
European Community (EC), 2–3, 16, 122–38, 163
and Eastern Europe, 137, 138
and EFTA, 136–7, 138
and pollution control, 229–32, 233–4
and services policy, 183–5, 186
Banking Directives, 62
budget contributions, 123, 125–6, 127
competition policy, 161, 184, 185, 186
environmental protection requirements, 229–32, 233–4
external economic policy, 136–7
harmonisation of standards, 2–3, 128–9
industrial policy, 161–2
industrial relations directives, 216–18
mergers policy, 161–2
regional policy, 130–2
structural policy, 132
tax harmonisation in, 253
trade diversion and creation in, 121
trade policy, 122, 154, 160–1
unemployment averages, 91
European Currency Unit (ECU), 127, 134
European Economic Space (EES) or Area (EEA), 136
European Free Trade Area/Association (EFTA), 117, 136–7, 138
European Investment Bank (EIB), 123, 132
European Monetary System (EMS), 5, 127
European Monetary Union (EMU), 39
European Regional Development Fund, (ERDF), 125, 132
European Social Fund (ESF), 123, 132
European Union Treaty, 217
exchange controls, 61, 62, 133
Exchange Rate Mechanism (ERM), 5, 8, 9, 15, 38–9, 56–9, 98, 108–9, 113–14, 127–8

exchange rates, 4, 5, 9, 15, 16, 102, 108–15, 125
  and inflation, 56–9, 111, 112, 114, 115
  and interest rates, 50–1, 111–12, 114–15, 116
  and monetary union, 134
  as monetary indicator, 112–13
  Deutschmark/pound, 110, 113, 115
  dollar/pound, 110, 112
  fixed, 113–14
Exchequer grants, 275–6
expectations about fiscal expansion, 38
exports, 11, 103, 144
external balance, 3
external sector, 102–16
externalities, 236–7

factor markets, 118–19
Fair Trading Act (1973), 149, 150
Family Credit, 252
Family Expenditure Survey, 46, 258, 259
Family Income Supplement (FIS), 252
financial innovation, 55, 59
Financial Management Initiative (FMI), 241–2
financial markets, 15, 61–85
  and corporate finance, 63–85 *passim*, 145
  and fiscal policy, 37
  de-regulation of, 7, 157
financial services,
  technological development in, 55
  trade in, 124, 129
  see also banks; building societies
Financial Services Act (1986), 61, 62
fiscal policy, 1, 3, 14, 146, 279
  and financial markets, 37
  and monetary union, 135
  and public sector deficit, 23–41
foreign direct investment, 77
foreign exchange market,
  intervention in, 109, 111, 115
  supply and demand in, 109, 11
foreign trade, *see* international trade
Foster, Sir Christopher, 272–3, 276, 277, 285
France, 13, 71, 77, 91
free trade areas, 118
  see also European Free Trade Area
full employment, 3, 88

gas supplies, 196
GATT (General Agreement on Tariffs and Trade), 3, 160, 163
GDP, 2, 11, 12–13
  /GD (government debt) ratio, 29–31
  /GGE (general government expenditure) ratio, 25, 27, 239–40

  /PSBR (public sector borrowing requirement) ratio, 24, 28, 39, 97
  /PSD (public sector deficit) ratio, 25–6, 27, 31–6, 39, 40
  tax share of, 25, 26
GDP deflator, 46
gearing, 74–5
general government expenditure (GGE), 26–7, 239–45
  /GDP ratio, 25, 27, 239–40
  see also public expenditure
Germany, 13, 58, 70, 77, 80, 91
Gini coefficient, 247, 258, 259, 262, 264
government debt
  /GDP ratio, 29–31
  interest-bearing, 29
government expenditure, *see* general government expenditure
Greece, 56
gross domestic product, *see* GDP

health and safety at work, 218
health service
  expenditure, 243–4
  privatisation of, 200
Heseltine, Michael, 272
high powered money, 29
housing,
  privatisation of, 7, 194, 199, 200–1, 245
  public sector, 245
  tax relief for, 248
Housing Benefits, 245, 252
housing expenditure, 242–3, 244–5
housing market, 7
  see also property prices
human capital, 89
hysteresis in unemployment, 95

import penetration, 144
imports, 103, 105, 108, 111
incentives and tax cuts, 32
income,
  distribution of, 48, 256–65, 270
  equivalised, 259, 262, 263
  gross, 259
  inequality of, 19, 257, 258, 259, 262–5, 270
  investment, 250–1, 265
  public sector, 26
  real disposable, 105, 106
  redistribution of, 260–5, 270
  replacement ratios, 95, 269
  effects of taxation on, 260–3
income smoothing, 34
income tax, 6, 8, 19, 26, 32, 249, 250–3, 260–1, 265
incomes/wages policies, 5–6, 264
industrial action, 211–12, 214, 218

industrial policy, 16–17, 141–63
    and EC membership, 126
    see also services policy
industrial relations
    EC directives on, 216–18
    legislation, 6, 18, 209, 210–16, 218–19
industrial restructuring, 130, 131
inequality of income, 19, 257, 258, 259,
        262–5, 270
inflation, 8, 63–4, 71, 78, 85
    and exchange rates, 56–9, 111, 112, 114,
        115
    and government debt/GDP ratio, 30–1
    and interest rates, 96
    and monetary policy, 44–59
    and monetary union, 133, 134
    and money, 49–52
    and unemployment, 47
    anticipated, 47–8
    control of, 5, 15, 47–9, 56–9
    cost push, 51
    costs of, 47–8
    demand pull, 51
    measurement of, 46–7
    rate of, 3, 5, 11, 14, 46
    redistributive effects of, 48
    unanticipated, 48
inflation tax, 49
information asymmetry, 69
information technology research and
        development, 159–60
inheritance tax, 267
insider trading, 61–2, 69–70
Institute for Fiscal Studies, 281
interest rates, 1, 8, 63, 71–2, 78, 107–8
    and exchange rates, 50–1, 111–12,
        114–15, 116
    and inflation, 96
    and money supply, 50
    long-term, 52, 53
    nominal, 64
    real, 52, 64
    short-term, 50, 52, 53
internal balance, 3
internal market, 128–30
international trade, 142–3, 144, 153–4,
        160–1
    and services industry, 124, 129, 173–4
intervention buying and selling, 123
interventionism, 4–5, 147
investment,
    foreign direct, 77
    in nationalised industries, 191, 192
    rates of, 11
investment expenditure, 26–7, 31
investment income, 250–1, 265
Italy, 13, 58, 91

Japan, 12, 71, 77, 91, 147, 148–9
Job Creation Programme, 98
job mismatch, 95
Job Release Scheme, 99
Job Splitting Scheme, 99
Jobshare, 99–100

Keynesian view of labour market, 91, 93,
        94

labour,
    mobility of, 118, 119, 124
    productive and unproductive, 166–7
    supply and demand for, 91–4
labour market and unemployment, 91–4
laissez-faire industrial policy, 147, 148
law of one price, 118
Lawson, Nigel, 106, 113
Layfield Committee, 273–4
liquidity, 66–8
local government
    finance, 272–86
    privatisation of services, 199–200, 201
Location of Offices Bureau (LOB), 180
Lorenz curve, 256–7
lump sum taxes, 277–8, 284
    see also Council Tax; poll tax

Maastricht, 24, 39, 135, 217
macroeconomic policy, 1–2, 3, 14–16,
        23–138, 146
Major, John, 8, 135
managed economy, concept of, 149
manufacturing industry, 126, 143
    employment in, 176, 186
    function of services in, 172, 173
marginal product of capital, 52
market failure, 147, 236–7
markets,
    factor, 118–19
    see also financial markets
median voter hypothesis, 276
Medium-Term Financial Strategy (MTFS),
        24, 53, 54
mergers, 107, 151–2, 155–6, 161–2
merit goods, 237
microeconomic issues, 2, 16–19, 141–286
minimum lending rate (MLR), 52
monetarism, 50
monetary base, increase in, 29
monetary policy, 1, 3, 15, 146, 279
    and inflation, 44–59
    and monetary union, 133, 134–5
monetary targeting, 52, 53–4, 59
monetary union, 119, 132–5
money,
    and inflation, 49–52
    demand for, 50, 55

money (*continued*)
  narrow, 54, 55
  velocity of circulation of, 49, 54
money demand function, 52, 54
money finance, 29
money supply, 1, 50–1
Monopolies and Mergers Commission
    (MMC), 149, 150, 151, 155, 156
monopolies and monopoly policy, 150–1, 155
moral hazard, 70–1

narrow money, 54, 55
National Audit Office, 242
National Health Service (NHS), 200, 243–4
National Insurance contributions (NICs),
    251–2, 263
National Rivers Authority (NRA), 229
nationalisation, 189–90
nationalised sector, 4, 17, 155
  investment in, 191, 192
  management of, 190–3
  pricing in, 191, 192
neoclassical view
  of industrial policy, 147, 148
  of labour market, 91–3, 94
New Earnings Survey, 259
new trade theory, 148
non-accelerating-inflation-rate-of-
    unemployment (NAIRU), 35, 88
non-tariff barriers (NTBs), 122, 123–4, 125,
    154

Office Development Permits (ODP), 180
office dispersal, 180–1
Office of Electricity Regulation (OFFER),
    194
Office of Fair Trading (OFT), 149–50, 152
Office of Gas Supply (OFGAS), 196
Office Industry Development Act, 180
Office of Telecommunications (OFTEL),
    196–7, 199
Office of Water Services (OFWAT), 196
oil market, 3, 44
Okun's Law, 89
Organisation for Economic Co-operation and
    Development (OECD), 225
Organisation of Petroleum Exporting
    Countries (OPEC), 3
output, 8
  stabilisation of, 1, 5
  and unemployment, 88–9
overseas sector, *see* external sector
ownership and privatisation, 199

patent system, 153
pay bargaining, 204, 218
Paying for Local Government (Green
    Paper), 273, 274–6

pensions, 269
  and financial markets, 81
  and redistribution of income, 264
performance indicators for public spending,
    242
Perrier company, 74
personal sector, 104–5, 106–7
petroleum revenue tax (PRT), 249, 250
Phillips curve, 4
picketing, 211
political pressures, 36–7
poll tax, 19, 272–3, 274, 275, 276–8, 280–1,
    282, 283, 285
Polluter Pays Principle (PPP), 225–6
pollution control, 18, 221–34
Portugal, 56
Post Office, 202n
poverty, 268–70
poverty trap, 252–3
preferential public procurement, 128, 129
price spread, 69
prices,
  and monetary union, 134
  and money supply, 50–1
  asset, 47
  consumer, 11, 14, 44, 45
  import, 111
  oil, 3, 44
  property, 8
  share, 75, 76
  stability of, 1
  target, 123
  see also inflation
pricing in nationalised industries, 191, 192
Principal-Agent problem, 70
private goods, 237–9
private sector, 2, 4–5
  financial position of, 104–8
privatisation, 2, 7, 17, 149, 155, 193–202
  and competition policy, 193, 199, 201
  and education, 200, 201–2
  and ownership change, 199
  of health service, 200
  of housing, 7, 194, 199, 200–1, 245
  of local government services, 199–200,
    201
  of public utilities, 17, 195–8
  of transport, 198, 199, 201
  see also public sector asset sales
producer services, 166, 172–3, 186
production, role of services in, 171–4
productivity, 143
  and trade unions, 207–8, 210
  and wages, 207
  in services, 174–5, 186
Programme Analysis and Review (PAR),
    242
property prices, 8

protection of domestic industry, 153–4
  see also trade barriers
public choice theory, 276–7
public expenditure, 4, 11, 19, 239–45, 254
  see also general government expenditure
Public Expenditure Survey Committee
  (PESC), 242
public goods, 236–9
public procurement policies, 128, 129
public sector,
  asset sales, 24–5, 26, 28–9
  consumption, 11, 26
  income, 26
  investment, 27, 31
  share of national income, 237–41
public sector borrowing requirement
  (PSBR), 23–4, 28, 39, 53, 55, 56, 97
public sector debt repayment, 24
public sector deficit (PSD), 14, 23–41
  /GDP ratio, 25–6, 27, 31–6, 39, 40
  financing of, 28–9
public utilities,
  privatisation of, 17, 195–8
  regulation of, 196–7
purchasing power, 64

quotas, 154

rates, 272, 274, 275, 280, 281, 282
rational expectations models, 4
Regional Development Grants, 158, 182
regional policy, 153, 158–9, 163, 180
  and services industry, 180–3
  within EC, 130–2
Regional Selective Assistance, 158, 181, 182
Regional Water Authorities, 228, 229
regulation,
  of public utilities, 196–7
  of services, 183–5
rent rebates, 245
replacement ratios, 95, 269
resale price maintenance, 152
Resale Prices Act (1976), 149, 152
research and development (R&D), 7, 143,
  153, 159–60, 163
Restart Programme, 96
Restrictive Practices Act (1976), 149, 152,
  157
Restrictive Practices Court, 149, 150, 152
restrictive trade practices, 152, 156–7
retail industry, 176
retail price index (RPI), 46
returns on financial assets, 72
risk, 64–5, 72
risk aversion, 64–5
risk capital, 67, 68
risk diversification, 65–6

River Purification Boards, 228, 229, 232
Rover Group, 194, 195
Royal Commission on Environmental
  Pollution (1976), 232–3

savings, personal, 104–5, 106, 107
Scotland,
  local taxation, 275
  pollution control in, 227, 228, 229
SEAQ (Stock Exchange Automatic
  Quotations) International, 81
secondary market, 66–7
sector theories of economic development,
  167
seigniorage, 29, 49
self-service economy, 173
service economy, 179–80
Service Industry Removal Grants, 181
services, 17, 165–86
  and competition policy in EC, 184, 185
  and technological development, 175, 176
  and the EC, 183–5, 186
  business, 176, 177–9, 186
  classification and characteristics of,
    166–71, 185–6
  de-regulation of, 184, 186
  employment in, 176–8, 186
    role in production, 171–4
  productivity in, 174–5, 186
  regional policy, 180–3
  restructuring in, 175–6
  trade in, 124, 129, 173–4
services policy, 180–5
Sex Discrimination (Amendment) Act
  (1986), 217
shareownership, 73–4
share(s),
  new issues of, 75, 76, 83
  prices, 75, 76
shocks, permanent and temporary, 34–5, 36
Single European Act (1986), 132, 217–18
Single European Market, 128–30, 131
small firms policy, 7
Smith, Adam, 166–7
'social chapter' of European Union Treaty,
  217
Social Charter, 216–17
Social Fund, 269
social security,
  benefits, 7, 243, 264–5, 268–9, 270
  and income distribution, 262, 263,
    264–5
  contributions, 249, 250
  see also National Insurance contributions
    (NICs); transfer payments;
    unemployment benefit
Spain, 56, 80
stabilisation policies, 1, 5

Standard Industrial Classification (SIC), 167
standards, harmonisation of, 2–3, 128–9
steel industry, 189
Stock Exchange, 66–7, 72, 75–6, 157
Stock Exchange, Automatic Quotations (SEAQ) International, 81
strike action, 211–12, 214, 218
structural policy within EC, 132
structure-conduct-performance rationale, 147, 148
Supplementary Benefit, 264–5, 269
Supplementary Special Deposits scheme, 61, 62
supply-side economics, 6, 96, 97
Survey of Personal Income (SPI), 258

takeovers, 71, 75–7, 81–2, 84, 85, 151–2, 155, 156
target prices, 123
tariffs, 154
  common external, 118, 120, 122, 160–1
tax base, 19, 248, 249
tax revenues, 32, 48, 249, 250
  and government debt/GDP ratios, 31
  as share of GDP, 25, 26
tax smoothing, 31–2
tax(es), 245–54
  ability to pay approach to, 246
  ad valorem, 247
  benefit principle approach to, 246
  capital gains, 251
  corporation, 6, 249, 250, 253
  cuts, 32
  effects of, 246–9
    on income, 248, 260–3
  income, 6, 8, 19, 26, 32, 249, 250–3, 260–1, 265
  indirect, 261–2, 263
  inflation, 49
  local, *see* Council Tax; poll tax; rates
  lump sum, 277–8, 284
  petroleum revenue (PRT), 249, 250
  pollution, 225, 233–4
  unit, 247
  value added (VAT), 6, 123, 129, 253
  wealth, 267, 270
Technical and Vocational Educational Initiative, 99
technological development,
  and financial services, 55
  and international economic integration, 121–2
  and services industry, 55, 175, 176
  and unemployment, 89
telecommunications industry, 194, 196–7, 199
Temporary Employment Subsidy (TES), 98

Temporary Short-Time Working Compensation Scheme (TSTWCS), 98–9
Thatcher, Margaret, 6, 127, 272, 283
trade, international, *see* international trade
trade barriers, 128–9, 153–4, 160–1, 479
  see also non-tariff trade barriers
trade creation, 119, 120, 121
trade disputes, 211, 214
trade diversion, 119, 120
trade policy, 3, 153–4, 160–1
Trade Union Act (1984), 211, 213
trade unions, 17–18, 204–16, 218–19
  closed shops, 204, 206, 212, 215
  and employment, 205–7, 209–10
  executive committees, 213, 215
  membership of, 204, 205, 206, 212–13, 215, 218
  political funds, 213, 215
  and productivity, 207–8, 210
  recognition of, 213, 215–16
  and unemployment, 95, 97, 206
  and wages, 205–6, 209
  see also industrial relations legislation
training and education policy, 6
transfer payments, 19, 26, 35, 262, 263, 270
transport services, 129, 198, 199, 201

unemployment, 6, 8, 15, 87–100, 143
  and aggregate demand, 93–4, 95, 98, 100
  and inflation, 47
  and labour market, 91–4
  and replacement ratios, 95
  and trade unions, 95, 97, 206
  classical, 93
  costs of, 88–9
  definition and measurement, 87–8
  frictional, 88, 93
  hysteresis in, 95
  long-term, 95, 96
  natural rate of, 88, 89, 92, 93, 94–5
  non-accelerating-inflation-rate-of, 35, 88
  policies, 97–100
  structural, 88, 93, 97
unemployment benefit, 95, 96, 264
unit taxes, 247
United States, 12, 71, 77, 91, 146–7
universities, 201–2

value added tax (VAT), 6, 123, 129, 249, 250, 253

wage settlements, 6
wages,
  and employment, 109, 205–7
  and productivity, 207
  and trade unions, 205–6, 209
  efficiency, 207

wages (*continued*)
   flexible money wage theory, 91–3
   minimum, 204, 207, 213–14, 216, 264
   money, 91–4
   real, 91, 92, 93, 94
   sticky wage theory, 93–4
wages councils, 204, 213–14, 216, 269, 270
wages/incomes policy, 5–6, 264
Water Act (1989), 228–9
water pollution control, 224, 228–9, 230–2

water services, 196
wealth,
   composition of, 51–2, 266–7
   distribution of, 19, 256–8, 265–7, 270
   taxation of, 267, 270
   transfer of, 267, 270
Wilson, T., 272–3, 277, 285
work-sharing, 99–100

Youth Training Scheme (YTS), 99